THE
BALKAN
WARS

THE
BALKAN
WARS

Conquest, Revolution, and Retribution
from the Ottoman Era to
the Twentieth Century and Beyond

André Gerolymatos

BASIC
BOOKS

A Member of the Perseus Books Group

•

Library of Congress Cataloging in Publication Data
Gerolymatos, André.
The Balkan wars : myth, reality, and the eternal conflict /
André Gerolymatos. — 1st ed.
[320] p. ; photos. : cm.
Includes index.
Summary: The history and mythology of the Balkans that has driven
the people to evict and kill their neighbors.
ISBN 0-465-02731-8
1. Balkan Peninsula — Politics and government. 2. Balkan Peninsula — History. I. Title.
949.6   21   2002   CIP

•

Every reasonable effort has been made to obtain reprint permissions. The publisher will gladly
receive any information that will help rectify, in subsequent editions, any inadvertent omissions.

Photographs of bombed areas courtesy Mrs. Verica Mustapic, custodian,
and Mr. Andrija Misic, co-director, of the Historical Museum of Yugoslavia.

Designed by Kinetics Design & Illustration

02 03 04 / 10 9 8 7 6 5 4 3 2 1

In memory of my father, Sotirios Gerolymatos,
who experienced war in the
Balkans and peace in Canada

CONTENTS

PREFACE

—❦❦—

History can serve the present
as a mirror of the past.

— Ssu-ma Kuang (1018–86), Chinese statesman
and historian of the Northern Sung dynasty

In 1989 I had just converted my doctoral dissertation on intelligence and guerrilla warfare in the Second World into a manuscript. And like most scholars, I had succeeded in elevating a turgid piece of writing into a tolerable academic publication. The fact that I managed the transition at all was due to the influence of Robert Vogel, certainly the greatest university teacher and historian I have ever encountered. Vogel was a military historian dedicated to the study of human conflict within the broad spectrum of history. The last time I saw him, in 1993, he suggested that I focus on the Balkan wars, suspecting that new conflicts in the region would be taken out of historical context. Robert lived long enough to be proven correct; he would have been amused by the avalanche of books published on the Balkans in the last seven years.

The primary purpose of *The Balkan Wars* is to demonstrate the continuity of war not as exclusive to this region but as part of the role of myth, history, and ethnic memory as a manifestation of conflict. To this end I have treated these subjects thematically and chronologically. Occasionally, it has been necessary to cover the same ground more than once, from the perspective of different countries, in order to comprehend events common to more than one part of the Balkan peninsula. Since war and violence are the predominant themes of this book I necessarily included graphic accounts of certain events in order to place them in historical and current context. If history teaches us anything, it is that war, especially ethnic strife, brutalizes society and, ultimately, that the survivors of violence become its living memory. The contagion of hate is simply transferred from one generation to the next.

Traditionally, books on the Balkans are either general histories covering the period from Byzantium to the twentieth century or renditions devoted to individual states. In addition, there are the national and semi-official histories, which, in effect, work backwards — they attempt to justify the current circumstances of a particular state by subtly redrawing the past to suit the present. We have also seen a recent spate of books focusing on the 1990s; with few exceptions, these are narrative accounts based on the writer's specific angle of vision of the Yugoslav wars. There are also anecdotal accounts by journalists who covered the Yugoslav crises and chose to capitalize on the sudden interest in the region. Some of these are well written and offer insight into events that all too often were covered only superficially by the media. Others are essentially polemics advocating justice for one Balkan group and denying it to another. Although personal perspectives are valuable, the quality of these works is uneven. A great many are hostages to the terrible images of the stories they followed and the locations they covered. In each case the reader is left confused and still wondering why after so many years people become willing executioners of their neighbors. Recent and notable exceptions are Lenard Cohen's *Serpent in the Bosom: The Rise and Fall of Slobodan Milosevic*; Misha Glenny's *The Balkans: 1804–1999;* and Stevan K. Pavlowitch's *The Balkans: 1804–1945*. The most comprehensive treatments on the general histories of the Balkans are John V.A. Fine's *The Medieval Balkans* and L.S. Stavrianos's *The Balkans Since 1453*. The fact that both works have been reprinted is testament to their contribution to the study of the region.

The Balkan story is long, complex, and covered by layers of mythology skillfully exploited by ambitious politicians and dictators

re-invented the past to fit conveniently with contemporary percep-
tions of historical injustices. I have attempted to review not only the
political developments that have shaped historical events, but the
regional sociological phenomena that characterize the Balkans. The
culture of violence is not unique to any of the southeastern
European states; rather it is a cycle of conflict that repeats itself from
generation to generation in regions where history, religion, and
nationalism overlap in limited territorial space.

Almost from their inception as independent states in the nineteenth century, the new Balkan countries adopted ambitious policies
of territorial expansion; in most cases they had little choice. After six
centuries of Ottoman rule, the human and political Balkan landscape
had become blurred but not homogeneous. During this period,
peoples with distinct cultures, religions, languages, and histories
shifted locations several times and most of the new states represented
an ethnic tapestry of disparate minorities. Independence failed to
bring prosperity or security, let alone liberal political institutions. All
such considerations had to take a back seat to the policy of territorial
expansion to incorporate all the lands associated with a particular
historical society. The Balkan states have paid and continue to pay a
dear price to match national borders with national history.

I have made some careful omissions in this book. It would be
redundant to recount the history of each Balkan state; it was more
economical to chronicle the evolution of the Balkans by elaborating
themes common to all societies in the region. Furthermore, the
accounts of the Balkan battles are confined to land warfare. The wars
at sea, the role of the island societies, as well as trade and pirates (the
maritime equivalent of bandits) deserve separate treatment,
although they did affect events in the Balkans. For example, during
the Balkan wars of 1912–13, the Greek navy dominated the Aegean,
thus depriving the Ottomans of any strategic or tactical opportunities throughout the conflict.

Whenever possible I have tried to place a face to an event to allow
readers to truly understand the human dimension of these Balkan
conflicts. I am fortunate that several people have trusted me with
their stories; I have tried to remain faithful to their accounts.
Research for this book has taken me to the Balkans on several occasions, when I was able to speak with politicians, soldiers, and

warlords. However, it was meeting with ordinary people — professionals, taxi drivers, waiters, shopkeepers, farmers, professors, and students — that gave me a chance to truly understand the Balkan conundrum. I have also relied on the rich bibliography available to any scholar interested in the region as well as the archival material at the Public Records Office in Great Britain. In addition, the remarkable collection of travel journals published at the end of the eighteenth and nineteenth centuries and in the early twentieth century proved invaluable. Written in most cases by curious European travelers, these journals are a font of topographical, sociological, political, and historical data, offering a valuable, yet sometimes overlooked source of information.

In writing this book I was assisted by a number of people who made useful contributions. My research was ably served by Sebastian Lukasik, whose assistance proved invaluable; his hard work and suggestions improved the final version of the manuscript. I wish there were more young scholars like him. I am grateful to Maria Rousou and Warren Mailey in particular for their hard work and diligence throughout the writing and some of the research phases of the book. Aleksander Petrovic was kind enough to transcribe the experiences of his grandmother Roksanda during the first night of the NATO air strike of Belgrade; Roksanda generously agreed to allow me to include them in the text. Vanessa Rockel contributed her time to examine some parts of the text; and Shannon McCallum designed the map. Milicia Marsten was kind enough to help secure some of the photos included in the insert and Dragisa Postolovic took the time and trouble to secure permission to publish them. I am thankful to Mrs. Verica Mustapic and Mr. Andrija Misic of the Historical Museum of Yugoslavia for the use of their pictures of the 1999 NATO bombings on Kosovo and Serbia.

I am indebted to Jack Stoddart, who, in a real sense, initiated this publication during our discussions about the causes of the Balkan crisis. Bill Hanna and Don Bastian offered invaluable suggestions and comments during the course of completing the manuscript. Jim Gifford shepherded the entire process from manuscript to book with effortless patience and diplomatic skill. I am very grateful to Janice Weaver, whose editorial work greatly enhanced this book. Her invaluable suggestions and comments added necessary polish. Any errors in the text are my own.

It is very exciting for me to have my work published in the United States, and I am thankful to Basic Books for making this book available to American readers. In particular, I am indebted to Lucienne Wu, who has been patient and encouraging as well as an excellent source of advice. Lucienne has been pivotal in making the transition of *The Balkan Wars* from Stoddart Publishing to Basic Books appear effortless. I thank her for her professionalism and enthusiasm. Basic Books could have no better ambassador.

Finally, Beverley, my wife and my best friend, has provided me with critical and thoughtful advice throughout the entire process. Her grace, patience, and understanding make all my work possible.

André Gerolymatos
Vancouver, British Columbia
February 2001

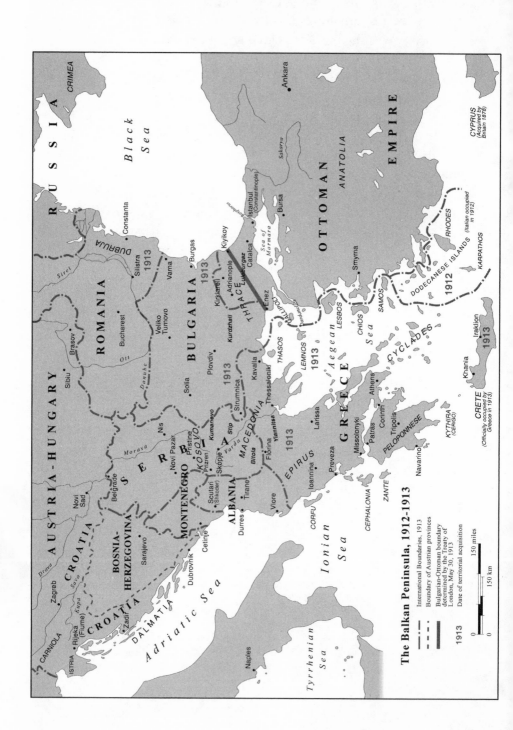

The Balkan Peninsula, 1912–1913

- - - International Boundaries, 1913
- - - Boundary of Austrian provinces
—— Bulgarian-Ottoman boundary
determined by the Treaty of
London, May 30, 1913
1913 Date of territorial acquisition

0   150 miles
0   150 km

RUSSIA

CRIMEA

Black Sea

Constanta

DUBRUJA

Silistra **1913**

Varna

Burgas

Kiyikoy **1913**

Istanbul (Constantinople)

Sakarya

Ankara

OTTOMAN EMPIRE

ANATOLIA

Bursa

Smyrna

Sea of Marmara

Çatalca

Enez

Gallipoli

Çanakkale

Adrianople

Kirklareli

THRACE

Luleburgaz

Kurdzhali

Plovdiv

Sofia

BULGARIA

Veliko Turnovo

Bucharest

ROMANIA

Olt

Siret

Brasov

Sibiu

Danube

Morava

Novi Sad

Belgrade

Zagreb

CROATIA

CARNIOLA

ISTRIA

Rijeka (Fiume)

Zadar

DALMATIA

Drava

Sava

Kupa

AUSTRIA-HUNGARY

BOSNIA-HERZEGOVINA

Sarajevo

Dubrovnik

Novi Pazar

Nis

SERBIA

Prizren

Pristina

KOSOVO

Skopje

Kumanovo

Stip

Strumnica

Vardar

MACEDONIA

Bitola

Florina

Yiannitsa **1913**

Thessaloniki

Kavalla

THASOS

Serres

Aegean Sea

LEMNOS **1913**

LESBOS

CHIOS

SAMOS

DODECANESE ISLANDS **1912**

RHODES (Italian occupied in 1912)

KARPATHOS

CYPRUS (Acquired by Britain 1878)

CYCLADES

Iraklion **1913**

Khania

CRETE (Officially occupied by Greece in 1913)

KYTHIRA (CERIGO)

PELOPONNESE

Tripolis

Corinth

Athens

Missolonyki

Patras

Larissa

Ioannina

EPIRUS

Preveza

Navarino

ZANTE

CEPHALONIA

CORFU

GREECE

Ionian Sea

Vlore

Durres

ALBANIA

Tirane

Scutari (Shkoder)

MONTENEGRO

Cetinje

Naples

Tyrrhenian Sea

Adriatic Sea

CHRONOLOGY

—◦/◦/◦/—

THE WORLD	THE BALKANS
1200	
1215 Magna Carta is signed	**1204** Fourth Crusade; Constantinople sacked
1225 St. Thomas Aquinas is born	
1232 Inquisition is established	**1261** Constantinople reclaimed by the Byzantines
1300	
1309 Papacy begins residency at Avignon	**1302** Territorial expansion of Muscovy begins
1325 Louis of Wittelsbach victorious against the Habsburgs	**1331** Rise of the Serbian Empire under Stephen Duscan
1337 Hundred Years War starts (ends 1453)	**1346** Duscan proclaims himself emperor of the Serbs and Greeks
1347 The Black Death in Europe (ends 1351)	**1355** Death of Duscan
1378 Start of the Great Schism in the Roman Catholic Church	**1389** Battle of Kosovo
1400	
1417 Council of Constance ends the Great Schism	**1453** Fall of Constantinople to the Ottomans under Mehmet II; end of the Byzantine Empire
1438 Albert II of Austria, a Habsburg, elected Holy Roman Emperor, beginning a dynasty that would last until 1806	**1454** Mehmet II invests new patriarch and grants the

1455 Gutenberg's Bible is printed	Orthodox Church greater privileges and authority
1492 Christopher Columbus lands in the New World	
1497 Vasco da Gama sails to India	

1500

1517 Martin Luther posts his 95 theses to the door of a church in Wittenberg	**1570** Venetian-ruled Cyprus captured by the Ottoman Empire
1588 Defeat of the Spanish Armada	

1600

1600 British East India Company is established	**1699** Peace of Karlowitz gives most of Hungary to Austria, begins Russian hegemony in the Black Sea area
1618 Thirty Years War (ends 1648)	

1700

1701 War of the Spanish Succession begins	**1739** Peace of Belgrade gives the Ottomans French support to check Russian territorial expansion in the Black Sea region
1713 Treaty of Utrecht divides territories between the Austrian Habsburgs and Philip V of Bourbon	
1756 Seven Years War (ends 1763)	**1768** War breaks out between Russia and the Ottoman Empire
1776 Declaration of Independence is signed	**1774** Treaty of Kutchuk-Kainardji forces the Ottomans to surrender the coastal areas of the Black Sea and give the Russian fleet access to the Straits
1784 Austria gains commercial access to the Straits	
1789 Start of the French Revolution	
1792 French revolutionary wars begin	**1783** Russia annexes the Crimea
1799 Napoleon Bonaparte seizes power in France	**1797** Smyrna Rebellion

1800

1807 Peace of Tilsit; Napoleon's "continental system" established	**1804** Serbs revolt in response to a massacre by the Jannisaries
	1805 The Battle of Austerlitz
1808 Peninsular War begins	**1806** Selim III declares a holy war against the Serbs
1815 Battle of Waterloo	
1848 Europe experiences revolutions and political upheavals	**1812** Treaty of Bucharest ends the Russo-Ottoman War
1861 American Civil War (ends 1865)	**1815** Second Serb uprising
	1821 Greek War of Liberation begins

1871 Franco-Prussian War ends in defeat for France and the establishment of the German Empire

1890 Battle of Wounded Knee

1832 Otto, a Bavarian, is crowned king of Greece

1853 Crimean War (ends 1856)

1872 League of the Three Emperors is formed

1875 Ottoman Empire declares bankruptcy

1876 First Ottoman constitution is proclaimed

1878 The Congress of Berlin

1885 Serbo-Bulgarian War begins; Alexander of Battenburg unites East Rumelia with Bulgaria

1897 Goluchowski-Murayev Agreement

1900

1904 France and Britain form the Entente Cordiale

1907 France, Britain, and Russia form the Triple Entente

1913 Peace of London cedes all Ottoman territories west of the Enos–Midia line and all of the Aegean islands

1914 Assassination of Archduke Ferdinand in Sarajevo

1917 Balfour Declaration advocates a Jewish national home in Palestine; Russian Revolution begins

1919 Treaty of Versailles ends the First World War

1922 Fascists rise to power in Italy under Benito Mussolini

1925 Locarno Pact establishes the boundaries of Western Europe

1929 Great Depression begins

1933 National Socialists, led by Adolf Hitler, rise to power in Germany

1936 Spanish Civil War (ends 1939)

1903 King Alexander and Queen Draga of Serbia are assassinated

1908 Austria-Hungary annexes Bosnia-Herzegovina; Young Turk Revolution begins

1912 Balkan League is established by Montenegro, Serbia, and Bulgaria; Montenegro declares war on the Ottoman Empire, which eventually leads to the First Balkan War

1913 Serbia concludes secret military pact with Greece regarding borders and the partition of Macedonia; Bulgaria and the Ottoman Empire conclude armistice

1915 Armenian massacre in Turkey

1919 Mustafa Kemal (also called Kemal Atatürk) lands at Samsun, Turkey

1923 Turkey becomes a republic, signaling the end of the Ottoman Empire

1940 Italian campaign against Greece begins

1938 Germany annexes Austria

1939 Germany invades Poland, initiating the Second World War

1940 Battle of Britain

1941 Japanese bomb Pearl Harbor

1942 Wannsee Conference and the adoption of the Final Solution

1944 D-Day invasion begins the liberation of Western Europe; Yalta Conference establishes the territorial division of Europe

1945 Founding of the United Nations

1947 India gains its independence from Britain

1950 Korean War (ends 1953)

1961 Construction of the Berlin Wall

1962 Cuban Missile Crisis

1964 Founding of the Palestine Liberation Organization

1967 Six Day War

1973 Yom Kippur War

1975 Vietnam War ends with the fall of Saigon

1979 Soviet Union invades Afghanistan

1987 The intifada begins in the Israeli-occupied West Bank

1988 Velvet Revolution leads to the breakup of Czechoslovakia

1989 Tiananmen Square massacre

1991 Soviet Union formally dissolved

1992 Civil war and famine devastate Somalia

1993 Rwandan genocide begins

1941 Tito organizes the partisan movement in Yugoslavia

1944 Churchill and Roosevelt agree to divide the Balkans into Western and Soviet spheres of influence

1946 Greek Civil War (ends 1949)

1948 Tito breaks with the USSR

1950 Turkish riots in Constantinople begin

1954 Balkan Pact between Greece, Yugoslavia, and Turkey

1965 UN peacekeeping force first sent to Cyprus

1974 Turkish invasion of Cyprus

1980 Death of Tito

1984 Winter Olympics in Sarajevo

1987 Slobodan Milosevic becomes president of Serbia

1989 Serbia proclaims a new constitution, which abrogates the autonomy of the provinces; six-hundredth anniversary of the Battle of Kosovo

1990 First free elections in Slovenia, Croatia, Macedonia, and Bosnia-Herzegovina

1991 Slovenia and Croatia declare independence

1992 War breaks out in Bosnia-Herzegovina

1995 Dayton accord attempts to bring peace to the Balkans

1999 Violence erupts anew in Kosovo; NATO bombings of Serbia begin

2000

2000 The collapse of Bill Clinton's Middle East peace initiative

2001 President George W. Bush inaugurated

2000 Milosevic loses national elections

2001 A new government is formed in Yugoslavia

INTRODUCTION

MEMORY
OF TERROR

—◦◦◦—

Roksanda Petrovic resided at 14 Decembra Street, just south of Slavija Square, in Belgrade. Her building was in the Crveni Krst neighborhood of the Vracar municipality, just three bus stops away from the center of the city. For many years, she enjoyed the view of the city from her apartment on the seventh floor. Petrovic could easily see the northern towns, including New Belgrade. From her balcony, she could watch people strolling on the streets of downtown Belgrade, going about their daily business. The neighborhood, defined by single and two-story houses and few high-rises, was characteristic of the architecture of postwar Yugoslavia; it was generally a good place to raise a family or, as in the case of Petrovic, retire in tranquillity and relative comfort.

On March 24, 1999, at 11 p.m., Petrovic was resting comfortably on her sofa when an air-raid siren initiated what would shortly become a night of terror. The sudden warning took her by surprise, and for a few seconds she imagined the high-pitched sound was a gigantic scream for help. Then her blood froze; reality had quickly set in. Petrovic rushed to her TV, turning it on just as the news anchor, with deliberate calmness, told people to shut down all electrical equipment, lock their doors and windows, and immediately find the nearest shelter. Almost as an afterthought, the visibly nervous man advised that sirens would also announce the end of the strike.

Instinctively, Petrovic stepped out onto her balcony and looked up, listening for the warplanes. The only sound that came back was her heartbeat. The siren continued wailing as she stood alone on the balcony, shaking with fear. When she regained control of herself, she went back inside and ran to her neighbors' apartment, only to catch them as they were closing their door, awkwardly holding blankets and bags of valuables. They tried to convince her, almost pleaded with her, to join them in the basement. But Petrovic refused. The thought of being trapped in a hermetically sealed space deep in the ground was more terrifying than the unknown and still-silent enemy high above.

Caught between two horrifying alternatives, she returned to her apartment and broke down in tears. But curiosity again forced her to the balcony. This time, she looked at the ground below and could see people running in panic, shouting and gesturing at passersby. The spectacle convinced her that the street was not an option. Frightened and confused, she noticed that the kitchen table was made out of a single piece of thick and strong wood; it seemed the only avenue of protection, and Petrovic slowly slipped underneath with the illusion of safety.

A few moments later, she could hear large thuds in the distance. The sound slowly came closer, and each thud became more intense with each passing second. Suddenly, the thuds metamorphosed into explosions. The sound of the detonations became louder and more clear, and she felt the building shake, or at least she believed the structure was beginning to vibrate. Again curiosity overcame fear, and Petrovic crawled out from under her table and peered down on the city. The Belgrade landscape was punctuated by thick columns of black smoke mixed with flames, and the sky was littered with streaks of brilliant light as anti-aircraft fire exploded in midair. Now she could hear the whining drone of the warplanes, but the machines of destruction continued to remain invisible to the naked eye.

Once again the voice from the television set warned that no one should be out until the air raid was over. Petrovic retreated under the table, this time too terrified to move. She was obsessed with the thought that she would get caught in a burning building. She prayed to God that if a bomb fell, she would be killed instantly and not suffer the slow decomposition of a lingering death among the flames and rubble.

Petrovic lost all track of time, and as the noise tapered off, she edged her way back to the balcony and was astonished to see that Belgrade was surrounded by a ring of fire and a wall of thick black smoke. In that surreal moment, the sound of the telephone brought her back to reality. She returned to the room, picked up the receiver, and heard her relatives from Canada, but she could not find her voice. They tried to calm her, assured her that all would be well. But Petrovic knew, just as the Canadians on the other end of the telephone line knew, that nothing could be done. It is the irony of contemporary technology in general — and the war in Yugoslavia in particular — that while some Canadians are dropping thousands of tons of bombs on a city, others can be talking on the telephone with those on the receiving end.

For the next seventy-eight days, Petrovic made her home under the kitchen table during the air raids, praying for deliverance or a merciful death. Her fate depended upon a NATO pilot miles above her home. If he shifted his targeting mechanism just slightly, her world would crash down around her, perhaps leaving the kitchen table as a temporary tombstone.

But Petrovic survived the NATO attack, and she eventually even managed to join her relatives in Vancouver.[1] She plans, nonetheless, to return home to Belgrade and resume living among the everyday surroundings that elevate life above mere existence. After all, home is a place where someone like Petrovic can speak her own language, be near her friends, and live in the comfort of physical familiarity. The tragedy of Yugoslavia is fundamentally a struggle to achieve security within a common physical space, language, religion, culture, and history. The NATO bombing was one act in a centuries-long theater of the macabre that has characterized war and violence in the Balkans and elsewhere.

—⟁—

If wars are what define the nature of a society at its worst, then the Balkans offer nothing new to the history of warfare in Europe — or anywhere else, for that matter. What does make the Balkan wars so striking, however, is that they have all been fought over the same problems: nationalism and religion. These are not new or exclusive Balkan phenomena, of course, but inexplicably they have appeared anew at the end of the millennium. Post–Cold War Europe and North America are at a complete loss to understand why these small countries are hostages to the past and seem so willing to fight the same battles all over again. In fact, most Western policy analysts had initially almost refused to consider the role of history in the Balkan crises, and they underestimated the forces of nationalism and religion after the collapse of the Communist system. After all, shouldn't half a century of Communist rule have toned down national consciousness and, at the very least, extinguished any vestiges of religious fervor? Indeed, some Balkan writers have attempted to explain the atrocities that resulted from the breakup of Yugoslavia as a recent experience and not as a Balkan legacy.

But if we want to comprehend the bloodstained fate of the modern Balkans, it is necessary to understand the impact and influence that war and its mythology have had on the region in the past. In fact, the history of the Balkan states is replete with heroes, villains, and most important, martyrs who offer an example of self-sacrifice for each succeeding generation.

Today, the very word "Balkans" conjures up images of intrigue, war, and human suffering on a scale abhorrent to Western society. To some people, the Balkan countries lack a clear Western orientation and carry far too much cultural baggage to belong in the European club. Western leaders refer to the region as the back door to Europe, the Balkan powder keg, or Europe's doorstep. What these euphemisms hide is, perhaps, the wish that the Balkans were located anywhere other than in Europe.

The Europe of today needs to move past its bloody history, and the events in the Balkans are a reminder of a previous dark age of war, mass killing, and destruction. The political, cultural, and economic development of the Balkan countries was interrupted and diverted by the Ottoman conquest in the fifteenth century. The five hundred years of Turkish occupation that followed suppressed the evolution of Balkan societies, so they failed to keep pace with the rest of Europe and North America. In effect, the march of European history and civilization skipped past, and the Renaissance, the Age of Enlightenment, and the Industrial Revolution made little impression on the region. As a result, the Balkan states emerged very late as modern societies and have lagged far behind the technologically advanced West.

The modern Balkans have captured the imagination and indignation of North Americans and Western Europeans because the atrocities there are taking place now and not half a century ago. But at the heart of all the Balkan wars is the clarion call of ethnic hatred served up as cultural heritage. The Balkan past is littered with the tribalism, ethnic nationalism, warmongering, mythmaking, and self-serving symbolism of oppression that scar most societies in transition, in the past as well as the present.

1

ASSASSINATION, MARTYRDOM, AND BETRAYAL

—❦—

*It has been said that though God cannot
alter the past, historians can.*

— SAMUEL BUTLER

The legend of the Battle of Kosovo
(1389) and the assassination of Archduke Franz Ferdinand in 1914
by the Serb Gavrilo Princip complement each other, and provide a
study in cultural contrasts. To Western Europeans, the assassination
of the archduke was murder and an abomination, while for Serbians,
the assassin became a national hero. The Kosovo legend, meanwhile,
has been the driving force of Serbian nationalism, but for those living
in Kosovo at the end of the twentieth century, the region's very name
represents the savagery of the Balkan wars. Remarkably, there is a historical line that connects these stories of assassination, martyrdom,
and betrayal with the development of the Balkan national state in the
nineteenth and twentieth centuries.

The man who shot Archduke Ferdinand in 1914 was a nineteenth-
century Serb nationalist who was attempting to invoke an ancient
heritage within the confines of twentieth-century international relations. The assassin did not so much aim a pistol at the heir apparent

to the Austro-Hungarian throne as repeat the sacrifice that had first been carried out by another Serb in 1389 at the Battle of Kosovo. In this respect, the story of the fate of the archduke is inextricably bound to legend and the fatalistic glory associated with a medieval battle between Serbian knights and Ottoman Turks. The story cannot be told without including some aspects of the complex world of the fourteenth century and the process that brought Ferdinand and his assassin to their fateful meeting in Sarajevo.

This particular Balkan tragedy unfolded on June 28, 1914, when Archduke Ferdinand defied several warnings of impending disaster and decided to visit Sarajevo. The day was sunny and warm and the crowds enthusiastic. Record numbers of Bosnians had turned out to get a glimpse of the royal procession and cheer the next ruler of the Austro-Hungarian Empire. Few were aware that the archduke and his wife, Sophie Chotek, had already survived one attempt on their lives earlier that day, and no one expected that the end for the royal couple was literally just around the corner. But the end did come when Gavrilo Princip aimed his pistol and shot and killed the archduke and his wife. What took only seconds to accomplish plunged Europe months later into the first global war, with consequences that were unforeseen by even the most pessimistic generals and politicians.

The archduke could have avoided the trip to Sarajevo, of course, and Princip could have missed or lost his nerve — but none of this happened.[1] Both men were trapped and driven by forces that had been set in motion centuries earlier. In the Balkan context, each man represented a reality that the other could neither recognize nor ever hope to understand. Ferdinand's visit to Sarajevo on that June day in 1914 indicated a degree of arrogance and certainly poor judgment.[2] For the Serbs in Bosnia, which had recently been annexed by the Austro-Hungarian Empire,[3] the visit of a Habsburg prince was perceived as an insult on what was their national day. The anniversary of the 1389 Battle of Kosovo was meant to remind all Serbs of the beginning of almost five hundred years of occupation by the Turks, who in Bosnia-Herzegovina were replaced by the Austro-Hungarians. Yet to a Habsburg like the archduke, there could be no comparison between the cruelty of the Ottoman conquest and the benevolent and civilized rule of the Austro-Hungarians.

The heir apparent had fulfilled his duties in Bosnia and had no substantive obligation to visit Sarajevo, except as consolation for his wife. Countess Sophie Chotek of Chotkowa and Wognin came from the ancient feudal aristocracy of Bohemia. Prior to 1815, the Chotek family had been allied by marriage with princely houses. Unfortunately, after 1815 the fortunes of the family declined, and they were excluded from the ranks of those eligible for marriage with members of reigning dynasties. As a result of the family's impoverishment and its decline in social standing, Sophie held the modest position of lady-in-waiting to Archduchess Isabella.[4]

Archduke Ferdinand was a man with a mercurial temperament; he oscillated between fits of anger and a charming personality. According to Ottokar Czerin, one of the closer members of his entourage, the explosive side of Ferdinand's nature caused considerable distress among officials, to the point that "ministers and other high officials rarely waited on the Archduke without beating hearts. He was capable of flying out at people and terrifying them to such a degree that they lost their heads."[5] In his monumental study of the causes of the First World War, Luigi Albertini, who was familiar with the major personalities of this period, wrote that Ferdinand "could only love or hate, and hatred was much more potent with him than love."[6] The archduke was a complex personality who was greatly misunderstood by his contemporaries, and as a result was unpopular with the palace courtiers and the social-political establishment of the empire.

The contrasts in the archduke's personality were also reflected in his choice of pastimes. Ferdinand had two great hobbies: hunting and gardening. As a hunter, he had few rivals. According to his personal physician, Dr. Victor D. Eisenmerger, more than half a million birds and animals fell victim to Ferdinand's ability with firearms.[7] Yet it was the archduke's love of horticulture that perplexed both his detractors and his admirers. Perhaps the same can be said of his devotion to and determination to marry a woman below his station. Within the strict and almost stifling Viennese society, Ferdinand managed to find and court Sophie under the nose of her formidable employer.

Archduchess Isabella, a lady not to be taken lightly under the best of circumstances, was overwhelmed to find her family the object of Ferdinand's interest. If the archduke had serious intentions toward one of her daughters, the implications were enormous. Yet the prospect was not unusual. Isabella and Ferdinand were first cousins, which meant that Isabella's family pedigree was sufficiently noble to warrant marriage between one of her daughters and the heir apparent. As the mother of a future empress, Isabella would rise to the pinnacle of the social ladder, both at home and abroad.[8]

The fickle nature of love, however, soon shattered Isabella's illusions. She discovered Ferdinand's pocket watch, which he had forgotten after a game of tennis. Unable to contain her curiosity over which of her daughters was the focus of his attentions, she sneaked a peak at the locket. To her horror, the picture inside revealed none other than Sophie, Isabella's lady-in-waiting. The archduchess was incensed and promptly fired her.[9] Ferdinand had not only bypassed Isabella's daughters for a lowly countess and an employee, but he was using the archduchess' household as a cover for his clandestine affair. The visions of imperial grandeur vanished and were replaced by the reality of humiliating national scandal. Isabella never forgave the archduke or Sophie, whose lowly status was an affront to the established nobility. The archduke also held a grudge, and even suspected the archduchess and her husband of harboring Hungarian politicians.[10]

Of course, Isabella wasn't alone in her disdain for Sophie. Because of her Czech origins and humble status, Sophie emanated almost an air of plebeianism, and the Viennese court often snubbed her. The archduke had chosen to marry for love, against the wishes of Emperor Franz Joseph and his inner circle. But the couple paid a dear price for ignoring tradition and underestimating the vanity of the Austro-Hungarian nobility. Although the archduke's claim to the throne remained unchallenged, his wife was forced to endure petty and subtle insults and occasionally outright hostility from the palace courtiers. The most glaring efforts to remind Sophie of her humble standing took place at official functions. At state dinners, the countess was not permitted to sit with her husband, but was placed at a separate table at a respectable distance from the official guests and members of the royal family. The same restrictions applied to public institutions, and at the opera or the theater. Sophie could not be seated next to her husband in the imperial box.[11]

This pattern of degradation began for Sophie on the day of her wedding on July 5, 1900. Ferdinand had to declare theirs a morganatic marriage, stripping both Sophie and their future children of the right to succession and all titles and privileges that were accorded to the so-called legitimate families of Austrian archdukes.[12] The emperor, a stickler for propriety, at first had even refused to consider a morganatic marriage, but he relented under pressure from Pope Leo XIII, Czar Nicholas II, Kaiser Wilhelm II, and his own empress.[13] Still, in keeping with his express wishes, the wedding itself was a low-key affair without representation from the royal family or the palace courtiers.[14] From that point on, Sophie and the archduke's life was a constant struggle against the carefully orchestrated barriers erected by the strict rules of court etiquette.

The guardian of the medieval Spanish court conventions inherited by the Habsburgs was the court chamberlain, Prince Montenuovo. Although Montenuovo himself was descended from a morganatic marriage between Archduchess Marie-Louise, Napoleon's widow, and Count Neipperg, he became the instrument by which the emperor and the court tormented Sophie.[15] Insofar as the court was concerned, Sophie was a non-person, and simply existed as an unwanted appendage of the archduke.

The fossilized Spanish court etiquette could reach absurd dimensions. On one occasion in the fifteenth century, a Habsburg emperor in Madrid collapsed and almost died while court officials argued about who had the right to provide help or call for assistance.[16] Even in the early twentieth century, medieval court etiquette superseded matters of life and death. While suffering from a severe asthma attack early one morning, Emperor Franz Joseph, for example, managed to screech, with almost his last breath, the word "tailcoat" upon seeing his personal physician, who had rushed to his aid wearing a mere dressing gown.[17]

Only outside the empire could the ostracized Sophie have a brief respite and enjoy the pomp and ceremony denied her by the Austrian court. During these trips, she was almost treated as the wife of the heir apparent. The German kaiser, in particular, was quick to exploit the archduke's sensitivity over Sophie's status, and he went out of his way to extend to the countess most royal privileges whenever they were in Berlin or he was in Austria. These simple courtesies cemented the friendship between Ferdinand and Wilhelm II, adding a personal as well as a political dynamic to the German–Austro-Hungarian military alliance.

In time, even the uncompromising Franz Joseph gave some consideration to Sophie's awkward status, and after a few years he began to elevate the unfortunate countess a few steps up the social ladder to the rank of duchess. Progress had been slow, but the unlucky couple continued to achieve acceptance and the recognition of Sophie's legitimacy in the other European courts. By 1914, Emperor Franz Joseph had relented to the point that Sophie was permitted to accompany her husband on official functions in the provinces.

In a twist of fate, the first such occasion was the visit to Bosnia. Ferdinand, as the inspector general of the Austro-Hungarian armed forces, had to attend the maneuvers of the 15th and 16th Army Corps in the mountains southwest of Sarajevo, the capital of Bosnia. Both the archduke and Sophie were reticent about the visit, and Ferdinand in particular was filled with foreboding. Bosnia, which was formally annexed in 1908, was one of the empire's restless provinces. It was seething with Serbian nationalists who despised the Habsburgs. In the past, the disgruntled Bosnian Serbs had missed no opportunity to embarrass or display their animosity toward the Habsburgs. Certainly violence was always a possibility.[18]

The archduke's concern was over the prospect of violent demonstrations and other ugly scenes from the Serb population. On the eve of his departure for Bosnia, Ferdinand expressed his fears to the emperor and even went so far as to ask if the trip should be postponed. Other witnesses have recounted that the archduke was overcome with pessimism, depression, and foreboding.[19] But the old emperor refused to order Ferdinand not to make the journey, and simply remarked, "Do as you think best."[20] Without a direct order from the emperor, it was unthinkable for the archduke to decline. After all, his sense of duty and the dignity of the royal family had to be upheld, and the inspector general of the armed forces was expected to attend army maneuvers.

For Ferdinand, his position was a significant honor and a major concession from the old emperor, who normally held the title.[21] Only once before had an archduke held that rank, thus underlining Ferdinand's growing status within the empire. So despite his premonitions and the volatility of the region, Ferdinand and his entourage set off for Bosnia, with the consolation that at least there Sophie would receive the pomp and ceremony denied her in Vienna.[22]

—◆◆◆—

The official part of the visit went well and without incident, and some members of the archduke's staff urged a speedy return to Austria. Honor had been satisfied, they argued, and a visit to Sarajevo did not technically fall within the obligations of the archduke. Baron Karl Freiherr von Rumerskirch, the head of Ferdinand's staff, was against continuing the trip. He was particularly concerned over possible hostile demonstrations against the royal party. Ferdinand almost cheated history and changed his mind, but ultimately he allowed himself to be persuaded that a visit to Sarajevo should be included in his itinerary.[23]

A great deal has been written about this fateful journey, as well as the near escapes that add a layer of intrigue to the events of June 28. For all that has been said, it remains that the shots fired by Gavrilo Princip proved to be the catalyst for yet one more Balkan tragedy.[24] For the rest of the world, the assassination of this couple caused a chain reaction that brought the Great Powers of Europe to the killing fields of the First World War. Although the causes of the Great War are complex and go beyond the deaths of the duchess and the archduke at the hands of a Bosnian Serb, the assassination is nevertheless woven into the tapestry of Balkan history. A mythology that has emerged has made this region synonymous with death and war. In the West, the great battles of the First World War and the inhumanity of the trenches have almost obliterated the memory of the assassination. In the Balkans, however, the name of Archduke Ferdinand always resumes its place in the panoply of war whenever a new crisis unfolds there.

In 1914, most Serbians were as horrified by the killing of a member of a royal house as anyone else. The Serbian newspaper *Samouprava* called the assassination an act of anarchist folly, and in Belgrade the murder was condemned — if only for fear of Austrian retribution. The Serbian prince regent and the government immediately telegraphed their condolences to the emperor, Count Berchtold (the Austro-Hungarian foreign minister), and the Austrian and Hungarian parliaments.[25] The elevation of Princip to the status of national hero and martyr came later, in part as a reaction to the belligerent attitude of the Austro-Hungarian government, which held the Serbian state as an accomplice to the assassination. Also, the horrors suffered by the Serbs during the First World War forced them to turn the events of June 28 into more than the simple murder of an archduke and his wife. Finally, it can be argued that after the war, the newly established Yugoslav kingdom required martyrs as well as national symbols. Princip the assassin was transformed into Princip the Serb, as well as into a Yugoslav patriot who sacrificed himself to liberate all South Slavs and resurrect the medieval Serbian kingdom.

Of course, the Serbs were not the only Balkan people who longed for the return of past glories and frontiers that encompassed ancient lands. Unfortunately, lost territories could be reclaimed only at the expense of the Ottoman Empire, Austria-Hungary, or other Balkan countries. This is why the region has two names. It's called the Balkans when it's at war and Southeastern Europe when it's enjoying a period of peace. Sadly, the past six centuries have marked the Balkans as a place of misery and suffering that is so often the lot of any region fortunate or unfortunate enough to have strategic significance.

The Balkan states stand at the crossroads of Asia, Europe, Russia, and Africa. Accordingly, the region has been the highway for armies large and small, many of which have cut a swath of destruction on their journey to empire building. This legacy of war has endowed the region with a tradition of fatalism that has guided the cultural heritage of the Balkan peoples. The memory of great defeats and great massacres has shaped at least part of the identity and commonality of each nation, tribe, or group in the Balkans.

Over the centuries, these upheavals have acquired a unique reality that often plays havoc with historical truth. It is not so much that events are altered to suit a particular political agenda, but instead that they are interpreted in the light of Balkan lore. In other words, Balkan national history does not represent a scientific reconstruction, or even a distortion of the past, but it does endow the current inhabitants with the ability to cast events in the context of a recurring theme of victimization and persecution. For each of the Balkan peoples, there is one particular event that reflects their own image of the past and practically dictates relations with their neighbors. Events in the cauldron of Balkan history are linked to war, and war is associated with victory for one group and defeat and humiliation for another.

Remarkably, in the kaleidoscope that is Balkan history, success and failure have almost the same significance. Both have provided the justification for future conflict. Great defeats are fodder for revenge and spectacular victories the prelude to further conquest. The Battle of Kosovo is a historical landmark, but more important, it's both a cultural icon to the Serbs and a glorious chapter in the history of the Ottoman Empire. Like most battles in the medieval period, it is shrouded in mythology and only partly accessible through facts. But its salient features are the themes of self-sacrifice, betrayal, and assassination.

—◦⁄◦⁄◦—

The harbinger of Serbian nationalism took place on June 28, 1389, when the Serb armies, led by Prince Lazar, set out to confront the forces of the Ottoman sultan, Murad I, on the field of Kosovo Polje.[26] Kosovo is a desolate mountainous plain where the frontiers of Serbia, Bosnia, Herzegovina, and Albania converge. The timing of the battle could not have been worse. At the end of the fourteenth century, the fortunes of the Ottomans were on the rise, and they occupied territory that ranged from Asia Minor to the eastern Balkans. Sultan Murad I had expanded the frontiers of the Ottomans in Anatolia and Southeastern Europe, reduced the Byzantine Empire to the status of a vassal state, and was now shifting the axis of his expansion to complete his conquest of the Balkans. In Serbia, internal division and feuding nobles had degraded the medieval kingdom to a mere shadow of its former self. Nevertheless, the Serbian nobles still loyal to Prince Lazar had to face an army of Turkish warriors, Muslim crusaders, and Christian vassals, led by Murad, one of the most competent sultans to rule the Ottomans in the fourteenth century.

In the previous century, the Serbs, under the leadership of King Stephan Uros I, had established an independent kingdom and expanded their territory to include present-day Montenegro and Kosovo. In the early part of the fourteenth century, they continued their expansion at the expense of the Byzantine Empire, and by 1331, on the death of Stephan Uros III, they had conquered northern Macedonia and controlled most of the Vardar valley. His successor, Stephan Duscan, continued the southern drive of what by this time had become a Serbian empire, and pushed his armies as far as the Gulf of Corinth. For a short time, Duscan, with his energy and ability to keep the Serbs united, threatened to replace the decaying Byzantine monarchy with a Serbo-Greek empire.

As the history of the Byzantine Empire indicates, this Serbo-Greek empire would have been possible. For almost a thousand years, the eastern Roman Empire and its capital, Constantinople, dominated the Balkans, North Africa, the eastern Mediterranean, the Black Sea coast, and the hinterland of modern-day Turkey. By the end of the sixth century, however, the empire had become Greek-speaking and had adopted Christianity as the official state religion. Despite these changes, the Byzantines continued to maintain the titles and symbols of imperial Rome, including the mechanism of succession. Succession to the imperial throne was passed from father to son or determined by revolutionary means. In other words, a challenger to the crown assumed legitimacy by overthrowing the current ruler or usurping the throne from the designated successor. If a coup was successful, the new emperor was recognized as the heir to the Caesars.[27] Such a process was essentially an act of constitutional revolution — as long as the challenger was successful. In the case of failure, it qualified as an act of treason.[28]

The Greek element had been further entrenched by the Great Schism of 1054, which separated Christianity into the Eastern Orthodox Church, led by an ecumenical patriarch in Constantinople, and the Roman Catholic Church, with a pope as its head. As a result, the Christian world was bitterly divided; after 1054, the empire faced threats from the West as well as from the East. Over the next few centuries, the Byzantines lost ground to the Slavs, the Bulgars, the Genoese, the Venetians, and the Turks. The empire not only had to defend itself against the encroachments of these new enemies, but was also plagued by dynastic quarrels. In 1204, the Fourth Crusade, though it was meant to be on its way to the Holy Land, descended on Constantinople, occupying the city for just over fifty years (from 1205 to 1261). But the Byzantines, still resilient, eventually pushed out the crusaders, reclaiming their capital and parts of the empire in Asia and Europe.

These upheavals created the opportunity for new peoples, such as the Serbs and the Bulgarians, to carve out, at the expense of Byzantium, their own kingdoms. By the time of Duscan's conquests, it was not inconceivable for the Serb king to achieve his grandiose scheme and place himself on the throne in Constantinople. For this purpose, he had himself proclaimed emperor of the Serbs and Greeks at Skopje on April 16, 1346. The Byzantine court naturally did not accept the Serbian king's new title, which meant that in order to establish himself on the throne of the Roman emperors, Duscan would have had to conquer Byzantium.[29] However, unlike the Western kings and princes, Duscan followed the Eastern Orthodox faith, thus meeting the primary requirement for a legitimate ruler of Byzantium. Should the Serbian ruler have succeeded in conquering the empire, he would have met less resistance than a Catholic or a Muslim prince.

Unfortunately for the Serbs and fortuitously for the Byzantines, Duscan died in 1355. Although the Serbian monarch had brought two-thirds of the Balkans under his rule, he had failed in his ambition to establish a new Byzantine dynasty. After his death, the feudal Serbian empire lacked competent successors who could maintain the momentum of conquest and unity. Serbia had reached its zenith under Duscan, and soon the empire that had risen so quickly began to tear itself apart. Indeed, it was the misfortune of the Serbs that competing nobles had fragmented the state at a time when they had to face the Ottomans, a new and far more dangerous adversary.[30]

Under the sultans Orkhan and Murad I, the Ottomans had conquered large parts of Asia Minor and established a solid foothold in the Balkans. The capture in 1369 of Adrianople, one of the largest cities in the region, provided the Ottomans with a base for further expansion and a strategic center to serve as their capital. Indeed, by 1370 the Turks occupied the region from Thrace to the Rhodopos Mountains. Yet even at this late date, not all of the Byzantine and Balkan Christian rulers fully appreciated the magnitude of the danger posed by the Ottomans. It may be that some Balkan rulers were more concerned with their own aggrandizement, while others, such as the Bulgarians who had waged war against the successful Murad, had already been reduced to the status of vassals.

Another possibility is that by the late fourteenth century, the Balkan principalities and the Byzantines, with some exceptions, had simply accepted the Ottomans as part of the internal political and military dynamic of the region. If anything, the Ottomans represented one more power that could be harnessed as an ally in advancing the interests of one or another of the competing principalities of the Balkans or Asia Minor. In historical hindsight, it is evident that at this time Serbia represented the last independent Balkan monarchy that could have prevented the Ottoman conquest of Southeastern Europe; certainly it was beyond the capability and resources of the Byzantine emperors.

By the middle of the fourteenth century, all that remained of the once powerful empire was the city of Constantinople, the capital and the center of the Eastern Orthodox Church. For a long time, the Byzantine Empire had ceased to shield Christianity from the westward march of Islam, and the leaders of the empire were consumed with conspiracies and counter-conspiracies for control of the throne. The combination of ruinous civil wars, the loss of territories to the Turks, and the impact of the bubonic plague had reduced Byzantium to a principality surrounding the city of Constantinople. As a result, the once proud inheritors of the Caesars had become dependants of the Ottoman sultans, and they needed their favor to continue the almost endless game of musical thrones that was consuming the limited resources of the empire. It is no accident that the term "Byzantine" — which refers to any labyrinth of treachery and conspiracy — originated with the complex intrigues and subtle machinations for power conducted by members of the Byzantine aristocracy.

Yet at this critical juncture, one Serbian noble, Ugljesa, the despot of Serres, understood that it was better to drive the Turks out of Southeastern Europe than wait and try to defeat the Ottoman armies from fixed fortresses. He also realized that the feuding Serbian nobles had to unite in order to defeat the Ottomans. Unfortunately, all other potential allies, including the Byzantines and the Bulgarians, refused to join forces and drive out the Turks. This left Ugljesa only a limited force with which to match the well-trained and battle-hardened army of Murad.

Regardless of this setback, in 1371 the despot of Serres advanced against the Ottomans in western Thrace, and on September 26 the two armies clashed at the Marica River. In the ensuing battle, the Serbian forces were annihilated and their commanders killed. Success on the battlefield now left the victorious Ottomans with half of the medieval Serbian kingdom and well positioned to continue their advance across Southeastern Europe. Perhaps the Battle of Marica, more than any other event in the fourteenth century, represented the beginning of the end of Serbian independence, and with it that of the entire Balkan region. It was only a matter of time before the Ottomans resumed their westward expansion.

After the battle, Serbian unity (or what was left of it) quickly disintegrated. The soldiers lost at Marica were the last vestiges of central authority, and those Serb nobles who had refused to fight now possessed forces far more powerful than the military resources of the monarchy. Despite the Ottoman threat, however, Serbian separatism prevailed, and the great nobles chose to carve out their own principalities rather than attempt to re-establish a unified Serbia. Most historians agree that the Battle of Marica had a far greater impact on the future of the Balkans than the better-known Battle of Kosovo would eighteen years later.[31]

Marica, in fact, was an unmitigated disaster for the Serbian kingdom. At least half the Serbian fighting men were killed. Furthermore, the refusal of the Byzantines and the Bulgarians to maintain Christian solidarity presented the Ottomans with a golden opportunity to maintain the intermittent war against their enemies indefinitely. This policy of divide and conquer was not so much an Ottoman stratagem as an exploitation of the disunity that characterized the region. As a result of the Ottoman victory, some of the Serb princes were forced to accept the sultan as their feudal overlord in 1371, as were the Byzantines in 1373 and the Bulgarians in 1376.[32]

In practice, Ottoman suzerainty meant that the vassals of the sultan had to pay tribute to their overlord and were obligated to furnish troops for Ottoman campaigns. These units had to be commanded by a member of the ruling family, usually the heir to the throne (in the case of kingdoms) or the head of the family (in the case of a principality). The Ottomans also occasionally required vassals to contribute a daughter or a sister in the ruling family to the sultan's harem. This was the fate of Tamara, the sister of Bulgaria's czar, John Sisman, who was given to Murad's harem as part of Sisman's vassal obligations.

Unfortunately for the Balkan Christian principalities, submission to the sultan did not necessarily guarantee security. Turkish raiding parties, some encouraged by the Ottomans and others on their own initiative, continued to ravage the countryside. The raids were a major source of instability in the Balkans, since the Turks destroyed crops, carried peasants into slavery, and helped themselves to small towns and even larger cities. In 1385, the Turks moved against Prince Lazar's territory. Lazar had inherited what was left of the Serbian kingdom, now reduced to a principality, but had failed to convince the nobility to accept one central authority. One year later, the Turks captured the city of Nis, and Lazar, according to some accounts, was forced to recognize the sultan as his feudal overlord.[33]

In 1388, the Turks raided as far as Hum (Herzegovina). This time, however, a Bosnian army led by Vlatko Vukovic wiped out the entire Turkish force. Murad could not afford to let this incident go unpunished. The Serb victory created a dangerous precedent for the Ottomans, since it proved that they could be defeated. At the same time, a quick campaign held the possibility of incorporating the rest of Serbia into the Ottoman domain and guaranteed the loyalty of the sultan's Balkan vassals. Despite the spectacular success of Orkhan and Murad, the ultimate Ottoman victory over all the Christian monarchies and principalities in Southeastern Europe was not a foregone conclusion. The Ottomans had indeed established a powerful state that included large parts of the European and Asian continents, but the emerging empire was far from secure.

The advance against the Serbs was both practical and opportunistic. By 1389, the few Serbian principalities in the Balkans did not represent much of an obstacle for the Ottomans in Southeastern Europe. Everything else had fallen to them or to the Hungarians. It is not clear whether the majority of Serb princes, including Prince Lazar, had already accepted the sultan as their feudal overlord, but if they had, some, including Lazar, renounced their pledge in 1389. This was an additional motive for Murad's advance against Serbia. According to custom, Murad demanded that Lazar accept or, as the case may be, re-accept the sultan as his feudal master, and pay tribute before initiating hostilities. The Serbian prince refused and managed to form an alliance with two of his neighbors, Tvrtko and Vuk Brankovic.[34]

As the two armies converged on the plain of Kosovo, the stage was set not so much for a pivotal battle, but rather for the foundation of a myth that would hang like a stone around the neck of most Serbs in the future. Accounts of the battle itself are sketchy, and as far as the events that took place before the battle are concerned, they belong more to the realm of myth and legend than to any accurate historical account. What is known is rather simple to summarize. There was a battle between the forces of Murad I, which included Serbian and other Christian vassals, and Prince Lazar's army of Serbs, Bosnians, and Albanians. During the course of the engagement, both Murad and Lazar were killed. Once again, the details of how they died are not clear. The reconstruction of the events before, during, and after the Battle of Kosovo relies partly on folklore and partly on the few extant accounts that offer some scraps of information.[35] In the best Balkan tradition, the notions of doom, betrayal, and premonition of defeat have been depicted by later accounts as actual events that forecast disaster even before the armies met in battle.[36]

The fate of Serbia and the future course of the battle began inauspiciously. Lazar's daughter, Mara, and Vukovasa, the wife of Milos Obolic, a well-known Serb nobleman and warrior, quarreled over the bravery of their respective husbands. When the issue could not be settled by rhetoric, Mara, who was married to Vuk Brankovic, Lazar's principal ally, slapped Vukovasa. Evidently, the slapping contest was inconclusive and Vukovasa promptly informed Milos, who then challenged Vuk to a duel. Despite Lazar's efforts to prevent a blood feud between the two nobles, honor had to be satisfied, and they proceeded to fight each other on horseback. When Milos knocked Vuk from his horse, however, the other nobles intervened and stopped the duel. Lazar managed to reconcile the two irate husbands, but their relationship remained uneasy. Vuk was determined to destroy Milos, and he mounted such a successful campaign of slander against him that Lazar became unsure of Milos's loyalty.[37]

The dilemma for Lazar was whether to believe Vuk, his ally and son-in-law, or trust his best warrior. The prince decided that precaution was the greater part of friendship and brought the issue to the test by publicly humiliating his best warrior. To ascertain the veracity of Vuk's accusations, Lazar held a dinner for his nobles and confronted Milos with the rumors of treason and betrayal that had permeated the Serbian camp. The hapless knight, faced with the prospect of dishonor and even execution as a traitor, exclaimed that in the forthcoming battle, he would prove his innocence and his loyalty to Lazar. After brooding all night, Milos made his way the next morning to the Ottoman camp and presented himself in Murad's tent.

The sultan, impressed by the countenance of the Serbian knight and pleasantly surprised that he was willing to change sides, summoned him closer. Milos, as was customary, prostrated himself before the sultan and, without the bodyguards noticing, pulled out a dagger and plunged it into Murad's belly. He tried to escape but was soon overpowered by the dying sultan's guards and killed. Some versions of the story have the assassination taking place before the battle, while other sources maintain that Murad was killed after the two armies were engaged in combat.[38] But if Milos had any hope of proving his loyalty by ensuring a Serbian victory, it made more sense for him to kill Murad before the battle, thus depriving the Ottoman forces of their leader. After the fighting had started, it would have been very difficult for Milos to break through the melee unscathed and reach the sultan. Certainly, assassinating the sultan after the battle would also have been a useless gesture.

Unfortunately for the unlucky Milos, the Serbs did not receive any news of the assassination until after the battle was over, and the poor man went to his grave believing his death secured victory for the Serbs. Lazar was also killed without knowing if his brave knight was a traitor or a hero — yet the tale could not end with so much uncertainty. Heroes and traitors are vital elements of a legend. It is not unusual, consequently, that more emphasis has been placed by written accounts on the fate of Milos and the assassination of Murad than on the details of the battle.

Meanwhile, the Ottoman officials who were present during the assassination decided to keep Murad's death temporarily secret.[39] It made sense to maintain the illusion of a living sultan rather than risk demoralizing the army. It was not unusual in medieval warfare for soldiers to retreat and disperse when a king or the leader of an army perished. Therefore, the Ottomans who were privy to the assassination gambled by letting one of Murad's sons assume command of the army, as well as the sultanate. Their choice was Bayazid, who was commanding the right wing of the Ottoman army. It is not clear why they chose this particular son, but as soon as Bayazid became apprised of the situation, he acted quickly and decisively. His first act as sultan was to order the death of his brother by gouging out his eyes and thus eliminating any future challenge to his authority.[40]

The outcome of the battle was by no means a foregone conclusion. Both armies were deployed in phalanxes on the flat field of Kosovo. Level ground was necessary, since most battles in the four-teenth century were essentially cavalry actions. Accounts of the size of the armies vary considerably depending on the source.[41] The Ottoman forces were composed of feudal cavalrymen wearing mailed armor and equipped with lances, as well as swords and maces for close combat. Some of the cavalry might have been horse archers, but the bulk depended on the spear as their primary weapon.

Murad's army was also supplemented by a small unit of regular infantrymen armed with bows and irregular cavalry and infantry detachments used for skirmishing. In addition, his forces included contingents of Serb, Bulgarian, and other Christian vassals. The Ottoman order of battle, before Murad's death, was based on a linear formation, with cavalry on the wings and the regular archers of infantry in the center. Christian cavalrymen formed the right wing, and were commanded by Bayazid, while the left wing was exclusively formed of Ottomans.[42] Before his assassination, Murad and his entourage had taken a position behind the center of the battle line.

It is a great irony, particularly in light of the significance that the Battle of Kosovo would have for future generations, that the armies facing each other on June 28, 1389, included contingents from almost all of the Balkan nations. There is one important distinction, however: they were not all on the same side. Lazar's army depended on three distinct detachments of Serbs, Bosnians, and Albanians, in addition to the Bulgarians, Hungarians, Romanians, Czechs, etc., who fought side by side to preserve Serbian independence. Opposing them were the Ottomans, and they were supported by Serb, Bulgarian, and other Christian troops who also fought side by side in order to subjugate the Serbian kingdom. This state of affairs, however, was not unusual in medieval warfare. Kings and knights often changed allegiances to suit their own interests and gain an advantage over their rivals.

The forces arrayed at Kosovo, it could be argued, were unusual only because of the mix of Christians and Muslims fighting against other Christians, yet even this was not necessarily remarkable. The Byzantines did not shrink from using Muslims as mercenaries against their enemies — and even against each other. The crusaders, though they were fighting in the name of a Christian God, did not hesitate to sack Constantinople in 1204, just as they had sacked other Christian cities in the Balkans, Asia Minor, and the Middle East. The strategic use of alliances was also not lost on the Muslims, who frequently fought with the Christians against other Muslims. Under these circumstances, it is improbable that either Lazar or Murad was aware that the battle he was about to fight had any dramatic implications for the future.

Lazar's army consisted of a feudal cavalry, but he had fewer cavalrymen and more infantrymen than the Ottomans. And unlike Murad, Prince Lazar commanded a coalition of forces led by rulers of autonomous principalities. The Bosnian contingent, led by Tvrtko, took position on the left flank, Vuk Brankovic's forces from Macedonia and Kosovo were on the right, and Lazar and his own knights led the combined armies from the center. Hostilities commenced after approximately 2,000 Ottoman archers attacked the Serb line. The Serbs responded with a full cavalry charge that hit the Ottomans left and center. However, the Serb attack lost much of its momentum after the cavalrymen encountered a pit of wooden palisades in front of the Ottoman line, a tactic commonly employed by the Ottomans in other battles.[43] The delay exposed Lazar's forces to an onslaught of arrows from Turkish archers that caused considerable losses among the Serb knights.

Despite the hail of arrows and obstacles, however, the Serb cavalry almost broke through the Ottoman left wing, causing some momentary panic among the Turks, many of whom began to fall back. The fighting was fierce and inconclusive until Bayazid and his troops traversed the length of the Ottoman line and counterattacked the right wing of the Serb army. This brilliant and difficult maneuver ultimately saved the day for the Ottomans. For a short time, the outcome of the battle still hung in the balance, but Bayazid's attack eventually succeeded in driving the Serbs back. Losses on both sides were heavy, but the Ottomans were able to maintain the cohesion of their forces and go on the offensive. The center of Lazar's line fell apart, and chaos and panic stalked the Serbs as they fled the battlefield. Lazar himself and several of his knights were taken prisoner and beheaded later that day.[44]

Vuk Brankovic managed to withdraw from the field with 12,000 men, thus saving one contingent of the Serb army. But many chronicles suggest that his motives were far from pure. His departure took place at the critical juncture of the battle, tipping the scales in favor of the Ottomans. Legend suggests that he had a prior arrangement with Murad, and that in exchange for unspecified rewards, Vuk agreed to betray his people. The withdrawal of his forces was the ultimate cause of the Serbian defeat, and thus the final element of the Kosovo legend was in place. Yet was this an act of betrayal, as one historian alleges,[45] or is it a myth that has mutated into historical fact? To some extent, the truth is irrelevant to the impact of the battle on the evolution of Serbian nationalism. Vuk's disloyalty, whether true or not, helps explain how an unremarkable military confrontation was elevated to the status of epic poetry.

After the engagement, the Ottomans remained in possession of the battlefield, which in a purely technical sense meant that the Turks won the battle. On the other hand, Bayazid did not pursue the defeated Serbs and conquer their lands, but instead withdrew his army to Adrianople. Thus it can also be argued, again in a purely technical sense, that the failure to complete the victory with a swift conquest of Serbia meant the battle was a draw, but only for a short time. Bayazid, instead, was eager to establish friendly relations with the Serbian principality, secure his position, and eventually move against the Muslim emirates in Anatolia, which had rebelled after the news of Murad's death.[46]

Nevertheless, the Serbian kingdom after the Battle of Kosovo was considerably weakened. Stefan Lazarevic, Lazar's successor, was a minor, and his mother, Milica, ruled in his place as regent. The prospects of the diminished kingdom offered little hope for the future. Serbia faced threats from Hungary, rival Serbian despots, and the Ottomans. In November 1389, Sigismund of Hungary took advantage of Serbia's weakness and captured fortresses and territory along the Serbian-Hungarian frontier. At the same time, Vuk Brankovic, who had managed to withdraw from the Battle of Kosovo with his forces relatively intact, had ambitions to absorb Lazar's territory and assume the position of ruler of all the lands that collectively defined medieval Serbia.[47]

Milica, in effect, had to deal with several challenges to the kingdom, almost all at the same time, yet she lacked both allies and the resources needed to defend what was left of her husband's kingdom. The only options available to the regent and her advisers were to surrender parts of the kingdom to the Hungarians, accept Vuk as Lazar's heir, or submit to the Ottomans. When Milica discovered that Vuk was negotiating with the Hungarians, the only choice left was an accommodation with the Ottomans. In 1390, when Bayazid resumed his advance in the Balkans, Milica, with the advice of the church, accepted Ottoman suzerainty. As vassals of the sultan, Milica and her son had to pay annual tribute, provide Serbian contingents for the sultan's army, and agree to the marriage of her daughter, Olivera, to Bayazid.[48]

In some respects, this was the lesser of two evils. Bayazid proved to be a devoted husband to Olivera and a friend to Stefan Lazarevic. In the spirit of the times, however, he equally devoted himself to a life of debauchery whose depravity is a favorite theme of Byzantine historians.[49] Regardless of the sultan's sexual predilections, however, he and Stefan became close friends, and they worked closely together in fighting Christians and Muslims alike. According to most accounts, Stefan was very attached to Bayazid and remained a steadfast ally to the end. Serbian knights fought alongside the Ottomans in the capture of Nicopolis and accompanied Bayazid in his campaigns to Asia Minor. In several battles, the Serbian auxiliaries played a key role in the Ottoman victories and made no attempt to abandon their Turkish overlord.

An important component of this devotion was that Bayazid offered his Serbian allies an equitable share of the booty and further ensured their loyalty by supporting the Orthodox Church.[50] The relationship between Stefan and Bayazid also enabled the Serbian prince to reclaim territories lost to Serbia even before the Battle of Kosovo.[51] The Ottoman sultan completed his campaigns by subduing the remaining independent Turkish emirates in Anatolia, and he was in the process of besieging Constantinople when he had to divert his efforts to deal with Timur the lame (or Tamurlane) and his Tartar armies.

This time, fortune went against the Turks, and Timur's forces crushed the Ottomans at the Battle of Ankara in 1402. Despite the overwhelming defeat, Stefan and Bayazid's sons managed to save themselves and part of the army by retreating from Asia Minor to the Balkans over the Dardanelles. Inexplicably, instead of taking the opportunity to destroy what was left of the Ottoman forces, the

Byzantines, the Venetians, and the Genoese provided transport that enabled the defeated Turks to cross the Sea of Marmora and find refuge in the Balkans.[52]

Bayazid, on the other hand, was captured alive and subjected to a series of humiliations and indignities that varied according to Timur's whims. In some accounts, he was forced to serve as Timur's footstool and was paraded around the camp on a donkey. In other versions, Bayazid was brought in whenever Timur had dinner with his officers so that the servants could throw bones at him. Whenever his army was on the move, Timur ordered Bayazid to be carried on a litter used for women, no doubt a humiliating blow to his pride. Finally, the unfortunate man had to watch the violation of his harem and endure the spectacle of his wife, Olivera, being forced to serve Timur and his guests naked.[53] This last degradation proved too much for the hapless Bayazid, who died of apoplexy on March 8, 1403.[54]

This was an ignominious and pitiful end to the career of Bayazid, and it marked the collapse of the Ottomans, who had been a major force in Anatolia and the Balkans for a decade. After the Tartar threat subsided, Bayazid's sons divided the territories of the Ottoman Empire between them, but they soon quarreled. The ensuing conflict between the brothers created a singular opportunity for the Byzantines and the Balkan principalities to drive the Ottomans from Europe, as well as from Anatolia. But neither the Byzantine emperor nor any of the Balkan rulers rebelled against the Ottomans.[55]

On the contrary, both the Serbs and the Byzantines ultimately played key roles in unifying the Ottomans by supporting Mehmed against the other sons of Bayazid, thus enabling him to bring together the fragmented Ottoman Empire under one ruler.[56] In effect, the rump Byzantine Empire and the remnants of the medieval Serbian kingdom of Stefan were the architects of their own destruction. The Christian monarchies, including the Venetians and the Genoese, failed to appreciate the gravity of the Ottoman threat to Asia Minor and Southeastern Europe. Even Timur the lame could not comprehend the ineptitude of the Byzantines in failing to take advantage of the situation and destroy their Ottoman enemies once and for all.

In essence, the Ottomans, at the most vulnerable period in their history, were given fifteen years of grace to work out the dynastic quarrels that plagued the empire after the defeat at Ankara. This was sufficient time for one leader to defeat the other contenders for the sultanate, reunify the Ottoman forces, and resume the offensive in Asia Minor and the Balkans. The Ottoman interregnum, from 1402 to 1413, invalidates both the significance of the Battle of Kosovo and the notion that in the fourteenth century, the world of Southeastern Europe was irrevocably divided between a monolithic Ottoman Empire and the defenseless Balkan monarchies. In fact, Stefan and his successors continued to increase the territories of Serbia at the expense of rivals, even after the reunification of the Ottoman sultanate.[57]

Certainly, one of the great "what ifs" of history is the refusal of George Brankovic, Vuk's son and Stefan's successor, to join the Hungarian coalition that almost defeated the Ottomans at the second Battle of Kosovo in 1448. If Brankovic had added his forces to those of the allies, it is plausible that the Ottomans would have suffered a major defeat. Instead, Brankovic refused to join the Hungarians or even allow them passage through Serbian territory. He remained a loyal vassal of Murad II and was rewarded by the sultan with additional territory.[58] Although vassals of the Ottoman sultan, the Serbs survived with partial independence until 1459, after which Serbia disappeared as a state until the nineteenth century.

The Kosovo ordeal of Prince Lazar and the Serbian knights is, among other things, a simple and convenient explanation for the Ottoman conquest of Serbia in the fifteenth century, a conquest that led to almost five hundred years of Turkish oppression. But the actual events before and after this "decisive" battle serve to undermine the impact it really had on the history of both Serbia and the rest of the Balkans. If the Battle of Kosovo is examined within the historical context of the period, it becomes simply one of many battles. It is hardly the strategic turning point that facilitated the Ottoman conquest of the region. The decline of the Balkan principalities and the collapse of the Byzantine Empire were both part of a long process, certainly one far more complex than the outcome of one or even several battles.

We can also view the Kosovo legend as a means of addressing a variety of national, sociological, and political factors that have manifested themselves in the identity of the Serbian people since the fourteenth century. In this regard, the legend basically underscores three concepts: assassination, martyrdom, and betrayal. Milos fulfills the role of the patriotic assassin, and Prince Lazar was eventually elevated to the status of martyr and canonized in the 1390s. Medieval chroniclers and bards attribute Lazar's ascent to martyrdom and sainthood to a dream the prince had on the night before the battle. In the dream, Lazar is offered the choice between a heavenly or an earthly kingdom — in contemporary language, glory and death or life and mediocrity. The noble prince naturally chooses death. In the same dream, it is prophesied that he will be betrayed in battle.[59] How else can the flower of Serbian knights face defeat at the hands of the ungodly Turks!

This provides the final element of the Kosovo legend, which of course means that the services of a traitor, in this case Vuk Brankovic, are required. After all, this Serbian prince escaped from the battlefield with his forces intact while braver men stood their ground and fought to the last. The fact that Lazar and a good number of his knights surrendered in a vain attempt to save their lives did not excuse Vuk's failure to continue fighting. However, Vuk was not the only Serbian prince who managed to withdraw unscathed. Tvrtko and the Bosnian contingent also fell back without suffering significant losses. Indeed, Tvrtko, as soon as he reached home, lost little time in telling anyone who would listen that Kosovo was a Serbian and Christian victory, yet he escapes the odium of treason in the Kosovo epics.

In truth, the story of Vuk's treason was the direct result of a propaganda campaign initiated by Milica's supporters as part of her quarrel with the prince. The heart of the charge against Vuk was the accusation that he retreated from the field of battle, abandoning Lazar and the other Serbians to their fate. However, Vuk withdrew his forces only after it was clear that the battle was lost. During the course of the fighting, his cavalry came close to breaking through the Ottoman left wing, and they fell back only when the Bosnian left flank and the Serbian center were in the process of disintegrating. Vuk was actually one of the last Serbian princes to become a vassal of the Ottoman sultan. But the oral tradition might have worked against him because he had the temerity to challenge Milica, the widow of Lazar the saint.[60]

Undoubtedly, Vuk had every intention of replacing the weak

dynasty of Lazar with one he himself headed, either by partitioning Serbia with the Hungarians or by direct intervention. This is likely why Milica and her advisers, too weakened from the losses at Kosovo to counter a move by Vuk, resorted to psychological warfare. By defaming her rival, Milica was able to both undermine Vuk's credibility and justify her own capitulation to the Ottomans.

It is no wonder that Milica accepted Ottoman suzerainty only after seeking the advice of the local clerics (advice that was endorsed by a special council organized by the Serbian patriarch). Once the accusation of betrayal had served its purpose and Milica had ensured her son's succession, relations with Vuk seemed to have returned to normal. By August 1392, the quarrel appears to have run its course, and Milica was visiting Vuk and her daughter, Mara, Vuk's wife, at their court in Pristina.[61] In fact, after the death of Stefan, Vuk's son inherited the Lazarevic lands and titles. Unfortunately for Vuk, the story of his betrayal became an integral part of the Kosovo epic.

—◈◈◈—

The Kosovo legend in its final form includes an assassin, a martyr, and a traitor. The three components have created a dramatic rendition of a less than epic battle, but more important, they have offered a convenient justification for the Ottoman victories over Serbia in the fourteenth and fifteenth centuries. The legend itself acquired momentum after the Turkish conquest of the Balkans and the collapse of the Lazarevic principality. The final Ottoman victory and the subjugation of the Balkans in the fifteenth century instigated the migration of large numbers of Serbs to the regions of old Serbia, Montenegro, Bosnia, and Herzegovina.[62]

In the years following the fall of Constantinople in 1453, more than 300,000 Serbs abandoned their homes, and as they re-established themselves in these regions, the Kosovo legend of courage and sacrifice inspired resistance to the Ottoman Turks. The Serbs, in an attempt to understand a world that forced them into a subservient role in their own country, made Kosovo the event that served as the "dramatic watershed"[63] between independence and subjugation. The collapse of medieval Serbia could thus be explained with one glorious defeat.

As the various epics of Kosovo evolved and began to be written during the centuries of Ottoman occupation, the events depicted acquired greater substance and, inadvertently, historical legitimacy. The printed word, certainly in earlier centuries, carried the perception of validity, which provided the Kosovo epic with a degree of authenticity. One 1601 history of the Slavs, *Il regno degli Slavi* (The reign of the Slavs), by the Ragusan monk Mavro Orbini, included a long passage on the Battle of Kosovo that offered all the basic themes of the story and was one of the first written accounts of the events outlined in the legend. Eventually, Orbini's history became the basic source for later chroniclers.[64]

In 1722, Orbini's book was translated and published in Saint Petersburg. The translation made the work accessible to a wider audience, and was a key factor in the emergence of Serbian nationalism and identity in the eighteenth century. A version published a few years before the Russian one offered a more elaborate account, and together the two works provided the complete rendition of the Kosovo legend.[65] During the nineteenth century, Serbian intellectuals began to group the various heroic folk songs and epic accounts of Kosovo into single publications, some of which were translated into several European languages.[66]

The most influential account of the legend, at least as far as Gavrilo Princip's generation was concerned, was that of a Montenegrin prince-bishop, Petar Petrovic Njegos. According to Vladimir Dedijer, who wrote one of the most important books on Serbian history, Njegos's version combined self-sacrifice, martyrdom, and patriotism. Dedijer writes that in this new interpretation, "the Kosovo martyrdom had a new, more optimistic character; it became an anticipation of the future. The tragic elements in the folk poetry became the most powerful incentive for the liberation of the South Slavs."[67]

In their final form, the Kosovo epic and the cult of Lazar became vital elements in the historical consciousness of the Serbian people.[68] The notions of self-sacrifice, bravery, and killing the hated Turks, as dramatized by Milos's assassination of Murad, were essential to stimulating rebellion against the Ottomans. Later on in the nineteenth century, the Kosovo legacy came to underscore Serbian irredentism. For the Serbian nationalists in Bosnia, the Habsburgs had simply replaced the Ottomans as the oppressors and the impediment to the new Serbian kingdom's achieving its natural frontiers. In Serbia itself, any obstacle to the renaissance of the Serbian state brought about the direst of consequences. If the Serbian patriots were determined to avenge the wrongs of the past, they were equally zealous in their efforts to expunge domestic enemies in the national interest. By 1903, the perceived threats to national integrity were the king and queen of Serbia. King Alexander Obrenovic and his wife, Draga, had earned the enmity of the Serbian military, which eventually led to their grisly deaths in the name of God and country.

The assassins saw their actions as part of a patriotic duty to remove a tyrant and redeem the dignity of the nation, but in reality the plot to kill the king was the culmination of several factors. One was the traditional rivalry between the Obrenovic and Karageorgevic families, and their respective claims to the throne. And then there were the actions of Alexander Mashin, the brother of the queen's first husband. Mashin held Draga responsible not only for his brother's death from alcoholism, but also for his own early retirement from the army.[69]

The radicalization of the army at the turn of the century, a reform instigated by Milan Obrenovic, also contributed to the intense dislike of the king and queen. Milan was Alexander's father, but he had abdicated in favor of his son in 1889 after a very public and messy breakup with his wife. The ex-king spent a few years in Paris and Monte Carlo, enjoying the good life, but he eventually returned to Belgrade and undertook the task of reorganizing and expanding the army. His reforms coincided with a series of radical changes implemented by the education minister, who reduced the number of high schools in Serbia to spare the kingdom from the development of "an intellectual proletariat." As a result, the sons of impoverished farmers and villagers lost the opportunity for a higher education, and many opted for a career in the new army instead.

The reforms dramatically altered the social composition of the officer corps, whose primary allegiance was now to the army and, by extension, to Serbia, and not to any particular monarch or politician. These changes, consequently, reduced the influence of the bureaucracy and the political leadership, and the military soon assumed the role of guardian of the state. In this new capacity, many officers took great exception when Alexander abolished the constitution and decided to rule as an absolute monarch. Several of his actions —

including the elimination of secret ballots, the abolition of freedom of the press, and the exclusion of representatives of the Radical Party from the senate and the council of state — alienated a significant element of the political establishment and earned the monarch the enmity of the military. The population in general was further offended in 1900 by Alexander's marriage to Draga Mashin, a commoner and the widow of an engineer, who was more than ten years older than the twenty-six-year-old king.[70] The situation continued to deteriorate after Milan Obrenovic quarreled with Alexander and was forced to leave Serbia and seek refuge in the court of Emperor Franz Joseph.

The king's reputation and credibility were further undermined when Draga's much-heralded pregnancy was exposed as a fraud. This, however, did not prevent Alexander from launching a campaign to elevate his wife by having villages, schools, and other institutions named after her at a time when Serbia was in a financial crisis. In addition, the country's financial problems had a severe impact on the army. Officers' pay was delinquent for long periods, and ordinary soldiers were reduced to a diet of bare subsistence. Incredibly, during these harsh times, the queen began to interfere in the military by promoting her favorites and demoting those officers she did not like.[71] Finally, rumors spread that Draga was planning to have her brother named as heir apparent to the throne. This proved to be too much, and on April 5, 1903, demonstrations in Belgrade had to be dispersed by gunfire from the police. Several young people were killed or wounded, and one hundred demonstrators were arrested, including two army officers. The king had initially ordered the army to deal with the demonstrators, but some of the soldiers chose instead to fraternize with the crowd.[72]

As early as 1901, a group of young officers began entertaining the notion of removing the unpopular monarch and his queen. One of them, Dragutin Dimitrijevic, nicknamed Aspis, shortly thereafter became the *éminence grise* of the Serbian political universe. More important, by 1914 Dimitrijevic was at the center of Serbian conspiracies in both Belgrade and the occupied provinces of Bosnia and Herzegovina, and he was also involved in plots against the Habsburgs and any other enemies of the Serbian people.

Like most amateurs, however, the Serbian officers at first failed to achieve success despite their determination and enthusiasm. On the other hand, their singular commitment to ridding Serbia of the unwanted king attracted many more recruits, so by 1903 the conspirators included 180 officers and civilians. Although they swelled the ranks, the newcomers brought little in the way of expertise in organizing a swift end for the king and his hated wife.

Initially, poison was considered the best means of disposing of Alexander and the unpleasant Draga. A substance was procured and tried successfully on a cat. This led to an elaborate plot. In May 1903, the conspirators hired a young Bohemian, the son of a tailor living in Belgrade. They arranged for the young man to find employment in the kitchen of the Grand Hotel in Belgrade, ostensibly to learn the art of cooking. The boy proved to be capable and was transferred to a position in the royal palace. Within a few months, he had demonstrated his culinary abilities and was charged with preparing the meals of the king and queen. One evening, while cooking the king's meal, he mixed poison with the food. Unfortunately, the head chef detected the young man's activities and promptly informed the authorities. The boy was immediately shot. His parents were brought to the palace, informed of their son's treason, and compelled, under the threat of execution, to tell all their relatives and friends that the young man had committed suicide.[73]

The conspirators were forced to accelerate their plans after rumors intensified that the king, under the influence of his wife, was moving quickly to appoint her brother, Nicolai Bunevitch, heir to the throne. Their fears were not unfounded, because by establishing despotic rule, Alexander had put himself in a position to have his rump Parliament rubber-stamp any decision concerning the succession to the throne.[74] This was the last straw. On the evening of June 11, 1903, at midnight, twenty-eight officers and their units surrounded the palace. They quickly disarmed the royal guard and attempted, without success, to break down the palace door with axes.

In a desperate measure, the conspirators then used dynamite, which not only blasted the door open but also blew out the fuses, leaving the palace in total darkness. They then proceeded from room to room, looking for the royal couple. Alarmed by the noise of the explosion, the king and queen had concealed themselves in a secret closet. After two hours of searching every room in the palace, the officers came upon Gen. Lazar Petrovitch, the king's aide-de-camp, and forced him to reveal the king's hiding place, which was behind a secret door in the bathroom.[75]

The conspirators finally cornered the royal couple, who were hardly in a dignified state. Alexander, wearing a dressing gown, was trembling from fear, and Draga, dressed only in a petticoat, white silk stays, and one yellow stocking, did not present a regal image. The officers showed their gratitude to Petrovitch by promptly shooting and killing him. Meanwhile, Alexander fell on his knees and begged that his life be spared, offering to yield to every demand, to sign any document, to leave the country or banish the hated queen — anything, as long as they would spare his life. The officers were not impressed; they simply replied that it was too late and opened fire.

The queen likewise fell on her knees and asked for pardon for any offense she may have committed in the past. Again the conspirators were not moved by the pleas, and after calling her several degrading names, they informed her that she had been queen too long. Next, they inflicted humiliations on the wretched woman, and one officer, obviously not a gentleman, drew his sword and cut part of her thigh. Immediately the others aimed their revolvers and shot her several times. Afterward, they turned their attention to Alexander, who was not yet dead, and proceeded to slash him with sabers. All twenty-eight conspirators took turns with sabers or bayonets to pierce the bodies.[76]

Unable to think of anything else, the conspirators dragged the naked bodies of the royal couple to the bedroom window and attempted to throw them over the balcony to the lawn in front of the palace. Draga was successfully tossed over. Alexander, however, refused to die. When the conspirators tried to pitch him over, he managed to clasp the balcony railing with his right hand. The officers were forced to cut off his fingers before he would fall to the ground, and there the fingers of his left hand clutched the grass. In the early morning, rain began to fall on the naked bodies lying among the flowers, yet the unfortunate Alexander and Draga lived for another hour or two before expiring.[77]

While the melodrama was unfolding in the palace, two officers in the conspiracy summoned Draga's two brothers to the home of the commander of the Belgrade division. Upon their arrival, they were offered a glass of water and then told to bid each other farewell. As the brothers embraced, the conspirators shot and killed them both. Other members of Draga's family were executed that day too, as were several government ministers, some in front of their families.[78]

In the morning, the conspirators rode through the streets of Belgrade shouting the news of the death of Alexander and Draga. The population responded with loud cheers, and every home displayed a large flag, lending an air of festivity to the capital.[79] In the capitals of Europe, the news was received with horror and indignation. *The Times* of London expressed in astonishment that

> Servia, the land of assassinations, abdications, pronunciamientos, and coups d'état has surpassed itself and caused all previous achievements to pale into insignificance [with] the tragedy enacted between midnight and the small hours of this morning at Belgrade. A Central Asian khanate, not a European city, would have been a fitting theatre for such ruthless and accurately planned regicide. France has seen her President, Austria her Empress, and Italy her King struck down by assassins within the last ten years; but no parallel can be found in recent European history for such wholesale extirpation of a reigning family and of its partisans. Fully and duly authenticated descriptions of the hecatomb are still waiting, but enough is known to characterize the tragedy at Belgrade as unique in contemporary history.[80]

It is not easy to comprehend the vicious manner by which the Serbian officers tormented and tortured Alexander and Draga before they killed them. One explanation is that the savageness exhibited by the officers was a result of their frustration at having spent so long looking for the royal couple. Each hour the conspirators wasted in searching for the king and queen diminished the chances of a successful coup. Of course, the Serbian officers also felt a great deal of repugnance for Alexander and, in particular, Draga. Her antics had diminished the dignity of the Serbian kingdom, which had emerged only after a long struggle with the Ottoman Empire, and by extension, they undermined Serbia's standing as a European state.[81] It should be noted that revolutionary fervor is often intertwined with the brutalization of the revolutionaries and the dehumanization of their enemies.

There are numerous examples throughout history of the inhumanity associated with civil conflicts and military and political coups. The treatment of Alexander and Draga was not altogether unique.

Finally, the nineteenth century was for the Balkans a period of occupation, resistance, and reprisals. The struggle of the Balkan societies to break free from the Ottomans, and later the internecine guerrilla war waged between these states over their respective claims to national territory, lent itself to conflicts characterized by atrocities. In this respect, the Balkan conflicts in the early nineteenth century represent not just wars of liberation against an imperial power, but struggles for survival. Revolutionaries had little expectation of humane treatment from their enemies. On the contrary, each failed conflict with the Ottoman authorities resulted in the massacre of the rebels and their families, often accompanied by small genocides within the regions associated with a particular rebellion. The vivid and detailed accounts of Turkish atrocities, whether real or exaggerated, set the standard of treatment meted out to enemies both within and outside the Balkan states.

This may partially explain the blood lust of the Serbian officers in 1903, but it also provides insight into the atmosphere generated in the Balkan states leading up to the 1914 assassination. The conspirators who killed the king and queen of Serbia later led the armies and the guerrilla bands that fought the Balkan conflicts of 1912 and 1913. A large number of the veterans of those campaigns provided the infrastructure for a multitude of secret and overt patriotic societies. Some of these organizations advocated the unification of the unredeemed Serbs, while others were committed to the concept of uniting all the South Slavs into a single state.

There would be an interval of eleven years before the Europeans would have to come to terms with the murder of another royal couple, only this time the consequences would reverberate beyond the borders of the Balkans. During those eleven years, assassination acquired legitimacy as a weapon to be used in the achievement of political ends. The pardon of the conspirators and their elevation to the status of national saviors contributed to this legitimacy, as did the Kosovo legend and Milos's assassination of Murad. In this age of war and political murder, a new generation of young patriots yearned to emulate the medieval knight by smiting the enemies of Serbia.

Between 1898 and 1913, forty-one major political murders were committed in Europe, the Near East, and the Americas; from 1792 to 1897, forty-eight assassinations took place in the same regions.[82] To many young Bosnian Serb radicals, terror and assassination became the instruments by which to free all Serbs.

—⁓⁓—

The assassins of Alexander and Draga and their followers had permeated the state apparatus and established the clandestine infrastructure that provided the training and logistical support for the champions of oppressed Serbs within and outside Serbia's borders. Without question, Gavrilo Princip was both patriot and martyr, as well as assassin and victim. As a Bosnian Serb, Princip was both a symbol of the unredeemed Serbians under the thumb of the Habsburgs and ultimately a casualty of war in the national struggle to unify all the constituent parts of medieval Serbia. In 1878, the Serbs living in Bosnia and Herzegovina had passed from the oriental despotism of the decaying Ottoman Empire to the subjugation of the autocratic Habsburgs. Under the rule of the Ottomans, the Serbs were treated as infidel serfs, and within the confines of the Austro-Hungarian monarchy, they were regarded as something less than second-class subjects. The Habsburgs had acquired the right to administer the Ottoman provinces as part of the settlement of the Congress of Berlin, which was organized to limit Russian gains as a result of their victories in the 1878 war against the Turks.

Thirty years later, in 1908, the Habsburgs formally annexed Bosnia-Herzegovina in order to enhance the status of Austria-Hungary. All this was lost on the Serbs, who simply changed one set of masters for another one. As the new subjects of this predominantly Catholic empire, the Eastern Orthodox Serbs saw no increase in their standard of living. Little effort was made by the Austrian authorities to improve the lot of the Serb population, and any attempts made by the Serbs to sustain their national and cultural identity were suppressed. The Austrians also failed to address the agrarian problem, which went a long way in perpetuating the ill feelings of the Serbs toward their new masters. During twenty years of Austro-Hungarian rule (1878–1908), 6,000 Muslim landowners still kept more than 100,000 Serb peasants under feudal conditions.[83]

It is no coincidence that Princip and several of his accomplices in the assassination plot were the children of Serb peasants who could not overcome poverty because of the Turkish land laws retained by the Hapsburgs. At his trial, Princip underlined the injustice of the Austrian failure to alleviate the plight of the Serb peasants.[84] Because of these conditions, Serbs lived in small villages and relied primarily on farming small plots to maintain a meager existence. There were few opportunities for them to rise above the level of mere subsistence, and even farming was not sufficient to provide for an average family. Many Serb farmers were forced to take on whatever odd jobs were available to supplement their income.

This world of poverty and limited prospects provided the backdrop for the formative years of Princip's childhood. Even his birth underscored the primitive conditions that characterized the life of Bosnian Serbs in the Austro-Hungarian Empire. On July 13, 1894, Princip's mother, although nine months pregnant, was working in the fields, carrying sixty-pound (27 kg) bundles of fresh hay. Later that day, she washed clothes in the nearby brook, and after milking a cow, she felt labor pains. Custom did not permit a woman to make any sign that she was going to have a baby — not even to shout or cry out. Princip's mother managed to reach her house in time to lie on the earthen floor and give birth to Gavrilo. Her mother-in-law rushed into the house and severed the umbilical cord by biting it off, washed the newborn, and wrapped him in a coarse hemp cloth.

Few expected the child to survive; the mortality rate among newborns was very high. The Princip family had nine children, and six had already died. But Gavrilo defied the odds and survived. As a child, he was small and appeared weak. He did not have the strong constitution of his father, but instead took after his mother. He had inherited her looks: curly hair, blue eyes, and pointed chin. Like her, he was less inclined to accept the absolutism of the Church, but rather regarded religion as part of traditional custom. Princip was a sensitive boy who kept to himself and demonstrated a natural affinity for books and learning. In some respects, he was a daydreamer engulfed by the heroic folk stories of Serbia's heroes and villains, which he often recited during evening parties.[85]

At the age of thirteen, he graduated from the local elementary school and was sent to join his older brother in Sarajevo to attend the city's military school. The older brother shortly rejected the notion of Princip's growing up as a Habsburg officer, and instead sent the boy to the merchant school. This also proved a false start, and after three years, the young Princip enrolled in the classical high school. Although the brother was disappointed that Princip had abandoned a career in business, he found consolation in the prospect of Princip's pursuing the legal or medical profession. However, the years Princip spent in high school steered him away from notions of a professional life and into the world of literature and Serbian nationalism.[86] By 1912, he had gravitated to the various secret societies mushrooming among the young Bosnian Serbs, and in the spring he was expelled from school because of his participation in anti-Habsburg demonstrations. With few prospects in Sarajevo, Princip moved to Belgrade, where he lived in extreme poverty but had the satisfaction of witnessing the onset of the Balkan wars that would free the Serbian lands still under Ottoman rule.[87]

Unfortunately, Princip's dream of participating in the crusade of liberation against the Turks was cut short. He failed to meet the minimum physical standards required to join the Serbian irregular units, and he was forced to watch from the sidelines as the Serbian armies, along with those of Montenegro, Bulgaria, and Greece, drove the Turks out of the Balkans. It must have been particularly galling for the young Serb nationalist to be a mere spectator as his friends took part in the liberation of Kosovo Polje and avenged the defeat suffered by the medieval Serbian knights at the hands of the Ottoman Turks. It has even been argued, by Vladimir Dedijer, that Princip's failure to join his comrades in the Serbian forces drove him to a grand gesture that would prove to his peers that he was their equal.[88]

Ultimately, the decision of Archduke Ferdinand to visit Sarajevo on June 28, 1914, the anniversary of the Battle of Kosovo, was the catalyst that transformed Princip from a struggling student into an assassin. He achieved the martyrdom he had read about in centuries of folklore and epic poetry by demonstrating that, like Prince Lazar and Milos, he had the courage to sacrifice his life. In so doing, he perpetuated the Kosovo legend into the twentieth century.

After the First World War, Vaso Cubrilovic, who had made the first attempt against Ferdinand on that fateful June day, recalled that Serbs "with the name of Milos Obilic, they bracket that of Gavrilo

Princip; the former stands for Serbian heroism in the tragedy of the Kosovo field, the latter for Serbian heroism in the final liberation."[89] But Cubrilovic was speaking as much for himself as for Princip. After his arrest, he freely declared that when he read in the papers of the archduke's impending visit, "this fact fired me with zeal to carry out the attempt. Our folklore tradition tells how the hero Milos Obilic was accused before Vidovdan [Saint Vitas] that he was a traitor, and how he answered: 'On Vidovdan we shall see who is and who is not a traitor.' And Obilic became the first assassin who went into the enemy camp and murdered Sultan Murad."[90]

Throughout his trial testimony, Princip remained steadfast to his conviction that terror and assassination were legitimate means of achieving the unification of all the South Slavs.[91] The use of assassination as a weapon was initiated by young Bosnian students as early as 1910, when Bogdan Zerajic unsuccessfully attempted to kill the governor of Bosnia-Herzegovina. Zerajic fired several bullets at the governor but missed. He then shot himself on the spot. Radical young Bosnian Serbs considered Zerajic a hero despite his failure, and his grave became an object of pilgrimages and a source of inspiration. Princip frequently went to the grave and placed flowers on the tombstone, vowing that he would follow Zerajic's example.[92]

It is not beyond the limits of credibility to say that the mystical legacy of Kosovo was pivotal in casting each of these young men in the role of assassin. Indeed, the members of the central committee that directed the secret society planning the assassination of the archduke called each other "spirits of the avengers of Kosovo."

It is still unclear precisely when Princip and the other conspirators decided to undertake the assassination of the archduke, and why they chose Ferdinand over another Habsburg or Austro-Hungarian official. At his trial, Princip testified that he had decided to assassinate Ferdinand when he first read about the archduke's proposed visit in March 1914. He also stated that the archduke was the embodiment of Austria-Hungary's oppression of the South Slavs, and he intimated that as the future emperor, Ferdinand would have prevented their unification.[93] The other conspirators gave reasons that ranged from the fear that the archduke would create a new federation, and thus prevent the unification of all the South Slavs, to the belief that the army maneuvers in Bosnia were a prelude to war with Serbia.[94]

Some of these fears were not unfounded. Ferdinand was an advocate of transforming the empire into a federal system, with equal rights for the South Slavs and all other minorities. The dual monarchy would have given way to a triple monarchy, one based on universal suffrage and proportional representation in a federal parliament.[95] In fact, contrary to the views held by many Serbs, the archduke did not see himself as an enemy of Serbia. If anything, he cared little for Magyars and believed that the Serbs could counterbalance the influence of the Hungarians. In the long run, however, Ferdinand's ideas about extending the franchise to all minorities posed a great threat to the unification of the South Slavs within a single state. Whether this was foremost in the minds of the assassins, we can only speculate. What is certain is that Ferdinand's visit to Sarajevo on the anniversary of Kosovo galvanized the young Bosnians into action.[96] Princip and his fellow conspirators, without much deliberation, agreed to kill the archduke both as a blow for Serbian nationalism and to exact vengeance as part of the Kosovo ritual.

Is it possible that Ferdinand was also drawn to Sarajevo by the allure of Kosovo? In other words, did the archduke choose the most sacred of Serb anniversaries as a sign that he accepted Kosovo as a symbol within the multinational empire he would soon rule? Surely ideas of accommodating the Serbs must have entered Ferdinand's mind as his convertible limousine made its way carefully through the crowds on that fateful day. However, any such thoughts were rudely interrupted by a loud bang that startled the royal entourage and the nearby spectators. The chauffeur saw an object moving through the air toward the automobile and stepped on the accelerator. The driver's alert action saved the archduke and duchess — at least temporarily. In a few seconds, a bomb bounced off the canvas top, rolled down the back of the limousine, and exploded with a deafening noise against one of the back wheels of the car behind the archduke's.

The explosion caused little harm to the royal couple, except for a slight graze on the duchess's neck, but it wounded one of the officers accompanying the governor of Bosnia. The unsuccessful bomber, Nedjeljko Cabrinovic, quickly made his escape by jumping into the Marica River, only to be overtaken by authorities and brought to the nearest police station. In the meantime, the archduke ordered his limousine to stop so he could ascertain what had happened, and he was informed of the wounded officer, who was taken to the hospital.[97] The royal procession, now reduced to three automobiles, resumed its journey and reached the town hall. The mayor and the assembled dignitaries, who had rehearsed the official ceremony of greeting for their eminent guest, were thrown into confusion by the attempted assassination. The mayor simply ignored the bombing incident and proceeded with his speech. However, as he began reading, the archduke cut him off sharply and said, "Mr. Mayor, I come here on a visit and I get bombs thrown at me. It is outrageous. Now you may speak."[98]

After the ceremony, the archduke asked Gen. Oskar Potiorek, the governor of Bosnia, if he thought there would be additional attempts. The general replied that he did not think so but advised the cancellation of the program and recommended that the royal couple proceed to the governor's palace or the Ilidze resort as quickly as possible. Ferdinand, however, decided that it was a point of honor to visit the wounded officer at the garrison hospital. Potiorek then suggested that they take a route that avoided the town, passing along the Appel Quay, where, according to the general, no one expected the procession to travel.[99] According to Luigi Albertini, in his book *The Origins of the War of 1914*, this was not true. The press had published the itinerary, which clearly indicated that after the town-hall meeting, the royal entourage was to pass along the Appel Quay as far as the Latin Bridge.[100] Although Sophie was to proceed straight to the governor's palace, she decided at the last minute to accompany her husband. As an additional element of safety, Count Franz Harrach stood on the running board on the left side of the car to shield the archduke with his body.[101]

Inadvertently, both the governor and the chief of police forgot to provide clear instructions to the drivers. The front car, which was carrying the chief of police, drove along the Appel Quay and, at the Latin Bridge, took a right-hand turn into narrow Franz Joseph Street. The archduke's limousine naturally followed, at which point Potiorek yelled at the driver to stop and turn back onto the Appel Quay. As the car came to a complete halt in the middle of a crowd of onlookers, Princip was brought within a few feet of his target. He raised his pistol and fired two shots almost at point-blank range. One bullet hit Sophie in the abdomen and the other struck Ferdinand in the neck.[102]

Princip was one of seven conspirators stationed along the route of the royal procession that day. At his trial, he said that when he heard the explosion, he assumed that the bomb had hit its target and Cabrinovic's attempt had been successful. When he saw Cabrinovic being taken away by the police, his first thought was to shoot his accomplice to prevent him from talking, then commit suicide.[103] However, Princip observed that the procession was resuming its journey, and it went right past him on its way to the town hall. At this point, since he knew the route of the royal procession from the newspapers, he decided that he would lie in wait for the archduke on the corner of the Appel Quay and Franz Joseph Street. It turned out to be the very spot where the car came to its abrupt stop. The unprotected right side of the car was directly in front of Princip.[104]

For a few seconds after the shooting, nothing happened. Then a thin stream of blood spurted from the archduke's mouth and hit the count's right cheek. As Harrach pulled out a handkerchief to wipe the blood away from the archduke's mouth, Sophie cried out, "In heaven's name, what has happened to you?" Then she slid off the seat and collapsed on the floor of the car, with her face between the archduke's knees. At this point, Ferdinand managed to cry, "Sophie, Sophie, don't die. Stay alive for the children." Count Harrach seized the archduke by the collar of his uniform to stop his head from falling forward and asked if he was in great pain. The archduke answered quite distinctly, "It's nothing." According to Harrach, Ferdinand's face began to twist, but he kept on repeating, six or seven times, "It's nothing." Then, after a short pause, there was a violent choking caused by the bleeding. By the time the limousine had brought the archduke and the duchess to the governor's palace, they were both dead.[105]

In the end, destiny was kinder to Princip than it was to the archduke. The young Bosnian Serb achieved what he wanted: martyrdom and glory. The spot where he fired the two shots has been preserved with impressions of his feet imprinted onto a concrete slab. The Latin Bridge was renamed the Princip Bridge, and the corner building where he stood during the assassination was remodeled as the Young Bosnian Museum and has a shrine in his memory.[106] It can also be argued that unbeknownst to Princip, the assassination sparked the First World War, which led to the defeat of Austria-Hungary and the unification of the South Slavs in the new state of Yugoslavia.

However, like his hero, Milos Obilic, Princip did not live to see these events. Charged with high treason, he was sentenced to twenty years hard labor, "intensified by one day of fasting each month and one day of solitary confinement in a dark cell on 28 June of each year."[107] Despite the rhetoric about the unjust regime of the Habsburgs, Austria's laws did not permit the death penalty for offenders under twenty. Although Princip missed the gallows, he had to spend the remainder of his life in chains. Two years later, on April 24, 1916, he died of bone tuberculosis.

Archduke Ferdinand and Sophie, on the other hand, were not spared the inequities of court etiquette, even in death. While they lay in state, the archduke's casket was placed eighteen inches higher than that of the duchess, whose coffin, although as ornate as Ferdinand's, was smaller.[108] After the official part of the ceremony, the remains of the royal couple were brought to the archduke's estate at Artstetten. When the coffins arrived at the train station in Vienna, the court chamberlain, Prince Montenuovo, relinquished any further responsibility for the former heir apparent and his consort. In effect, the coffins were simply loaded onto the train, which reached its destination of Pochlarn at 2 a.m. There, Ferdinand's friends, members of his staff, ex-servicemen, and the fire brigade had to take charge and complete the burial ceremony.[109]

—◦◦◦—

Outside of those in the archduke's immediate entourage, there were few tears shed for Ferdinand and Sophie. In fact, there was a sense of relief for the Viennese establishment. The Hungarian political elite in particular was prepared to celebrate the archduke's demise, though members refrained from any outward displays of joy in deference to the emperor. For a man whose death was the trigger for a world conflagration, Ferdinand was quickly forgotten. The death of one man, even an archduke, was completely eclipsed by the millions of corpses generated by the killing fields of Europe during the Great War.

The Great War, as the First World War was called before the world conflicts were numbered, had less to do with the little drama in Sarajevo than with other complex geopolitical factors beyond the borders of the Austro-Hungarian Empire. For a brief time after the war, however, the assassination of Ferdinand and Austria-Hungary's ultimatum to Serbia served as useful fodder for both the advocates and the critics of Germany's war guilt. Considerable ink has been spilled by all parties in an attempt to prove or contradict Serbia's involvement in the assassination of the archduke, and by extension assign responsibility for the outbreak of war.[110]

Ferdinand's legacy is one of "what might have been." If the archduke had had the opportunity to restructure the Austro-Hungarian Empire, would this have led to a different future for the Habsburg dynasty? Princip, however, assumed his place in the pantheon of Serbian heroes and martyrs. And in a macabre twist of fate, German planes were among the hundreds of NATO warplanes bombing Yugoslavia and Kosovo in 1999. Perhaps the German contingent will in the future come to represent for the Serbs the ghost of Archduke Ferdinand seeking revenge. In effect, the recent devastation of Yugoslavia, as well as the ultimate failure of a federation that included all South Slavs, becomes just another stanza in the Kosovo epic.

The Kosovo myth will continue into the next millennium, sustaining a new generation of Serb patriots, who will themselves endeavor to liberate the historic heartland of ancient Serbia and demonstrate once again the enigmatic power of legends. In the history of the Balkans, each state, nation, ethnic group, and tribe has its own Kosovo ethos, and over the centuries this has perpetuated the need for a specific identity, exclusive from that of any other people in the region. Indeed, myth and mythmaking are an integral part of Balkan historiography, and they are the yardstick by which each Balkan society measures its national consciousness.

2

THE OTTOMAN ERA:
THE BIRTH OF BALKAN MYTHOLOGY

*Better the turban of the sultan than
the tiara of the Pope in Constantinople.*

— GRAND DUKE NOTARAS, CONSTANTINOPLE, MAY 1453

In the early hours of Tuesday, May 29, 1453, the people of Constantinople were shaken from their sleep by a cacophony of drums, trumpets, cymbals, and fifes, accompanied by the terrific battle cries of 80,000 Ottoman soldiers approaching the walls of the great city.[1] The sudden noise was startling and terrifying, as it was intended to be. The Ottomans were quite adept at using psychological warfare, and their battle for the conquest of the remnants of Byzantium was no exception. The sound of thousands of pounding drums and trumpets, when combined with shrill battle cries from soldiers moving to the attack, was designed to paralyze and weaken the enemy's resolve. For the inhabitants of Constantinople, the terror was further enhanced by a decree from the Ottoman sultan, Mehmet II, who had pledged to reward his troops with three days of unrestricted pillage and mayhem after the capture of the city.[2] The troops defending Constantinople expected no quarter from the Ottomans as they silently waited for the attack to begin.[3]

Shortly after the symphony of war had heralded the onset of a fresh attack, the watchmen guarding Constantinople saw the Ottoman war machine approaching the walls and sounded the alarm. In turn, each church throughout the city began ringing its bells, and their haunting sound was a harbinger of impending doom.[4] The men who had chosen to fight quickly took their positions on the walls. Women, including nuns, joined the men and helped to buttress the defenses, some by dragging stones and wooden beams to strengthen the fortifications; others simply brought fresh water to the soldiers. But in spite of the imminent peril, a large number of able-bodied men refused to take part in the fighting. They were furious because Emperor Constantine, in a desperate move to save the pitiful remains of Byzantium, had reaffirmed the union of the Eastern Orthodox Church with the Church of Rome.[5]

The emperor's decision to unite the churches alienated many Orthodox priests, who feared the pope more than they did the Ottomans. Many of the dissident priests publicly denounced the emperor and refused to offer, from their rich treasuries, any financial support for the defense of the city. For them, debacle was preferable to submission to Rome.[6] The same mean-spiritedness was exhibited by a number of Byzantine nobles, who pleaded poverty when the emperor beseeched them for loans to pay for additional mercenaries, cover the cost of repairing the fortifications, and allow them to stockpile more weapons. In one example, marauding Turks found more than 30,000 ducats in the possession of just one noble. When the battle was over and the Ottomans occupied Constantinople, these very same nobles promptly sent their daughters to Mehmet, along with gifts of money, in a pathetic effort to curry favor with their new Turkish master. Unfortunately, their new-found spirit of generosity failed to impress Mehmet, and the victorious sultan ordered their execution, partly because he could not trust them and partly to literally decapitate the Christian leadership of the defunct Byzantine Empire.[7] A short while later, the Ottoman sultan realized that his support for the Orthodox Church would prove a better weapon against the West, and at the same time would ensure the loyalty of his Christian subjects, including what was left of the nobility. There were priests, monks, nobles, and laypeople who believed that union with Rome was a greater affront and heresy than submission to the Turkish sultan.[8]

The deep-rooted sentiments of these hard-core Orthodox fanatics were best summed up by Grand Duke Notaras, who openly stated that he would rather see "the turban of the sultan than the tiara of the Pope in Constantinople."[9] The ancient Greeks believed that "those whom the gods wish to destroy they grant their wishes," and Notaras got his wish when Mehmet, wearing his turban, rode triumphantly through the streets of Constantinople. On that day, Notaras could finally be assured that the hated Catholics would not impose the rule of the pope over the faithful Orthodox, but his joy was short-lived. The sultan initially treated the grand duke with courtesy, especially after Notaras provided a list of all prominent citizens marked for execution, but then Mehmet demanded Notaras's young son for his sexual entertainment. When Notaras refused, Mehmet ordered the beheading of the grand duke, along with his older son and his son-in-law; the young boy was spared for the sultan's pleasure.[10]

The ill feelings harbored by the Byzantines toward the Roman Church led to strained relations with Constantinople's Catholic mercenaries, most of whom were from Venice, Genoa, and Spain. Some priests and monks said that the Ottoman siege was God's retribution for the union of the two churches, in fact, and they counseled passivity and acceptance of divine punishment.[11] The venerable monk Gennadius, who after the fall of Constantinople was made ecumenical patriarch by Mehmet, warned his supporters that deviation from Orthodoxy and alliance with the Franks (the Catholics) would lead to the loss of the city and the enslavement of the inhabitants to the Turks. The monk's obstinate refusal to accept the union of the churches, along with his condemnation of the emperor, influenced many in Constantinople to riot, and many more to refuse to take part in the fighting.[12]

Further examples of defeatism emerged. The priests and monks saw signs and portents that they conveniently interpreted as proof that the end of the empire was near. During a religious parade through the city three days before the attack, for example, the icon of the Virgin Mary fell from the hands of the priests, who seemed to have considerable difficulty lifting the portrait back up from the ground. This incident was instantly interpreted as evidence of impending doom. Later that day, a sudden thunderstorm swept over the city. The priests explained the storm as a signal of the coming fall of Constantinople to the Ottomans. The day before the siege, a dense fog fell over Constantinople; according to the priests, the fog represented the image of the "Divine Presence departing, and its leaving the city in total abandonment and desertion."[13] Mehmet could not have arranged for a more effective propaganda campaign if he had designed it himself. After the conquest, the sultan showed his appreciation for the power of the Orthodox religion and its priests (at least those who had survived) by granting the Eastern Christian Church and its clergy considerable rights and privileges.

But some extremely optimistic scenarios competed with these evil portents. Those who flocked to the churches during the siege expected divine intervention and waited for the saints and angels to provide protection against the heathen Turks. A large number sought refuge at the great Church of Saint Sophia (the Church of Holy Wisdom). Some, in desperation, placed stock in an old prophecy that said that although "the heathens might penetrate the defenses of the city right up to the sacred building, the Angel of the Lord would appear and with his shining sword consign them [the Turks] to annihilation and damnation."[14]

The congregation in Constantinople's holiest of shrines continued to pray for deliverance during the course of the battle, as did all the worshippers in all the churches throughout the city. But more than prayer was needed to beat off this particular siege. The Byzantine Empire, which had stood for one thousand years, had been reduced to one city and a handful of defenders. Almost everyone, including the most exuberant optimists, must have known that it was only a matter of days before the Ottoman Turks would breach the walls. Knowing something and accepting it, however, are very different things. Occasionally, the population would rejoice at the sight of a Christian galley on the Sea of Marmora, assuming it was the forerunner of a rescue fleet. They would then fall into despondency when the sighting proved to be only a lone ship returning home with bad news — or worse, with no news whatsoever — of the expected reinforcements from the West.

Even if help did arrive in time, the demise of the empire was a foregone conclusion. The historian G. Ostrogorsky estimates that "had the West intervened its aims would certainly not have been to save the Byzantine Empire."[15] The walls of Constantinople had withstood twenty-nine sieges over almost two thousand years, and succumbed to only eight. After each assault or capture, the city had recovered and the empire had managed to survive, and occasionally even expand. In 1205, Constantinople fell to the Fourth Crusade, which effectively gutted the empire.[16] Western crusading knights, with the financial backing of the Venetians, soon abandoned the cause of liberating the Holy Land for the much easier and substantially wealthier prize of Constantinople. Certainly the treasures of the last great city of the Roman Empire held a stronger allure than a long and hard campaign against the fervent Muslim warriors of the Middle East. In the end, the fall of Constantinople to the soldiers of God in 1205 had dealt a lingering but ultimately mortal blow to the Byzantine Empire.

Indeed, the line in the sand had first been drawn by the Great Schism of 1054, which divided Christianity into a Catholic Church in the West and an Orthodox Church in the Balkans and the East. Over the next four centuries, the schism evolved into a religious abyss that led some Orthodox faithful to believe that Ottoman rule was preferable to submission to the pope in Rome. Although fine points of dogma and differences over liturgy and the nature of the Holy Trinity fueled the religious antagonism between the two churches, it was really the fate of Constantinople during the Fourth Crusade that had destroyed any possibility of genuine reconciliation with the Western Christians. "Their barbarity left a memory that would never be forgiven them," writes Steven Runciman. "In the hearts of the East Christians the schism was complete, irremediable and final."[17]

Unlike the Ottomans, the Norman and German knights had not been compelled to attempt a long siege; after a short battle, they entered Constantinople, with the connivance of some members of the Byzantine nobility, to install a rival emperor.[18] When the new ruler, Alexius IV, was unable to fulfill his extravagant promises of rich prizes and money for the crusaders, the warriors of Christ wreaked their vengeance on the population. The Church of Holy Wisdom was plundered. The crusaders ransacked the building, looking for valuables, and paused only to massacre the Eastern Orthodox inhabitants with greater gusto than the Turks would do in 1453. Priests were hacked to death by medieval broad swords and nuns raped on the altar of the great church. To add insult to injury, the knights placed on the throne of the patriarch a prostitute who sang a lewd French song for their entertainment.[19] Pillage, rape, and plunder spread to the rest of the city, and the inhabitants of Constantinople were forced to endure the sack for three days. (More than two hundred years later, the Ottomans would be satisfied with a paltry twelve hours of looting.[20]) Afterward, the Western knights carved up the empire and a Catholic assumed the throne of Byzantium. The final indignity for the Orthodox Christians was their forcible conversion to Catholicism and the submission of their church to Rome. Fifty years later, the Byzantines were able to expel the crusaders and recover their capital, but the empire that re-emerged was a mere shadow of its former self. In this condition, it was incapable of resisting the onslaught of Turkmen tribesmen who overran Anatolia and Asia Minor in the 1400s.

The Turks, who had emerged from obscurity in Central Asia, came in waves of various Turkmen tribes and in disparate groups displaced from their homelands. Many coalesced into new societies that included combinations of fervent Muslim crusaders, bands of nomadic tribesmen, adventurers, and mercenaries in search of booty. But they did not represent a unified force that could impose a single social, political, and economic system on the new lands they conquered. Their appearance in the lands adjacent to the Byzantine frontier was not part of any calculated design. It was instigated instead by the Mongol conquests of Central Asia, and accelerated after the Mongols overran Persia and finally captured Baghdad in 1258. The Seljuk Turks, who had re-enacted the Mongol invasions, were the first to drift westward, and by the end of the eleventh century, they had established powerful principalities (called emirates) as well as a Seljuk Empire in Anatolia and Asia Minor. Meanwhile, the migrations of the Turkmen tribes and bands of roving warriors continued. Many of these new Turkmen nomads quickly fell under the domination of the established Muslim emirates in Persia, Anatolia, and Asia Minor, and they were employed as religious warriors (Ghazis), either defending or infiltrating the border between Byzantium and the Muslim principalities.[21] In the words of the historian Fernand Braudel, the "troubled frontiers of Asia Minor [were] a rendezvous for adventurers and fanatics. For Asia Minor was a region of unparalleled mystical enthusiasm: here war and religion marched hand in hand."[22] Ultimately, the journey led them to Constantinople.

In this cauldron of religious war, Turkish Ghazis and their Christian counterparts (Akritai) waged a relentless, three-century struggle along the frontier of the Byzantine Empire in the name of their respective religions. The Christian and Muslim warriors fought a seemingly endless conflict with their own codes of behavior and belief systems. This frontier culture, comments Peter Sugar, represented a "Christian and Muslim mixture of superstitions, mysticism, traditional, and in some cases, even pagan beliefs — [and these] were more similar to each other than they were to officially correct versions of the creeds. These folk-religions began to fuse and gradually became dominated by Muslim characteristics."[23]

After the Byzantines reclaimed Constantinople in 1261, the emperors made a fatal strategic blunder by concentrating their efforts in the Balkans against the emerging Slav kingdoms.[24] Succeeding emperors neglected the defenses of Anatolia and Asia Minor, and committed the limited military resources of the empire to Southeastern Europe. Consequently, the eastern frontier fell into a state of anarchy. The emperors lacked the resources to maintain law and order, let alone stem the tide of fresh waves of Turkmen tribesmen pouring over the frontier. The Turkmen warrior nomads quickly overwhelmed the eastern frontier regions of the Byzantine Empire, destroying its urban centers and settling in what had become a rural environment. The emperors in Constantinople, meanwhile, abandoned the Akritai to their fate. Some joined the Turkish Ghazis, while others managed to escape from Anatolia and find employment in the European possessions of Byzantium.[25] The Byzantine rulers kept on surrendering parts of Anatolia and Asia Minor, so that by 1300 most of the region had fallen under the control of the Turks.

As in the eleventh century, the conquest of the territory did not unfold as part of a master plan, but was instead pursued by independent bands of Turkmen soldiers, tribesmen, and Ghazis. During the course of the fourteenth century, these tribal chieftains and Ghazi leaders managed to organize the nomadic Turkmen into principalities that owed their existence to the jihad waged against the Byzantine Empire. In other words, the relations between the early Muslims in general (and later the Ottomans in particular) and the Christians were based on mutual hostility and intensified by religious differences. Although there would be periods of peaceful coexistence and even cordial relations, these were truces of mutual convenience, and the situation quickly returned to a state of aggression and war.

———◦∿◦———

In this region of decaying empires and emerging nations of the early fourteenth century, a mix of Turkmen nomads, soldiers of fortune, and renegade Byzantines gravitated to the banner of Osman, an obscure tribal chieftain and Ghazi warrior whose descendants would reach the gates of Constantinople. At first, Osman and his forces served as auxiliaries to the Seljuk Turks, and eventually, they established their own emirate (principality) in Bithynia, just opposite the rump Byzantine Empire.[26] The location was fortuitous because the new and small emirate could plunder the nearby wealthy Byzantines rather than having to compete with the other Turkish principalities over the limited resources of Anatolia. The Ottomans, or Osmanlis, as the followers of Osman came to be called, absorbed or conquered over the next half century what was left of the Seljuk Empire and brought their formidable army to bear against the last vestiges of Byzantium and then Europe.[27] Under the leadership of Orkhan, Osman's successor, the Ottomans almost completed the conquest of Asia Minor, and by the middle of the fourteenth century, they had established a firm foothold in the eastern Balkans. During the same period, Byzantium underwent a series of natural upheavals and internal rebellions that made it impossible for the empire not only to contain the Ottomans in the East and prevent their expansion into the Balkans, but also to counter the threat from the Serbian medieval empire.[28]

When Orkhan died in 1361, after ruling for thirty-seven years, Murad I inherited a powerful army and an embryonic feudal state that depended on both Muslim and Christian vassals of the sultan. The secret of the Ottoman feudal system was flexibility and the policy of transplanting military colonists to newly conquered territories. Unlike its Western equivalent, Ottoman feudalism was designed to provide the sultan with a military force on demand. In the West, feudal lords could expect only forty days of service from their vassals, which limited their ability to wage long campaigns. For the Ottomans, however, war was the vital element that sustained continuous growth, thus affording each sultan the means to provide his followers with land and booty. Nonetheless, land given to Muslim warriors was rewarded only for the lifespan of the individual, and successors could claim territories for themselves only in exchange for their own exemplary service to the sultan.[29]

The Ottoman rulers had to perpetuate this cycle of war, conquest, and distribution of new lands, and this created a momentum that attracted fresh Turkish recruits to the Ottoman camp, which in turn necessitated additional campaigns to reward the successful warriors. Viewed from another perspective, the Ottoman armies were like a brush fire that moved forward as long as there was fuel and oxygen to sustain the blaze. New lands and the spoils of war provided the fodder and energy of the Ottoman drive to the West. But the critical flaw of the Ottoman phenomenon was that loss of movement meant stagnation and eventual disintegration. Two centuries later, when the Ottoman Empire ceased to grow, the process of decline was initiated automatically. Although historians cite several reasons for the decay of the empire, most agree that the termination of successful campaigns altered the military and socio-economic structure, which eventually ushered in the empire's demise.[30] One vital factor was that the military establishment, represented by the Sipahi cavalry and the elite Janissary corps, eventually evolved into a hereditary land-owning class. When these soldiers began inheriting their own land, there was no longer any use for the policy of awarding estates on the basis of military merit, which had been the mechanism that reinvigorated these units in the past. By the late sixteenth century, this transition had also led to corruption (in the form of extortionary land taxes and bribery).[31] To maintain the flow of land and booty for his followers, Murad I had to continue expansion by war or by manipulating the Balkan Christians, either as allies or as vassals, until they were ripe for conquest.

By the fourteenth century, the Ottomans had established a pattern that led to the gradual conquest of the Balkans. First, Turkish irregular bands moved westward from Thrace, wreaking havoc and establishing a forward base of operations, which was later exploited by the Ottoman army. In this manner, Demotika was seized from the Byzantines in 1360–61, Philopolis from the Bulgarians in 1369, and Adrianople in 1369; by the middle of the fifteenth century, the Ottomans were masters of the Balkans and all the territories of Asia Minor and Anatolia. Only Constantinople and a few small towns remained — the last Byzantine foothold in an otherwise hostile land of Turkish kingdoms and principalities. It was in 1359, however, that Byzantium first lost all vestiges of independence and dignity to the Ottomans. In March of that year, John Palaeologos, king of the Greeks and Roman emperor, had to present himself at Scutari as a vassal of Orkhan, the Ottoman sultan. The humiliation of the Roman emperor was made complete when Orkhan forced the reluctant John V to give his ten-year-old daughter in marriage to Orkhan's son, Halil.[32]

To a great extent, the Byzantines had set in motion their own demise when they failed to see the danger posed by the Ottomans. Initially, the Turks were invited into the empire as mercenaries and later as allies to counter the encroachment of new adversaries such as Serbia, Bulgaria, and the Italian city-states. The Byzantine emperors did not hesitate to use the Ottomans in their dynastic wars, and they effectively facilitated the entrenchment of the Ottomans in both Asia and Europe, which of course was at the expense of the empire's territories and subjects. The process was initiated in 1345 during a dynastic struggle between John Cantacuzenos, regent of Emperor John V, and the young emperor's mother, Empress Anna. Cantacuzenos had decided to appoint himself co-emperor in order to seize the throne, and at first he sought help from Duscan, the king of Serbia. Empress Anna, for her part, turned to Orkhan for military support, which created the opportunity for the Ottoman sultan to exploit the divisions not only within the empire, but also between the Christian monarchies.

Cantacuzenos, however, proved a better military commander and quickly defeated the Ottoman forces sent against him. What took place afterward was graphically described by Ducas, the Byzantine historian. According to his account, after the battle, all captive Turks were put to the sword. But the Roman prisoners were spared, and after their clothes were taken away from them, they were permitted to return home naked.[33] The Turks who had escaped, however, soon turned to plunder and succeeded in capturing a large number of Roman women, men, children, priests, and monks. These prisoners were tied together in single file to be sold in Constantinople. When buyers did not materialize, the Turks flogged their captives, whose cries it was assumed would arouse the sympathy of the onlookers. But despite tears and pity from the citizens of Constantinople, none came forward to free the unfortunate prisoners, and they were transported to the slave markets of the East.[34]

When the fortunes of war turned against Cantacuzenos, who by this time had discovered that he had little support for his claim to the imperial mantle, the cunning ex-regent decided to outbid the empress for an alliance with the Ottomans. Cantacuzenos, in exchange for 6,000 Turkish cavalry, proposed the marriage of his daughter, Theodora, to Orkhan, along with a hefty dowry. In later periods, Western historians were appalled by the practice of giving young Christian women to the Ottoman sultans and having them reduced to little more than slaves or concubines. In time, the image of beautiful Christian women being used as payment and sacrificed to the sexual depravity associated with the sultan's harem became an important ingredient in the mythology of the Ottoman period in Southeastern Europe.

Such impressions were fostered by Byzantine writers such as Ducas, who described the Ottomans as an "intemperate and lustful people, incontinent beyond all races and insatiate in licentiousness and dissolute from having intercourse by both natural and unnatural means with females, males, and dumb animals."[35] Ducas even called the marriage of Orkhan and Theodora an "abomination."[36] The images of Turkish debauchery and sexual degradation conjured up by Byzantine and Balkan writers later offered a model for the portrayal of the Ottomans during the nineteenth and twentieth centuries. The Ottomans were given no redeeming features whatsoever, and there was always considerable emphasis placed on the slaughters and other cruelties inflicted on the Balkan peoples when the empire was in decline.

Despite the prejudices of the Byzantines, it was not uncommon for Muslims and Christians to marry as a means of sealing alliances. In some cases, the marriages proved to be successful unions, as happened with Orkhan and Theodora. They were married in Selymbria in the summer of 1346 and had one child, Halil, who died shortly after Murad became sultan in 1362. According to most accounts, Orkhan was passionately in love with Theodora, and he allowed his Christian bride to maintain her Orthodox religion (although he made several attempts to convert her to Islam). When Orkhan died, Theodora probably returned to Constantinople and lived with her sister, Empress Helena. The marriage of Orkhan and Theodora aside, however, most such unions were not happy. Nevertheless, women and especially children continued to be handed over in what was effectively a child tax. The notion of paying the Ottomans in human currency became even more prevalent after the conquest of Constantinople, since the sultans needed no more allies, and thus had no need for dynastic marriages.

With the military aid of the Ottomans, Cantacuzenos became emperor for eight years, but during this time he remained in power only with Orkhan's support. In 1349, more than 20,000 Ottoman forces were deployed around the major Balkan port of Thessaloniki to fight Cantacuzenos's battles. The Ottomans used the opportunity to plunder the area, but they also became familiar with the lay of the land, which proved useful when Orkhan's successors decided to conquer the region. In 1353, the Ottomans captured Gallipoli, which gave them a foothold in Europe. Despite Cantacuzenos's demand that the city be handed back to Byzantium, the Ottomans refused and used this new acquisition to initiate their expansion in the Balkans. Cantacuzenos was overthrown one year later, but the new emperor, John VII Palaeologos, did not have the military resources to force the Ottomans to give up the city. The Ottomans were in the Balkans to stay. Indeed, in 1916, Herbert Gibbons, a historian of the Ottoman Empire, wrote in disgust that "John Cantacuzenos introduced the Osmanlis [Ottomans] into Europe, [and] John Palaeologos accepted their presence in Thrace [in the eastern Balkans] without a struggle. There is little choice between these two Johns."[37] During the course of the fourteenth century, the decay of Byzantium was hastened by the impact of the great plagues and compounded by the ruinous competition between powerful families whose greed for power left them squabbling over what was left of the imperial corpse.

—◦◦◦—

In the end, the Ottoman armies proved irresistible, and victory after victory confirmed their military superiority — but they still failed to conquer Constantinople. For more than a century and a half, succeeding Ottoman sultans fed their ambitions by trying to master the great city — only to face defeat and disappointment. In 1453, however, Mehmet II vowed to capture Constantinople for the glory of

Islam and at the same time assure his place as one of history's great conquerors. The sultan had assembled an army of more than 80,000 fighting men and 325 vessels of all types. By the end of April 1453, the Ottoman fleet had managed to seal the entrance to the Golden Horn[38] and cut Constantinople off from the sea.

The defenders, on the other hand, numbered approximately 7,000 mercenaries and volunteers, spread across fourteen miles (23 km) of walls, while the naval contingent included only fourteen ships. Lack of funds had left the mercenaries without pay for long periods, and some, such as the Hungarian engineer Urban, abandoned the Byzantines and instead offered their services to Mehmet. During the siege, which lasted almost two months, the cannons designed by Urban hammered the walls of Constantinople, causing major breaches and demolishing towers. Although damage was quickly repaired, the wear and tear took its toll on both the fortifications and the soldiers manning the walls.[39] Each day the number of thinly spread men was shrinking. The Byzantines could not afford even minimal casualties — the siege had become a war of attrition, and it was only a matter of time before the defenders, regardless of their bravery, would be overwhelmed. Indeed, on Tuesday, May 29, Mehmet calculated that he could end the siege with one last massive assault.[40]

The sultan organized the attack against the city in three stages. First, Mehmet commenced the battle with his irregular troops, the Bashi-Bazouks. This strange assortment of mercenaries, cutthroats, and adventurers consisted of several thousand Turks, but it also included many more Slavs, Hungarians, Germans, Italians, and Greeks, who fought against their fellow Christians for pay and booty promised by the sultan. In addition to carrying scaling ladders, they were armed with an odd collection of scimitars, bows, slings, and harquebuses. Under the best of circumstances, the Bashi-Bazouks were unreliable and poorly disciplined, more concerned with pillage than fighting. They were usually formidable in the first onrush, but quickly lost momentum and became disorganized if that attack failed. Afterward, they fell behind as a disorganized mass and could rarely be inspired to mount a counterattack.

On this occasion, Mehmet was not taking any chances. He placed reliable troops just behind the irregulars, with orders to use force to keep them from falling back. If any Bashi-Bazouks managed to get past this line of "military police," they would be killed by the sultan's Janissaries. For more than an hour, the Bashi-Bazouks rushed the fortifications all along the line, but they were easy prey for the better-armed professional soldiers manning the walls. One problem was that they advanced close together in a disorganized fashion, which only put them in each other's way and caused more confusion. The defenders were able to destroy large numbers of Bashi-Bazouks by hurling stones on the massed clusters of them, thereby killing several at a time. Even the few who managed to climb the ladders were cut down before they reached the top. Although the attack was a failure and the Bashi-Bazouks were ordered to retreat, they had accomplished their primary mission: to wear down the defenders as a prelude to the second assault.

Before the Byzantines had time to reorganize, Mehmet ordered the advance of the Anatolian heavy infantry. This attack too was preceded by a concentrated cannonade against the walls, which tore considerable gaps in the fortifications and brought down several towers. The Anatolian troops at first moved slowly and in close order, accompanied by the sound of trumpets, drums, and pipes. As they approached the walls, they attempted to rush the defenses, determined to be the first Muslims to enter the city. With considerable tenacity and religious zeal, these soldiers set their ladders and began the grueling task of scaling the walls. Their very discipline worked against them, however. In an effort to overcome the obstacles presented by Constantinople's fortifications, they massed against a narrow front and continued to maintain their cohesion despite the barrage of missiles and rocks hurled down on them by the defenders. Stones flung from above the walls killed hundreds; others died when their ladders were pushed off, and many more while fighting hand-to-hand on top of the walls.

Regardless of the casualties, the Anatolian infantry continued to maintain closed ranks, which in turn enabled the defenders to sustain the slaughter and destroy almost entire units. Just as the Anatolians were beginning to lose ground, however, a ball from one of the cannons created a major breach. For a brief moment victory was in sight, and 300 Turks managed to enter the city, only to be massacred by the quick response of the Byzantines. After about an hour, the attack was called off.

With the almost constant fighting, the defenders had had little opportunity to rest and only time enough to partially regroup. Despite a ten to one numerical disadvantage, the Byzantines and their allies had held the walls against waves of suicidal assaults and a constant barrage of artillery that periodically caused serious damage to segments of the outer walls. The effective use of cannonade by the Ottomans frequently created sudden breaches, forcing the defenders to move their tired troops back and forth to plug new holes in the fortifications.[41]

After more than two hours of hard fighting, two-thirds of Mehmet's army had already spent itself against the walls of Constantinople. The sultan remained impervious to the large number of casualties, however, all the while mindful that the purpose of the first attacks had been to soften the defenses and wear down the enemy. It was a steep price to pay, but the Turkish sultan could not afford to end the carnage. If he failed to capture Constantinople, the blow to his prestige and authority would be irreversible. Like his predecessors, Mehmet had few illusions about his fate if he suffered a major defeat.

—◦◦◦—

The status of the sultan and the absence of a rational means of succession were at once remarkable features of strength and fundamental flaws in the political structure of the Ottomans. To a great extent, the Ottoman Empire was organized and established by freemen but ruled by the children of slaves. Each sultan assumed the throne by virtue of his ability to influence the army and eliminate any challengers. In keeping with the Muslim custom of polygamy, the sultan maintained a harem of hundreds of women. Some, as we have seen, were the daughters of Christian monarchs or influential Turkish families. But this practice fell into decline after 1453. By then, the sultan had no need of Christian allies, and it had proved dangerous to marry into the families of prominent Turks, thus granting them direct access to the imperial family. Indeed, reducing the power and influence of the great Turkish families became official policy, and the ultimate aim was to eliminate any potential claimants to the throne.

The use of slave girls offered greater control of dynastic lineages. None of their offspring could mount strong claims to the throne, and thus they represented no threat to the power and absolute authority of the sultan. The sultan's agents scoured the slave markets of the Balkans and the Middle East for beautiful and totally powerless females. These women and their children were entirely at the mercy and whim of the sultan. In fact, these convenient and non-committal liaisons endowed most sultans with a reservoir of potential heirs from which to choose. There was no legal tradition of succession from father to eldest son, and so all of the sultan's male children were on an equal footing.

In other words, any one of the sultan's male offspring could aspire to the throne, regardless of the status of his mother. Most successors were either so designated by the sultan or secured the support of the army and the Muslim establishment. Any of the other potential heirs could challenge the new sultan, of course, and the most convenient and effective means of removing claimants to the throne and preventing dynastic quarrels was to have them murdered. According to some Ottoman sources, Bayazid initiated the practice when he had his brother killed right after the Battle of Kosovo to guarantee a smooth transition and avoid any potential civil war.

To some extent, the absence of a system of succession and the cruel practice of killing all of the new ruler's male siblings ensured that the sultanate went to the strongest man. But such traditions and customs also meant that defeat or failure in war would completely undermine a sultan's position as ruler and leave him vulnerable to challenges from other powerful Turkish leaders. Mehmet, in particular, was by no means a popular sultan, and at the age of twenty-three, he had had little opportunity to fashion a reputation as a soldier. Furthermore, his senior advisers and military commanders were divided. The political group, led by Grand Vizier Halil, advised ending the siege of Constantinople, arguing that it would fail and that the Ottomans might then face war with Venice and Hungary. But the sultan and the military, whose future depended on the outcome of the battle, preferred to continue with the siege.[42]

In the early hours of the morning, Mehmet finally decided to commit the Janissaries, the elite and most reliable force in his army. He gambled that it was the right moment to intensify the battle, since the Byzantines and their allies would be close to exhaustion. The Janissaries, the best soldiers in the medieval world, were also unique. Almost all of them were Christians, and most had been taken as prisoners or handed over to the Ottomans by their parents as a form of child tax. The best and strongest of these children were converted to Islam and, from the age of twelve, trained as soldiers. Their lot was a lifetime of military service and absolute devotion to the sultan. They were not permitted to marry and remained segregated from society, living in barracks and always ready to execute their master's orders. In fact, the Janissaries represented the first professional standing army. Despite their Christian upbringing, they became fanatical Muslims and earnestly maintained their faith as warriors of Islam.

This cruel practice of what today can be defined as the "brain cleansing" of the Christian populations of the Ottoman Empire is perhaps the most inhuman Turkish legacy.[43] The advantages gained by those chosen for conversion and a better life in Constantinople cannot militate against the odium of taking children away from their parents. The Ottomans periodically sent their agents to exact the child tribute, depriving the Christian villages of their strongest and most intelligent boys and girls, whose vitality then augmented the human resources of the sultan. The Ottoman child collectors were the most hated manifestation of Ottoman rule, and the memory of these men continues to stigmatize the Turks in the Balkans.

It is the tragic irony of the siege of Constantinople that the Janissaries, who had once been Christians, were the ones to strike the fatal blow against Constantinople, the very symbol of Christianity in the East. The Janissaries represented not only the *crème de la crème* of the Ottoman forces, but also the flower of Greek youth. Many of the sultan's generals, senior officials, and advisers were also converted Greeks; several, in fact, were renegade Byzantine nobles who had conveniently switched faiths to preserve their estates.[44] Perhaps only an ancient Greek tragedy could do justice to the surreal spectacle of a Greek army preparing to assault a Greek city defended by Italian and other mercenaries in order to bring down what was left of the Roman Empire. In another time and age, it could be argued that the Greeks simply adjusted from a Roman to an Ottoman universe. But the critical and insurmountable reality was a religious fault line that permanently segregated Christian and Muslim societies. Although many of the Janissaries were Greek, their conversion and adherence to Islam severed them forever from the Hellenic consciousness of Greek society.

On the morning of May 29, 1453, as the Janissaries started their advance against Constantinople, they represented more than an army of Greeks with a different religion — they were a human abomination already consigned to the grave by their families. In effect, they were dead to the society of their birth and now marched as the undead against the city of Eastern Greek Orthodoxy. In the fifteenth century, language and culture no longer defined the Greek world, and its classical antecedents had been damned as vestiges of the pagan past. Even the word "Greek" (Hellene) was associated with paganism, and the word "Roman" was used to define a Christian Greek. As the Greeks progressively fell under the sway of the Ottoman Empire in Europe and Asia, the cultural and political currency of the Greek world had been replaced by religion. Although some individual Greeks achieved prominence and wealth, the predominant Greek regions of Asia Minor, the Aegean Islands, and mainland Greece underwent a cultural metamorphosis, emerging as self-contained and inward-looking societies. The slow death of Byzantium had already fragmented Greek society, rendering it easily susceptible to Ottoman administration and, after the fall of the empire, incapable of mounting a collective resistance against the vicissitudes of Turkish domination.

As secular authority collapsed in regions conquered by the Ottomans, the Orthodox Church filled the political and cultural vacuum until Greek identity and Orthodoxy became one and the same. According to a memorandum dated 1437, out of the sixty-seven metropolitan sees that were dependent on the patriarch of Constantinople, only eight remained within the territory of Byzantium. Many Orthodox theologians and politicians in the fifteenth century had few doubts that Byzantium was doomed. They believed that the only hope for reuniting the conquered Greeks with the Orthodox Church in Constantinople, and thus for preserving Greek identity, was to accept Ottoman rule. Otherwise, even if Constantinople were rescued, the Orthodox Greeks would constitute a small fragment attached to the edge of the Western world and severed from the majority of their co-religionists, who would remain within the Ottoman Empire.[45] But as long as there was a Christian emperor in Constantinople, every Greek in Ottoman lands continued to hold out hope for salvation from Turkish captivity. The last act of the siege of Constantinople, however, an act that was initiated by the forward movement of the Janissaries on the morning of May 29, was to shatter for half a millennium any such notions.

Although the Janissaries, like the Bashi-Bazouks and the Anatolian contingents, marched in double step and in closed order, they resisted the temptation to rush the fortifications. Loud martial music, the pounding of drums, and the blast of cannon fire almost drowned out the noise of battle as each unit marched past the sultan in one last desperate effort to breach the fortifications. With their banners flying in the early morning breeze, these grim warriors of Islam approached the walls, impervious to the barrage of arrows, fire, burning oil, and stones that rained down on their ranks from the equally determined men on top. Hundreds managed to climb the scaling ladders and struggle to the top of the walls, and as each rank was defeated, a fresh contingent replaced them. They remained indifferent to the mangled bodies of their comrades and were determined to press on with the attack.

Despite the ferocious tenacity of the Janissaries, they fared little better than the previous units. Nevertheless, the city could not escape its destiny. At the corner of one of the walls, there was a small gate half hidden by a tower. These types of gates were designed to enable the defenders to harass besieging armies. In fact, raiding parties attacking the flanks of the Ottomans had used this particular portal on more than one occasion. Unfortunately, someone returning from such a raid forgot to close and bar the door. Later, conspiracy theories abounded on whether this was carelessness or a deliberate act of betrayal. Whatever the case, a few Janissaries noticed the opening and rushed through the gate to the courtyard behind it, which they also found unguarded. They managed to climb a stairway that led to the top of the wall. When the defenders became aware of the presence of the Turks inside the fortifications, they attempted to retake the gate.

In the melee that followed, some fifty Turks were left inside the wall, but before they could be dispatched, the Genoese commander of the Byzantine garrison, Giovanni Giustiniani-Longo, was wounded.[46] Giustiniani, a professional soldier from Genoa with considerable experience in defending cities, had been the heart and soul of the resistance against the Ottomans; his sudden withdrawal from the fighting was a serious blow to both the Byzantines and his own followers. As the commander-in-chief of all military forces in

Constantinople, Giustiniani was the very image of the brave and skillful soldier always at the forefront of the battle. Although the wound he suffered was not lethal, it bled profusely, sapping Giustiniani's strength and courage. He pleaded desperately with his men to carry him to the safety of his ship, ignoring the emperor's entreaties not to leave the field of battle and cause a general breakdown of morale. Unfortunately, the sight of Giustiniani's own blood had reduced the brave commander to a pitiful state. In the end, he chose ignominy over a gallant end to his career by deserting at the critical moment of the battle. Escape did not save his life, however. It only stained an otherwise exemplary career.[47]

The departure of Giustiniani and his men caused general panic among the remaining mercenaries and the Byzantine troops. Although some continued fighting, a large number abandoned the fight and sought to protect their families. Taking advantage of the confusion, the Janissaries made one last surge. Led by a giant named Hasan, one company of thirty Janissaries climbed over the corpses left behind by earlier attacks and hacked their way to the top of the wall. The defenders struck back with equal ferocity. Hasan had his head crushed by a large stone, crumpled to his knees, and shortly expired, alongside seventeen of his Janissaries. The remainder, however, held the position and, with fresh reinforcements, managed to break though the defenses. The Byzantines fought with considerable tenacity to stem the flood of Ottomans now pouring through the breach, but they were overwhelmed by the sheer volume of numbers. When Emperor Constantine realized that all was lost, he discarded his imperial insignia and threw himself into the battle. Unlike many of the other Byzantine nobles, Constantine chose to die with honor rather than end his days facing either the ignominy of execution or a life as a slave of the sultan. Soon, additional Ottoman forces broke through other gates and gaps in the walls and fanned throughout the city — the very incarnation of death and destruction foretold by apocalyptic prophecies.

At first, the Janissaries and the other Ottoman troops did not believe they had destroyed what was left of the Byzantine army, and they continued to butcher anyone they found in the streets. When the Ottomans finally accepted the reality of victory, they turned their attention to the business of massacre and pillage. On Tuesday, May 29, the clarion call of death beckoned the helpless civilians of Constantinople. Thousands were butchered to satiate the Ottomans' craving for revenge for the sacrifices they had suffered to capture the city. During the course of the siege, it had been common for the Byzantines to behead their captured Turks on the walls in full view of the Ottoman army. Nothing inhibited the conquerors from inflicting the cruelest forms of retribution on the Byzantines for these acts. As the morning wore on, Mehmet's soldiers pillaged the vanquished in a general slaughter that sunk to new depths of depravity. Women, regardless of age or vocation, were raped repeatedly, many on the altars of churches, and those who survived, even young nuns, were carried off to the Ottoman camp as booty. Some were literally torn apart as their captors fought over them to claim their human spoils.[48]

The troops in their frenzy ransacked churches, palaces, and houses. They killed the old and the sick, as well as the very young — anyone who had no immediate utilitarian purpose or any value as booty. Those who had crowded into the Church of Holy Wisdom, hoping for divine intervention, now found themselves trapped. The Ottomans broke down the door and, with little warning, pounced on the terrified Christians. Remarkably, no one offered any resistance or attempted to flee; all preferred to remain as docile as spectators until their turn came to face slavery, death, or rape.[49] Almost all the priests were butchered at the altar as they continued chanting, but a handful managed to hide in the nooks and crannies of the building. At the last moment, according to the testimony of those present, a few of the priests grabbed some of the holy vessels and objects and moved to the southern wall of the sanctuary. The wall opened, they entered, and it closed behind them. This story later became an integral element of the myth surrounding the fall of Constantinople, and legend still has it that the priests will reappear only after the building is once again sanctioned as an Orthodox church.[50]

The killing came to an end by dusk. Gradually, greed replaced vengeance as the Turks realized that their captives were more valuable alive and could be sold as slaves. Thereafter, the Christians who had crowded into the Church of Holy Wisdom faced a new torment. Men, women, and children were herded together, regardless of rank or status, and carted off to the Ottoman camp, swelling the ranks of human booty being assembled by the victors. Families were separated, most never to be reunited again, while thousands ended up in the slave markets of the Middle East and even as far away as Central Asia.

The orgy of plunder, rape, impalement, decapitation, and other forms of butchery finally came to an end by eight in the evening. Mehmet, surrounded by his bodyguards and senior Ottoman officials, entered the city and proceeded to the Church of Holy Wisdom. Before entering, he sprinkled dirt over his turban as an act of humility to Allah, and then he ordered the consecration of the great church as a mosque. Later that evening, the Muslim calling of prayers in the church echoed the last convulsions of Constantinople as the capital of a Christian empire. Mehmet ordered the cessation of any further pillaging and invited all the Christians who had survived to return to their homes, guaranteeing their lives, property, and religion.[51]

Although statistics of casualties are not precise, it is estimated that approximately 4,000 civilians and soldiers were killed. Some sources say about 50,000 civilians and a few hundred soldiers ended up as captives and potentially as slaves.[52] This last statistic is doubtful, however, since the entire population of the city was less than 50,000. What is certain is that not all who were captured were consigned to a life of slavery. A great many were either purchased by the sultan himself and set free or bought by sympathetic Balkan nobles and despots.[53] Mehmet, who now wished to establish Constantinople as his capital, more than likely encouraged the manumission of the captured inhabitants. After all, a depopulated city would offer few advantages to what was to become the center of the Ottoman Empire.

The sack of Constantinople and the graphic descriptions of Turkish cruelty have contributed to a literary and historical tradition that cast the Ottoman Empire as a shameful chapter in the history of Western civilization. After 1453, Byzantine writers sketched out the last days of Constantinople in images more inclined to tap in to a reader's emotions and less committed to historical detail and proportionality. This theme of Ottoman barbarism was really a subtle jibe at the failure of the West to make any attempt to save Constantinople. From Gibbon's time to the present, writers dealing with this period do not fail to mention the hypocrisy of the Western monarchies, which failed to aid their fellow Christians and yet still considered the collapse of Byzantium a major blow. Gibbon writes: "The importance of Constantinople was felt and magnified in its loss: the pontificate of Nicholas the fifth, however peaceful and prosperous, was dishonoured by the fall of the Eastern Empire; and the grief and terror of the Latins revived, or seemed to revive, the old enthusiasm of the crusades."[54] Steven Runciman, one of the foremost authorities on Byzantium, offers a different and more poignant perspective:

> For eleven centuries Constantinople had been the center of the world of light. The quick brilliance, the interest, and aestheticism of the Greek, the proud stability and administrative competence of the Roman, the transcendental intensity of the Christian from the East, welded together into a fluid sensitive mass, were put now to sleep. Constantinople was become the seat of brutal force, of ignorance, of magnificent tastelessness.[55]

More recent writers and popular historians still react viscerally to the fall of the Byzantine Empire. Part of the reaction may be historical romanticism, but another possibility is that the clash between Muslims and Christians in the Balkans in the 1990s awakened old memories. Paul Fregosi's description of the end of the Byzantine Empire is an excellent example of such sentiments. In his book *Jihad in the West*, he bitterly commented:

> The fall of Constantinople is, after the Crucifixion, the greatest human calamity to have befallen Christianity. Poor theology, I know. The Crucifixion was the inevitable prelude to the Resurrection. But it's good imagery, and it conveys the feelings of Christians at the time. Today, more than half a millennium later, if one is a Western European, one can still cringe in shame when one remembers how this bastion, however flawed, of European civilization, religious tradition, and culture, in spite of its desperate calls to Christendom for help, was allowed by the rest of Europe to disappear into the maw of a then cruel nation while the West wrung its hands and twiddled its thumbs.[56]

In much the same way as the Battle of Kosovo served (and still serves) as the linchpin for Serbian national identity, the sack of

Constantinople and the conquest of Byzantium by the Ottoman Turks provided a dramatic end to universal Hellenism and, conversely, the genesis of Greek national consciousness. All the Balkan peoples have had some affinity with Constantinople, yet for the most part, the fate of the city in 1453 and its future liberation evolved more as elements of Greek historical anguish. In Greek school texts, today as in the nineteenth century, the motifs of redemption and divine intervention continue to sustain the myth and notions of fatalism, defeat, and humiliation linked to the fall of the city. The thrust of the story of Constantinople in children's history books is that the Ottoman victory, and by extension the Greek defeat, was a qualified Turkish success. In other words, the Greeks (i.e., the Romans) were overwhelmed by masses of Turks (not Ottomans), whom Emperor Constantine fought off by the thousands single-handedly. His end is depicted in almost biblical terms. "And just as he was about to be felled by a 'black' [a Muslim], the Angel of the Lord came and carried off the king deep in a cave below the earth (from an entrance near the Golden Gate). There the king waits while transformed into marble counting the hours when the angel will return and reawaken him."[57] According to the same legend, the Turks are fully aware of this situation, and they have taken steps to prevent any potential resurrection by sealing the gate to prevent the "king from returning and retaking the City." However when God wills it, the angel will return to the cave and transform the king from marble into human form. The emperor then will attack the Turks, and "there will be a great slaughter so that the calf will be able to swim in blood."[58]

For half a millennium, the once great Roman city and spiritual center of the Eastern Orthodox faith remained a melancholy place dominated by the specter of the Church of Holy Wisdom as a mosque. The implication then, and perhaps even now, was that the church was a symbol of Ottoman greatness over Byzantium and a constant reminder of the inferior status of Greek Christians. After the Ottoman Empire collapsed in 1924, the new Turkish republic, still hesitant to part with the vestiges of Ottoman glory, turned the mosque into a museum. They refused to consider restoring the church to the Orthodox patriarchate. Even today, the Hagia Sophia (as it's now called) continues to evoke memories of Ottoman supremacy and the subjugation of Orthodox Christians, and it remains a reminder of the great cataclysm that brought the curtain down on the Byzantine Empire. A by-product of this religious and historical mindset sustains the cultural chasm that divides the Turks from Southeastern Europeans. In Greece and the other Balkan states, this underscores lingering fears of potential Turkish aggression in the Eastern Mediterranean. This, at least, is the perception of some Balkan nationalists, and their suspicions are often reinforced by zealous accounts of iniquitous deeds against the Christian inhabitants of modern Turkey.

It is a unique feature of the Balkans that the Ottoman period is defined as a negative and regressive historical experience, while the earlier Roman conquest of the same area is characterized as benevolent and a positive contribution to Western civilization. This is partly because the impact of ancient Greece and Rome on Balkan society led to the synthesis of the Greco-Roman world of Byzantium. The Ottomans, on the other hand, represented an alien people who had little in common with the customs and cultures of the ancient Greeks and Romans.

Additionally, the Roman wars in the Balkan peninsula and Asia Minor were relatively quick, and afterward the indigenous populations were integrated and eventually given equal status within the Roman Empire. Reports of outrageous cruelties during the sack of cities by Roman legions are relatively limited, and they're certainly less descriptive than in the case of the Ottomans. One exception was the sack of Carthage in the third century B.C., during the Third Punic War. The Romans massacred all the men of the city and sold the women and children into slavery, scattering them to diverse slave markets. Finally, the city itself was erased from the map, and after the Romans had collapsed all the remaining structures, they removed the stones and covered the ground with salt to exterminate any plant life. All that was left of the once proud city was a dark stain on the shores of North Africa.

The fate of Carthage at the hands of the Romans is certainly equal to, if not on a greater scale of destruction than, the usual Ottoman treatment of captured cities, whose depictions nevertheless are far more gruesome. Byzantine and Italian accounts, as well as those of European historians in the nineteenth and early twentieth centuries, offer vivid testimony of Turkish behavior during the sack of Constantinople. In contrast, the Roman, ancient Greek, and

Byzantine equivalent mass killings are understood as taking place within the confines of a single civilization.

Ottoman outrages, on the other hand, are generally treated as the work of foreigners. The chronicles of Ottoman barbarism, supplemented by stories of continued Turkish brutality during the Ottoman period, have in essence excluded the Turks from mainstream European carnage. The Balkan stories of Turkish atrocities, in other words, reinforce the sentiment that their behavior was specifically Ottoman and exclusively oriental — that is, they were foreign elements grafted on to the Balkans and adopted by the inhabitants only during times of conflict.

The Battle of Constantinople and the protracted war against the Ottomans in the early nineteenth century have been seared into the historical memory of the Greeks. Both events have evolved as salient features of modern Greek historiography, and even as literary themes. Early modern Greek ballads, poems, songs, and prose pieces are peppered with poignant tales of suffering and stories of Turkish savagery.[59] Indeed, the downfall of Hellenism in 1453 and the cruelty and humiliation of the Ottoman occupation were an integral part of early Greek nationalist rhetoric, a sentiment equaled only by Turkish nationalist breast-beating in the twentieth century.

In fact, all the Balkan peoples, including the Turks, engage in a relentless tally of the horrors their ancestors suffered. This, in turn, has often served as justification for the mistreatment of other religious groups. History is fraught with crimes against humanity implemented in the name of religion, nation, or race. The Crusades are but one horrific example of the cruelty that Muslims, Jews, and even other Christians endured at the hands of the soldiers of Christ. More recently, the Turkish genocide of the Armenians in 1915 perpetuated the tradition of blood lust against an unwelcome and inconvenient minority.

The Balkan crises of the 1990s, and the accounts of atrocities and terror associated with the region, are often explained as a manifestation of Ottoman influence. In point of fact, the Ottoman Empire was the first multiethnic state that practiced a degree of toleration for minorities, which would have been unimaginable in medieval Europe — and for that matter, in many parts of the world at the end of this millennium. At the same time, however, the Ottoman Turks were not adverse to subjecting towns, villages, and cities to the sword, which translated into mass killings, torture, rape, mutilation, forcible conversions, and wonted destruction for its own sake. In the end, it is not so much the excesses of Turkish atrocities but rather the manner of implementation that distinguished the particular brand of suffering endured by the Balkan peoples during the Ottoman period.

—◈◈◈—

The Ottoman era in Southeastern Europe was marked by periods of not only great upheaval and hardship, but also benevolent administration and prosperity that enhanced the living standards of all Ottoman subjects. These two extreme patterns of behavior can also apply to other empires, and more often than not, the day-to-day reality lay somewhere in the middle. In the case of the Ottomans, early reports of their magnanimity toward conquered societies were greatly overstated. At the same time, later reports of Turkish outrages, while probably at least partly true, were matched by the savagery of the Christians in their struggle to expel the Turks from Southeastern Europe.

This inexplicable and paradoxical behavior permeates both the European and the Muslim accounts of the Ottoman presence in the Balkans until the beginning of the twentieth century; it is then reintroduced in the 1990s. A rational approach to the Ottoman period in the Balkans, consequently, has meant coming to terms with a host of contradictions and fallacies in order to provide some explanation for such unspeakable human cruelty. The challenge remains to try to interpret these ingrained dispositions. To this day, references to religious minorities or nations conjure up images of unrelenting cruelty and inexplicable human suffering (or in modern parlance, ethnic cleansing and genocide). To paraphrase Count de Talleyrand, Balkan and European ethnic groups, whether Christian or Muslim, have learned nothing and remember everything. Memory, however, especially when viewed through the prism of national history, offers a distorted and selective view of the past. Fundamentally, the first task is to demystify the Ottoman period. The stages of the empire represent different thresholds in the evolution of the Balkan societies, and these are integral to the culture of the region today.

In this respect, the Turkish factor in Balkan history is hostage to several fundamental questions. Were the Ottomans simply one more in a series of conquerors who annexed the Balkans to their respective empires? Was the Turkish, and by extension Muslim, presence in the region an aberration, stifling and diverting the future course of Balkan history? And did the Turks themselves perpetuate an Asiatic legacy, or did they transform the Balkan peninsula into the first European Muslim state? Finally, how did the wars between the Ottomans and the Christians manifest a distinct Balkan mythology nurtured on hate and fostered by territorial competition?

There is no single answer to any of these questions. The conundrum of the Balkans, as is the case with the evolution of all societies, is part of a complex set of variables intertwined with the history of the region. Those variables include the social, political, economic, and military dynamics generated by the indigenous people of the region, and these also helped shape the development of the Southeastern European states in the nineteenth century. But the Ottoman component certainly cannot be disentangled from the evolution of the Balkans, for it is as prevalent as the contribution of the Hellenes and the Romans to the region. And then, of course, there is the Asian influence, which can be seen today in many Turkish habits, traditions, laws, and social institutions.

In effect, the Ottomans were not a single society but a synthesis of several distinct cultures, traditions, customs, and peoples. The Ottoman Empire, in fact, was the culmination of several forces that instigated mass movements of tribes across continents, and these in turn swept away old empires and created new dominions that supplemented the secular and religious absolutism of Byzantium. But did the Ottomans simply borrow extensively from Byzantium and recreate the old empire within an Islamic context as a hybrid state? Or did the Turks establish a new and unique empire with only superficial references to Greek and Roman institutions?

Without doubt, the collapse of the Roman Empire in the East is identified as the end of an era. By 1453, the great city that bridged the East and West had ceased to hold any moral or political sway over the monarchies and city-states of Europe. The Greek Orthodox, for their part, soon came to terms with the new conquerors. After the initial shock and pillage, the Turkish occupation held few terrors for the survivors of Constantinople, who became the Orthodox subjects of the sultan. In fact, Mehmet assumed the role of the defender of the Orthodox faith and undertook to re-establish the Church on solid foundations.

Mehmet's regime attempted to create two essentially parallel yet unequal communities, each with its own social, economic, and political hierarchies, but both under the absolute control of the sultan. Although Mehmet severed the influence of the old Turkish families over the sultanate, he conversely institutionalized the position of the Greek Orthodox Church within the empire, for those at both the apex and the nadir of the social and political structure. Ottoman society was categorized within intersecting horizontal layers. The professional Ottomans, members of the sultan's personal household, the military establishment, the bureaucracy, the ulema (Muslim doctors of sacred law and theology), and members of the educational institutions formed the ruling elite. Almost all of these were Muslims. The rest of the population, collectively known as the *reaya*, or flock, made up the bottom layers. Upward mobility for this group depended on a stratified system of opportunities that differed for Muslims and Christians.[60] Under the new regime, all the non-Muslim subjects of the sultan were organized into religious communities known as millets, which permitted a considerable degree of local autonomy. The strictly religious structure of the millets excluded any notions of national, ethnic, linguistic, or cultural identity, and created, to a great extent, artificial communities. The Armenians, for example, were divided into Catholic and Gregorian nations, while all the Orthodox peoples in the Balkans, Asia Minor, and the Arab provinces of the empire were placed within the Greek Orthodox millet, and thus came under the jurisdiction of the patriarchate of Constantinople. For the first time since the heyday of Byzantium, all the Orthodox Christians were assembled under a single religious and civil administration.[61] This enhanced the power of the Greek patriarch, who, along with the group of families that revolved around the Church, had direct access to the sultan's court and formed the Greek Orthodox hierarchy within the Ottoman establishment.[62]

This privileged position of the Orthodox establishment, and of the Greek Orthodox patriarch in particular, was inaugurated when the new conqueror of Constantinople secured the election of the monk Gennadius as the new ecumenical patriarch. In the process, Mehmet redefined himself, and by extension the sultanate, as the inheritor of Byzantium.[63] Mehmet, in a traditional ceremony that had been performed by the Roman emperors in the past, invested the patriarch with a staff and a cross and granted the Orthodox Church greater privileges and authority than it had had under Byzantine rule.[64] The clergy and the Church were exempt from taxation, and were given direct responsibility for the welfare and good conduct of the Greek Orthodox people. Bishops assumed the right to establish courts to adjudicate matters of civil law between Christians, while criminal law and disputes between Muslims and Christians came under the jurisdiction of Ottoman officials.[65]

The patriarch, in effect, assumed a status equivalent to that of an Ottoman vizier.[66] Indeed, the expansion of the Ottoman Empire complemented and enhanced the power of the patriarch.[67] The earlier establishment of the Serbian and Bulgarian empires also saw the creation of Serbian and Bulgarian Orthodox churches that were independent of the patriarchy in Constantinople, but these disappeared when these lands fell under Ottoman rule.[68] For just over a century, the patriarch in Constantinople reigned as the supreme leader of the sultan's Orthodox subjects.[69] In fact, the Ottoman conquests of the Balkans, Asia Minor, and Anatolia in effect created a cohesive Orthodox community by bringing within one empire almost all the followers of the Orthodox faith.[70] In this way, the Ottoman Empire consolidated and even expanded the frontiers of the Eastern Orthodox Church. The Ottomans also coalesced as a society by absorbing Byzantium. The religious and educational infrastructure remained uniquely Turkic, but other parts of Ottoman society borrowed or adapted Byzantine institutions, customs, and habits. Both societies covered their women, for example, but the oppressive yet elegant Byzantine veil made a stronger fashion statement. As a result, after 1453 Turkish women abandoned the linen hoods they had long worn. The Byzantine veil was a gentler way of limiting the female identity.[71]

In practice, however, the Ottoman system could not reinvent itself as a universal empire with equal status for all the subjects of the sultan. As generous as Mehmet was toward the defeated Christians, he couldn't bridge the gulf of religious chauvinism and intolerance that placed the Muslims ahead in the social, economic, and political hierarchy of the empire. Christians were obliged to permanently display their secondary status by wearing distinctive clothing so that they could not be mistaken for Muslims. They were forbidden to ride horses[72] or bear arms, their homes had to be lower in height than those of Muslims, and they were required to pay a special head tax (literally to keep their heads), in place of military service.[73] And until the seventeenth century, Orthodox subjects, except for Jews and Armenians, were forced to pay the repulsive child tax.

It can be, and has been, argued that on the whole, the Christian subjects of the Ottoman Empire fared considerably better than did other groups in Western Europe.[74] The limited privileges and the fact that the Ottomans did not embark on wholesale forcible conversions enabled the Balkan peoples to maintain their identities into the nineteenth century. Mass conversions to Islam did take place in some Balkan regions, but these were in reaction to particular circumstances. In Bosnia, for example, a large portion of the population turned to Islam because of the persecution and harassment of both the Orthodox and the Catholic churches. The inhabitants of certain regions in Bulgaria also turned to Islam, along with half the population of Crete and a large part of the Albanian population. In these cases, the conversions were in part to avoid taxes and in part to benefit from the advantages afforded the Muslims.[75] With these exceptions, however, the Balkan societies survived with their identities intact and the status quo prevailed. As long as the Ottomans provided a degree of security and avoided interfering extensively in the daily lives of the Christians, the Greeks, Serbs, Romanians, and Bulgarians accepted their lot.

In fact, during the first two hundred years of Ottoman rule, the influence of the West and the ideas emerging out of the Renaissance were both perceived as greater threats to the Orthodox Church and its control over Balkan Christians. Until the czars of Russia began offering an Orthodox alternative, the Ottoman Empire was the only bulwark against Western intervention and penetration of the Orthodox world. The Eastern Orthodox Church was anti-Western, and it rejected vigorously everything the Renaissance represented. L. S. Stavrianos, a historian of the Balkans, asserted that the Orthodox Church was repelled by the "exaltation of reason in place of dogma, the turn to Greek antiquity. . . . In short, Balkan Orthodoxy opposed

the West not only because it was heretical but also because it was
becoming modern."[76] Undoubtedly, modernity offered a direct challenge not only to the predominant position of the Orthodox
theocracy, but also to the wealthy and primarily Greek families centered around the Phanar (lighthouse) district in Constantinople.

To a great extent, the golden age of the Ottoman Empire was also
the age of Orthodox supremacy in the secular affairs of Balkan societies. The Ottoman armies not only kept the Western heretics out,
but also protected the privileged position of the Church and the
clergy within the confines of the empire. This security and purity of
the faith came at a price, however. Balkan societies stagnated and suffered a radical decline in material wealth. Literacy and intellectual
life in general practically vanished, and schools were not maintained,
which, contrary to some of the myths generated in the post-Ottoman
period, was not the result of Turkish prohibition. (The tales of secret
schools for Greek culture and language being operated by the
Orthodox Church under the very noses of Ottoman officials is
another essential feature of the Balkan myth.[77]) Instead, the degeneration of learning was a result of the monopolization of education
by the Church and the reluctance of most communities to support a
scholastic system. The Patriarchal School in Constantinople, founded
in the sixteenth century, was one exception, and with its focus on
ancient Greek, philosophy, and mathematics, it quickly became the
center of higher learning for the Greek Orthodox people. By the end
of the sixteenth century, the Church had also funded new schools in
various parts of Greece, but it could not establish the network of educational institutions that was needed to satisfy all the Greek
community centers. The Ottomans, for their part, remained indifferent to the educational needs of the Christian communities and
left the matter to the Church.[78]

—◦◦◦—

The definition of the Ottoman occupation of the Balkans as a period
of darkness, slavery, and oppression evolved in the nineteenth century and crystallized in the first half of the twentieth century. This
negative record was in part a natural reaction to foreign domination
and the cycle of repression, massacres, and reprisals that characterized the wars of liberation fought by the Balkan peoples, first against

the Ottoman Turks and later against each other. Stavrianos summed up the notion of five hundred years of slavery and darkness as "part of the folklore of Balkan nationalism. Turkish rule in the early period was in many respects commendable. It provided the Balkan peoples with a degree of peace and security that previously had been conspicuously absent. It permitted them to practice their faith and to conduct their communal affairs with a minimum of intervention and taxation."[79] This type of folklore so often distorts the historical reality. But that doesn't mean myths and legends offer no insight into the past. The story of Euphrosyne of Ioannina is just such a blend of fact and fiction.[80]

Euphrosyne was the niece of Gabriel, the archbishop of Ioannina, and the wife of a prominent businessman who should have spent less time on the road and more time at home.[81] Euphrosyne, as a relative of a prelate of the Church, had had an excellent education and became attracted to the salacious elements of the classics. In particular, she decided to revive the lifestyle of the ancient Greek *hetairai* (courtesans) and indulge in conduct unbecoming a lady of her time and stature. During her husband's frequent absences, Euphrosyne turned her home into a resort for Ioannina's educated and wealthy Christian and Muslim young men, including Mukhtar, the son of Ali Pasha, who very quickly also developed a taste for the "classics." This unusual behavior elicited imitation from other young married women, who sought to follow in Euphrosyne's footsteps and enjoy the forbidden fruit of liberal sexual relationships. Their antics, however, quickly earned the condemnation of their husbands, as well as the wives of their patrons. Soon a strange alliance of Christian husbands and Muslim wives had formed, and these people set out to destroy Euphrosyne and her accomplices. The outraged husbands of these new *hetairai* and the wives of their Muslim lovers appealed to Ali Pasha for justice, and the Albanian Ottoman had all the practicing *hetairai* rounded up. They were arrested and sentenced to death for adultery. In another version of the story, it was the wife of Mukhtar, Ali Pasha's favorite daughter-in-law, who precipitated the execution of the women when she complained to her father-in-law that her husband ignored her because he had found new female interests. At Ali Pasha's request, the lady wrote down, quite at random, the names of seventeen women, both Christians and Muslims, who had diverted Mukhtar's affections.[82] These women were promptly condemned to death. According to other versions, however, Ali Pasha's harsh treatment was motivated by revenge, since he was denied the affections of one or more of the *hetairai*. In the Greek version, Euphrosyne is cast as a beautiful Greek woman who is a victim of Ottoman atrocity perpetrated by an avaricious and degenerate Ali Pasha (although the instigators were in fact Albanian Muslims and Greek Orthodox subjects of the sultan).

When the women were first arrested, they had little concern, and assumed that their spouses or other relatives would offer the necessary bribes for their release. Yet to a man, the husbands, brothers, fathers, and cousins failed to make any effort to buy their freedom or commute the death sentence. Later that evening, all seventeen hapless women were carried to the middle of a lake in small boats, and with their hands tied, they were tossed into the water. Most of the victims accepted their fate with resignation, but some attempted to cling to life by thrashing about in the water. A few others managed to latch on to the side of the boats, only to be driven away in a most savage fashion.[83] For a short time, the screams and shrieks of the women could be heard for miles and even unnerved some of the executioners. It took several days to collect all the bodies, which had the effect of prolonging the distress of the general population, who indicated their outrage by attending the funerals in record numbers.

The fate of these women is often cited as an example of the cruel habits of Ali Pasha and, by extension, the Ottoman regime. But Ali Pasha argued that he proceeded with the death sentences only because no one spoke out on behalf of the women — not even their own relatives. The end result was that the Christian husbands of the victims and the Muslim wives of their admirers were delivered from further scandal, and the blame fell squarely on the Ottoman authorities. If some of the stories are to be believed, the conduct of at least one of the Christian husbands was not only self-serving, but also quite reprehensible. He, according to some accounts, was fully aware of Ali Pasha's intention to execute the women, but rather than warn his wife, he encouraged her to answer a summons from the man, which was in fact a death sentence. The husband convinced the unfortunate wife that Ali Pasha had invited her for the purpose of awarding presents. He then told her to appear before the pasha without her finer jewelry and garments, so as to induce Ali to grant more expensive gifts. In truth, the husband was simply trying to save as much of his wife's trinkets and best clothes as possible.[84]

As the example above illustrates, some of the most graphic acts of inhumanity associated with the Ottoman period resulted from the convergence of several local interests. In this instance, Christian husbands and Muslim wives worked together to fend off the permissive elements of Greek antiquity that had invaded their society. But it is Ali Pasha who has been demonized. Later in life, the old pasha complained that his counselors had failed him, since he would have spared a few of the victims in exchange for ransom. Euphrosyne, meanwhile, is celebrated in song and poetry. After Greek independence in 1830, her story became a source of pride for the Greeks of Ioannina, and it was lauded as an example of their cultural and intellectual superiority over the rest of Greece.[85] The local inhabitants most certainly would not have approved of the liberated liaisons encouraged by Euphrosyne. But her demise at the hands of the Ottomans elevated her from courtesan to revolutionary icon in spite of this fact.

Mutual self-interest also made possible the collusion between the patriarchate and the Ottoman regime, and this, along with the absence of any secular leadership in the first two centuries of occupation, left the Church as the principal authority over the Christian communities. Although the sultans were initially content to leave Church affairs alone, the position of patriarch was later sold to the highest bidder (as was the case with most high offices in the Ottoman Empire). By the end of the seventeenth century, the cost of assuming the patriarchal throne was 20,000 piasters, or 3,000 gold pounds. Three decades later, the price rose to 5,600 gold pounds, but after 1727 it declined, as did the authority of the patriarchate in Constantinople. The Ottomans exploited the situation by arranging frequent vacancies, and thus raising the price for prospective candidates. Between 1595 to 1695, there were sixty-one nominations, but in the eighteenth century, the rate dropped to thirty-one appointments.[86]

The cost of appointments naturally was passed on to the members of the Church, which meant that in addition to their other taxes and encumbrances, the peasants had to subsidize the revolving patriarchal throne.[87] In addition, the Orthodox Church had the power to collect taxes of its own and also to excommunicate anyone who failed to pay the sultan's share. Later, the Church used its spiritual and secular authority to condemn anyone who opposed the Ottoman regime. George Finlay, shortly after the Greek revolution, wrote, "The most observant traveler who visited Greece before the Revolution declares that it is a common sentiment among the laity that the bishops have been a great cause of the present degraded condition of the Greek nation."[88] Another observer, William Martin Leake, recorded in his travel journals that "although the clergy were often the instruments of oppression, and a bishop could hardly avoid acting like a Turk in office, the regular clergy kept the Greek language alive and perhaps prevented the dissolution of all national union."[89]

But Church leaders were not always able to resist the sometimes unreasonable demands of Ottoman officials. One story involving the same Ali Pasha highlights the weaknesses of the Church in the face of Ottoman supremacy. Ali Pasha had noticed that the Orthodox bishops had considerably more authority than his own tax collectors. Accordingly, the ambitious and clever pasha ordered Ignatius, the metropolitan of Arta, to assume the duties. The Orthodox primate, fearing for his life, executed the pasha's orders with considerable enthusiasm — to the point that it created unrest in the region. Ali Pasha, always careful not to cause rebellion, agreed to scale down the taxes and ordered a remission of 2,000 gold pounds. The unfortunate Ignatius was forced to make restitution from his own resources while the wily pasha retained the original funds collected. Ali Pasha garnered goodwill for his gesture, but the metropolitan was tainted as an avaricious tax collector and received little credit for the refund.[90] Later, Ignatius escaped to Italy, but Ali's actions deprived the Ottoman regime of an affective ally and eroded the influence of the Church.

The patriarch, his bishops, and his priests needed to collaborate with Ottoman officials like Ali Pasha if they wanted to survive and thus maintain the identity of the Greeks. If the Church had failed to submit to the will of the sultan, it would have forfeited its privileged status and lost all means of sustaining the Hellenic consciousness. By the early nineteenth century, however, the failure of the sultanate to control the provincial governors also compromised the authority of the Church, which in turn was losing influence to a new generation of secular leaders.

Regardless of its shortcomings, the Church remained, for the first 250 years of Ottoman rule, the only legitimate source of authority in the Greek communities within the empire, and as such it was largely responsible for the preservation of the Greek nation under foreign rule. Indeed, the members of the Phanariot aristocracy, the only other possible leadership candidates, were co-opted by the Ottoman system and infiltrated the Church hierarchy (largely because the Church remained the only political bridge between the Ottomans and Orthodox Christians).[91] The Phanariots grew rich and powerful as administrators of the Ottoman Empire, and were by and large oblivious to the fate of their compatriots. Indeed, with their elegant and spacious homes in the Phanar district of Constantinople, they had little in common with mainland Greeks. The latter scratched out a meager existence while the Phanariots increased their material and political gains within the empire. After the Ottoman decline in the seventeenth century, some of the Phanariots filled part of the leadership vacuum and ultimately joined the rebellion against the sultan.

After Greek independence, both the Orthodox clergy and the Phanariot aristocracy had to find a place outside the mantle of Turkish subjugation. The roles both had played during the Ottoman period made them incompatible with the ethos of the new Greek state. It became necessary and expedient, therefore, to find a way to erase or excuse what was later defined as their collusion in the almost five hundred years of Turkish slavery. To this end, the Ottoman period began to be viewed not in the context of the times, but through the perspective of the nineteenth century. As a result, the collaboration of the clergy and the Phanariots was explained away as the result of the omnipotence of a Turkish empire that left few opportunities for opposition and mercilessly crushed any resistance. Under these terms, the Church hierarchy and the Greek aristocracy in both Constantinople and mainland Greece could shed their Ottoman heritage and be integrated with the revolutionary movement that achieved Greek independence in 1830. Without them, the modern Greek state would have been brought into existence by an unlikely alliance of illiterate bandits (who did the actual fighting), the Greeks of the diaspora (who funded the war), and the Great Powers (whose intervention ultimately forced the sultan to concede defeat).

The historical rapprochement naturally required the Ottoman

Empire to play its part and demonstrate sufficient cruelty in the nine-teenth century to accommodate tradition and legend. Thus through the prism of national history, the Phanariots and the higher clergy are viewed as heroes and martyrs. However, the Great Church (as the ecumenical Orthodox patriarchate of Constantinople was labeled) never fully renounced its place in the Turkish republic. Though the Greek community in Constantinople eventually shrank to just a few thousand members, the ecumenical patriarchate never relocated to any part of the Orthodox world. It is the irony of history that the ecumenical patriarch, the spiritual leader of all the Orthodox faithful, must even today be a Turkish citizen.

—*✺✺✺*—

Byzantium may have provided the intellectual foundations of the Orthodox faith, but the Ottoman sultans ensured the survival of the Church and instituted the mechanisms for its secular authority and wealth. Still, the spectacle of what was once the Church of Holy Wisdom being reduced to a museum and the ecumenical patriarchate finding itself perpetually at the mercy of capricious Turkish regimes cannot help inducing melancholia in most Orthodox believers. Indeed, the very helplessness of the Orthodox institutions in Turkey invokes what can be aptly described as the power of the victim.[92]

Although at the end of this century the Church has lost ground in Greece, its shadow continues to reach out from Istanbul and spread across the Greek communities of the diaspora, as is also the case with the Orthodox churches of the Balkan and Russian minorities in Europe and North America. Today, these communities are caught in the whirlwind of mass information technologies, and they face cultural and linguistic oblivion. This has a direct bearing on the survival of the Orthodox Church, which is also partially tied to the perpetuation of the Balkan and Ottoman myths. Nevertheless, the Orthodox communities of the diaspora continue to recreate the Balkan past around replicas of the Great Church in small and large community centers around the world. On May 29, 1453, the walls of Constantinople resisted the onslaught of the Ottomans for the last time. Today the barbarians at the gate are not the Turks but the forces of globalization and assimilation. Only time will tell whether these faceless threats will be able to breach the defenses of the new Constantinople.

3

BANDITS WITH ATTITUDE

Everyone is in debt to the robber.

— NINETEENTH-CENTURY GREEK BANDIT

he Balkan mountain ranges have acted as a place of refuge for some and a remote graveyard for others. Despite the brilliant light of early spring, the stark and desolate mountains appear cold and inhospitable. At dusk, the rugged Greek landscape offers a dramatic yet melancholic picture. These defiant hills have provided the backdrop for centuries of human turmoil. On Thursday, April 21, 1870, the mountains once again bore silent witness as a bloody tragedy unfolded. Less than sixty-five miles (100 km) north of Athens, death stalked among the craggy footpaths and thorny bushes of lower Mount Pentilicus. At five o'clock in the afternoon, the silence of the jagged foothills exploded with gunfire.

The first shots came from Greek troops chasing a dozen or so bandits who were attempting to escape deeper into the mountains, carting along their human booty of foreign hostages. That first volley brought down two of the bandits. The survivors quickly realized that speed was their only avenue of escape. The hostages had now become useless and a burden to the bandits. Fear, desperation, and panic transformed the colorful ruffians into butchers, and three Englishmen and one Italian met a cruel and untimely end. Even before the first shots of the Greek soldiers had faded into the mountains, two of the brigands drew their swords and approached the first victim, Edward Herbert. The young man instinctively put up his right arm to protect his face, but the blade hacked right through the bone. A few seconds later, two more slashes cut across Herbert's face, slicing the maxillary artery and exposing the jawbone. Herbert staggered for a few feet and then collapsed, falling face down across a thorn bush. The bandits attempted to serve a *coup de grâce* by firing three bullets into his back. They failed to end his agony, however, and the young man eventually bled to death.

The Greeks soldiers retaliated, and the second volley brought down five more of the bandits. In response, the survivors dispatched the second hostage, Edward Lloyd. A short while later, six of the bandits were captured. The leader of the band, with a handful of his followers and the remaining captives, managed to slip past the soldiers and vanish into one of the countless mountain passes. At dawn, two more shots shattered the evening air as the last hostages, Frederick Vyner and Count Alberto de Boyl, were each executed with a bullet to the back of the head.

News of the ghastly murders caused shock and dismay across Europe.[1] *The Times* of London of April 26, 1870, offered just one example of the depth and ferocity of the rage that rained down on the Greek kingdom and its inhabitants:

This murder of our countrymen has been committed in a European country, among men calling themselves Christians, within a few miles of a capital the name of which is associated with all that is highest and noblest in our recollections. Greece is a country whose very existence as an independent State is in great part the work of England; in its cause one of the greatest of English poets [Lord Byron] risked and lost his life, and as if inspired by his example, our statesmen have watched by the cradle of its nationality, and borne with patience its perverse and forward childhood. We have laid on our overtaxed people a burden of no small weight for its sake; we have abandoned in its favour our traditional policy when the cannon of Navarino shattered the Turkish Navy; and never since, except when provoked by schemes manifestly culpable, have we refused Greece countenance and help. . . . It is in this Greece, to which we have given independence, protection, a reigning

House, and one of the fairest portions of its territory, that three of
our countrymen, including the Secretary of the British Legation
[Edward Herbert], have been foully murdered within a few miles
of the capital.[2]

The vituperative harangue against the Greeks continued for
weeks, and the tone of the invective became considerably darker. On
June 3, 1870, *The Times* provided a summary of the abuse that had
been heaped upon the Greek state:

> The Greeks have been roundly abused by every press in Europe.
> They have been told that they are not Greeks; that they are at best
> a mongrel race, with a very little admixture of the classical blood.
> They have been told that the foundation of their kingdom was a
> mistake. . . . Their morals, social and political, their statesmen,
> their constitution, have had to bear a storm of obloquy. We do not
> pretend for a moment to say that any of this is undeserved; on the
> contrary, it is for the most part nothing but the literal truth, which
> has long been visible to those who have watched them intelligently,
> though it may have been unperceived by Philhellenic eyes dazzled
> by phantasm of classic glory. But it would be a great misfortune if
> European opinion were to content itself with mere wordy condem-
> nation.[3]

Various solutions to the Greek problem were bandied about in
the press and in the British Cabinet. Recommendations ranged from
military intervention by the three protecting powers[4] to imposing
changes on the Greek government and constitution. After several
months, however, an avalanche of diplomatic notes and judicial
inquiries had obscured the entire affair. Despite the rhetoric of the
newspapers, none of the three protecting powers had any inclination
to intervene in the internal affairs of Greece, at least not at that particular time. William Gladstone, the British prime minister, was
content to limit Britain's demands to insisting that the Greek government hold an official inquiry and prosecute the people responsible.[5]

What most Europeans really objected to, of course, was the idea
that banditry, abduction, and murder could take place in civilized
Europe. Almost a century and a half later, in the 1990s, Europeans

would once again have to come to terms with the ugly and brutal notion of Europe as a theater of war. Not surprisingly, the graphic images of the Yugoslav crisis have again spawned indignation and consternation. One journalist, Simon Winchester, in a memoir of his travels during the recent Balkan conflicts, was quite forthright in stating that the carnage he saw in Europe had a stronger impact on him than the misery he had witnessed in other parts of the world. In describing the refugee problem during the Kosovo crisis in 1999, Winchester stated, without hesitation:

> I feel no shame in confessing that it was as much as anything the evident Europeanness of the thousands on this field that struck me first: for while I have in a life of wandering just like this seen many thousands of refugees and displaced and dispossessed unfortunates in Africa and Cambodia and Bengal and Java and elsewhere, and have felt properly sorry and ashamed that such calamities should befall them, my instincts on that April day at Blace-Camp were very much those of a European man, looking at men and women and children who could very well, from the simple fact of their appearance, be cousins or friends or acquaintances, in a way that no one in the refugee fields in Bengal or the Congo could ever really have been.[6]

Despite Simon Winchester's feeling of kinship with these people, the Balkans have often been described as the back door to Europe or as Europe's doorstep. The implication is that the Balkan states are not part of Europe proper, or that the region is at best the dividing line between the West and the Near East. The hesitancy to embrace the peoples of the southeast as cultural equals is often confounded, however, by memories of classical Greece. The glory that was ancient Greece is a cornerstone of European history, but accepting Greece as a historical and geographical landmark means incorporating the Balkan peninsula into European civilization. Hence the conundrum.

Of course, it would be impossible to fold the Balkans into the history of the rest of Europe without first coming to terms with the phenomena of war, occupation, liberation, and the search for national identity. War, more than anything else, has marked the evolution and decline of Balkan empires and societies, and the use of violence as a political, cultural, and economic mechanism has been a key factor in the Balkan powder keg. For more than a millennium, and certainly in the past five hundred years, the agents of death in the Balkans have come in the form of conquerors and the less grandiose bandits. Over the centuries, both have dominated Southeastern Europe, leaving a historical legacy that has been painfully revived in the current Balkan crisis.

In the twentieth century, the human disaster zone that is the Balkans has been the battleground of bands of private armies, skillfully employed to spearhead irredentist claims, and almost an equal number of lawyers, ever ready to apply the label of "war criminal" as a sop to European and Western sensitivity. There is no question that crimes against humanity took place during the Balkan crises of the 1990s, but is it possible that Europeans grasped at international justice to compensate for their failure to prevent the Balkan debacle in the first place? Are the present-day warlords and private armies simply our modern equivalents of the bandit chiefs who were the arbiters of military power in the Balkan mountain societies of the nineteenth century?

—⟨∞⟩—

Perhaps European reaction to atrocities in the former Yugoslavia had its historical antecedents in the killings in the Greek mountains in the 1870s, an event that unhinged the notions of Hellenism held by classical scholars, European aristocrats, and that strangest character of all — the philhellene.

Originally, the term "philhellene," which literally meant "a lover of Greeks or a friend of Greeks,"[7] was coined during the Greek War of Liberation (1821–30). It defined those Englishmen, Frenchmen, Germans, Italians, and even one Cuban who rushed to Greece to liberate the land of Plato, Aristotle, and Homer — or in a word, classical Greece. Early travelers to Greece, such F. S. N. Douglas, believed that it was possible to "discover the countrymen of Pericles in the inhabitants of modern Athens, or the sturdy mountaineer of Maina with the disciple of Lycurgus."[8] William Leake, in *Travels in the Morea*, his monumental topographical and geographical survey of Greece, wrote, "The women of Mistra and the plain are taller and more robust than the other Greeks, have more colour in general which agrees also with Homer's beautiful women of Lacedaemon."[9] One British traveler, Edward Dodwell, commented that there were classical Greek parallels for the "respectable occupation of brigandage," and suggested that acts such as "depriving people of their ears and noses is a practice common to most parts of Turkey."[10] (The reference to Turkey is actually to the European possessions of the Ottoman Empire and their Christian subjects.)

Some of these men were romantics seduced by visions of ancient Athens, as symbolized by the Parthenon and other antiquities. No doubt, they pictured themselves fighting alongside the descendants of Leonidas and the Three Hundred Spartans, or as the successors of Alexander the Great, pitting themselves against the barbarian Persians (as played by the Ottoman Muslims). Others were adventurers who were attracted to any war for booty, fun, or simply because they were no longer welcome in their own countries. Some of these so-called philhellenes were soldiers and officers in Napoleon's armies who had turned into mercenaries after the demise of the emperor.

But most philhellenes who arrived in Greece after 1821, whether they were in search of toga-clad Greeks discussing philosophy in the ancient marketplace or simply the spoils of war, were disappointed. As Col. Leicester Stanhope observed, "All came expecting to find the Peloponnese filled with Plutarch's men and all returned thinking the inhabitants of Newgate more moral."[11] European aristocrats, flaunting their facility with ancient Greek, failed to elicit any coherent response from the local inhabitants. The Greeks not only did not measure up to their ancestors in the eyes of the Europeans, but also displayed singular Balkan and Turkish habits. Indeed, they appeared to lack any of the graces associated with classical Athens, as it was preached to young aristocrats in European schools. Even in the manner of their dress, the Greeks reflected the orientalism of the Ottomans. Greek fashion in the nineteenth century saw men dressed in the Albanian kilt while women followed the Muslim tradition of covering themselves up, including the face and eyes.

To the dismay of the Europeans, the Greeks were also marked by other negative characteristics inherited from the Levant, such as the nasty habit of misplacing the truth, at least as truth was understood by Europeans. Romilly Jenkins has described the Greek notion of veracity as observed truth versus "ethnic" truth. According to Jenkins, the Greek of the nineteenth century lived simultaneously on two levels of consciousness,

> the level of factual, observed truth, on which he had to conduct his everyday life. And there was the upper level of ideal truth, on which he claimed to appear in the eyes of the outside world. These levels of truth seldom approached one another, and were often sharply divergent: and this led to a dichotomy in the Greek mind which contemporary, secularized Europe could not understand at all, and attributed, rather unfairly, to an inherent deceitfulness of character.[12]

Practically speaking, the "observed truth," Jenkins noted, was the reality of the Greek kingdom in the late nineteenth century. Greece occupied territory in the southern Balkans that was mountainous and infertile. The country's independence rested on the guarantees of the three Great Powers: Great Britain, Russia, and France. Greece lacked a strong army and a police force, and maintained a very small navy. The state was poor and in debt to the Great Powers, and its political life was dominated by a minority of powerful families who had retained their wealth and privilege from the Ottoman period. "These persons," Leake wrote with contempt, "interested in the continuance of ignorance and Turkish tyranny, were, together with the some of the higher clergy, the greatest obstacles to national improvement."[13]

Outside the main towns and Athens, groups of bandits practiced extortion, theft, murder, and kidnapping, and generally terrorized the shepherds and small farmers in the countryside. When they were not engaged in plunder, these bandits acted as hired guns for regional and national political leaders. For nineteenth-century Greece, as is the case today for the newly minted national states carved out of the former Yugoslavia, Mao's maxim "Political power grows out of the barrel of a gun"[14] was a way of life. The temporary groupings that constituted the political parties at the time used armed bands to guarantee victory at the polls. In exchange, the bandits were given the freedom to pillage and kill with impunity.

The bandits responsible for the kidnapping incident described at the beginning of this chapter resorted to violence because they had become accessories to the political intrigues of Athenian politicians.

Although the leader of the band, Christos Arvanitakis, was initially content to accept a ransom of 50,000 pounds for the victims, he was persuaded to up the ante by Alexandros Koumoundouros and Demetrios Bulgaris, the leaders of the Greek opposition party. Both politicians convinced the bandit chief to help bring down the government by holding out for a pardon in addition to the ransom. According to the constitution, the king of Greece had the power to pardon those convicted of political crimes, but not those convicted of criminal offenses. If King George amnestied the bandits, the government would be forced to resign in deference to the constitution. This was the ultimate goal of Koumoundouros and Bulgaris, of course, and they had promised Arvanitakis far more generous rewards if the actions of the bandits brought about the fall of the current regime. The bandits, consequently, stubbornly clung to their demand for a pardon and announced that they were also willing to accept a little more than half of the requested ransom.[15] Unfortunately, the Greek government was backed into a corner. Resigning over a point of constitutional law was not an option, and the only other choice was a military raid, which resulted in the tragic murder of the captives. Sadly, this would not be the last time that Balkan politicians exploited outlaws and paramilitary forces to achieve their own ends.

Some of the bandits themselves turned to politics in place of their outlaw activities. According to S. G. W. Benjamin, an American traveler to Greece and Turkey in the 1860s, the end of the Greek war of independence left many bandits without employment: "When that heroic struggle was over, it became unlawful to rob and murder the Turks, [and] they found their occupation gone. Some of them settled down into scheming, restless politicians, while others . . . sighted for new adventures, sometimes attempting . . . to raise an insurrection, sometimes returning to their evil ways."[16]

John Koliopoulos, in *Brigands with a Cause*, his exhaustive study of Greek bandits, attributed the 1871 law that suppressed brigandage to what Jenkins defined as "ethnic" truth. Koliopoulos described the law, which was enacted to appease Europeans, as a collection of the harshest provisions to be found in the legislative and administrative measures of Greece. He wrote, "More than any other law of the time perhaps, the law of 1871 . . . reflected the capacity of official Greece to react to criticism with selective severity, disregard of humanity, discrimination, and misplacement of responsibility."[17] Thanos Veremis, a Balkan specialist, remarked that "perceived truth and reality, or 'ethnic truth and truth,' were not always reconcilable."[18] Jenkins himself argued that this other level of truth was intended to serve the myth sustaining the Greek kingdom. He wrote:

> It was formed by the transcended and mystical concept of the Nation, the "ethnos," a term which comprehended everybody inside or outside the kingdom who was of, or wished to claim, Hellenic descent. According to the "ethnic" truth the modern Greek was at once the spiritual heir of all the splendid intellectual endowments of the classical age, and the political heir of all the vast pretensions, both religious and imperial, of Byzantium. From the first of these he derived his genius and culture, from the second his natural right and fitness to resume the Empire over all the nations of the eastern Mediterranean; and from this evident superiority, in intellect and capacity, over the members of any other race. It followed from these premises that his conduct was above reproach, and his country a paragon of order and enlightenment.[19]

In Serbian history, truth also has two meanings. According to the historian Tzvetan Todorov, there is "'truth adequation' (factual truth) and 'truth-disclosure' (more or less truth)."[20] Julie A. Mertus, in her book *Kosovo: How Myths and Truths Started a War,* examined the notion of truth and concluded that "to understand how wars start, we need to . . . unravel the more or less truths."[21]

When defining truth within the Balkan context, and by extension, distinguishing the myriad shades of meaning underwriting Balkan history, we must remember that truth was a luxury limited to those with power. Four centuries of Ottoman rule and eleven hundred years of equally authoritarian Byzantine government had taught the Balkan peoples to avoid direct confrontation with authority and follow the path of least resistance. Although for the first two hundred years the Ottomans showed considerable religious toleration and permitted Christians a degree of self-government, they lapsed into corruption and sporadic acts of violence against non-Muslim communities after the onset of the empire's decline in the seventeenth century.

In these circumstances, the economic, cultural, and even physical survival of the Balkan Christians depended on their skillful use of subterfuge, which was often interpreted by Europeans as docility. All authority, to them, was synonymous with Ottoman mismanagement and foreign rule. Even as each of the Balkan states achieved independence or administrative autonomy in the early nineteenth century, they somehow maintained the notion that the authority of the state was alien. In effect, the European institutions that were transplanted to the newly established Greek kingdom and other Balkan countries remained distinctly foreign to the indigenous political culture. This was chronicled by William Mure, an English traveler in post-independence Greece, who wrote:

> I had frequently heard it said by intelligent foreigners settled in Greece that its inhabitants, in spite of their obstinate struggle for independence and amid a good deal of native spirit and ferocity, had not yet been able to shake off some of those defects, which Homer, as if in prophetic anticipation of the future fate of his own countrymen, assures us slavery never fails to entail on the character of its victims; that the same abject cringing to any thing in the shape of a superior, which during the Turkish despotism had been a matter of necessity, still continued to display itself towards rank, or constituted authority, as a matter of habit: and that to this day, consequently, the proper mode for a traveller to secure justice or respect in his dealings with the natives, was the employment of the cane or the horsewhip.[22]

In the case of Greece, and later Romania and Bulgaria, even the monarchs appointed by the Great Powers were foreign. Otto, the first king of Greece (1832), was a Bavarian. When he was deposed in 1862, he was replaced by George I, the second son of the king of Denmark. In the countryside, meanwhile, the wealthy landowners and their families continued to hold sway over the small farmers and shepherds, very much as they had done during the Ottoman period. For the citizens of the new Greek state, independence itself was an "ethnic" truth that promised future redemption while mortgaging the present to the past. In this surreal social and political architecture, the dreams of ancient Byzantine glory converged with the stark reality of the paucity of the Greek kingdom, and truth was an elusive and dangerous commodity indeed. People survived by the time-honored mechanisms of shifting blame, deflecting responsibility, and paying homage to authority.

These realities were glossed over by the European press during the course of the Greek war of independence; they preferred to cast the Greeks in a more romantic and Euro-friendly light. The illusion was useful because it enabled the European philhellenes to plunder whatever antiquities came their way in the guise of protecting ancient artifacts from the careless natives. In this manner, Lord Elgin, to give just one example, helped himself to the sculptures of the Acropolis, which eventually came to be housed in the British Museum in London.[23] Some Englishmen at the time argued that it was an act of barbarism to remove the artifacts, but others claimed, and continue to do so, that Elgin saved the marbles from Turkish neglect. The sculptures, known as the Elgin Marbles, are still at the British Museum, where, according to some, they are protected from the ravages of Athenian pollution.

Nineteenth-century Greeks themselves never tired of covering up their inadequacies by hiding behind their glorious past. After all, in their war against the sultan's armies, all they had had was a motley collection of bandit units and history. (And the latter was a far more potent weapon than the disorganized irregular forces of the various provisional Greek governments.) Even the Europeans responded more to the appeal of ancient Greece than to emerging Balkan nationalism. In other words, to create a modern country and justify a war against the Ottoman Empire, the British, French, and Russians found it convenient and necessary to pretend that the Greeks of the nineteenth century were the reincarnation of the Greeks of antiquity. And for their own sake, the Greeks let them pretend.

—◦∾◦—

These illusions were shattered, albeit temporarily, by the murder of the three Englishmen and one Italian on April 21, 1870. The very complacency of the victims can be attributed to a general conviction that the Greece of 1870 was the inheritor of the customs and traditions of the city-states of the classical period. Indeed, the victims, along with their friends and families, were in Greece hunting relics of classical antiquity. They had set out on April 11, 1870, to discover Marathon, some twelve miles (19 km) east of Athens. The group included Lord and Lady Muncaster; their friend Frederick Vyner; Edward Herbert, the third secretary of the British legation; Edward Lloyd, an English lawyer involved with the Piraeus railroad company; and Count Alberto de Boyl, a young Piedmontese nobleman, first secretary at the Italian legation. These distinguished tourists were oblivious to the fact that the countryside in Greece was notoriously dangerous for travelers. The Greek authorities, in the exercise of "ethnic" truth, had given them assurances that the area outside of Athens was safe. To admit that this was not the case would have been cultural suicide. Tragically, the unsuspecting tourists received few warnings of the true dangers of traveling in the area. The party felt so confident, in fact, that Lloyd also brought along his wife, Julia, and their daughter, Barbara. In the morning, the group happily trotted off toward Marathon in two horse-drawn carriages.

In actual fact, Attica, the region outside Athens, like most of the Greek countryside, was infested with armed bandits who earned their livelihood through kidnapping, extortion, and murder. For centuries, bandits were a sociological and cultural fixture in the Balkans, heroes to a few and scoundrels to most. Above all, they were, as we have seen, a useful element in national and transnational Balkan politics. The armed bands were an easy and usually unattributable weapon for Balkan politicians to use against domestic and foreign enemies.

By 1870, the pattern had been set for the bandits and their foreign victims. Hapless travelers would routinely find themselves hostage to a particular bandit group. According to a tried and proven protocol, the unlucky captives would end up living for a few days or weeks with colorfully dressed and usually courteous ruffians, feasting on roast meat and other delicacies in the fresh mountain air. Occasionally, the hostages would be forced to endure some hardship, such as walking long distances over the rocky mountain paths as the bandits sidestepped police or army patrols, and sometimes they were forced to sleep outdoors. Meanwhile, family members, friends, or business associates would collect the demanded ransom, bringing the excursion in the rugged Greek mountains to an end that was uneventful for the hostages and profitable for the bandits.

On December 8, 1865, Lord John Hervey, Henry Strutt, and Mr. Coore, who crossed in a yacht from Patras to Dragomesti to hunt red deer, ended up as prizes to a band of eight thieves led by Capt. Spyro Dellis. The three Englishmen were promptly relieved of their valuables, and their yacht was boarded and thoroughly looted. The industrious Captain Dellis then sent a letter to the British vice-consul at Patras, demanding one thousand pounds in gold for each hostage and the termination of all pursuit of the bandits. As was the usual custom, one of the hostages stayed behind with Dellis while the other two sailed back with the terms of the ransom. Fortunately, on this occasion, the local British authorities understood the gravity of the situation and managed to meet the demands of the bandits before the eight-day deadline expired. Coore, who had volunteered to remain with Dellis and his men, was freed. Despite a few close encounters with Greek militia and the hardships of moving quickly over the Greek mountains, the young man was none the worse from the experience.

Unfortunately, such incidents tended to create a false sense of security among foreigners. They were convinced that capture by the colorful Greek desperadoes was a relatively harmless outdoor experience. The only risk was death by boredom — at least for the friends of the victim, who were often forced to endure listening to the tale over and over again at dinner parties. But the romantic image of the bandit as a kind of Balkan Robin Hood disguised a desperate, ruthless, and sometimes cruel individual who had forsaken society and accepted violence as a way of life. Even though these men had rejected the conventions of traditional law and order, they were zealous in enforcing their own rules, which had evolved over centuries.

In addition to presenting a centuries-long challenge to law, order, and internal stability, the outlaws of Southeastern Europe left a deep imprint on the cultural heritage of the Balkan peoples. Endemic banditry, brigandage, and irregular warfare are pivotal elements of Balkan folklore and history. Indeed, the exploitation of the bandit ethos became an integral part of the national strategies adopted in the nineteenth century by the newly created Balkan states. Such policies were meant to realize the irredentist aspirations of each Balkan nation. At the same time, the traditions of brigandage and guerrilla warfare directly influenced the evolution and character of the regular armed forces of the modern Balkan states, as well as shaping the attitudes of their citizens toward obligatory military service. Standing armies were an expensive yet critically important aspect of the push to expand each Balkan state to its national frontiers.

Banditry was a distinct military, social, and cultural institution whose deep and enduring roots originated in classical antiquity, took hold in Byzantine times, and developed extensively during the Ottoman period. By the early nineteenth century, bandits had become the foot soldiers of the Balkan independence movements and the only military force to counter the armies of the Ottoman Empire. In the process, the bandits were transformed from outlaws and murderers into freedom fighters — at least in the post-independence national history of each Balkan state.

—◦◦◦—

The peculiar features of Balkan geography provided the ideal environment for banditry and irregular warfare. In geographical terms, Southeastern Europe is defined by prominent mountains, cut by narrow river valleys, and interspersed with a relatively small number of isolated and widely scattered lowland plains.[24] The mountainous terrain had a twofold significance in the history of the Balkans. First, it provided the indigenous populations with a place of refuge in times of war or social and economic upheaval. (Later, it also became a natural base for resistance movements opposing foreign invaders.[25]) Second, the mountains and the plains shaped the evolution of two distinct and often antagonistic socio-economic organizations. The first of these was based on the sedentary agriculture of the plains. The other was founded on the economically insecure and less rewarding practices of nomadic pastoralism in the mountains.[26]

During those periods when the region was not under the control of a single empire or divided among several strong kingdoms, the competition for scarce resources led to the development of a culture of violence among the mountain tribes. Force was often used to acquire or defend limited resources, and thus the circumstances favored robbery, theft, and the possession of arms.[27] Not surprisingly, a society based essentially on the struggle for survival tended to distrust and resist all forms of central authority, and placed its primary loyalty in the institution of the patriarchal family.[28] In this sociolog-

ical context, the family took responsibility for the resolution of conflicts and disputes, the punishment of crimes, and the preservation of
individual and collective honor, and revenge was often exacted by
means of the blood feud.[29] Ultimately, these societal trends led to the
rise, by the time of the Ottoman conquest, of a military class guided
by an ethos that extolled manliness, loyalty, courage, and strength
above all else.[30]

Members of this military class frequently resorted to plundering
the more prosperous agricultural communities in the lowlands in
order to supplement their own meager economic assets.[31] But while
most bandits were shepherds, the life of brigandage attracted many
other types as well, including fugitives from justice, debtors, common
criminals, and victims of real or imagined injustices.[32] Throughout
the Ottoman period, groups of bandits known as *klephts* in Greek-
speaking areas and as *hayduks* or *uskoks* in Serbian and other
Slavic-dominated communities earned their livelihood through
plunder, pillage, and kidnapping. Their primary victims were local
villagers and traveling merchants, regardless of their religious or
"national" identity. In time, banditry expanded to such a degree that
it posed a serious threat to the internal stability of the sultan's
European possessions and a direct challenge to Ottoman authority
in the region.[33]

The problem of banditry was not caused by the Ottoman conquest of the region, however. Over centuries, outlaw bands had
operated throughout the Balkans. In the early modern period, groups
of *klephts* or *hayduks* varied in size from two to three men to more
than one hundred.[34] The right to command such bands rested not so
much on military competence, but on personal courage, initiative,
strength of character, and most important, ruthlessness. Experience
counted for little among brigands unless it was combined with a
strong personality.[35] The activities of these outlaws were concentrated
on the vital crossroads of the commercial routes that traversed the
mountains, forests, and swamps — terrain that was advantageous to
the guerrilla-type operations favored by the Balkan bandits.[36]

Typically, a band of outlaws followed a hierarchical structure
based on rank and status. Usually each band was organized on three
levels. The first included only the chief (called *kapetanios* or
boulouksis). The second tier comprised a small number of his trusted

lieutenants (*protopallikaria*), and these men were usually related to the chief. The third included all the rest. Those at the bottom of the structure were regular brigands and teenage "novices" (*psychogioi*) who served as the chief's servants or adjutants. These hierarchical arrangements were meant not only to ensure proper deference to the band's leaders, but also to provide a system for the division of booty and plunder according to rank.[37] The booty was divided into three parts, with one part going to the leader of the band, one part equally divided among those in the second rank, and the final part divided among those in the third level.

Occasionally, the bands operated in parties of smaller groups and kept in touch through a primitive but effective system of communication that involved piling stones in small cairns or on pillars; the number of rocks and their arrangement would convey a particular message. While on the move, the bandits avoided following paths or roads for any length of time, and after two or three miles, they would break up into small groups and divert their journey through the mountains, later reuniting at a prearranged location. When they traversed a road, they would march in single file and the last two or three men would drag a bush behind them to erase their footsteps. The same cautious approach was applied to campsites, and great care was taken to eliminate any evidence of their presence. Fires were built in such a way as not to leave a black mark on the ground, and the ashes were disposed of in the woods, some distance from the campsite.[38]

From the nineteenth century onward, nationalist Balkan historians and intellectuals have been attempting to prove that the *klephts* and the *hayduks* were champions of social justice and equality. According to such writers, these "freedom fighters" were inspired by patriotic and religious sentiments. They were hailed as liberators and admired by the Balkan peasantry, who allegedly viewed the bandits as the only force capable of protecting local freedoms from subversion by the Ottoman government and the indigenous elites. The advocates of such arguments frequently make reference to the degree to which Balkan folklore reflects the peasantry's admiration for the brigands and their activities. Greek popular ballads and the great epic poems of Serbia are frequently singled out as evidence of the peasantry's sympathy for the bandits.[39] Indeed, the brigands are traditionally endowed with the attributes of patriotism, religious duty, and a spirit of independence. They are also depicted as victims of Ottoman oppression who were forced to flee to the mountains.

But the argument that brigands were nationalists or freedom fighters is open to question. For one thing, the conviction that the bandits were consciously and deliberately "anti-Ottoman" is true only because they carried out their activities within the boundaries of the Ottoman Empire. However, the bandits were indiscriminate in their choice of victims.[40] They robbed rich and poor, Muslim and Christian alike, "preferably those who had more to take from but generally those whom they feared less."[41] In the words of one brigand, "Everyone is in debt to the robber."[42] Whatever support they were able to obtain from the peasantry was a result not of admiration, but of fear.[43]

Henry M. Baird, a nineteenth-century travel writer who was generally sympathetic to the *klephts*, recorded that "the elders of a village presented large sums, and furnished provisions to the band, to secure immunity from plunder."[44] A favorite activity of the *klephts* was plundering the stores of a monastery, although they would rarely molest the local parish priest. (He might be needed to read prayers or give last rites to a dying comrade.[45]) On the other hand, peasants who earned the enmity of the bandits could face mutilation, decapitation, or other unpleasant and cruel punishments. In reality, most brigands had only contempt for the peasantry, which further contradicts the notion that they were inspired by a devotion to the cause of social justice.[46]

The brigands' lack of political- or class-consciousness was matched by their lack of awareness of the cultural and historical heritage of the nations to which they belonged. Their ignorance in this regard is effectively illustrated by an episode that took place during an encounter between the Greek historian Koumas and the great nineteenth-century *klepht* Nikotsaras. When the scholar drew parallels between Achilles and Nikotsaras, the latter took offense at being compared to someone he had never even heard of: "What nonsense is this, and who is this Achilles? Did the musket of Achilles kill many?"[47]

Even after the establishment of the independent Greek state and the Greek government's attempts to exploit the bandits in the cause of irredentism and patriotism, these concepts remained little more than abstract notions for most brigands. Occasionally, irredentism could serve as a useful justification for the mounting of plundering forays into Ottoman territory, where "the burden of the brigands' depredations" commonly fell upon the shoulders of Christian and Greek-speaking subjects of the Ottoman Empire.[48] However, patriotism was an alien sentiment for the majority of bandits. They even joined the Ottoman security forces just as readily as they would the Greek armed forces. John Koliopoulos explains that "as a rule they were ready to sell their services in return for military employment with the additional prospect of booty."[49]

A good example of this self-interested attitude is to be found in the group of brigands who operated in southern Macedonia in the late 1870s. When the Greek consul at Thessaloniki attempted to inspire them with a sense of patriotic fervor, in an effort to guide them away from banditry and back to Greece, he was told, in a reply liberally peppered with insults, "that Greece was, as far as they were concerned, no different from Turkey — in both they were hunted, when not needed, like wolves — and that for them there could be only one fatherland, the mountains, and only one guide, their own interests."[50]

Even though the bandits were not motivated by nationalist or class ideology, the Ottoman administration regarded them as a serious threat to the internal, and later the external, stability of its European possessions. The empire, however, lacked the resources to garrison all of its territories, and it was able to maintain only a modicum of authority over the less accessible regions. The only alternative was to organize local militias to enforce and maintain law and order.[51]

The Ottoman security system itself was of a dual nature. The defense of strategic mountain passes (called *derbends*) was made the collective responsibility of the inhabitants of nearby villages (*dervenochoria*).[52] In exchange for the duties they performed, the villagers were granted privileged legal status and tax exemptions.[53] At the same time, the Ottomans commissioned Christian irregulars (known as *armatoli*) to enforce the sultan's authority and collect taxes on behalf of the government within the bounds of an administrative district known as an *armatolik*. Unlike those in the *dervenochoria* villages, which were answerable to Constantinople, the *armatoli* were responsible to the Ottomans, and the settlements in which they lived were not granted preferential treatment.[54] The precise origins of the *armatolismos* system are obscure, and it is regarded, variously, as a Byzantine, Venetian, or Ottoman innovation.[55] What is known for certain is that the first *armatolik* was established during the reign of Sultan Murad II (1421–51) in the Agrapha region, and between the fifteenth and nineteenth centuries, the number of *armatoliks* ranged from ten to twenty, depending on the period.[56]

Each *armatolik* was commanded by a *kapetanios*, normally an amnestied *klepht* who had been hired by the Ottomans to combat his own kind.[57] In time, this position was institutionalized within the Ottoman system, becoming the hereditary privilege of a small number of families.[58] The hierarchy of the *armatolik* bands was identical to that of the *klepht* bands, with the *kapetanios* assisted by *protopallikars*, who were usually kinsmen, while the rank and file consisted of ordinary *armatoli*.[59] The similarities were more than just coincidental. The line between *armatoli* and *klephts* was blurry at best, with individuals frequently changing from one role to another.[60]

The concept of sending a thief to catch a thief was fundamental to the *armatolismos* system itself.[61] This system was meant to contain, rather than eradicate, brigandage. And in practical terms, the Ottomans had few other choices, since only bandits had the military skills and experience needed to fight against other bandits. But this created an interesting paradox: the *klephts*, in order to obtain employment as *armatoli*, had first to achieve as much notoriety as possible, so as to make the authorities all the more eager to terminate their criminal careers by granting them the cherished amnesty. And ironically, the *armatoli* could not suppress the *klepht* bands completely without eradicating their own raison d'être. Ultimately, the *armatolismos* system was little more than a finely balanced game, a game played by the *klephts* and the *armatoli* at the expense of the peasants, who survived either by accepting extortion as a way of life or by taking to the hills and turning to banditry themselves, thus perpetuating what was already a vicious circle of violence and disorder.[62]

―――◈◈◈―――

While the *armatolismos* system was principally a feature of the Ottoman period, banditry antedated the arrival of the Ottomans in the Balkans by centuries. As early as the fifth century B.C., Thucydides noted that brigandage on land and piracy on the sea were common occupations among the inhabitants of Greece.[63] Following the Roman conquest of Dalmatia between the first and second centuries A.D., Illyrian pirates and mountain tribesmen conducted frequent plundering expeditions against the urban centers established by the Romans on the coastal plains of the Adriatic.[64] Even after they extended their authority over the rest of the peninsula, the Romans were able to control only the principal communications routes, with the indigenous Illyrians populating the rest of the region.[65] The failure of the Romans to manage the less accessible parts of the Balkans ultimately created conditions favorable to banditry. This situation repeated itself in the period between the third and fifth centuries when frequent Goth invasions into the Balkans resulted in social and economic dislocation, the decline of commercial activity, and the erosion of the tax base. Large segments of the population were even forced from the cities and towns into the countryside and mountainous areas to escape the ravages of the invaders. Eventually, some of these migrants became bandits.[66]

In the sixth century, Justinian I (527–65) managed to stabilize and reconquer the lost territories of the empire in the West, as well as extend Roman authority over the eastern frontiers, but this newfound security was temporary. To finance his wars and his ambitious building program, Justinian had to increase the tax burden on his subjects. This forced many peasants to flee their farms in desperation and turn to a life of brigandage.[67] The situation continued to deteriorate in the following years, and was compounded in the middle of the sixth century by the onslaught of Slavic invasions. The waves of Slavic tribes uprooted or assimilated the peasants from the countryside and eventually rolled back the frontiers established by Justinian's wars. During the same period, plagues and earthquakes killed countless people and contributed to the depopulation of the cities and towns.[68] By the ninth century, according to the account of St. Gregory the Decapolite, land traffic across the peninsula had virtually ground to a halt, and even major roads such as the Via Egnatia had become unsafe for travel.[69]

It is more than likely that by this time, the links between the nomadic shepherds and brigandage were already being forged. For example, in the twelfth century, Benjamin of Tudela, the Jewish traveler, wrote that the Thessalian Vlachs were renowned for banditry. The Vlachs, who by the late medieval period became synonymous with shepherds, also dominated routes throughout the Balkans and had established a lucrative business protecting merchant caravans from the attacks of brigands — and other Vlachs.[70] By 1189, banditry was so widespread in the region that the Byzantine governor of Branicevo hired many of these bands to harass Frederick Barbarossa's army. The bandits, serving in irregular units, performed well and caused considerable difficulties for the German emperor as he led the Third Crusade through the thick forests of Serbia's Sumadija region.[71]

The problem of brigandage continued to escalate in the following centuries. By the middle of the fourteenth century, it was serious enough to merit detailed treatment in Stephan Duscan's Law Code of 1349. The code made individual communities responsible for maintaining law and order, and held them liable for any crimes committed within their jurisdictions.[72] The provisions of the code, aside from demonstrating the steady deterioration of state authority, reflected the conviction that brigands could not operate without the support of the local community. Dusan believed that brigands depended on villagers not only for supplies, but also for information about potential targets. His rationale was that any community that shared in the brigand's crime should also share the punishment.[73] But the code's strict legal injunctions against banditry were of little practical use in eradicating what must already have been a well-established social problem. In the long run, Dusan was able simply to contain the activities of the brigands.[74] This became evident in the initial stages of the Ottoman conquest of the Balkans, when banditry escalated once again throughout the peninsula.

For the Byzantine emperors, the only solution to the problem of increasing political instability resulting from lawlessness was to employ more and more soldiers to protect roads, bridges, and mountain passes, and frequently they were forced to hire brigands to provide local security.[75] Unfortunately, this led to a self-perpetuating cycle of soldiers turning into brigands and the reverse. When the highway guards were underpaid, or not paid at all, they would supplement their incomes by plundering the merchant caravans and travelers they were supposed to protect.

Throughout the late fourteenth and fifteenth centuries, for example, the merchants of Dubrovnik experienced difficulties as the result of an infestation by Bosnian brigands of the trade routes leading into the interior of the Balkan peninsula.[76] The soldiers of the regular Byzantine army, unsatisfied with the terms of their service, had also deserted and often took up brigandage, either on their own initiative or in the service of a local potentate.[77] These bands of disaffected individuals trained in the use of weapons further disrupted the economic and social conditions of the region, driving many peasants off their farms to join the already considerable ranks of brigands.[78]

Byzantine authorities appeared helpless, and imperial property was just as vulnerable to plunder and pillage as private possessions and estates.[79] To many Byzantine subjects, their government, in its inability to address this particular problem, must have seemed to be abdicating its responsibilities. Not surprisingly, individuals and groups of all sorts began to fall back on their own resources to protect their interests, effectively taking the law into their own hands, and often using force or persuasion to settle disputes. Even property litigation between monasteries was, more often than not, settled through the force of arms, as was the case in 1315, when a violent confrontation arose between the Vatopedi and Esphigmenou monasteries on Mount Athos.[80]

The Ottoman conquest and the establishment of the *armatolismos* system at first provided a measure of stability in the region. But its usefulness declined along with the empire. Despite the harsh punishments meted out by the Porte (a term that was originally used to describe the gates of the sultan's palace, but that eventually came to refer to the sultan and his government) to those who had been unlucky enough to be caught, brigandage continued to be a serious destabilizing force in the Balkans, even if its practitioners did not, as some authors have suggested, actively pursue the cause of "anti-feudal resistance."[81] The auxiliary Christian militias on which the Ottomans tended to rely were effective only as long as the Ottoman state itself remained strong and could maintain control over such forces. With the corrosion of central authority, however, the *armatolismos* system began to work against the Ottomans; it was, after all, providing potentially subversive elements of society with weapons, military experience, and a firm foundation for anti-governmental and ultimately revolutionary activity.[82]

The danger the bandits posed to the stability and integrity of the Ottoman Empire became all the more acute when the Western powers began to realize the bandits' military potential and sought to harness it for themselves. In 1593 and again in 1606, during the Austro-Ottoman War, many *hayduks* enlisted in the service of the Austrians, for example, and were used to harass Ottoman lines of communication and supply, and tie up substantial Ottoman forces in subsidiary theaters of operations.[83] In 1598, *hayduks* also made up a substantial part of the army that Michael the Brave of Wallachia led into Bulgaria in an effort to "liberate" the Christian subjects of the Ottoman Empire. But with no sense of patriotic duty or religious sentiment, the *hayduks* proceeded to plunder those they were supposed to liberate, thus motivating the hapless Bulgarian peasants to co-operate with their Ottoman "oppressors" in ejecting the invaders.[84] Between 1792 and 1793, the Ottoman authorities organized the first regular Serbian troops to combat renegade units of Janissaries, and after their victory near Kolar in 1793, they began to distribute weapons to any Serb who was willing to fight on behalf of the sultan.[85]

In effect, the Habsburg–Ottoman competition along the Danube and the mass population movements in the Balkans defined the future course of Balkan national, territorial, and state demarcation. The great Serb migration in 1690 provided the opportunity for the Austrians to establish a new military frontier manned by refugee settlements. The Serbs offered the Habsburg emperors a ready pool of recruits for border units and irregular forces, and these same units for many centuries participated in the wars and skirmishes between the Austrian and Ottoman armies. The new Habsburg military frontier, which was first established in Croatia during the sixteenth century, extended to Vojvodina and later to Transylvania. In fact, the ongoing aggression between the Muslim and Catholic empires proved a training ground for future Serbian, Bulgarian, and Romanian revolutionary armies. In the aftermath of the disintegration of the Yugoslav federation in the 1990s, the successors of these frontier communities, such as Croatia and Krajina, became the epicenters of the Balkan crisis, and the new bandits, in the form of warlords with private armies, answered the clarion call of guerrilla war.

The seventeenth century brought yet another escalation of banditry. In Romania, heavy tax burdens forced many peasants to their traditional refuge in the mountains, where they too opted to join the brigands. In Greece, the Sublime Porte's inability to pay for the

upkeep of the *armatoli* also contributed to an increase of brigandage.[86] Yet these outbreaks of banditry were once again not
necessarily synonymous with revolutionary activity. In fact, brigandage would not assume revolutionary connotations as long as the
Balkan peasantry continued to regard the *hayduks* and the *klephts* as
enemies rather than as friends. In addition, most Balkan peoples did
not view local abuses as evidence of a deliberate anti-Christian bias
on the part of the Ottoman government, and thus the empire's
external enemies were unsuccessful in their attempts to enlist their
support against the Porte. This, too, meant the brigands were not a
revolutionary factor.[87]

—⟡—

The process of Ottoman decline, which began in the sixteenth century and accelerated throughout the following two hundred years,
gradually became the catalyst for revolutionary activity, however. This
eventually transformed the Balkan desperado into a freedom fighter.
At the same time, the decline of central Ottoman authority, coupled
with the transformation of the land-holding system and the emergence of local power centers, created conditions of discontent
among the European subjects of the Ottoman Empire.[88] These factors, which were accentuated by several new intellectual trends
espoused by Western-educated Greeks and Serbs, eventually led to
the national liberation struggles that took place in the beginning of
the nineteenth century.[89]

In these struggles, the *klephts* and the *armatoli* formed the main-
stay of the armed forces of the Greek and Serb insurgents, and later of
the Romanian, Bulgarian, and Albanian revolutionaries. In the Greek
War of Liberation, they filled the role of irregular light infantry,
which excelled at defensive guerrilla-style operations, a method of
warfare they had been practicing for centuries.[90] The *klephts* especially preferred skirmishes of short duration on ground of their own
choosing. These tactics had evolved partly as a result of the mountainous terrain they inhabited and partly from the limited range and
inadequacy of the firearms available to them. To overcome these limitations, Balkan guerrillas had become expert at waging mountain
warfare that allowed them to use local terrain to ambush superior
forces as they traversed narrow defiles or mountain passes.[91] The

notion of challenging the enemy to a stand-up fight over open ground was abhorrent to the *klephts*. For one thing, the process of loading a musket was a long and complicated one, and handling the weapon in the open rendered its owner vulnerable to the enemy. Furthermore, because a typical band was relatively small, all of its members had an obligation to keep body and soul together, thus enabling them to fight another day.[92] For these reasons, personal bravado and unnecessary exposure to enemy fire were regarded as acts of criminal folly that jeopardized the collective safety of the band.[93]

In practical terms, the stress on survival manifested itself in the bandits' skill for exploiting natural cover in battle; when such cover was not available, the brigands would frequently construct small waist-high earthworks (called *tambouria*) to protect themselves from hostile fire.[94] If the band found it necessary to withdraw from combat, the warriors would attempt to fall back to a new defensive position using fire-and-movement techniques to cover each other's retreat.[95] The act of running away from a battle that was going badly carried none of the connotations of cowardice and dishonor attached to it by Western military tradition. On the contrary, *klephts* regarded such action as simple common sense.[96] Not surprisingly, philhellenes who fought in the Greek War of Independence were often puzzled by the tactics of the *klephts*, and even thought of them as cowardly and dishonorable.[97] For their part, the *klephts* could scarcely comprehend the logic behind the linear tactics employed by nineteenth-century Western European armies. The notion that Westerners considered it honorable to blast one another with musketry fire for hours on end, all the while standing straight up, shoulder to shoulder, in orderly and neatly deployed ranks, was regarded by the *klephts* as the height of absurdity.[98]

Survival was as important to the *klepht* as his honor. He could advance, withdraw, hide, use subterfuge, even change sides, and still emerge with his honor intact. His main objective was to live to fight another day. To this end, the use of lies and disguises was considered cunning, not cowardly. The *klepht* who changed sides, especially for large sums of money, was thought to be endowed with so much prowess that the enemy had been compelled to purchase his services. He could not change his religion or betray his band, however, without soiling his name and reputation. One of the favorite ballads of the *klephts*, which has remained a popular story in Greek schoolbooks and folklore, was the tale of Athanasios Diakos. The unfortunate Diakos fell into a trap; after losing all his men, his musket, and his sword, he was taken prisoner by the Turks. His bravery, according to the ballad, so impressed his captors that they offered not only to spare his life, but to promote him within their own army, if only he apostatized. The brave Diakos chose to die by impalement rather than deny his faith, at least according to the version given by Henry Baird.[99] In the official Greek ballad, Diakos is impaled and roasted over a fire.

Many Greek and Balkan accounts of the period have victims first impaled and then roasted. Of course, impalement would result in instant death, and thus roasting the victim was a pointless exercise. Yet this did not mean that roasting served no purpose. The historian George Waddington contrasted the Greek and Turkish approaches to torture and execution, and noted that

> Greek brutality imitates the character of French republicanism. A Turk is more manly in his rage; he is content to be serious when he is savage; his fury seeks only the death of his victims; he sees nothing ridiculous in the spectacle of human agony. In the midst of his wildest madness, reeking and steaming with blood, he is at least free from the horrible infusion of frivolity, which can extract amusement from massacre, and convert the real tragedy of revolutionary abomination into a fete or a farce.[100]

After centuries of empire, in other words, the Ottoman approach to brutality had become calculated. As Waddington commented, "Impalement is a legal punishment, and I have never heard that it has been inflicted except deliberately, and by the order of a superior." On the other hand, the Greeks, it seemed to Waddington, were inclined to exact a measure of entertainment and humiliation in the middle of their blood lust. They had not acquired the centuries of experience the Ottomans had in using human suffering as a technique to humble and subdue their opponents. They had inherited from the Turks the means of inflicting pain, but it seems they had yet to master the political subtleties of using torture as a political end. For the Ottomans, grisly death after unspeakable mistreatment was not a source of entertainment, but was a ritual intended to instill fear

Left: The Suliot dance of death. Rather than capitulate to notorious Balkan warlord Ali Pasha, the Albanian Suliots chose suicide. They danced in concentric circles; at the end of each revolution, one jumped, until all had fallen to their deaths.

Bottom: Greek resentment over the almost 500 years of Ottoman rule reached a bloody climax in 1821, with the Greek War of Independence. Here, revolutionaries vent their wrath on Turko-Albanians.

Top: According to tradition, the Orthodox Church operated secret schools to keep alive Greek language and culture throughout the Ottoman occupation.

Bottom: In March 1913, the Greeks finally took Ioannina after a long and savage assault. Here, the Greek army liberates the town whose capture marked the union of Greece with the region of Epirus.

Top: Serbian cavalrymen, 1908. Serbia, like many other Balkan nations, gained some independence in the wake of the Greek War of Liberation. But the new state's irredentist claims set it on a path that led directly to the Balkan wars of 1912–13.

Bottom: The Church of Holy Wisdom *(Hafia Sofa)*. Built by Byzantine Emperor Justinian I in the fourth century, the Church is a symbol of the Eastern Orthodoxy. It was sacked during the Fourth Crusade by the Warriors of Christ.

Right: When Emperor Constantine realized that Constantinople was about to fall to the Ottomans in 1453, he threw off his imperial insignia and tried to defend the city with his own hands. He preferred a death of dignity to a life as a slave of the sultan.

Middle: The Janissaries were the best soldiers in the medieval world. Most were Christians appropriated as children by the Ottomans, converted to Islam, and trained as soldiers. They led austere and solitary lives of absolute devotion to the sultan.

Bottom: In 1205, the knights of the Fourth Crusade cut a wide swath through the Balkans. They quickly abandoned the cause of liberating the Holy Land for the more lucrative prize of Constantinople.

Top left: To many people, the *klepht* was a romantic figure inspired by patriotism and religious duty. In reality, he was a ruthless brigand who terrorized the peasants he ostensibly protected.

Top right: Ottoman Sultan Mehmet II, the Conqueror. The capture of Constantinople in 1453 was among his greatest victories.

Left: The lawlessness of the Suliots gave Ali Pasha an excuse to attack their region in what he hoped would be the first step toward the creation of his autonomous empire.

Above: Although they were Greek Christians, Phanariots assumed important positions within the Ottoman administration. They disproved of revolution and the ensuing social and economic upheaval.

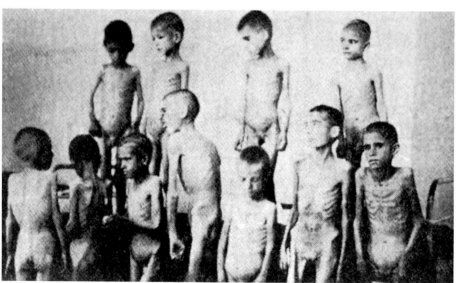

Top: *Evzone* (highlander) battalions were a key part of the Greek ground forces during the Balkan wars of 1912–13. Their primary mission was the capture of Thessaloniki.

Bottom: These boys were victims of the 1941–42 famine in Greece. During the occupation, the Germans confiscated all food and livestock. The resulting famine claimed more than 100,000 lives in Athens alone.

Left: Essad Pasha was the Ottoman commander charged with the task of holding Ioannina, one of the two greatest Ottoman fortresses in the western Balkans, in 1913.

Below: These Bulgarian irregulars take a break between skirmishes during the Balkan wars. The geography of the region made irregular warfare key to the success of all the Balkan armies.

Top: These natty Turkish officers were the last gasp of the Ottoman Empire. The "sick man of Europe" was in such financial chaos that it had to declare bankruptcy in 1875. The Balkan wars were the final nail in the empire's coffin.

Above: Greek irregulars, 1900. The Greeks' successful battle for independence in 1870 fed their dreams of securing Constantinople, Asia Minor, the Aegean islands, Crete, and Macedonia.

and helplessness in the victims, and thus paralyze other opponents into submission. The atrocities associated with the Balkan crisis of the 1990s surely demonstrate that all sides in these conflicts have since learned to reach deep into the reservoir of the Ottoman experience and attempt to recreate the architecture of terror to achieve political goals.

The *klephts* favored another curious element of ritual as well. Skirmishes were frequently preceded by exchanges of verbal abuse. Slanders against the honor of the opponents' womenfolk, couched in the appropriate sexual terms, appear to have been a favorite of the brigands. Boasts and name-calling were also quite popular.[101] Occasionally, these exchanges were accompanied by obscene gestures. References exist to *klephts* who had been wounded in the buttocks while "mooning" their opponents.[102] In most cases, however, a strict and unwritten code of honor forbade either side to open fire so long as the trade in expletives was in progress.[103] The same policy applied to mutually accepted superstitions. Both Christians and Muslims in mainland Greece had a morbid fear of rabbits, for example. On one occasion, according to the account of Edward Blaqueiere, an English observer during the Greek War of Liberation, some Greeks and Ottomans who were engaged in a firefight paused when a rabbit happened to pass between them — and all turned their fire on the unfortunate hare.[104]

The use of foul language remained a favored behavior of the *klepht* even after the war of independence was over, and such language was often directed at hapless peasants and later on at the Greek police or military forces. The most common expletive was "*keratas,*" which literally translates as "cuckold" but, according to Koliopoulos, meant "bastard." Other abusive terms included "*Ovrios,*" the popular version of "*Evraios*" (Jew), and "*Antichristos*" (Antichrist). However, the *klephts* really liked to get under the skin of those they held in contempt by insulting the honor and chastity of their unmarried daughters or sisters. These disparaging sexual comments, says Koliopoulos, were often accompanied by references to the manliness of the *klephts.*[105]

Yet for this enthusiastic articulation of sexual practices, the bandits must have relied on their imaginations, since few had contact with women. Their society was strictly male, and the bandits were self-disciplined about their sensuality, if not completely averse to female company. *Klephts* seldom married or carried on romantic liaisons. Those few who actually developed relationships rarely made reference to them.[106] Of course, their lifestyle left little or no opportunity to form lasting relationships. And Greek society prohibited sexual contact for women before marriage. Indeed, women were, for the most part, kept cloistered and could not speak to or be seen with any male who was not a direct relation. In public they were compelled to cover up as much as possible, and in their homes they had to maintain a discreet distance from visitors. Although customs varied from region to region, sexual abstinence remained a common denominator.

The bandit who was interested in a sexual relationship had two choices: marriage or the disgrace of a local virgin. The former was made extremely difficult by the brigand's way of life and the latter led to severe complications with the villagers.[107] The *klepht* extorted money or goods from the villages and in exchange provided a degree of security, even if that meant protection from himself and his band. But when he interfered with the female relatives of the villagers, they had little choice but to betray the *klepht* or turn to another band for justice. In either case, the sexual predilections of one bandit could impact negatively on the fortunes of the entire band. The ethos of the *klepht* was to fight, oppose all authority, and survive through plunder and extortion. In those circumstances, abstinence was the safer and more honorable way of life.

—◦◦◦—

Although by the early nineteenth century, the guerrilla warfare of the *klepht* was common throughout the Balkans, it had its roots in Albania.[108] The Albanians had a reputation as military innovators, a distinction associated particularly with the Orthodox Christian Souliot tribe of Epirus.[109] In the eighteenth century, as the military efficiency of the Janissary corps continued to decline, the Ottoman authorities began to rely on Albanian mercenaries with increasing frequency.[110] Eventually, their military reputation rose to such heights that it invited emulation of method, and soon, as mentioned earlier, the Albanians even set the fashion for Balkan warriors with their kilts. Eventually, many Ottoman notables also adopted the Albanian look, as did the Greek *klephts* and the *armatoli*.[111] The popularity of the costume was enhanced during the Greek War of Liberation, since those who wore it could claim to fight for the Greek cause and draw pay from the various Greek governments.[112] Today, this Albanian fashion statement of the eighteenth and nineteenth centuries is instantly recognizable as the Greek national costume, and it's proudly worn by the men guarding the tomb of the Unknown Soldier in front of the Greek Parliament.

Recently, most Albanians have been viewed as either victims of Serbian oppression or armed insurgents destabilizing Kosovo and northern Albania. However, in the nineteenth century, Albanian customs and traditions made considerable inroads into the society of the Balkan mountain villagers. Although Albania is the smallest country in the Balkans, it has a powerful military legacy. As a region, it lacks natural resources, and this absence of a strong material infrastructure is perhaps one reason why Albanians, according to L. S. Stavrianos, "cannot look back to an earlier period of glory and greatness. Their homeland has been too poor and restricted to enable them to expand and to found an empire comparable with those of the medieval Byzantine, Serbian, and Bulgarian emperors."[113] During the Ottoman invasions of the fifteenth century, however, the Albanians managed to unite for a brief period. Led by the legendary George Kastriotis, they defied the armies of the sultan. From 1444 to 1466, Kastriotis fought thirteen campaigns against the Turks and kept them away from Albania, much to the delight of Christian Europe, states Stavrianos.[114] But that was their high point, and they soon receded into the Ottoman Empire, remaining in relative obscurity until the Kosovo crisis of 1999.

The absence of cultural chauvinism and adaptability were the keys to the survival of the Albanians as a distinct people both during and after the Ottoman period. In fact, even before the Ottoman invasion, the Catholic and Eastern Orthodox churches had waged a relentless struggle for the hearts, minds, and souls of the Albanian tribes.[115] When the Ottoman armies first subdued the region, they discovered a people divided between the Orthodox Church in the south and the Catholic Church in the north. Characteristically, the Ottomans exploited these differences, and the Albanians called on their instincts of survival to adjust to the new economic and political realities. The Albanian feudal landlords were the first to renounce their respective faiths and embrace Islam, an act that allowed them to keep their estates and privileges. In 1468, the Ottomans implemented large-scale Islamization, which triggered both a mass exodus of Catholic Albanians to southern Italy and countless conversions to Orthodoxy. Not for the first time had the sultan and the Orthodox Church found common ground. The Ottomans, who viewed the Catholics as a potential security problem, saw in conversion to Islam a means of containing the Catholic threat. The Orthodox Church, in the meantime, which had despaired over the Catholic encroachment in the Balkans following the decline of the Serbian Empire, was grateful that the Islamization program had also produced new Orthodox converts. The sultan did not object, since the Orthodox Church was now part of the Ottoman establishment and looked to the empire for protection.

Economic factors and the tax advantages of Muslim affiliation ultimately produced a net population benefit for the Ottomans, since Albanians continued to convert to Islam, even some of those who had first piously adopted the Orthodox faith. Some groups remained Eastern Orthodox, of course, and a few even maintained their Catholicism. Yet despite their different religions and the social upheaval, the Albanians preserved their identity as one people.[116] Almost all, for one thing, adopted Greek as a common language. To a great extent, their proficiency in Greek facilitated the migration of Albanians to Macedonia, Thessaly, the Peloponnese, and the Greek islands. At the same time, these migrations, argues Stevan Pavlowitch, contributed to the Islamization and Albanization of many Slav and Greek territories.[117] Indeed, the mass migration of Muslim Albanians to Kosovo during the eighteenth century was the genesis of the later Serbian–Albanian tug-of-war over who is entitled to the region. Albanians from the surrounding mountainous areas had drifted to Kosovo as early as the fifteenth century and formed small farming settlements. This migration had a domino effect, with one group of migrants moving into the towns while another took their place in the villages they left behind. Miranda Vickers, in her book *Between Serb and Albanian*, argues that as a result of the "Treaty of 1489 between Venice and the Ottoman Empire almost half the population of Albania moved to Italy and to evade the Turks thousands more retreated into the inaccessible mountain regions."[118]

The exodus of Albanians to Europe followed earlier similar migrations in reaction to Serbian pressure from the north. In some regions of Europe, distinct Albanian minorities survived well into the twentieth century. For example, in 1901 there were more than 200,000 Albanians in Italy and small communities of them in the Greek mainland and the islands. The Albanian colonies in Italy were more advanced culturally, and by the late nineteenth and early twentieth centuries, they were in a position to make a significant contribution to the development of modern Albanian nationalism.[119]

The Albanian migration into the Greek regions in the sixteenth and seventeenth centuries was facilitated by a combination of geopolitical factors and natural phenomena such as plagues. Initially, people abandoned the towns and cities to avoid the advance of the Ottoman armies; those who remained adjusted to the new sultan's administration. Later, particularly after the Ottoman decline, the urban centers became battlegrounds between the sultan and his European enemies; some also suffered the ravages of indigenous rebellions. Many Albanians sought refuge in the mountain communities of Greece, while others fled to the coastal regions. The outbreaks of plagues and higher taxes imposed by local potentates accelerated the depopulation process, which left many parts of the Greek hinterland empty and desolate. The end result of these population upheavals, writes Pavlowitch, was that "the Balkans had a floating population of soldiers, deserters, bandits — men who had lost land, home or kin as Ottoman rule retreated or retaliated."[120] The Albanians moved into the abandoned spaces, either encouraged by the Ottoman authorities (who wanted to increase the Muslim element) or of their own volition (because they were fleeing their own homes on account of their Orthodox faith). Such was the case for the Albanians who settled in Boiotia, Attica, Argolis, and the island of Hydra in the sixteenth century.[121] Soon, the southern and eastern inland regions of Greece had become a mishmash of "Hellenic, Slav, Romance [Romanian], Turkish, and Albanian — of a people of an ambivalent identity and with a floating consciousness."[122]

Eventually, those in Greece, at least the Albanians who remained Orthodox, adopted a Greek identity.[123] They did so partly because they would then be allowed to intermarry with the indigenous Greeks, and partly because integration brought with it a higher level of economic opportunity. The Albanians living on the Greek islands adjusted even more quickly, since they were exposed to the influence of maritime travel and trade. As a result, many of them played a significant role in the Greek War of Liberation and achieved leadership positions with the post-revolutionary governments. Of course, Albanians and Greeks also fought on behalf of the sultan. For example, the dragoman of the imperial Ottoman fleet was a Greek, directing operations against his compatriots. He, like the Greek Wallachian and Moldavian despots, sought wealth and power within the Ottoman system.[124]

Remarkably, the Albanians also had a disproportionate level of influence in the Ottoman Empire. In the period from 1453 to 1623, eleven of the forty-nine grand viziers[125] were Albanian, eleven were South Slavs, and only five were actual Turks. By the nineteenth century, the palace guard and the First Army Corps, which guarded the capital, consisted of Albanian troops.[126] For the most part, it was their legendary military prowess, as well as their willingness to serve in foreign armies, that established the Albanians as the hardiest and toughest recruits for the Ottoman forces. Two tribal divisions separated the Albanians into the Ghegs in the north and the Tosks in the south. The Tosks are, even today, shorter, more somber, and more urban, a result of both a less harsh physical environment and closer contact with Byzantine culture (which fostered a greater acceptance of central authority). The Ghegs, on the other hand, were mountaineers in both culture and habit. Taller, tougher, and warlike, the Ghegs, at least in the nineteenth century, were resentful of any authority. In their remote villages high above the plains, the Ghegs evolved a socio-economic structure based on banditry. Initially, this structure was a reaction to the vicissitudes of foreign conquerors, whether Byzantine, Serb, Ottoman, or Albanian; as it evolved, however, it was transformed into a culture of violence tempered by an indigenous concept of right and wrong.

All Albanians in the nineteenth century carried arms. Usually they were equipped with a musket, pistols, and a sword. This made it easy for those who were not in league with the bandits to defend their homes and property against them. For years, the pattern of bandit activity remained relatively unchanged. In the early summer, armed groups of as few as two or as many as a couple of hundred would assemble under the leadership of a single chief. In the winter, most of the bandits would disperse and take refuge in their respective villages. During their operating season, some would find shelter in caves, but many simply lived outdoors with only their capes for cover. The local shepherds, either out of fear or in collusion, would supply the outlaws with meat and other necessities, while at night the bandits would descend on villages and collect a primitive "bread tax." The nocturnal visitor would knock softly on the door of each house and whisper, "*Psome, psome*," meaning "bread." This was the signal to the villager that it was time to give the bandit whatever he wanted.[127]

The bandits maintained an excellent system of security, and also identified potential victims through a network of spies in nearby towns and villages. Once they had decided on a target, they would lie in wait, taking cover in thickets, behind stones, in water, or by covering themselves with leaves. First, they had to determine if the target was armed, and if he was accompanied or alone. When they knew the situation was favorable, they would open fire from their hiding place until their victim surrendered or was killed. If the party under attack proved to be formidable, the bandits would beat a hasty retreat. If the victim gave up, he would be tied and gagged. Once the captive had been relieved of any valuables, the bandits would determine if he was someone of substance. In such a case, the unfortunate man would be forced to write to family or friends, begging to be ransomed, at a sum that was dictated by the bandit chief. If the money arrived, the prisoner would live to be captured another day. If the family and friends were unable or reluctant to raise the money, however, or if they simply saw an opportunity to get rid of an unwanted relative, they might neglect to pay the ransom. The bandits would then, more often than not, behead the unfortunate man, though occasionally they would keep the victim with them until they dispersed for the winter. The fate of the prisoner often varied depending on the mood and whim of the bandits. Most exchanges, however, were without bloodshed. After the first shots were fired, most people submitted, and if the bandits faced stiff opposition, they would often just melt away into the mountains.[128]

In his book *Journal of a Tour in Greece and the Ionian Islands*, William Mure provided a detailed account of one typical bandit attack. The victim was a cotton dealer who was returning home after collecting outstanding debts in the northern Peloponnese. He was traveling on foot, alone, with a considerable sum of money. The attack took place in a thicket where the road narrowed and was flanked by steep banks on both sides. Bandits had prepared the ambush by lying in wait on both sides of the higher end of the road banks, hidden by brushwood. First, a single pistol shot was fired at the victim, presumably a warning for him to stop and surrender his valuables. The man, however, started to run toward the open plain; the bandits fired a second shot but once again failed to hit their target. They then chased their quarry across the field, and when they caught him, they stabbed the man with their knives. The more the poor fellow tried to fight off his assailants, the angrier they got. After receiving several cuts, he fell to the ground. The bandits then slit his throat to such an extent that his head was almost severed. They proceeded to take anything of value, and then disappeared into the interior of the country.[129]

Years of such illegal activities, as well as service in the Ottoman forces, created a pool of irregular soldiers who had learned to live under considerable hardship. Many were skilled in hit-and-run tactics and knew how to wage long guerrilla wars with limited supplies. Some were even able to practice a crude form of medicine for treating a wound or setting a broken bone. J. C. Hobhouse, in *A Journey through Albania*, tells the story of a French diplomat who suffered from a hernia that was so painful he was persuaded to trust an Albanian healer. According to Hobhouse, the consul not only lived to tell the tale, but was cured of his condition.[130]

The legend of the bravery and success of the Albanian bandit created a model for other Balkan brigands. A bandit's value was based on his skill with weapons and the degree of courage he displayed. Any kind of central authority was treated with disdain, and rugged individualism was celebrated. But what most distinguished the Albanian bandit was his willingness to carry and display a weapon.

It is not unusual that the cult of the weapon also assumed such importance among the Greek *klephts* and other Balkan bandits. The Ottoman administration prohibited non-Muslims from carrying arms, a mark of their inferior status. Furthermore, Christians were, as we have seen, forced to pay extra taxes and avoid any displays of extravagance. Not surprisingly, the legend of the Albanian mountain warrior often proved irresistible to young men and nationalist historians alike.

In this way, the bandit was transformed into a romantic desperado in search of freedom. In practical terms, of course, most Christian land-lords, whether Albanian, Greek, or Serb, lived as ostentatiously as their Muslim counterparts, made their wealth through tax-farming, and ultimately offered a tempting target for bandits. Indeed, brig-andage increased in the nineteenth century not because of a growing revolutionary ardor among the bandits, but because the decaying Ottoman Empire was unable to offer the level of security it once had in the mountainous regions and passes and later in the urban centers.

Until the outbreak of the Greek and other Balkan revolutions, relations between the Ottoman central authority and its Christian subjects were based on a pattern of mutual corruption. Nationalist sentiments were confined to members of the Balkan elites, especially those educated in Europe. Their compatriots remained oblivious to such notions, and the bandits had no inclination to view the world in terms of Ottoman versus Christian.

Eventually, though, nationalist ideas generated by the French Revolution, along with the advent of mass print communications (especially newspapers), set the stage for a new period of upheaval in the Balkans. The combination of Ottoman decline and the emerging national consciousness of the Greeks, Serbs, Bulgarians, Romanians, Albanians, and Turks proved irresistible. Ultimately, it was the Great Powers that actually sanctioned the creation of new states in Southeastern Europe. But most nationalist rebellions were really instigated by an unlikely alliance of urban intellectuals and illiterate bandits. The intellectuals created the historical, sociolog-ical, political, and moral framework for each revolution (a framework that continues to permeate the foundations of each of the modern Balkan states), while the bandits secured victory by virtue of their ability to survive against the regular armies of the sultan. This enabled the revolutionaries to wait out the initial hesitation of the Great Powers, which were loath to upset the European geopolitical security that had been established in the wake of the Napoleonic Wars. Survival, after all, was the fundamental skill that characterized every Balkan bandit.

4

ETHNICITY VERSUS
THE NATION-STATE

———∞∞———

My father will roast your father,
or brother, if he catches them.

— THE RESPONSE OF A YOUNG ALBANIAN CHRISTIAN
TO THE NEWS THAT HE WAS TO BE ROASTED ALIVE

Typically, February draws cold winds
from the north that relentlessly whip the mountain peaks of southern
Albania and north-western Greece. These thrashing winds then
descend to lower altitudes, engulfing the few isolated communities
nestled in the deep valleys. The temperature drops to below freezing,
and the bone-chilling cold seeps through the walls of the villagers'
humble homes.[1] In the early eighteenth century, most such houses
offered only modest cover against the cold. During the winter
months, the mountain villages and towns were often snowed in for
weeks on end. The dwellings near Lake Ioannina, in northern Greece,
were less exposed, but occasionally the frigid winds from the mountains buffeted the fishing hamlets by the water. The monastery of St.
Panteleimon, which is located on one of the small islands dotting the
lake, was fortuitously placed in a sheltered nook beneath a rock and
thus was spared the violence of the harsh winds. This humble cloister

became the stage setting for the final act of Ali Pasha, one of the most colorful and notorious Balkan warlords.

On the afternoon of February 5, 1822, a handful of men cautiously approached the gate of the monastery. The small island had become the last domain of the Muslim governor, once the most powerful official of the sultan's territories in Europe. The Old Lion, as Ali Pasha had come to be known, was confined to this remote spot. After a lifetime motivated by lust for power and wealth, Ali Pasha was now under house arrest. The pasha, with his personal bodyguards and his favorite wife, had reluctantly retired to the monastery and patiently waited for his master, the Ottoman sultan, to pronounce sentence.[2] He had committed high treason and was anathematized by the mufti of Constantinople. Yet the arrogance of power had seduced Ali into believing he could cheat his fate. The phantom authority he exercised within the environs of the little monastery was typical of the kinds of illusions desperate men create to avoid reality. He was clinging to the idea that he would win a reprieve, and indeed he lived within an empire whose vicissitudes left some reason to hope. The Ottoman sultans, from the eighteenth century, had become accustomed to ignoring the betrayals of ambitious satraps. Ali believed that the capriciousness and corruption of the sultan's court would mitigate the gravity of his treason to the empire. Ultimately, his hubris was the instrument of his own demise.

During his reign, the Ottoman pasha had waged a series of political and military campaigns against fellow pashas, *klephts*, Christian and Muslim Albanians, Greeks, and anyone else who stood in the way of his efforts to carve out for himself an independent principality in the Balkans. In the end, he succumbed to defeat. Ali was abandoned by the Albanian Muslims and even betrayed by his own sons. All but his closest bodyguards deserted him. Essentially, he was the victim of his own unscrupulous political dexterity, a friend and an enemy to everyone.[3] At times, the pasha would shift loyalties within a matter of hours, proving himself so slippery that no one trusted him.

In January 1821, Kurshid Pasha, the Ottoman commander-in-chief in Europe, reduced all of Ali's fortresses and finally compelled the Old Lion to surrender. At first, Ali refused to capitulate, threatening to blow himself up in his last stronghold of Itch-Kale on Lake Ioannina. After torturous negotiations, however, he agreed to give up on the condition that he be permitted to present his case personally to Sultan Mahmut. Kurshid Pasha accepted the terms of the armistice only after Ali surrendered the fortress and retired to the little monastery. For a short while, Ali lived in relative comfort, holding court for visiting pashas and other Ottoman dignitaries. He was permitted to maintain a retinue of his own bodyguards and pass the time in luxury while awaiting the sultan's decision. The Old Lion believed he would be able to ingratiate himself with Sultan Mahmut by distributing generous bribes to the sultan's advisers. This tactic had been successful in the past, but this time the sultan was convinced that Ali Pasha was far too dangerous a threat to Ottoman rule in the Balkans.

On that cold afternoon of February 5, when Ali saw the Ottoman officials pass through the gate, he quickly concluded that his fate had been sealed. He managed, in spite of his circumstances, to summon enough courage to challenge the men. Unfortunately, they ignored his command to halt, displaying the gilded front piece of the case containing the sultan's firman. One of the somber officials advised Ali to "submit to fate; make your ablutions, address your prayer to God and the Prophet; your head is demanded."[4] Before the official could finish, however, Ali pulled out his pistol and fired. He wounded one emissary in the thigh and killed a second, while his faithful guards dispatched a few more. But these grand gestures of defiance were to no avail. Within a few minutes, the Ottoman soldiers on the perimeter of the monastery had killed several of Ali's guards and wounded the pasha himself in the chest.

Still the Old Lion refused to die or surrender. As he turned to one side then another, desperately seeking a place to protect himself, musket balls rained down on the sides of the building. Ali received a second wound, this one to his side, and then a third shot shattered his spinal column. The old pasha tottered, caught himself by the window, and finally collapsed on the sofa. "Run," he told one of the few bodyguards left alive. When the man hesitated, Ali pleaded, "Go, my friend, and kill poor Vasiliki [his favorite wife], so that the unhappy woman may not be outraged by these wretches."[5] It was Ali's last command — all resistance had come to an end.

Ali's remaining men jumped from the windows, and the Ottoman officials commenced with the grisly task prescribed by Ottoman custom and tradition. Ali, remarkably still alive, was seized by his beard and dragged to the staircase. Without much ceremony, his head was roughly slammed on one of the stairs; the executioner then proceeded to swing his sword in order to sever the head from the body. However, the makeshift scaffold and the hurried manner used to complete the task made it very difficult to decapitate the old pasha. The executioner could not effect a clean cut, and he was forced to hack away repeatedly at Ali's neck until the head finally gave way.[6]

For sixty years, Ali Pasha, vizier of Ioannina, had been the military and political authority of the southwestern Balkans. The son of a minor Ottoman official, Ali skillfully combined guile and the manipulation of Muslims and Christians alike to achieve control over large parts of northern Greece and southern Albania. But he unintentionally turned himself into the Greeks' secret weapon in their revolution in March 1821. With substantial Ottoman forces attempting to put down Ali's own private rebellion, the various and often divided Greek rebels were able to unite long enough to sustain their initial drive for independence.

——◦◦◦——

The pugnacious regionalism of nineteenth-century Balkan societies, such as was at the heart of the Greek revolution, was a by-product of the Ottoman policy toward non-Muslim peoples, a policy that recognized religious communities but not secular "nations." This approach had, in tandem with Balkan geography, created clusters of disparate communities. By the early modern period, these communities based their identities on religion and affiliation with a specific region. The Ottoman regime, as the Communists would do after the Second World War, had kept the Balkans essentially isolated. Ottoman absolutism did not encourage political integration, nor did it force a new culture upon the conquered Balkan societies. As Steven Pavlowitch underlines, "It had prevented the development of the countryside but enabled its survival and preserved old values. Living in the past blurred reality, but maintained hope."[7]

The major cities of the empire, on the other hand, were more affected by class division than religious segregation. Wealthy Christians and Jews, especially the Phanariots, exercised as much influence as their Muslim counterparts and maintained all the trappings of a powerful elite.[8] In the provinces, the primates (who included Christian landlords, tax farmers, and Ottoman administrators)[9] formed an oligarchy that set them apart from the landless peasants and poor Muslims. With some notable exceptions, these regional and metropolitan aristocrats clung to the privileges they had, and concentrated on wresting further concessions from the Ottomans.[10]

In addition to the political, religious, and social stratification brought by Turkish rule, the Balkan region also suffered from ethnic fragmentation. The Balkans formed the frontier between the Christian kingdoms of early modern Europe (later the Great Powers) and the Ottoman Empire. During the Ottoman period, Croatia served as a buffer zone between the armies of the sultan and those of the Habsburg emperors. The region effectively became a permanent battleground for the Ottoman and Austrian armies, as each conducted extensive raids and waged wars that completely devastated and depopulated large parts of the country. Bosnia-Herzegovina, for example, was alternately a transition area between the Orthodox Serbs and the Catholic Croats.[11] Slovenia, meanwhile, came under Habsburg control in the course of the fourteenth and fifteenth centuries, and remained Catholic and part of the Austro-Hungarian Empire until the end of the First World War. The Slovenes never achieved any form of independence, but they also suffered none of the upheavals that afflicted their fellow Slavs in the southeastern Balkans. The social and political development of the eastern Balkans, on the other hand, was greatly influenced by the proximity of these regions to Constantinople, as was also the case with Bulgaria and Romania.[12] Bulgaria's nearness to the center of Ottoman power meant direct rule, an attraction for large numbers of Turkish settlers.

Romania emerged from the medieval period as the semi-autonomous principalities of Wallachia and Moldavia. The Ottomans, at least in form, maintained the quasi-independence of these territories, but power was exercised through regional rulers, *hospodars*, or princes appointed by the sultan. Most of these quasi-independent princes were foreign, and in the eighteenth century the position of *hospodar* became the exclusive prerogative of the Phanariots. In the principalities and Constantinople, this Greek aristocracy achieved power and wealth, as did their lesser counterparts in Greece. This was not the case with the Serbs, however. The small number who succeeded in the Ottoman capital were absorbed by the Phanariots and maintained few links with Serbia.

Equally significant was the fact that the Greek merchant class and those serving as Ottoman administrators acquired considerable skill and practice in government. This became a salient feature of the revolution in Greece. Serbia, by contrast, lacked experienced leaders and individuals with managerial expertise. In Bulgaria and Romania, foreign rule also meant domination by fellow Christians. These regions were particularly controlled by Greek Orthodox administrators and prelates, and their tenure generally deprived the regions of the opportunity to cultivate an indigenous political, economic, and ecclesiastical elite. The administration of the Phanariots over the principalities, with few exceptions, was an exercise in fiscal exploitation meant to satiate the increasing demands of the sultan. R. W. Seton-Watson, in his history of Romania, maintains that "it is impossible to conceive a more disheartening task than that of recording in detail the history of these hundred years in Wallachia and Moldavia, and the western reader would only read it with impatience and under protest."[13] There is little doubt that the Phanariot rulers were absolutist and resented by the local notables. And of course, collecting taxes was not the way to ingratiate themselves with the indigenous population.

The cumulative effect of these factors was that the concept of the nation-state was at first alien to both the general population and the Christian elite, while the notion of multi-ethnic communities remained a legacy of Byzantine and Ottoman rule. It took time for all the various regional and distinct communities of the Balkans to coalesce into individual national entities, and in some cases this is still an ongoing process. In the eighteenth century, the intellectual revival of the Greeks began within the circles of the Phanariots of Constantinople and the Phanariot rulers of the Danubian principalities. Ironically, many Phanariots were themselves opposed to the revolutionary aspects of Western intellectual liberalism, and most later found the radical ideas emanating from the French Revolution equally abhorrent.[14] But they employed the Greek intellectuals and professionals of Constantinople and the principalities, thus inadvertently financing the first tentative steps toward rebellion.

The Phanariots had, by this time, assumed most senior positions within the central Ottoman administration, and they controlled a significant share of the empire's trade and maintained almost a stranglehold over the commercial life of non-Muslims. At first, they had served only as imperial interpreters, but with their superior education and political skills, they were soon elevated to the status of senior advisers to the sultan and his ministers in matters of international affairs. Indeed, the Phanariots administered Moldavia and Wallachia with the absolutism and enlightened despotism they had learned first-hand at the court of the Sublime Porte. Their sometimes harsh use of power was articulated by Athanasios Ypsilantis, a Phanariot historian, in this way:

> What harmful innovations have occurred in these unhappy lands
> . . . on account of the Greeks! I pass over in silence all the things
> I know. . . . This only I say that the Greeks have destroyed the old
> privileges of these two principalities that were beneficial to their
> inhabitants, and they will surely see at God's tribunal Who it is they
> have sinned against.[15]

Over time, the Phanariots extended their influence over the Orthodox Church and came to dominate the ecumenical patriarchate in Constantinople, and by so doing, writes Pavlowitch, "politicized the patriarchate which, in turn, provided them not only with an identity, but with a sense of historical continuity through its unique relation to Byzantium."[16] On the other hand, they did protect the Orthodox Church, intervening on its behalf in countering the encroachments of the Catholics in the Balkans and Jerusalem.

While the Phanariots attempted to refashion Balkan society from within the Church, members of the Greek intelligentsia were promoting a different type of reform. They were inspired by the principles, if not the violence, of the French Revolution, and they attempted to modify these principles for home consumption. Revolutionaries such as Rigas Phereos advocated the creation of a Hellenic republic of Balkan and Asia Minor Christians. Some Phanariots, meanwhile, such as the Ypsilantis brothers, Alexandros and Constantinos, whose ancestors had ruled the Danubian principalities, appealed for Balkan unity through the restoration of the Byzantine Empire. The Phanariots loathed social and economic upheaval, preferring instead either the Ottoman status quo or the establishment of an equally authoritative imperial regime.[17] But in effect, both attempts to reconstitute the Balkans were variations on a theme, the ultimate aim of which was the resuscitation of a Byzantine multi-ethnic state. In the final analysis, the Phanariot aristocrats and the intellectuals associated with them were all fundamentally anti-national.[18] For these early revolutionaries, the concept of the nation-state lacked cultural and historical precedent. The closest parallel was to be found with the ancient Greek city-states, which nevertheless did not conform to the ideal of a multinational and multi-denominational federation.

Not surprisingly, these early revolutionaries became the first casualties of the Greek insurrection. Rigas Phereos was arrested by the Austrians for advocating revolution and handed over to the Ottomans, who promptly executed him in Belgrade. Alexandros Ypsilantis was forced to seek asylum in Russia, while the rough and pragmatic politicians of mainland Greece and the pre-eminent *klepht* chieftains eclipsed Constantinos's political and military role in the Greek War of Liberation. He joined the fight to establish a Greek state after failing to rouse the Balkan communities to a struggle for the resurrection of a multi-nation Byzantine Empire. None of this ended the Phanariot influence in Greece, however. After the creation of the modern Greek state, the Phanariots provided the conservative leadership and backbone of the Greek monarchy.

Ottoman degeneration also inspired other wealthy Greek Christians to contemplate the creation of some kind of state for the Orthodox subjects of the sultan. The activities of these quasi-revolutionaries and nascent nationalist intellectuals revolved around two organizations that were set up at the turn of the century. Men who believed that education was the precursor to a struggle for liberation founded the Philomuse Society at Athens in 1812. Many of the leaders of the Greek independence movement were trained in Europe as a result of funds raised by this society.[19] Greek merchants in Russia, meanwhile, established the second hub of revolutionary activity in Odessa in 1814. The Philiki Hetairia (the Society of Friends), in an attempt to shroud itself in secrecy, adopted loose Masonic rituals involving covert signals and a hierarchy of membership. The very layers of mystery masked the society's paucity of influential adherents and lack of support from or contact with any of the Great Powers.

In the late eighteenth and early nineteenth centuries, the prevailing wisdom among Greek and other Balkan radicals and intellectuals was that the Ottoman Empire was on the brink of collapse, and that imperial Russia was destined to become the agent of Ottoman demise. The leaders of the Philiki Hetairia were able to convince a great number of people in the Balkans that the patron behind their society's veils of secrecy was the Russian czar, Alexander I. Through this ruse, the Hetairia hinted that it enjoyed the unequivocal support of Russia, and that it was only a matter of time until the czarist armies swept away the degenerate forces of the sultan and restored Byzantium. This careful sleight of hand enabled this relatively small and obscure group of merchants to raise considerable funds and plant agents in every major Ottoman urban center.[20]

Yet in matters of national affiliation, the founders of the Hetairia were either unable or unwilling to differentiate between Orthodoxy and nineteenth-century egalitarian nationalism. To some degree, this was reflected in the hierarchical structure of the organization. George Finlay, in his *History of the Greek Revolution*, scornfully writes that "the traders who framed its organization called the popular class of initiated brethren [i.e., the lowest-ranking members of the Hetairia] by the barbarous appellation of Vlamides, from the Albanian word *vlameria*, signifying brotherhood."[21] This derogatory word was used to refer to the society's more simple and illiterate members, and it perhaps points to the social and intellectual snobbery of some of the society's leaders.

Modern Greek historians describe the Hetairia as an organization not only committed to Greek independence, but also determined to support insurrections in Romania, Bulgaria, and Serbia.[22] Balkan specialists such as Steven Pavlowitch suggest that "without a public program, it [the Hetairia] meant different things to different people."[23] Greek and Serbian merchants, Romanian *boiers*, Phanariots, *klept* leaders, doctors, lawyers, and other professionals all found political space within the Hetairia's poorly defined ideology. Given this, it is possible to view the use of non-Greek appellations as an attempt to suggest the pan-Balkan aspirations of the society's leaders. On the other hand, the confused and haphazard aims of the Hetairia and the failure of its leaders to see past religious affiliation as a national common denominator were the legacy of the Orthodox and Byzantine traditions. When Alexandros Ypsilantis assumed the leadership of the Hetairia, he carried with him the intellectual baggage of the former until the Greek revolution gave voice to distinct national aspirations after 1821.

In general, the difficulty with the Phanariots and the Greek intellectuals was that they were cut off from the realities faced by lesser Orthodox notables in the provinces. These lesser officials were dependent upon the regional idiosyncrasies of the rural communities, as well as the military might provided by the bandits, who turned freedom fighters after the insurrections broke out. These Western-educated professionals and merchants also saw little merit in replacing the stagnant Ottoman system with an equally repressive Byzantine autocracy. And such imperial notions held little weight with the Greek diaspora in Western Europe, whose fortunes and political influence were critical to the success of the 1821 rebellion. Adamantios Korais, like many other members of the diaspora, believed that education was the key to liberating the Greeks from both Ottoman domination and the dead hand of their Orthodox Byzantine heritage.

Conventional Balkan historiography suggests that the cohesion of the Orthodox establishment was what preserved language, culture, and identity during the Ottoman period. But there are problems with this theory. For one thing, the higher clergy communicated in archaic Greek, while their Serbian counterparts relied on a variation of medieval Slavonic. Therefore, only a small minority of educated Christians could understand the foundational elements of Church culture. The village priests, too often poorly educated, confined their activities to weddings, baptisms, funerals, and other rituals that, more times than not, remained incomprehensible to them and the members of their flock. But if the clergy members were not the key, how did any of the Balkan communities maintain their language, culture, and history, and ultimately form their respective national identities?

One tentative explanation is that popular culture survived through folk music, stories, epic poems, and the oral tradition. In effect, a type of cultural memory was passed from generation to generation. The Ottomans, without realizing it, made their own contribution to the sustentation of the distinctiveness of the Balkan communities by simply applying laws that reminded Christians they were conquered peoples. Every rule that forced Christians not to wear certain articles of clothing, to refrain from keeping weapons, or to pay special taxes was a constant reinforcement of their distinctive identity and their inferior status. This policy of exclusion was perhaps the single most important contributing factor in maintaining the sultan's Orthodox subjects. The Balkan Christians might not have understood the finer points of Orthodox dogma, but for centuries Ottoman practices served to persuade them that, both by default and as victims of persecution, they were members of a distinct Orthodox community.

Violence was also a determining factor in promoting segregation and distinctiveness. Most Balkan folklore revolves around the theme of death, either through sacrifice or at the instigation of enemies. Killing and destroying opponents, massacres, torture, and mutilation are all at its core. In the preserved litany of catalogued horrors, Christians are impaled, roasted, flayed, drowned, decapitated, and burned individually or en masse. Women and men are raped, forced into the harems of pashas, sold with their children into slavery, and demeaned in one form or another. The objectives of war as understood then, a pattern that seems to have been repeated in the recent atrocities in the former Yugoslav republics, were to humiliate, degrade, and finally exterminate the enemy, whether by mass killing or expulsion. Karl von Clausewitz's maxim that war is an extension of politics by other means has little meaning in the context of total war. The ultimate characteristic of all Balkan conflicts, and what makes some European and North American journalists uncomfortable and occasionally hysterical, is the application of total war.

The sum total of these characteristics shaped, at least in part, the evolution of modern Balkan nationalism. The finishing touches of Balkan identity were then added by the post-revolutionary governments of each new country in the form of state culture. In matters of language, literature, music, dance, folklore, and history, these regimes attempted, with varying degrees of success, to instill their own interpretation of identity, which was often a caricature of the culture that predated the Ottoman conquest. Indeed, to some extent, popular culture was sacrificed in order to revive some vestiges of the Byzantine legacy. The chaos that followed the outbreak of the wars of independence reduced most Balkan communities into economic, social, and cultural wastelands. The only avenue available to their post-revolutionary governments was to centralize cultural institutions and impose a systematic program of national standards across a landscape distorted by regional disparities and identities inscrutable to the political elites.

Through this process of cultural regeneration, only those elements of literature, language, and history judged authentic were enshrined; everything else was consigned to the dustbin as alien appendages. Adamantios Korais was one who strove to eliminate Turkish and other foreign words from the Greek language. By combining elements of classical, Byzantine, and demotic Greek, he created the *katharevousa* (purest), an artificial language that looked and presumably sounded like ancient Greek. Despite the work of scholars and popular writers, who proved that the simple spoken Greek and the written demotic version represented the natural evolution of the language from antiquity, the state preferred to err on the side of archaisms.

Ironically, the written form of the demotic language found a welcome home in the court of Ali Pasha.[24] Under the pasha's protection, proponents of demotic Greek had the freedom to use the language without fear of either retribution from the patriarchate in Constantinople or the intellectual tyranny of neo-classicists. But sadly, only a Muslim Albanian tyrant was able to truly appreciate the work of Greek-language revolutionaries. For more than a century, newspapers, books, laws, and any official documents were published in *katharevousa*, yet only a small percentage of the population had the facility to use the artificial language. Inevitably, the politics of language created opportunities for demonstrations, violence, and a mushrooming of literary and nationalist societies that rose up in the name of cultural salvation.

But the twists and turns of language and culture as exercises of national affirmation and national purity were not enough. The independence movements had to fulfill the goals of the ecclesiastical establishment in order to secure a continuum with the inheritance of Byzantium. Yet once the fighting had started, the original program of replacing Ottoman subjugation with Byzantine cultural and political hegemony temporarily fell by the wayside; indeed, the allure of a future modern state dissipated any notion of Balkan unity. The success of just one Balkan rebellion was enough to spur people to seek their own nation-states and corresponding historical territory. And of course, the Pandora's box of ideas from the French Revolution presented a new vision of nationhood, one molded to reflect the historical identity of each individual Balkan community.[25] History offered a justification for great defeats and an explanation for Ottoman subjugation. After all, those five centuries of Ottoman rule needed to be rationalized to mitigate the helplessness of the Balkan peoples.

Unfortunately, the problem created for future generations was that the nineteenth-century Balkan states either ignored or failed to accommodate the ethnic groups that had become an indigenous minority within the boundaries of the historic space claimed by the dominant majorities. Often, these minorities were inconveniently located adjacent to the frontier of their own historic homeland, a situation that was essentially a guarantee of perpetual friction, violence, and ultimately national wars of liberation. The blueprint for the present-day Balkan conflicts was drawn up by nineteenth- and twentieth-century European and Balkan politicians, who tried to balance the interests of the Great Powers with autochthonous ethnic and national expectations.

From the early nineteenth century on, the Balkan wars of liberation have been complex mixtures of emancipation from Ottoman rule, manifestations of Balkan unity, and rebellions against Christian and Muslim Ottoman administrators. At first, rebellions against the sultan lacked both the cohesive political platform and the military resources needed to achieve any measure of success. In Greece, and later in Serbia and Bulgaria, salvation was expected to come from abroad. Local insurrections often began as a result of Habsburg and Russian intrigues and promises of liberation during periods of war with the Ottoman Empire. However, when the Russians or Austrians were defeated, reached an accommodation with the sultan, or faced constraints from the other Great Powers, the Balkan Christian cause was quickly jettisoned. The Ottomans always exacted terrible retribution in the form of massacres, depopulation of towns and villages, and forced conversions. Indeed, such Ottoman reprisals constitute a recurring theme in Balkan history and literature, and have often served as justification for counter-atrocities.

Of course, neither the Russians nor the Habsburgs would have been able to stoke the fires of insurrection unless an initial spark already existed. That spark, more often than not, was a reaction to the inequities of regional conditions. In Serbia, for example, the road to independence began as support for the sultan's reforms. In Romania, meanwhile, insurrection began as opposition to Greek Orthodox princes, while the Greek revolution was served handsomely by the rebellion of Ali Pasha.

At first, even the radicals themselves were not always clear about their goals. In the absence of historical national states, as understood in the nineteenth century, a post-Ottoman Balkan world held several possibilities. Some, especially members of the professional and merchant classes, argued for a united Balkan state or federation with Constantinople as the capital. The wealthy Phanariot class looked to the Russian or Habsburg rulers to replace the Ottoman regime and recreate the Byzantine Empire with a Christian emperor (which was also the secret ambition of the Orthodox Church hierarchy).[26] But this was not the dream of those in the meager mountain villages and small rural communities of the Balkans. Most of the individuals who entertained these notions had senior positions in the Ottoman administration or had served in the Russian Empire, and thus construed government as a function of absolute and imperial authority. Cyril Mango wrote that "the Phanariot . . . was a man who fed on the existing system, while the merchant fed himself by circumventing it. The former tended to be a reactionary, the latter a liberal."[27] The intellectual and material advantages separating the Phanariots from their simple compatriots, however, also considerably limited any influence they carried outside their immediate circle of supporters. The Phanariots continued to believe in an evolutionary historical cycle that would reform the Ottoman Empire from within and give them either constitutional political control or the rebirth of Byzantium. In hindsight, these ideas appear unrealistic, but in the context of the early nineteenth century, the convulsions that beset the Ottoman world allowed for any possibility.

Within the Balkan political landscape, the regional Christian notables understood liberation not as the destruction of the social order, but simply as a means of replacing the Ottoman system with an Orthodox hierarchy (in effect, themselves). Most of the *klepht* and *armatoli* chiefs, if they had considered the long-term implications of fighting against the sultan at all, were equally opposed to radical change and preferred the status quo — though under Christian control. In the early nineteenth century, it was the intellectuals who entertained ideas of establishing a liberal society with a constitutional government. They lacked, however, the economic and human resources to assume the direct leadership of the liberation movements and their corresponding military forces.

In part, the rebellions achieved momentum because of their early success against the Ottoman forces. Another important factor was fear. After the sultan failed to contain the initial outbreaks, he declared a holy war. For the rebels, and their willing or unwilling co-religionists, this represented a line in the sand; defeat was tantamount to complete annihilation. The revolutionary program of equality, universal suffrage, representative government, and land reform, consequently, fell by the wayside, and would be picked up again only after the Balkan states achieved independence. It can be argued that in some of the current Balkan states, the process of realizing this program is still ongoing.

Perhaps the intricacies of Balkan political, social, and military history can best be seen in the way the ambitious Ottoman governors' attempts to carve out independent fiefdoms intertwined with the convoluted "national" aspirations of the early revolutionaries. This is how Ali Pasha's rebellion not only paved the way for the Greek revolution, but also rescued the Philiki Hetairia from languishing in the futile exercise of obscure plots and conspiracies while waiting for the next Russian–Ottoman war.

—◦◦◦—

Ali Pasha began his climb to the upper echelons of Ottoman administration as a bandit. At the age of fourteen, he established a successful sheep-stealing operation that generated enough wealth for the young man to increase the strength of his band. After twenty years of extortion, robbery, kidnapping, and assassination, he was a small powerbroker in his region and had gained credibility by becoming an official of the sultan. Ali managed to present his betrayals and murders of local Ottoman officials as acts of service to the sultan. In return, the grateful sovereign appointed him guardian of the passes of Rumeli and governor of Thessaly.

During this period, these regions were infested with dozens of outlaw bands that had brought trade almost to a standstill. Ali Pasha did not eliminate banditry as much as bring it under control by setting himself up as the only robber. As a former bandit, Ali was familiar with the tactics and major hideouts of the brigands. For several years, he waged ruthless campaigns against his former associates and opponents. Random acts of kidnapping, highway robbery, and murder were replaced by the systematic extortion of merchants, travelers, and townspeople who used the passes. In actual fact, Ali's monopoly brought both security to the region and wealth to the coffers of the wily Albanian. According to one writer, T. S. Hughes, who in 1819 traveled through the territory administered by Ali Pasha:

> There exists at present a security in these dominions, which we should seek for in vain elsewhere where the baneful influence of the crescent extends. A police is organized, robbers are extirpated, roads and canals are made or repaired, rivers are rendered navigable, so that the merchant can now traverse the Albanian districts with safety, and the traveler with convenience. Agriculture, in spite of all obstacles, improves; commerce increases; and the whole nation advances, perhaps unconsciously, towards higher destinies and greater happiness.[28]

The Ottomans' tendency to prey on regional particularism proved to be an essential component of their power. The policy of divide and rule also served as a useful mechanism to contain ambitious governors. But Ali successfully exploited this administrative tradition by playing one Ottoman pasha against another. As a result of his success suppressing brigands and ferreting out Ottoman officials who had grown too independent, the sultan awarded him the *pashalik* of Ioannina, one of the most important imperial provinces in the Balkans. Ali was only too aware that his tenure of office was temporary, however, and at the mercy of the whims of the sultan. He knew he had to find a way to eliminate the Ottoman element from his administration if he wanted to hang on to the reins of power.

Ali's plan was to centralize all power in his own hands, but to do so he had to weaken the influence of the Ottoman Turks, especially those with considerable property in the region and influence in

Constantinople. To this end, he planned the destruction of the most powerful Turkish pashas and great landlords. Forever mindful of their influence in the sultan's court, however, he did not attack them collectively; instead, he tried to reduce them individually. Ironically, Ali's tactic was to accuse his rivals of treason or of conspiring with the *klephts* to promote themselves at the expense of the sultan. He instigated quarrels among the powerful Turkish families and encouraged the Greeks to complain to the Sublime Porte of acts of injustice. If all else failed, he did not hesitate to use assassination to get rid of a powerful rival. After almost a quarter of a century, Ali's program had significantly reduced the Turkish presence in Thessaly and southern Albania. Many Turks were impoverished, and several of those who exercised the power of Ottoman privilege had lost their fortunes. According to George Finlay, as a result of Ali's policy, "towns everywhere showed signs of decay; the best houses in the Turkish quarters were often tenanted by Greek or Vlach traders, or occupied by Albanian officers."[29]

Ali Pasha was the sum of his contradictions: cruel and impetuous one moment and a benefactor to the Christians the next. "The boasted ability of Ali was displayed in subduing the Albanians, cheating the Ottoman government, and ruling the Greeks," Finlay wrote.[30] By the early nineteenth century, Ali's machinations had made him the unlikely catalyst for the Greek revolution. His every calculated move to outmaneuver the sultan enhanced the position of the Greek revolutionaries in general and those in the Ioannine *pashalik* in particular. He used Greeks in civil administration and Muslim Albanians in the military, and forged a complex series of alliances with the French and the British — all in an attempt to consolidate power in his own hands. Geography was another element that was essential to Ali's success. The region covered by southern Albania and northern Greece, and dominated by the town of Ioannina, enjoyed a unique convergence of disparate ethnic and religious communities, as well as strategic access to the West. With its formidable landscape of mountains and narrow valleys, the terrain was ideally suited for defense and guerrilla warfare.

At the end of the eighteenth century, Ioannina was one of the most important urban centers in Greece and Albania. The town had a population of 30,000, and had evolved into a major hub of commerce and banking in the Balkans. Under Ali's governance, Ioannina was also transformed into the literary capital of Greece, and it soon became a place of refuge for Greeks and other Christians fleeing Ottoman authority. In fact, Ali Pasha became almost a patron of the arts and a protector of those persecuted by the Ottoman and Orthodox administrations. He encouraged and supported the founding of schools, colleges, and libraries, and provided generous endowments to maintain these institutions. Greek quickly assumed prominence as the literary language of southern Albania, and it was studied by Christians and Muslims alike.[31] Yet Ali Pasha had no real interest in either Greek or Albanian nationalism; he was simply using everything at his disposal to degrade Ottoman authority. If his actions served the interests of the Greek revolutionaries, it was completely unintentional. His only real interest was in maintaining and expanding the sphere of the Ioannina *pashalik*, and to do that, Ali had to eliminate all potential challengers to his rule. In practical terms, this meant that in addition to destroying the neighboring Turkish governors and local Turkish notables, he also had to reduce the military capability of the *armatoli*, squash the quasi-independent Albanian Christian villages, and destroy any significant *klepht* bands that could be used against him.

Ali proceeded randomly in any direction provided by circumstance and chance. His first goal was to reduce the Christian Albanians of Suli, a group that had managed to achieve some measure of independence through a combination of geographic inaccessibility and Orthodox opposition to the Catholic West. The Suliots were a branch of the southern Albanian Tosks, and until the end of the seventeenth century, their territory belonged to an Ottoman *timariot* (a landholding lord) based in Ioannina. When the Venetians gained possession of the Peloponnese through the Treaty of Carlowitz in 1699, however, anarchy took over in the rest of the Balkans. Orthodox Albanians formed armed bands to defend themselves against brigands whose numbers and activities thrived as a result. Instead of forcing the Christian Albanians to give up their arms, the pashas of Albania and northern Greece found common cause in combating the Catholic menace that had become established in southern Greece.

By the first quarter of the eighteenth century, the Suliots had been awarded control of a small Christian district in southern

Albania. Remarkably, they numbered no more than one hundred families at the time. By the early nineteenth century, though they had increased their numbers to no more than 450 families, they had the ability to field a military force of 1,500 men.[32] The real strength and advantage of Suli, however, lay in the formidable geography of the region. The clusters of villages and hamlets that constituted Suli were situated in southwestern Albania, opposite the island of Corfu. The district itself consists of steep ranges of bare and precipitous mountains towering 2,000 feet (600 m) over the river Acheron. A short distance below, the Acheron joins with the river Cocytus and forms a marshy lake, which in the eighteenth and nineteenth centuries rendered the surrounding area extremely unhealthy. The Suliot community was entrenched in a lateral valley covered by two rocky hills; the main approach was through a gorge called the Kleisura.[33] Nestled on top of the precipitous peaks, Suli was impervious to a frontal assault, protected by the deep ravine formed by the Acheron, and easily defended by highly skilled marksmen who could hide themselves in the rocks or stone buildings of the Suliot villages.

For almost a century, the Suliots dominated the surrounding villages and offered protection to Christian Albanians who fell victim to the rapacious demands of local Ottoman authorities. The ethos of the Suliot was to fight, and war was the only honorable occupation. Suliot women were also trained to use muskets, and on occasion they took part in the fighting. Usually, they supported their men by carrying provisions and supplying them with ammunition during the course of battle.[34] This lifestyle, of course, left very few means of support, so if protection dues were not forthcoming, the Suliots exacted tribute by force from the nearby Christian villages. By the time Ali Pasha took over Ioannina, there were numerous complaints coming from Christians and Muslims over the frequency of plundering activities and the general lawlessness of the Suliots. Ali saw in this an opportunity to tackle the autonomous Suliot community, which fit perfectly into his personal campaign to eliminate all possible centers of future resistance. The fact that the Suliots were Christians made it possible for Ali to disguise his motives as a defense of the sultan.

Ali was operating under the assumption that no one would offer support to the Suliots, but he soon discovered that nearby communities, both Christian and Muslim, were more afraid of him than they were the Suliots. "When he attacked them, all their neighbors were alarmed, recent injuries were forgotten, and new alliances formed," explains Finlay. "Mussulman beys and the Venetian governors of Parga and Prevesa supplied them secretly with aid."[35] The campaign ended in failure, but the sultan, incensed at the continued intrigues of the Russians in the Balkans, ordered Ali to resume the offensive in 1792. Although his soldiers were, by sheer weight of numbers, able to break through the Kleisura from the south, they were driven back and eventually abandoned their positions. At one point during the attack against Suli, Ali threatened to roast alive the son of one of the chieftains he was holding hostage. The threat made no impression on the parents whatsoever. The young Suliot's mother, Moscho Tzevellas, simply replied that she was young and would have other children. She even said she would rather eat a bit of the roasted flesh than betray her people. The young man to be barbecued, Foto Tzevellas, was equally unfazed, and when he was informed that he would be roasted, he replied, "My father will roast your father, or brother, if he catches them."[36]

In the face of such determined opposition, Ali's troops suffered heavy losses and the ensuing retreat turned into a rout. The Suliots had seventy-four killed and ninety wounded, while Ali lost 2,500 in the actual fighting and hundreds more during the retreat. Most of the survivors tore off articles of clothing in order to hasten their flight through the mountains and reached Ioannina half-naked. With desertions, Ali returned with only one thousand of the 8,000 troops he had mustered for the attack.[37]

For the next six years, Ali Pasha concentrated on easier targets and found new allies. In 1798, with support from the French at Corfu, he captured a coastal Christian community that had been supplying the kingdom of Naples with recruits. He slaughtered the entire population. In the fall of 1798, Ali double-crossed the French. After defeating them at Nicopolis, he gained possession of Preveza and Vonitza, which the French had originally taken during the Napoleonic Wars.

A year later, Ali again turned his attention to the Suliots. This time, the crafty pasha used treachery to undermine his opponents. Through secret negotiations and bribery, he managed to hire away several Suli chieftains. These chieftains represented a loss of seventy families to the Suliots, which translated into one hundred warriors. The attack in 1799 was spearheaded by George Botzaris, a Suliot renegade in command of 200 Christian troops. Unfortunately, he was quickly defeated, and died soon afterward. Ali continued his efforts to recruit additional Suliot chieftains, but he was unsuccessful. Evidently, his reputation for treachery surpassed the greed of the mountain warriors.

Since he couldn't weaken the Suliots through defections, Ali decided instead to lay siege to the area. During 1799–1800, his forces occupied several easily defendable positions that enabled him to cut off the Suliots' supply routes. By this time, the neighboring villages had become dissatisfied with Suliot hegemony and had grown tired of paying them tribute. Ali Pasha raised the stakes in 1801 by forcing the senior Orthodox clergy to condemn their Suliot brethren. Ignatius, the metropolitan of Arta, issued a circular forbidding the Christians in his diocese to support the Suliots and threatening to excommunicate those who failed to comply. Ali went a step further, dictating a letter from Ierotheos, the metropolitan of Ioannina, to the bishop of Paramythia. The letter ordered the bishop to use all his influence to have the Suliots declared a predatory and rebellious tribe.[38]

The final act of the struggle between Ali and the Suliots unfolded in 1803. On September 3 of that year, Ali's forces gained control of one of the two hills guarding access to the Suli hamlets. The Albanian troops, however, succeeded not out of military skill, but through Ali's use of bribery. The jealousy fostered by the competitive nature of Suliot society meant there was always someone willing to betray his compatriots. In this case, the traitor was a Suliot named Pylio Gousi. For a bribe equivalent to 300 pounds, he agreed to conceal in his barn 200 of Ali's troops. With the help of additional Suliot defectors, the next attack proved irresistible.

The Suliots surrendered their fortress on December 12, 1803, and in exchange the survivors were permitted to evacuate to the lowlands. Unfortunately for them, Ali was not prepared to let them live in peace. One group of survivors escaped by changing their route, thus avoiding an ambush organized by Ali's men; the others were not so fortunate. Even the Suliots who had found employment in Ali's service were either killed or reduced to slavery. Two hundred of those who had accepted Ali Pasha's promise of immunity and had resettled in Zalongo, west of Ioannina, were also attacked as soon as Suli fell. Of those, 150 men and women were forced into slavery, while twenty-five men died defending themselves.[39] The remainder chose suicide over surrender. According to Albanian soldiers who had witnessed the event, six men and twenty-two women first tossed their children over a precipice behind the village and then themselves jumped over the edge. The spectacle captured the imagination of painters, poets, historians, and especially nationalists, who glorified the suicide pact by embellishing the story with heroic Suliot women singing and dancing before they leaped into history. In fact, not all the women died. Some fell on top of their dead children and were saved, and a few were spared when their garments were caught in the edges of the rocks, thus preventing their fall.[40]

According to the version of the tale provided in Greek school books, the Suliots retreated from the fortress only after capitulation, not by betraying their compatriots before the battle was lost. On the road, the Albanians surrounded them. They held out for two days and nights, until there was no ammunition, food, or water. At that point, the women climbed the hill, kissed their children, tossed them over the cliff, and broke into song and dance. They continued dancing in concentric circles, and at the completion of each full turn one jumped, until they had all fallen to their deaths.[41]

The Suliot dance of death is an integral image of the Greek revolution, and it has been seared into the consciousness of Greek schoolchildren for generations. Many youngsters pay homage to the memory of these Orthodox Albanians each year by recreating the event in their elementary school pageants. Every March 25, the day that also commemorates the outbreak of the Greek revolution, children offer a performance in which they dance around in a circle; at each turn, one child drops off to represent the Suliots who leaped off the precipice. The dance continues until all the children have left the stage.

The demise of the Suliots completed the disarmament of all the Christian villages in the *pashalik*. Ali Pasha was now virtually the only military power in the region. Over the next seventeen years, he continued to consolidate his power, but when he began to exterminate Muslim communities, it became apparent to the sultan that the Old Lion had intentions other than fidelity to the Ottoman Empire.

Ali's ambition, however, was not to be constrained by religious, ethnic, or cultural scruples. After the sultan declared him a traitor, the wily pasha resolved to co-opt the Albanians and the Greeks into his schemes. He considered himself the natural chief of the Albanian Tosks, and he assumed that he could easily become the political leader of the Greeks. Ali was aware of rumors about Greek plans for revolution, and he was familiar with their desire for their own constitution and general assembly. In fact, he expected to create a strong national feeling in his favor by promising the Greeks a constitution, and according to one account, he even offered to convert to Orthodoxy to make himself more acceptable as the future head of a Greek state.[42]

Although he was not quite sure of what was meant by a constitution or a national assembly, he convened a meeting of Albanian chieftains, Greek notables, and Orthodox clergymen. To avoid insulting his Muslim delegates, he called the meeting a divan (council) and said it was to discuss the question of supplies to the province. In this manner, he was able to bring together Muslims and Christians on equal footing, and at the same time preserve the dignity of Islamic custom and tradition. The divan met, and Ali addressed the assembly in Greek.[43] (It is an interesting aspect of the social and economic dynamics of the period, and of Ottoman–Christian relations, that a Muslim like Ali Pasha could offend his co-religionists simply by discussing political matters in front of Christians. And yet, when he spoke in Greek instead of Turkish, no offense was seemingly taken.)

Ali proceeded to describe his plans for rebellion, and in a move uncharacteristic of an Ottoman ruler, he condescended to ask for their help. He claimed to be opposing the sultan because he was being persecuted by the viziers of the Sublime Porte for his vigilant support of Albanian interests and for the protection he offered the Christians from the ruinous demands of the sultan's agents. As the Kafkaesque assembly unfolded, the Muslim Albanians, who were all connected to Ali in one form or another, agreed with everything the pasha said. The Greek secretaries, meanwhile, assured Ali that it would be easy to incite the Greeks to rebel against the sultan. But the rest of the Greek delegates remained silent. Few of them believed the pasha's sudden concern for the welfare of the Orthodox, and those who had contacts within societies like the Philiki Hetairia were averse to trusting Ali with any information that he could later use against them.[44] He was thus unable to gain a consensus.

In the end, Ali Pasha failed because, despite his political agility and acumen, he was not able to rise above the position of regional strongman. Essentially, he remained a bandit chief. Yet he was only one of countless provincial governors who exploited the congenital weaknesses of the Ottoman system for their own gain.

———⟆ɷɷ⟆———

The Ottoman Empire was essentially a series of segregated religious communities ruled by an Islamic elite. As long as the Ottomans continued to expand and generate wealth from conquest, the system remained self-generating. Once the era of expansion passed, however, the empire came under pressure from the periphery. The activities of provincial governors such as Ali Pasha were a symptom of a decay that could be arrested only if the system adapted to change. There was no question of transferring power to satiate provincial interests, since the theocratic regime revolved around the absolute authority of the sultan. The only viable recourse for the Sublime Porte was to reassert its ancient power base by centralizing all authority in Constantinople and adjusting to modernity by reforming the economic, social, and imperial administration of the empire. But members of the Ottoman establishment feared that any changes would erode their traditional advantages, and thus they stubbornly clung to the past and violently opposed reform. Other fossilized institutions such as the Janissaries also refused to accept improvements, and indeed were convinced that any modification would undermine their privileged military, social, economic, and political status. Although the success of the French under Napoleon proved the superiority of Western military technology, these entrenched interests resisted, jeopardizing what was really the key to the survival of the empire.

Sultan Selim III, who auspiciously assumed power in 1789, was profoundly influenced by the ideas of the French Revolution. He was also impressed by the military innovations that had secured victory after victory for the French armies during the Napoleonic Wars. Their military stood in direct contrast to the archaic and ineffectual Ottoman forces, and Selim was determined to change that. First, he attempted to reform the economy, the civil administration, and the tax structure. He improved education, expanded trade, and curtailed the power of the provincial pashas. Most important, he wanted to organize and equip a modern army to be led by officers with Western military skills. Timing, however, worked against the reforming sultan. By the turn of the century, Selim was facing a host of mutinous pashas and rebellions by the Whahabites in Arabia, the Druzes in the hills of Syria and Palestine, and the Mamluks in Egypt. He also had to deal with Ali Pasha's engineering of the Suliot insurrection. The Ottoman Empire, for all practical purposes, had collapsed as a unitary state.

Selim's attempts at military reform also led to mutinies and outright rebellion. The Janissary corps remained the most intractable problem, and Selim became determined to keep these difficult troops out of Constantinople by sending them to the provinces. According to the authoritative study *Islamic Society and the West*, by Sir Hamilton Gibb and H. Bowen, the Janissary corps was not so much a standing army as a standing menace.[45] In Serbia, the Janissaries were a destabilizing element, and they proved detrimental to Muslims and Christians alike. They seized the lands of legitimate Ottoman landlords in the province, and under their tenure, conditions for small farmers declined considerably. In other parts of the empire, particularly the cities, the mercurial temperament of these imperial scavengers had disastrous and deadly consequences for Christians. Spencer Smith's account of the Smyrna Rebellion of March 1797 illustrates the capricious cruelty and volatility of these recalcitrant part-time warriors. After a minor incident involving some entertainers, the Janissaries, in a frenzy of violence, massacred 1,500 Greeks and destroyed most of the property of the French merchant community in the city.[46]

The Janissaries, with their immunity from prosecution, can only be considered another manifestation of the Ali Pasha syndrome, which continued to plague the Ottoman Empire. Ali's Bulgarian counterpart was Pasvanoglou Osman Pasha. Like the crafty Albanian, he was determined to achieve his own state. Pasvanoglou attracted an army of bandits, Janissaries, and renegade Ottoman soldiers, and with their help, he usurped the *pashalik* of Vidin. Success brought additional troops, including Albanian irregulars, mercenaries,

Janissaries from Bosnia and Serbia, and radical Turks opposed to Selim's reforms.[47] In 1795, Pasvanoglou declared his independence from the sultan, and just as Selim's forces were about to restore Ottoman authority, Napoleon's invasion of Egypt gave the rebels a new lease on life. Pasvanoglou had rightly judged that the Janissaries were valuable allies, and to maintain his own security, he did everything in his power to keep them in control of the Belgrade *pashalik*. The Janissaries, in turn, used Vidin as a staging area for their attacks against the Ottomans in Serbia.

Events in Serbia at the end of the eighteenth century and beginning of the nineteenth, it can be argued, were less determined by the outcome of the Ottoman–Habsburg wars and later conflicts between the Ottomans and the French than they were by the internal convulsions of the Ottoman regime itself. That is not to say that there were no tensions with the Austrians, however. For one thing, many of the Serbians who fought as irregulars in the Austrian army believed that the Habsburg emperor would intercede on their behalf in the event of an Ottoman victory. But after the signing of the Treaty of Sistova (1791), which ended the war, the Serbians were left to their own devices. Most Serbian leaders then turned to the progressive Selim in an attempt to establish some degree of tranquillity in the countryside and perhaps secure recognition of local autonomy. Selim did give them the right to collect taxes, bear arms, and organize a militia, and he also promised that his representatives would endeavor to limit the excesses of the Janissaries in the countryside. Although the Serbians did not achieve autonomy within the empire, they had come a long way in defining a new relationship with the Sublime Porte. The settlement might even have paved the way for a new relationship between the Ottoman Empire and the disgruntled Christians. But Selim had no real power to effect change in the provinces, let alone bring to heel ambitious pashas bent on establishing their own principalities. Nor could he reform the unruly Janissaries, who were convinced that change undermined the pillars of Islam and, more important, their way of life.[48]

Not surprisingly, then, the first successful insurrection against the Ottoman Empire took root in the rustic province of Serbia, a region thinly inhabited and covered with layers of thick forests. A large proportion of the population lived in the countryside and depended on pig farming, but a growing number were abandoning the plains for a life of banditry in the wooded mountains. The oppressive and corrupt rule of the Janissaries had swollen the ranks of the outlaws, who found that a life of plunder and war was preferable to mere subsistence under Ottoman tutelage. The province was centered on the *pashalik* of Belgrade, which by the beginning of the nineteenth century was a federation of village communities self-administered by the Serbians. The *pashalik* had a population of 300,000 to 400,000, including approximately 20,000 Slav-speaking Muslims, urban Bosnians, and about 900 *sipahis* (horsemen who represented the dominant Ottoman property owners).[49] The pasha of Belgrade, Hadji Mustafa, was a competent Ottoman official who maintained good relations with the Christians and earnestly tried to implement Selim's reforms. Mustafa's relations with the Christians were so cordial, in fact, that he was called "the mother of the Serbs."[50] Belgrade had long been immune to the tyranny of the Janissaries because it once was occupied by the Austrians. After the city was recovered by the Ottomans, the sultan had barred the Janissaries. Though they did lay siege to the city in 1797, Christians, Muslims, and loyal Ottoman forces together successfully defended Belgrade and contained the Janissaries in other parts of the province.

Just when the sultan's loyal followers had established control over the region, however, Selim had to divert whatever forces he had at his disposal to deal with the French invasion of Egypt in 1798. Without any credible military assets, he was forced to come to terms with the renegades. Accordingly, all was forgiven, and the Janissaries were allowed to live in Belgrade as long as they accepted the authority of Hadji Mustafa Pasha. The Janissaries did not intend to respect the will of their sovereign, of course. Once established in the city, they murdered the pasha and installed their own puppet as governor. They then appropriated the lands of the *sipahis* and partitioned the *pashalik* among four of their leaders. Their rule was characterized by tyranny against the Muslims and open extortion of the Christians. The Serbians sent a deputation of their local mayors to Constantinople to plead with the sultan for protection against the rapacious regime. Selim, still lacking a force strong enough to subdue the Janissaries, could do little except issue warnings and threats to the rebels.

On a blistering cold morning in January 1804, one of the four

Janissary leaders sped through the countryside on his splendid Arabian mount. Mehmed-aga Focic was headed toward Valjevo. The condition of the region outside the Belgrade *pashalik* had degenerated so much that at least 200 cavalrymen had to accompany the Janissary to ensure his safety. A few hours later, the party reached the village of Ljubenino Polje, thirty miles (48 km) from Belgrade, and picked up the local Serbian chief, Aleksander Nenadovic, and one of his friends, Ilija Bircanin. A few miles outside the village Nenadovic and Bircanin were bound in chains, and the Janissaries then continued their journey to Valjevo. Nenadovic's crime was smuggling. He and his family were transporting weapons from Austria to supply Serbian peasants who were preparing an insurrection against the Janissaries. Valjevo, according to the information procured by the Janissaries, was the center of the conspiracy, and Mehmed-aga had intercepted a letter from Nenadovic's son that proved the family's link with the rebels.[51]

In Valjevo, the Janissaries dragged the hapless Serbs in front of a crowd that had been attracted by the arrival of the Janissaries and the subsequent commotion. Mehmed-aga solemnly displayed the letter and cried out, "This letter has killed Aleksa. He conspired with the Germans and denounced us, the Janissaries, to our own sultan. It would be a sin to leave his head upon his shoulders. Cut it off."[52] After the decapitations, the bodies were left in the open. Mehmet-aga kept Nenadovic's head in a storeroom until one of the Serb's servants stole it and placed it in the grave with the body.[53] The Christians and Muslims of Valjevo were terrified, and each group sought safety in its own way. In his book *The Balkans: Nationalism, War, and the Great Powers, 1804–1999*, Misha Glenny writes, "The Muslims locked their doors, fearing the reaction of the Serb villagers; the Serbian men grabbed their weapons and took to the forest."[54] But the Janissaries went on a rampage of torture and death.

The Slaughter of the Knezes, as the event is called in Serbian history, resulted in the killings of anywhere from seventy-two to 150 prominent Serbs, often under grim circumstances. For example, in Belgrade the Janissaries captured Hadzi-Ruvim, a monastic priest who had managed to escape from Valjevo and take refuge with the Greek bishop of the city. But the latter handed him over to the Janissaries. The priest was tortured in an attempt to make him reveal the details of the Serbian rebellion, but he refused to talk. The leader of the

Janissaries, Aganlia, used a pair of pliers to strip layers of skin from the unfortunate man, but to no avail. In frustration, the Janissaries decapitated the priest in public at the Belgrade city gate.[55]

Later that same year, the Janissaries staged another massacre of Serbs in an attempt to pre-empt a Christian and Ottoman coup. Instead, they incited a general uprising.[56] Selim, once again, had to sanction what appeared to be a strange alliance of Serbian Christians, local *sipahis*, forces loyal to the pasha of Bosnia, and a few Turkish regulars. This motley collection, with the sultan's blessings, rose against the Janissaries and quickly defeated them. The triumphant campaign was celebrated with the exhibition of the four severed heads of the Janissary leaders. The bloody trophies were proudly displayed in the Serbian camp, in what was both a crowning victory for the sultan and the beginning of the Serb quest for independence.

With the defeat of the renegade Janissaries, the Serbs found themselves in possession of most of Serbia (with the exception of Belgrade and a handful of fortresses garrisoned by loyal Ottoman troops). The Serbian leader, Karageorge (Black George), was a *hayduk* who at one time had commanded brigands serving as Austrian auxiliaries and had eventually retired to Ottoman Serbia as a prosperous pig farmer. The Serbian forces were composed primarily of other *hayduks* who, like Karageorge, had learned to fight as outlaws. Many had augmented their military experience as mercenaries in the Austrian and Hungarian armies. Indeed, some of these bandits had even fought with the Janissaries. For nine years, Karageorge kept the Ottomans at bay and defeated every army sent by the sultan to reclaim the insurgent province.

Although Greek, Bulgarian, Albanian, and Montenegrin volunteers joined the Serbs, who also received financial support from wealthy Serb merchants in Croatia and abroad, they were still unable to achieve internal unity or secure backing from any of the Great Powers. In the past, the Russians, the French, and the Austrians had encouraged the Serbs with promises of support, but the Serbian uprising took place in the middle of the geopolitical and strategic fluctuations of the Napoleonic Wars. In succession, the French, the Russians, and the Austrians forged alliances with the Ottomans, and that meant forsaking the Serbians.

Napoleon's victory at Austerlitz in 1805, which gave the French

Venice, Istria, and the Dalmatian coast, brought into question the tenuous security of the sultan's maritime hegemony over Southeastern Europe, and in particular the future of the Straits. For millennia, the Dardanelles and the Bosporus, the two narrow bodies of water collectively referred to as "the Straits," have been the gateways to the Black Sea, and hence to the markets of Central Asia and Russia. After the Ottomans conquered Constantinople and assumed mastery of the Straits, it became a cardinal policy to keep the Black Sea closed to all foreign shipping. Even during the decline of the Ottoman Empire, the Europeans agreed not to let any one power have the advantage of controlling the Straits. They were content even then to leave the sultan with sole jurisdiction over the strategic passageway.

Although all the Great Powers eventually had designs on the possessions of the Ottomans, control of the Straits was of critical concern to Great Britain and Russia. To the British, the Straits offered access to Russia's virtually unguarded frontier along the north coast of the Black Sea and also protected the imperial lines of communication in the Far East from attack by Russian squadrons stationed in the Mediterranean. But Russia also had serious economic and military reasons for wanting to gain control of the Straits. (Between 1901 and 1910, 87 percent of Russian wheat and 45 percent of all other exports were transported through these narrow strips of water.[57]) Consequently, the goal of Russia's foreign and strategic policies from the eighteenth century onward was to establish total or partial control over the Dardanelles and the Bosporus, while at the same time keeping other powers from gaining access to the Black Sea.

During the eighteenth century, under Peter the Great and Catherine the Great, the Russians had wrested from the control of the sultan the territory along the north shore of the Black Sea. This foreshadowed what was to become known as the Eastern Question: the strategic riddle of when the Ottoman Empire would collapse and which power would fill the resulting vacuum. The problem of the Ottoman Empire and the issue of the Straits have left in their wake a trail of international conventions and treaties. These not only offer an insight into the politics of the major European powers, but also represent a significant chapter in the evolution of international and maritime law. The Treaty of Carlowitz in 1699 was the first sign of the beginning of the end for the Ottoman Empire and the beginning of

Russian hegemony in the Black Sea region. The terms of that agreement forced the Ottomans to secede Hungary and Transylvania to the Habsburgs, the Ukraine and Podalia to Poland, and Azof to the Russians. The 1699 convention was also a milestone for the Phanariots. Alexander Mavrokordatos, a wealthy Greek from Constantinople, negotiated the treaty on behalf of the sultan, and this began the process that led to the predominance of the Phanariots in the Ottoman administration.[58]

But Carlowitz alone wasn't enough to spell the end for the Ottomans. During the early years of the eighteenth century, the sultans were able to recoup some of their losses. In 1710, the Russians, after losing a ten-year war against the Ottomans, had to surrender all their earlier gains. And almost three decades later, under the terms of the Treaty of Belgrade (1739), the sultan, with the backing of France, succeeded in blocking Russian expansion in the Black Sea, as well as preventing Russian ships from crossing the Straits. However, later in the century, Catherine the Great mounted a second assault against the Ottoman Empire's northern frontier, which ended in total Russian victory. One of the conditions of the Treaty of Kutchuk-Kainardji (1774) forced the sultan to surrender the coastal area of the Black Sea. More important, the Ottomans had to give the Russians access to the sea through the Straits.[59]

The Treaty of Kutchuk-Kainardji (the little fountain)[60] created a new dynamic in the Balkans. By bringing to an end Turkish control of the Straits and gaining access to the Black Sea, the Russians, under Catherine the Great, created a maelstrom in international relations whose shadow extends to the present day. At first, the Russian success was essentially a commercial victory. In fact, all the Great Powers were able to profit from the opening of the passage to the Black Sea, and thus the increased access to the markets of Central Asia and Russia.[61] Austria gained free passage through the Straits in 1784, Great Britain in 1799, France in 1802, and Prussia in 1806.

For the Balkan Christians, meanwhile, the treaty underscored Ottoman decline, and they found in Russia a potential patron and a military ally. One of the treaty's articles, article 7, was interpreted by the Russians to mean that the czar had the right to protect the Eastern Orthodox subjects of the sultan. In other words, they believed they had legal grounds to interfere in Ottoman affairs.

Ultimately, this led to the Eastern Crisis in 1853, and indirectly to the Crimean War (1853–56). In actual fact, article 7 stipulated that the Sublime Porte would protect the Christian faith and its churches in the Balkans. Furthermore, the sultan agreed to allow the Russians to build a church in Constantinople, and to let the Russian ambassador make representations about this church to the Porte. It was this reference to a "Russian church" in Constantinople that future czars claimed was a right to defend all Eastern Orthodox Christians and their churches throughout the Ottoman Empire.[62]

The treaty also gave the Russians the right to maintain a permanent embassy in Constantinople, as well as consulates in every major port of the Ottoman Empire. Effectively, this allowed the Russians to establish centers for future intrigues and secure direct access to the Orthodox communities in Asia Minor and the Balkans. If the Treaty of Carlowitz had marked the end of Ottoman expansion and the empire's slow retreat from Europe, the Treaty of Kutchuk-Kainardji exposed the chronic weaknesses of the empire and signaled the emergence of Russia as a major player in the Near East and Central Asia. The Austrian ambassador to the sultan's court assessed the treaty as "a model of skill on the part of the Russian diplomats, and a rare example of imbecility on the part of the Turkish negotiators."[63]

In the nineteenth century, with the Ottoman Empire tottering on the brink of disintegration and the Russians poised to pick up the pieces, the other Great Powers became determined not to surrender any strategic advantage to Russia. The European states feared the Russian ambition to resurrect the Byzantine Empire and disputed their claims to be the sole beneficiaries of the sultan's territories. From the Russian perspective, Constantinople was the future capital of a new eastern Christian empire to be ruled by a Romanov. These grand dreams, however, would remain just that unless Russia was able to gain control of the Straits and the adjacent territories. While the Treaty of Kutchuk-Kainardji guaranteed Russians the right to move commercial traffic through the Dardanelles and the Bosporus, the Ottomans continued to retain the right to prohibit the passage of warships. Thus the Russians had to end the bottleneck of their Black Sea fleet either by direct conquest or by turning the sultan into a Russian puppet.

Unlike the other European monarchs, the czars were able to

claim their only ambition was to protect all the Eastern Orthodox in the Ottoman Empire. This image of the czar as the imperial and secular patron of the Balkan Christians gave the Russians a moral rationale for expanding their territories at the expense of the Ottoman sultans.

Nonetheless, the Christians who mattered for the Russians were the Romanians, the Greeks, and the Bulgarians, not the Serbs. The lands of these people impacted directly on the future control of the Straits and Constantinople, while Serbia was peripheral to the long-term interests of the Russians. In this geopolitical context, the fate of the Serbian uprising was of consequence to the Russians only in that it could offer the French or the Austrians an opportunity to get a foothold in the Balkans. The Serbs, for their part, had only a small window of opportunity to secure their independence. Thus a delegation was dispatched to Saint Petersburg in September 1804, with the aim of securing military aid from Czar Alexander I. The Russian emperor was ambivalent, but the possibility of the French expanding into the Balkans from Italy caused him to hedge his bets. He feared that if he turned them down, the Serbs would go to the French or the Austrians for help. Thus Czar Alexander cautioned the Serbs to "be discreet and prudent" and reach an accommodation with the sultan.[64] He even offered arms, Russian officers, and diplomatic support to smooth the way in the negotiations with Selim.

The Serb uprising against the Janissaries initially had been less an insurrection than a genuine effort to restore the legitimate authority of the sultan. The leaders of the Serbs, though, also believed that they could avoid a repetition of the Janissary oppression only by securing considerable autonomy from the Porte. Karageorge, the leader of the Serb forces, insisted that the sultan recognize him as the ruler of Serbia, effectively turning the Ottoman province into an autonomous principality. Each one of the subsequent items on his list of demands proposed, in effect, to strip another layer of Ottoman sovereignty. In petition after petition, Karageorge requested from Selim the right to collect taxes, control customs and the judiciary, and establish garrisons with equal numbers of Ottomans and Serbs. Finally, Karageorge insisted that he and the pasha, who would be only a figurehead, be given the power to decide which Turks could live in Belgrade.[65] But the sultan was in no mood to surrender any part of his sovereignty over Serbia. The negotiations collapsed, and Selim declared a holy war against the Serbs.[66]

Karageorge once again displayed the natural talents of a guerrilla fighter and brilliant strategist. Small mobile units of both bandits and volunteers harassed the Ottomans the moment they crossed the frontier. In the meantime, Karageorge had organized the bulk of his forces into a strategic core that advanced against any point threatened by the Ottoman armies. In 1805 he defeated one unit that was advancing to the Morava valley from Nish, and in the following year he crushed three more that were attacking from the south, east, and west. During December 1806 Karageorge took Belgrade, and by June he had captured every Ottoman fortress in Serbia.[67] Selim compounded this setback by gambling on Napoleon. While the remnants of his forces were retreating from Serbia, he joined the French alliance, which placed the Ottoman Empire at war with Great Britain and Russia.

From 1804 to 1806, the Serbs had been left to their own devices. None of the Great Powers showed any interest in the prospect of an independent Serbia, and by extension, the first sovereign Christian state in the Balkans. The Austrians did not support Serbia for fear of giving the Russians or the French an excuse to use Serb territory as a stepping stone to Constantinople and the Straits. The Russians, the French, and the British, meanwhile, had their own objectives, none of which included the Serbs. Only when the Ottomans had thrown their lot in with the French and declared war against the czar did the Russians urge the Serbs to defy the sultan. Their reasoning was that a Serbian rebellion would tie down Ottoman forces in the Balkans. Most Balkan specialists today agree that the Austrian–Russian rivalry, the Russian intervention in the Danubian principalities, the declining fortunes of the Ottomans in the Balkans, and finally the Napoleonic Wars together brought Serbia into the international arena.[68] The future of Serbia, not for the first time, was hostage to events unfolding in Europe, and the fate of the Serbs was only a matter of strategic expediency. Lawrence Meriage, in his book *Russia and the First Serbian Insurrection*, comments that "in a very real sense the fate of the Serbian people was placed in the hands of capricious rulers in the major capitals of Europe."[69] The Serb leaders could neither keep up with the pace of the European alliances nor understand the dramatic shifts and fragile agreements that characterized international relations during the Napoleonic period.

Whether it was because of naiveté or lack of political experience, Karageorge gambled on a Russian alliance.[70] He and the other Serb leaders failed to read the subtle hints of the Russian envoys, and they assumed that the agreement they signed actually and honestly reflected the policies of the czar's government. In June 1807, the czar's emissary, Marquis F. O. Paulucci, had arrived in Belgrade with instructions to assess the situation, but not to conclude a regular agreement.[71] Instead, he proceeded to sign a formal treaty binding Russia to assist Serbia in the present as well as the future.[72] The tragedy for the Serbs was that once Selim III faced a combined Russian-Anglo attack by land and sea, he was prepared to concede to all the Serbian demands. Unfortunately, Karageorge and his followers had instead put their faith in Russia.[73]

The Russians, of course, abandoned the Serbs just as easily as they had urged them to fight. In fact, Czar Alexander was forced to reach accommodation with the sultan in order to deal with the impending French invasion of Russia. In 1812, he ended the war with the Ottomans and quickly concluded the Treaty of Bucharest. The Russians managed to include in the agreement an article that essentially called for a return to the status quo before the rebellion.[74] Karageorge was desperate to forestall the terrible punishments that would be inflicted on the Serbs when they fell back under the control of the Ottomans. He turned to the Habsburgs and offered to annex Serbia to the Austro-Hungarian Empire, but the Viennese government had overextended itself and could not divert any units to the Balkans. On August 16, 1809, the frustrated Serb wrote to the French emperor and pleaded for the "powerful protection of the Great Napoleon," assuring him that the Serbs would follow his lead.[75] But Napoleon ignored the entreaties, fearing that any kind of support for the Serbs would undermine his relations with the Ottomans.[76]

The paper guarantees of the Treaty of Belgrade were the only paltry result of the Serb alliance with Russia, and even these provided only a brief respite for the Serbs. In the summer of 1813, while the Europeans were embroiled in another war with Napoleon, the sultan's forces attacked Serbia from three directions and, after much hard fighting, crushed the rebellion.[77] The Serbs had come full circle.

Their uprising had begun in 1804 in reaction to the reign of terror of the Janissaries, and nine years later their landscape was the scene of another round of Ottoman atrocities.

The sultan's victorious armies occupied the towns and cities, but the officers quickly lost control of their men, who proceeded to indulge in an orgy of plunder and pillage. The circus of destruction turned into frenzy as soldiers fought over the spoils. At least 300 Ottomans were killed by their fellow soldiers in the furious competition for the choicest slaves and valuables.[78] For twelve days, Serbia was put to the sword. Ottoman raiding parties scoured the countryside, killing all men and boys over the age of fifteen; women and children were spared for the slave market. The bounty of slaves reached such proportions, comments Michael Petrovich, that "Belgrade became a vast slave market. On one day alone, October 17, 1813, some 1,800 Serbian women and children were sold. The forests were full of refugees and marauders. The roads were crowded with humans and cattle alike being led to the market."[79]

The Ottoman commander-in-chief, Grand Vizier Hurshid Pasha, finally announced a general amnesty on October 21 and offered leniency to all rebels who returned to their homes.[80] It was only a matter of time, however, before the Ottoman military occupation degenerated from the chaos of plunder to the inevitable application of systematic brutality. Within months, a malignant pattern of torture and death had been established. The mixture of fear, revenge, and wounded pride won over the policy of moderation that the Ottoman commander had tried to implement. At first, the new pasha of Belgrade, Suleyman Uskuplu, had followed a conciliatory course. In fact, the entire feudal Ottoman system was reinstated, and superficially life had returned to normal. In April 1814, approximately 30,000 Serbs and an equal number of livestock made their way back from their refuge in Austria. But the situation soon began to deteriorate, partly because the new pasha had a deep loathing of Serbs and partly because law and order, as often happens in a postwar environment, were replaced by individual acts of aggrandizement and vengeance. At least one-third of the Ottomans who terrorized the Serbs were Bosnians, thus adding one more entry to a ledger of atrocities that would continue to have impact in future Yugoslav crises.

The international situation also contributed to Ottoman insecurities. Napoleon had been defeated, and there were rumors of a new coalition rising against the Ottoman Empire. The Ottomans rightly feared potential Austrian or Russian intervention in Serbia, and decided that it would be prudent to confiscate all weapons. But this attempt at disarmament backfired, since thousands had already fled to the forests and swollen the ranks of the *hayduks*. Those who remained were generally unlikely to take up arms against the Ottoman administration. Nonetheless, the process exposed the weaknesses of the Ottoman system and increased the desperation of the Serbs. Ottoman officials fanned out into the countryside to look for weapons and to extort any assets squirreled away by the Serbs. They enthusiastically beat and tortured the peasants, while indiscriminately executing bandits and local leaders. The Serbs hiding in the forests then retaliated by ambushing and killing Muslims in the countryside.[81] The reprisals, even by the standards of the day, were barbaric. Thousands were butchered and entire villages were destroyed. Petrovich's account, which is based on eyewitness reports, is a catalogue of horror and abomination:

> Men were roasted alive, hanged by their feet over smoking straw until they asphyxiated, castrated, crushed with stones, and bastinadoed. Their women and children were raped and sometimes taken by force to harems. . . . Outside Stambule Gate in Belgrade, there were always on view the corpses of impaled Serbs being gnawed by packs of dogs.[82]

Karageorge was not there to see it, or to face the penalties for the insurrection. During the course of the Ottoman attack, the Serb leader lost his nerve; he fled over the Danube and sought asylum in Russian Bessarabia. In fairness, he was sick during the fighting, and more than likely just as sick of the bickering, intrigues, and disunity that had plagued the nine years of Serbian independence.[83] The expulsion of the Ottomans had left the Serbs to their own political devices, without a system of government or a civil administration. There was no administrative elite that could replace the Ottoman regime. The mechanisms of law and government, as well as key state institutions such as the police and the military, forces that bind a society, had eroded over centuries of foreign occupation. The Serbs had little choice but to graft on to the Ottoman system their individual and idiosyncratic version of authority.

Karageorge's leadership was in theory based on his election by an assembly of *knezes* (the appointed or elected heads of villages) in February 1804. In practice, his ability to rule Serbia for nine years depended on military success and Russian support.[84] Real power rested with the armed bands that loosely constituted the Serbian army. Each unit was raised from a particular region and its loyalty was to the local leader. Initially, these regional barons did not challenge Karageorge, but they did resist any attempt on his part to centralize political and economic authority. Inevitably, conspiracies were hatched against him, and he retaliated by executing the culprits. Political and military power in Serbia was an unequal and chaotic contest between the centralizing efforts of Karageorge, oligarchic and regional monopolies, and the constitutional notions of the small class of merchants, professionals, and intellectuals.[85]

Without a native model of government, or for that matter the means by which to display ostentatious power and wealth, the Serbian leaders soon fell back on Ottoman customs. The new powerbrokers even adopted the fashion of the Turks. Members of the new Serbian military and political elite were soon observed wearing embroidered green silk and turbans, as well as displaying an appetite for wealth that often exceeded the rapacious practices of the Ottoman officials.[86] The Serbian experiment in statehood collapsed not only because of their defeat at the hands of the Ottomans, but also because the Serb leaders could not match their military ability with political acumen in the constitutional sphere. After nine years of intermittent warfare, the Serbs were reduced to fighting the Ottomans in the summer and each other during the rest of the year.

Almost five centuries of Ottoman rule also left little in the way of a Serbian intellectual and professional elite. "With no far-reaching intellectual background or political project," comments Pavlowitch, "the 'Serbian revolution' had begun in an obscure territory at a time of general fermentation. For a while it seemed as if it might become a Balkan revolution, but it had attracted little attention in Europe and the price of that period of freedom had been high."[87] The tragedy of Serbia is that it was not strategically significant enough to attract the attention of the Great Powers. The Serb capacity to endure war and its accompanying hardships meant little to the Europeans and even less to their Russian co-religionists.[88]

In contrast, the Greek War of Independence captured the imagination of European liberals, poets, and romantic intellectuals, who saw in Greece a rebirth of revolutionary ideals. The result was a groundswell of support whose force kept the possibility of a Greek state alive long enough for the politicians and generals to catch up. In Greece, as everywhere else in the Balkans, independence was not possible without the support of at least one European power. And that support was not forthcoming as long as the Ottoman Empire was able to exhibit any degree of control over its vast and diverse territories. Ultimately, the Ottoman decline was triggered by the inability of the Muslim establishment to shed its ancient institutions and come to terms with Western technology in both the marketplace and the military. When the realization hit that clinging to the past was equivalent to hanging on to a corpse, it was too late.

5

FIRE, SWORD, AND BLOOD:
THE BIRTH OF THE BALKAN STATE

—⟨∾∾⟩—

An untoward event.

— THE REACTION OF THE DUKE OF WELLINGTON
TO THE NEWS OF THE DESTRUCTION OF THE OTTOMAN FLEET
AT NAVARINO IN 1827

The congregation of affluent and privileged Greeks stood in silence as the patriarch officiated over the most holy of Christian ceremonies. On the eve of Easter Sunday, 1821, in Constantinople, the ecumenical patriarch of the Eastern Orthodox Church, Gregorius V, was conducting the solemn Easter ceremony. He was adorned with spectacular robes and held the religious instruments of his office. But this particular Easter service had more than just a spiritual significance. The Greeks of the Ottoman Empire were, at that time, facing a potential tidal wave of change, for they had risen in rebellion against the sultan.

Gregorius V believed that by condemning the leaders of the uprising, he could keep the Greeks of the Ottoman Empire out of harm's way. Accordingly, he had excommunicated the rebel leaders from the Church, and thus from the Greek Orthodox community in general. Once again, during that eventful Easter service, he had the excommunication document read out to reassure the sultan of the Church's loyalty to the empire. But just as the service ended and people began to disperse, Ottoman guards burst in and pushed their way to the altar. They seized the patriarch and his priests by their collars and dragged them to the hall of the synod. The patriarch's sole Janissary bodyguard attempted to protect his charge, but he was stabbed to death in the ensuing scuffle.[1]

The imperial dragoman, Stavrakis Aristarchos, produced a firman from the sultan and declared that "Gregorius, having acted an unworthy, an ungrateful and a treacherous part, was degraded from his office."[2] This humiliation occurred in the synod chamber, before senior clergymen, leading Phanariots, and various heads of Greek associations. The soldiers then seized Gregorius and a number of bishops and priests, bound them with ropes, and dragged them to the gate of the patriarchate in the Phanar district.

By the next morning, Easter Sunday, a crowd had gathered outside the main gate of the Phanar, the entrance to the Greek Orthodox district in Constantinople. The spectators jostled for better positions, for those in the back could not get a clear view of the unusual execution. Word had spread throughout the capital, and the curious arrived in record numbers so as not to miss the main event. The impending spectacle had Muslims excited, Christians frozen with fear, and foreigners both attracted and repulsed. The executioners, who had explicit orders to humiliate as well as kill, felt a proper scaffold was not necessary. They simply threw a rope over the hinge that fastened the folding doors of the Phanar gate, placed a noose around the neck of Gregorius, and pulled the body up — slowly.[3] The patriarch, resigned to his fate, maintained his dignity throughout the ordeal.

Gregorius choked to death slowly. The patriarch struggled with his robes and kicked his legs in the air in a vain attempt to gain a foothold. The witnesses nearest the tormented cleric could hear him wheezing as he gasped for air. Gregorius was a slight old man, which meant it took him hours to die. But the end was inevitable — each breath got shorter and shorter until there were no more. By nightfall, he had finally expired, though the body continued twitching until the nervous system shut down. Shortly after, two of the remaining priests were dragged to the other gates of the patriarchate and hanged in a similar fashion. Indeed, Sultan Mahmut had no intention of depriving the rest of the population of similar spectacles. He had three bishops hauled through the streets with ropes around their necks and hanged in different locations throughout the city.[4]

George Finlay writes that after the execution, the grand vizier, Bendierli Ali, walked to the patriarchate, accompanied by only a single attendant. On reaching the gate, he sat on a stool and calmly looked at the hanging body. After a few minutes, he left without saying anything. Finlay assures us that the grand vizier was contemplating the finer points of Ottoman justice, which held that senior officials were responsible for the welfare of the sultan's dominions and would be sacrificed to atone for the crimes of their charges.[5] This Ottoman interpretation of ministerial responsibility was based on the notion of collective guilt and collective punishment. It was a concept enforced as stringently for religious and ethnic groups as it was for towns, villages, and hamlets. A community, whether Muslim or Christian, could be held liable for the actions of its individual members, both near and far. This approach to crime and punishment had permeated the culture of Balkan societies, which often used guilt by historical association to justify "judicial" retribution. Both the innocent and the guilty were held accountable for past and present ethnic altercations.

In this case, the sultan's rage knew no bounds. The patriarch's corpse remained at the gate of the Phanar for three days, and the pungent odor reminded passersby of Mahmut's fury. Even Gregorius's hastily elected successor, Eugenios II, who was on his way to the palace to be confirmed as the new patriarch, could pass through the gate only after his Ottoman escort pushed the body aside to make way. The Ottoman official used the ghoulish exercise to remind the new patriarch of the fate of his predecessor.[6]

Initially Mahmut had been satisfied with the position the Church took with respect to the uprising. But when several of Gregorius's close associates, as well as a few leading Phanariots, left Constantinople in a hurry, the already paranoid sultan concluded that a revolt of the Christians in the capital was in the making. At the very least, he reasoned, those who had fled were in league with the insurgents and were being protected by Gregorius. So when in doubt, he thought, massacre the Christians.

Of course, Mahmut II had some reason to be so paranoid. The effort to destroy Ali Pasha had left the Ottomans with only limited resources with which to defend the rest of Greece. Dimitrios Ypsilantis's efforts to launch a Balkan independence movement in the Danubian principalities had also used up considerable Ottoman forces, leaving most of the remaining areas of mainland Greece vulnerable. Reports soon reached the sultan that the Muslim communities in Greece and the Danubian principalities were under attack. These were followed by stories that detailed the pitiless and wholesale killing of thousands of the sultan's subjects and co-religionists in other parts of Greece and Moldavia. According to these accounts, men, women, and children were being tortured and brutally put to death by Greek revolutionaries.

Constantinople was then beset with rumors that the Philiki Hetairia planned to assassinate the imperial family. The society's so-called grand project involved not only the killing of the sultan, but also the destruction of the Ottoman arsenal and the burning of the capital.[7] Unfortunately, some members of the Hetaira felt compelled to put their plans in writing. Michael Soutzos, the prince of Moldavia, sent letters to Hetaira members in Constantinople urging his fellow conspirators to "let fire consume the capital. Encourage the sailors to take control of the arsenal. Try every means to seize the Sultan at the moment he goes to the fire. Let the voice of the fatherland be heard." Such indiscreet communications soon came into the possession of the Ottoman authorities.[8]

The rumors were accorded more credence with each new report of Greek attacks against Muslims in the Balkans. Mutilated survivors from Moldavia appeared in the streets with their noses and lips cut off, decrying the Greek rebels. Some brought back a Greek standard bearing an inverted crescent with a cross superimposed on it, a symbol of the triumph of Christianity over Islam.[9] Mahmut, meanwhile, saw conspiracies everywhere. He knew his position as sultan was not secure, and he remembered only too well the fate of his predecessor, Selim III. The Janissaries, meanwhile, were not only useless in suppressing the revolts, but also remained a threat to Mahmut's tenure on the throne.

With so many bewildering events buffeting his empire, Mahmut overestimated the gravity of the situation in Greece and underestimated the long-term impact of his actions in Constantinople. He sought advice on Islamic law from the mufti of Constantinople so he could declare a holy war against the Greek Christians throughout the empire. The mufti, however, was a man of deep religious conviction and probity who would not accept that the uprisings in Greece warranted a holy war. He turned Mahmut down. But the mufti was to pay with his life for maintaining the integrity of Islamic laws and traditions in the face of a determined sultan. Mahmut, meanwhile, instigated a self-defeating spree of violence and retribution. Naturally, he turned to the Eastern Orthodox Church to initiate the process of establishing control through terror.

—*◌◌◌*—

On Easter Sunday of March 1821, Sultan Mahmut II effectively ensured that the sporadic uprisings in Greece would be transformed into a cohesive war of independence. The first act of his reign of terror was to execute Gregorius, probably the only man who had the power to stifle the uprising. The patriarch, indeed, had done his duty as both a senior Ottoman official and a clerical and secular leader, anathematizing the Greek rebels in order to distance the Church and the entire Greek Orthodox community from the events in Greece. But despite the patriarch's immediate repudiation of the rebels, the sultan proceeded with a pogrom in parts of the empire still under Ottoman control.

The sultan also resolved that even in death, Gregorius would be deprived of both dignity and martyrdom. A group of Jewish criminals were ordered to cut down the body and drag it by the neck through a particularly dirty section of the market to the shoreline. The hapless Jews sweated in the noonday heat, pulling the corpse from one end of the market to the other while their Ottoman overseers directed them to specific areas stained with human and animal waste. Afterward, they were ordered to weigh down the corpse with stones and dump it into the harbor. But this was not to be the final resting place of the Greek Orthodox patriarch. Gregorius V ultimately eluded the oblivion of a watery grave and secured the martyrdom that the sultan had tried to deny him. The body of the Greek cleric did not decompose in the filthy waters of the harbor, but instead was carried by the undercurrent of the Bosporus to the Sea of Marmara.

A few days later, a miracle was reported: Gregorius's body had risen to the surface near a Christian ship bound for Russia. Just before sundown, a fugitive from the Easter slaughter spotted the body floating on the water and identified the patriarch from his vestments. The ship's captain had the corpse recovered and covertly brought to Odessa, where Gregorius's mysterious reappearance was taken as proof of divine intervention. He was given a state funeral and finally achieved the martyrdom he had almost been denied by the obscure depths of the Golden Horn.[10]

For the Greeks in Constantinople, the death of the patriarch signaled the start of a week of hell. During the Christian Easter, mobs of Muslim fanatics indulged themselves in an orgy of plunder, rape, torture, and murder. Churches were looted and some destroyed, and homes were ransacked. Many Christians were set upon by faceless mobs held together by mass frenzy. They burnt, decapitated, hanged, or stabbed their victims to death, mostly at random. Robert Walsh, the chaplain of the British embassy, wrote of the fate awaiting the victims of the mob. In *A Residence at Constantinople*, the British minister describes what happened to a young man who was caught by his pursuers:

> He was forced upon his knees by two Turks pressing on his shoulders, and in that position a third came behind him with his kinshal. This is a curved-bladed sword, with the edge on the concave side, and exceedingly sharp, used always as the instrument of decapitation. With a single horizontal stroke he severed his head from his neck; his body was thrown into the puddle in the middle of the street for passersby to trample on, and his head was laid contemptuously between his thighs. The executioners then hastily passed on, leaving both to be torn by the dogs who were gathering around.[11]

Outside the gate of the imperial palace of Topkapi, there were piles of heads, noses, ears, and lips. The Ottoman commanders who had captured the city of Patras, in southern Greece, had sent these human souvenirs. The grisly mementos remained on display and were slowly trampled by the public. Occasionally, some of the remains would stick to the heels of the passersby, who would walk for hours without caring about or even noticing the added features of their footwear. Above the gates, vultures circled the bodies, and in the streets young boys played by kicking the heads of the victims.[12]

In truth, fewer than one hundred were killed at Patras, but the display of the ears and noses intensified the hatred between the Greek revolutionaries and the Ottomans. The scenes of mayhem described by the British chaplain were meant to instill terror in every Christian in the empire. But at times, even the professional Ottomans were just as afraid. The new grand dragoman, Stavrakis Aristarchos, for one, was the very picture of terror. Aware that his predecessor had been executed on Mahmut's orders, Aristarchos behaved with great trepidation whenever in the presence of the sultan. During the British ambassador's first official visit to the sultan, according to Walsh, Aristarchos trembled so violently and dripped so much sweat on the ambassador's letter of credentials that he had difficulty making out the words.[13] As it turned out, he had reason for concern: a short while later, the terrified official was decapitated.

The Ottoman authorities also cast a wide net over the Phanariots, wealthy merchants, and any other obvious targets or sources of possible financial gain. Hundreds of Christian notables and merchants were apprehended, relieved of their gold, tortured, and summarily executed. Death was either prolonged or came suddenly and without warning. A Greek architect, for example, was beheaded immediately after he completed the office he had designed for the Ottoman navy at Galata. But a few escaped, and some were even released by their captors. In Smyrna, the city's chief mullah (Islamic scholar) and some of the local Turkish authorities tried to intervene on behalf of their Christian neighbors; the mob remained deaf to their pleas, however, and simply butchered them as well.

The pogrom might have satisfied Mahmut's primordial and authoritative appetites. The crude efforts to pit Jews against Christians might even have hinted at a Machiavellian side of the sultan's character. But ultimately, exacerbating tensions was no clever domestic policy. Alan Palmer, in *The Decline of the Ottoman Empire*, suggests that

the sultan fatally miscalculated in failing to recognize the long-term significance of the Easter killings. In sanctioning the execution of the Patriarch and the vilification of his remains at such a moment in the Church's calendar, Mahmud alienated a quarter of his subjects. The Orthodox millet was thrown into permanent opposition to the Sultanate, thereby weakening the Ottoman Empire throughout the last century of its existence.[14]

But some scholars, such as William Cleveland, argue that Mahmut has received bad press from Western diplomatic historians because he ruled during a period of increased Ottoman decline.[15] Later in his reign, Mahmut did display considerable talents as a reformer, but he nevertheless continued to combine his administrative improvements with periods of terror. On June 15, 1826, for example, he ordered the massacre of thousands of Janissaries on the streets and in their barracks, consigning them to the same fate they had meted out to Christians and Muslims alike.

The Greek uprising was initially a series of uncoordinated insurrections, not a single event. But Mahmut's campaign of humiliation and terror in Constantinople legitimized the rebellions and helped turn them into a nationalist movement. The sultan had failed to understand that martyrs fuel revolutions, and thus that his execution of Gregorius had symbolically freed the Greek Orthodox Church from its bond with the Ottoman Empire. In the words of Steven Runciman, "The contract between the Conquering Sultan and Gennadius had been broken by the Patriarchate [after the killing of Gregorius]."[16] The Ottomans would no longer trust the Orthodox, and the Greek Christians lost their faith in the security of the empire. Indeed, the Church was now free to reinvent itself and come to terms with the nationalism that permeated the Balkan region.[17] The Phanariot class, which had been integral to the supremacy of the Eastern Church in the Orthodox world, was dispersed and its monopoly over imperial positions and privileges abolished, leaving a critical intellectual and professional gap in the Ottoman administration.

Of course, Mahmut was not the only one to usher in a reign of terror. The Christians in Greece exacted their own pound of flesh in dozens of villages and towns, on the roads and on mountain trails. The Peloponnese, where the Muslim population numbered approximately 40,000, was one such spot. Most of the Peloponnese Muslims had converted to Islam centuries earlier, but all spoke Greek as their primary language. The Muslims owned 750,000 acres (300,000 ha) of cultivable land, while the estimated 360,000 Christian Greeks had to make do with 375,000 acres (150,000 ha), most of which belonged to a small group of wealthy Greeks.[18] The majority of the peasants worked as laborers for Muslim or wealthy Greek landowners, though a small number scratched out a modest existence on tiny plots of their own. These conditions, not surprisingly, gave rise to a notion of exterminating the hated Turks (as all Balkan Muslims were called), a process that would conveniently create opportunities for the land-hungry peasants. As Stavrianos baldly states, "Many peasants supported the revolution as a means of getting land."[19]

—◦ʔ/ʔ/ʔ—

Modern Western policy-makers trying to unravel the Balkan conundrum of the 1990s have often failed to understand the significance of land as a determinant of ethnic strife. Urban dwellers also often underestimate the value and emotional sentiment placed on land by peasants and farmers. In pre-war Bosnia, Muslims were concentrated in cities and towns, as doctors, bankers, lawyers, clerks, secretaries, and merchants. Serbs, on the other hand, were more often engaged in farming and other rural pursuits, and thus naturally occupied more land space than the Muslims. Indeed, on September 9, 1992, Tanjug, Belgrade's official news agency, reported that the Serbs in Bosnia owned 51.4 percent of the overall land, even though they represented just one-third of the population.[20] Opportunistic politicians of all stripes were soon focused on this issue, and Bosnia quickly fell victim to the lethal dynamic of land, ethnicity, history, religion, and nationalism.

Both sides in the debate wanted to push out the unwanted communities — in effect, ethnic cleansing — and claim land to which they had a historic link. But initiatives to carve up Bosnia were interpreted by local Serbs as attempts to appropriate parts of their farms. Certainly politicians in both Serbia and Bosnia were quick to feed the anxiety of Serb farmers. On July 11, 1993, the president of the Bosnian Serb Republic, Radovan Karadzic, claimed, "They [Muslims] ought to get approximately 30 percent of the territory of former Bosnia-Herzegovina, because two-thirds of the land in B-H has always been in possession of the Serbs, who are farmers, and because we need a corridor between east and west for the defense from aggression, whichever side it may come from."[21] Thus throughout the war in Bosnia, nationalist Serbs continued to claim some 51 to 66 percent of Bosnia's land mass, even though they represented 31 percent or less of the population. The political leaders might have had dreams of a Greater Serbia, but the local farmers were simply concerned with the future of their agricultural property.

The Western solution to the Bosnia problem was to divide the country into Serb, Muslim, and Croat sectors based as much as possible on the percentage of the population represented by each ethnic group. During the Bosnian war, however, the various peace plans consistently attempted to allocate a greater portion of land to the Serbs, largely because they, through the force of arms, had conquered more territory. The Western approach failed, in part, because it did not take into account the socio-economic realities of the region. Even worse, the realpolitik tack served to undermine the credibility of the international peace efforts. Western governments were either unprepared or unable to understand the complexities of Yugoslav disintegration, and they appeared to be rewarding aggression.

Of course, the situation in Bosnia was by no means unique. Land seizure and the application of collective responsibility have been cornerstones of both domestic and foreign policy in Europe and North America for centuries. In 1919, for example, the German government was forced to accept the "war guilt" clause of the Treaty of Versailles as part of the settlement to end the First World War. Throughout the nineteenth century in America, and especially after the Civil War, African Americans were routinely and indiscriminately executed to answer for offenses committed by unknown individuals. In 1923, the Great Powers, under Turkish pressure, forced Greece to accept a compulsory exchange of populations with Turkey. In fact, the population agreement was intended to prevent the return of more than a million Greek Christian refugees who had left Turkey prior to 1923.[22] Indeed, the ultimate goal of the Turks was to eliminate all minorities, through either expulsion or extermination.

The Turkish pogrom against the Greeks was, to a limited degree, the result of revenge. During the Greco-Turkish War (1920–22), the Greek army did engage in harsh treatment of some Muslim communities in Turkey. To a greater extent, however, the pogroms were aimed at creating Turkish homogeneity, and they followed the age-old pattern of eviction facilitated by terror. Although the Turkish nationalists disdained their Ottoman heritage, they had no difficulty following the example of Mahmut II in once again choosing a cleric as the first official victim.

On Monday, September 11, 1922, Archbishop Chrysostomos was summoned to the headquarters of Noureddin Pasha, the commander of the 1st Turkish Army, who had taken control of Smyrna. Chrysostomos was escorted by a French naval detachment of twelve men. The navy men had orders not to intervene, but their mere presence, it was hoped, would serve as a deterrent. When the archbishop faced the Turkish officer, Noureddin first spat upon him. The general then informed the archbishop that the court in Ankara had found him guilty of treason and condemned him to death. All that remained was to determine the manner of his execution. With that, the priest was thrown outside the building and seized by a mob. Noureddin, standing on the balcony, extolled the crowd of close to 1,500 men and women to "give him what he deserves."[23]

There are conflicting reports on what exactly took place, but all accounts agree on the substance of the event: the archbishop was practically torn to pieces. Once the mob got hold of the cleric, they dragged him about half a block to the nearest barbershop. The proprietor was pushed aside and the establishment instantly turned into a shop of horrors. Someone tied a white sheet around the archbishop's neck and yelled, "Give him a shave!" Then the ordeal commenced. Some of the mob took turns tearing out his beard and hair, while others cut off his ears and nose. In due course, his eyes were gouged out, his tongue removed, and his hands severed. The grotesque violence served only to excite the crowd, and they used any sharp implement they could find to secure a souvenir of the event.

The archbishop did not survive long. According to one account, a Turk he had helped in the past shot him and ended his agony. The mob then chained the body to an automobile and dragged it around the city square.[24] Through all this, the French marines who had accompanied the archbishop to his meeting with Noureddin remained inactive. Initially, a couple of the navy men had lunged forward in an attempt to protect the archbishop, but they were compelled at gunpoint by their commanding officer to keep out of it. They stood by in helpless frustration, some physically shaking, all revolted by the impotency of their position.

The incident at Smyrna in 1922 would have a gruesome echo in Bosnia in 1995. Dutch peacekeepers had been handed responsibility for Srebrenica, one of the UN-designated safe areas of the Bosnian war zone. Thousands of Muslim refugees had flocked to Srebrenica, placing their faith and their very lives in the hands of the UN. Soon, however, the 600 lightly armed Dutch troops, of which only 300 were actual infantrymen, found themselves caught in a maelstrom of human despair. On July 6, 1995, the Serbs began shelling the town and attacking from the south. Those at UN headquarters dithered, then ordered the Dutch not to fire and to withdraw. The troops fell back to their compound in the city, accompanied by a near-hysterical crowd of Muslim refugees. Srebrenica fell on July 11, and the killing commenced. The Dutch stood by while the Serbs separated the Muslim men of military age from the women and children. Later, these men were executed. Even those Muslims who had sought safety within the UN camp itself were driven out by the Dutch to meet certain death at the hands of the Serbs. The pleas of the Dutch commander to UN headquarters were drowned out by resolution after resolution. The Dutch then tried making a list of some of the men they had surrendered to the Serbs, assuming that this exercise in bureaucracy would somehow prevent their execution. It did not.[25] More than likely, it helped the Serb killers identify their intended victims.

In Smyrna in 1922, similar scenes involving frantic refugees and well-meaning but neutral Allied forces were played out again and again. In most cases, the Allied soldiers found themselves in the same position as the French marines who had observed the unimaginable torture of the archbishop and done nothing. Throughout the city, Christians were subjected to gross brutality, and at least 25,000 perished at the hands of the mobs or members of the Turkish army.[26] And the Turks did not limit themselves to Greek Christians. They also exacted a bloody tribute from the Armenians. First, Turkish irregulars and some members of the Turkish army sealed off the Armenian quarter of Smyrna. Then every house was broken into and the inhabitants slaughtered. In one neighborhood, 300 women were strangled, while in another section the younger and more attractive Armenian girls were sequestered in large abandoned homes and made available to passing troops. None of these women survived.[27]

Mass rape and military brothels were used not only for revenge, but also to symbolize total defeat. Military success on the battlefield was not enough. The vanquished had to endure abject humiliation, and each new degradation provided another layer of security for the victor. The enemy had to be eradicated, and therefore it was deemed necessary to dehumanize the victims. Unfortunately, the Armenians in Smyrna, unlike the Greek refugees (who found a safe haven in Greece), had nowhere to go, and were thus consigned to oblivion. Their continued presence, in the minds of the Turks, represented a threat to the cohesiveness of the new Turkish republic.

The Armenians are a people with a common language, culture, and history who unfortunately lived in a defined territory that was part of northeastern Turkey. As a people with legitimate and ancient claims to the region in a period of time when world leaders were acknowledging the right of self-determination, they could — and did — demand the restoration of ancient Armenia at the cost of Turkish territory. The Greeks had asserted their own ancient claims for parts of Turkey, but these were put down along with the Greek army in Anatolia in 1922. The Greeks, however, unlike the Armenians, had a homeland in mainland Greece. Once the Turkish soldiers and their bloodthirsty civilian counterparts were sated, the survivors could be expelled. The Armenians were not so lucky.

After two days of plunder and murder, the Turks torched Smyrna and forced its residents to the shoreline, where they waited for salvation that never came. The reports Ward Price wrote for the *Daily Mail* painted a vivid and almost surreal picture of Smyrna's last hours. "Picture a constant projection into a red-hot sky of gigantic incandescent balloons, burning oil spots in the Aegean, the air filled with nauseous smell, while parching clouds, cinders and sparks drift across us," he wrote, "and you can have but a glimmering of the scene of appalling and majestic destruction which we are watching."[28]

Remarkably, the fleets of Britain, France, the United States, and Italy stood by in the harbor as the city was consigned to ruin. Geopolitical considerations and rivalry kept the Allies from interfering, and no concerted effort was made to save the population. The special representative of the American Near East Relief Organization, Mark O. Prentiss, at first could not believe the atrocity stories he was hearing. When he went to see for himself, he was so shocked by what he observed that he penned an article for the *New York Times*. "I have seen terrible sights until my senses are numb," he wrote, "but the sight of 200,000 people, mostly women, and little children, being penned up and burning and those escaping being driven to a barren, devastated country for starvation is past all comprehension."[29] An account by Bertram Thessiger, the British captain of the battleship *George V*, sounded like a scene from Dante's *Inferno*:

> About 1:00 a.m. the fire broke through [the] front houses almost simultaneously. It was a terrifying thing to see even from the distance. There was the most awful scream one could imagine. I believe many people were shoved into the water simply by the crowds nearest the houses trying to get further away from the fire. . . . I went in with our boats and made for the place where the fire seemed worst. It was certainly a horrible scene; mothers with their babies, the fire going over their heads, and many of the bundles of clothes also on fire, and the people all screaming.[30]

It is certain that the fire was a deliberate act, but the identities of the arsonists has remained a mystery all these years. There is no question, however, that he was a Turk. The Turkish and Jewish quarters were spared (the Jews were considered loyal to the new Turkish republic), along with buildings that had the phrase "Islamic structure" painted in red on the front.[31] In his *New York Times* article, Prentiss testified:

> Many of us personally saw and are ready to affirm the statement — Turkish soldiers, often directed by officers, throwing petroleum in houses and streets. Vice-Consul Barnes watched a Turkish officer leisurely fire the custom house and the passport bureau, while at least fifty Turkish soldiers stood by. Major Davis saw Turkish soldiers throwing oil into many houses. The naval patrol reported seeing a complete horseshoe of fires started by the Turks around the American school, forcing a panicky evacuation.[32]

The destruction of Smyrna was aimed at ridding the new Turkish republic of as many of its unwanted minorities as possible. And the Turks were not unsuccessful in this. For example, early in 1922, 150,000 Greeks left Constantinople to avoid the grim prospect of Turkish retaliation. This policy was affirmed by Gen. Refet Pasha, who informed Neville Henderson that "the Greeks if they were not actually expelled would be well advised to leave, as in future in a new Turkey they would be unable to make a living here. The Turks were going to take the commerce into their own hands."[33]

Of course, the Turks and Greeks were not the only people who engaged in forced population movements. Early in the twentieth century, the Ottoman and Bulgarian governments also used population exchange as an instrument of frontier security. Under the terms of the 1913 Treaty of Peace between Bulgaria and the Ottoman Empire, 48,500 Muslims were moved from Bulgarian territory to Turkey and 46,700 Bulgarians were relocated to Bulgaria. The treaty, according to the political scientist Harry Psomiades, was the first interstate agreement in modern history to include a provision for the voluntary exchange of populations. In effect, however, the treaty simply confirmed the "ethnic cleansing" that had already taken place in the zone during the course of the 1912–13 Balkan wars.[34]

After the Second World War, forced population exchanges in Czechoslovakia, East Germany, Romania, and Russia were considered an acceptable means of addressing the upheavals caused by the Nazis and the Fascists. But Tito's Yugoslavia did not take advantage of the postwar circumstances by indulging in mass population reconfigurations in 1945. The new Yugoslavia emerged as a multi-ethnic federation of six republics and two independent provinces. The republics were not entirely homogeneous, however, and some included large pockets of historical minorities, which proved unwelcome after Tito's death in 1980. For the Serbs and the other former Yugoslavians, what was eminently commendable in 1945 became reprehensible after 1991. In 1821, however, the Greeks and the Ottomans were able to freely implement such policies; the condemnation of historians only came later.

George Finlay was particularly offended by Greek atrocities against the Muslims, and in his monumental *History of the Greek Revolution*, he expresses at some length his disgust with the behavior of the Greeks. According to Finlay, the Greek campaign against the Muslims culminated with the capture of Tripolis, a town in southern Greece, and he writes in dismay that

> human beings can rarely have perpetrated so many deeds of cruelty on an equal number of their fellow-creatures as were perpetrated by the conquerors on this occasion. Before the Greek chiefs could enter the place, the whole city was a scene of anarchy, and their misconduct had rendered them powerless to restore order, or to arrest the diabolical passions which their own avarice and dishonorable proceedings had awakened in the breast of their followers. . . . After the Greeks had been in possession of the city for forty-eight hours, they deliberately collected together about two thousand persons of every age and sex, but principally women and children, and led them to a ravine in the nearest mountain, where they murdered every soul. The writer saw heaps of unburied bones bleached by the winter rains and summer suns in passing this spot two years after the catastrophe; the size of many of which attested to the early age of the victims.[35]

Finlay's outrage over the excesses of the Greeks in Tripolis stands in stark contrast to Lord Strangford's observations of events in Constantinople (such as the killing of Gregorius), and this is perhaps an early insight into the origin of the confused European love-hate relationship with the Balkans. Strangford, a contemporary of Finlay's, was the British ambassador to the Sublime Porte. He initially reported to Viscount Castlereagh, the British foreign secretary, that the Greeks of Constantinople were being punished as rebels and not as Christians. Later, however, he changed his tune, and claimed that the sultan had brought troops to the city to check the fury of the mob. Reports of the rampage were greatly exaggerated, he said; out of seventy-six churches, only one had been destroyed, and only thirteen injured or plundered. He then informed his government that order had been restored, and to further downplay the degree of violence, he added that Turkish children were being disarmed. "[The] little miscreants under seven years of age, and armed with daggers and pistols, had till now the privilege of robbing, shooting and stabbing with impunity."[36]

Inset: This sign in front of the Terminal Hotel in Daruvar, Croatia, prohibits entry to soldiers of the Yugoslav National Army, Chetnik soldiers, and dogs. It calls to mind similar signs that barred Jews from various European establishments in the years leading up to the Second World War.

Just as the knights of the Fourth Crusade plundered the Church of Holy Wisdom in the thirteenth century, Croatians desecrated this monastery in Pakra, Croatia, in 1992.

Right: Three bombs hit the Belgrade thermoelectric plant on April 4, 1999. This is the same scene that Roksanda Petrovic would have faced when she dared to emerge from under her kitchen table.

Below: To avoid losing planes to Serbian anti-aircraft fire, NATO pilots were ordered to conduct high-altitude bombing runs. As a result, they could not avoid hitting civilian structures, such as this hospital, which had the misfortune of standing next to the Ministry of the Interior of the Serbian Republic.

Above: Modern weapons can create spectacular pyrotechnics, but they have dangerous consequences for the local population, as was demonstrated by the destruction of this oil refinery in April 1999.

Left: The innocent victims of war. A woman contemplates the destruction of her home, bombed April 8, 1999.

Opposite, top: The surreal images of modern war. Pancevo (about eighteen miles [30 km] east of Belgrade), June 1999.

Above: Modern warfare sometimes seems more like a video game than a life-or-death struggle. This is the view from the targeting system of a NATO plane aiming at a bridge.

Left: Although the West went to war to protect the Albanians in Kosovo, NATO bombers could not always differentiate between friend and foe. This Albanian refugee column was bombed by NATO planes on April 14, 1999. Seventy-six people were killed.

Left: It is still not clear how a post office in Kosovo would have aided the Serbian war effort, but in the absence of any tangible military targets, NATO bombers sometimes seemed to believe that any government building would suffice.

Above: Amid the destruction, a man goes about the daily task of survival.

Above: Twin brothers Miladin and Radivoje Stepanovic survey the remains of their Chuprija home, bombed April 8, 1999.

Left: In times of war, no one is safe. When this Belgrade hospital was bombed on April 3, 1999, mothers and their newborn babies had to be evacuated to the basement.

Horror is routinely downplayed or enhanced to reflect the interests of the observer. That is how we can have the strange spectacle of one British historian lambasting the Greeks for their massacre of Muslims while at the same time a British diplomat minimizes Mahmut's atrocities by putting children's faces on the attackers.

More often than not, however, massacres like the one in Constantinople are motivated by profit and excused to save national face. The siege of Tripolis in 1821 and the subsequent slaughter of the Muslim population was the result of a combination of fear and the army's sense that it had been cheated. For six months, the Greeks had laid siege to the city, and the troops had been promised booty to make up for their not being paid. At the same time, the leaders of the Greek forces were engaged in negotiations with the Muslims, but they could not reach agreement on the terms for surrender. This did not prevent some of the Greek commanders from selling provisions to the besieged inhabitants and making separate arrangements with the wealthier Muslims to guarantee their safety — in return for money and jewels, of course.[37] The Albanian contingent of the Ottoman garrison, meanwhile, managed to negotiate its own capitulation and retired unharmed from the city, thus abandoning the inhabitants to their fate. Tripolis was finally taken by storm when the Greek soldiers rushed one of the main gates and broke through the defenses. The soldiers feared that the negotiations of their commanders were about to result in the capitulation of the city, and that they would be deprived of the promised booty.[38]

The Greek insurgents stumbled onto brutality because they lacked the professionalism needed to conduct disciplined killing. For the Ottomans, on the other hand, savagery was the mechanism of imperial control. Yet Mahmut's actions were also in keeping with Oriental despotism, and they were even similar to instruments of repression that had been employed by European monarchs for centuries. However, the advent of nationalism meant that Mahmut was no longer a ruler practicing terror against his subjects. Indeed, the sultan's real intent was to address the breach of an ancient contract with his Greek Orthodox subjects. Patriarch Gregorius had failed to restrain his flock, Mahmut believed, and thus he was in default of the formal and informal agreements between the Ottoman Empire and the Eastern Orthodox Church. But while it is true that the Church's role as the spiritual and secular guardian of the Orthodox Christians had long been intertwined with the well-being of the Ottoman Empire, the sultan had failed to appreciate that the concept of political identity had eventually overtaken religious affiliation. And Mahmut made another fatal error. By executing the patriarch, he inadvertently lifted the veil of anonymity that disguises the identities of the victims of mass killings. The body left hanging from the archway had a name and a personality that was recognizable to every Greek Christian in the Ottoman Empire and beyond. The sultan was essentially demonstrating that no one was safe and there was no turning back; he effectively cast the die for the Greek War of Liberation.

—◦◦◦—

In 1821, events in Constantinople were being observed by mainland Greece and the Great Powers, which were reluctant to intervene. The Russians, however, had a direct interest in Greece, both strategic and moral, and could not stand by for too long while their co-religionists were eradicated. Thus the period during which the European leaders were able to ignore the events in Greece was short lived. Soon the fate of the Greeks was reverberating from the halls of power to the general European public.

Unfortunately, the Greeks were not in a position to launch a coordinated revolution. They lacked unity of command and were plagued by regional divisions. The leaders they did have were uncertain how to implement a political and military strategy against the Ottomans. Even the Hetairia was divided on how to proceed and when to strike, with some members favoring immediate action and others advising delay and careful preparation.

Nevertheless, the Ali Pasha rebellion proved too tempting an opportunity to ignore, and Alexandros Ypsilantis, with little planning or forethought, seized the moment to try to ignite a general uprising in Moldavia and Wallachia. On March 6, 1821, he crossed the river Pruth into Moldavia, hoping that his presence would inspire the Romanians to join the rebellion. In Jassy, Ypsilantis proclaimed the liberation of all Christians in the Ottoman Empire, and hinted that the czar would intervene on their behalf. Ypsilantis's Romanian ally, Tudor Vladimirescu, also exhorted his compatriots to join the rebellion and assured them that Russia would protect them. The Hetairia, meanwhile, had sent Karageorge to Serbia, but he was promptly arrested and executed by the order of Milos Obrenovic. His head was sent to the sultan as a demonstration of Obrenovic's genuflection. And anyway, the Serbian leader could not be convinced of the merits of another uprising. Obrenovic had skillfully achieved autonomy for Serbia in 1815, and it seemed to most Serbs that continued loyalty to the sultan offered a better future than the uncertainty of another attempt at independence.

In Moldavia, meanwhile, years of Greek oppression had quenched any desire for rebellion on the part of the local inhabitants, who saw little difference between the Ottomans and their Greek masters. The Greek rebels tried massacring Muslims and Ottoman officials, but this too failed to interest the Danubian Christians. For the rebels, this was just one more setback. The Romanians would not join the uprising, the Serbs had abstained, and the czar had disowned Ypsilantis and the Greek insurgents. By the end of June 1821, Ypsilantis's forces had been defeated and he abandoned his followers and took refuge in Austria. The rebellion continued to sputter along until all resistance was snubbed out a few weeks later.

Events after this went into free fall. Poorly disciplined troops, bandits, and predatory gangs of looters made up most of the forces that were fighting for both the Ottoman Empire and the Greeks, and this inevitably increased the tempo of violence. The Ottomans dominated central and northern Greece and Turkey, which meant that a large portion of the Greek population remained hostage to the Ottomans and had no hope of ever joining their compatriots in Greece proper. The Greek rebels, meanwhile, were strongest in southern Greece and the islands closest to the mainland. When Kurshid Pasha had assumed command of the Ottoman forces ranged against Ali Pasha, he'd discovered that his lines of communication with the Peloponnese, the islands, and a great part of mainland Greece were cut off because of the Greek uprising.

During the summer of 1821, Kurshid's operations were severely curtailed, and he was forced to choose between two equally dangerous options: sustaining the siege against Ali Pasha or trying to fight his way back to southern Greece. He had little choice but to adopt the former, however, since his army of 20,000 also included a large number of Christian troops, who could not be trusted to fight against their own kind. In addition, he was reluctant to weaken the Ottoman defenses in northern Greece — and thus potentially lose direct access to Constantinople — by drawing additional troops from units in Macedonia and Thessaly. And of course, Kurshid was obliged to execute Mahmut's orders, which were to destroy Ali Pasha before anything else. In hindsight, however, Kurshid made a critical mistake; in the end, the Greek rebels proved a far greater threat than Ali.

The Ottomans made another fatal error in underestimating the leaders of the bands that formed the core of the Greek armed forces. Many of these men, prior to the rebellion, had served in foreign armies. During their occupation of the Ionian islands in the first decade of the nineteenth century, for example, the Russians put together a unit of 500 Greeks on Corfu. After the islands passed into French hands in 1807, members of this unit were enrolled in the Bataillon du Chausseurs à Pied Grècs.[39] A similar unit, the Duke of York's Greek Light Infantry, existed in the British army. Commanded by Sir Richard Church, a philhellene who would play an important role in the Greek War of Liberation, this regiment saw combat against the French and their Greek allies in the Ionian Islands.[40] Indeed, the spectacle of Greeks fighting other Greeks while serving in foreign armies was not uncommon. If anything, it was a natural and perfectly acceptable occurrence, with precedents that went back at least to the medieval period, when Balkan peoples would routinely fight against one another on behalf of foreign conquerors.

Yet even though service in the armed forces of the Great Powers did prepare many Greeks for leadership roles in the War of Liberation, it is doubtful that the tactical experience they gained proved relevant against the Ottomans. It appears that in spite of their regimental designations, the units in which the Greeks served were deployed mainly as line formations. In other words, these regiments used conventional tactics that stood in direct contrast to the guerrilla techniques that later dominated the War of Liberation.[41]

Conventional warfare had played a much more important role in the Serbian struggle against the Ottomans. In its initial stages, the Serbian revolution was sustained by the activities of *hayduks* armed with weapons smuggled in from Austria or captured from the Ottomans.[42] As the conflict escalated, however, the Serbs were compelled to adopt conventional methods that relied on European tactics and standardized military organization, discipline, and drill.[43] They were able to do this because Serbs had for centuries served in the Ottoman, Austrian, Hungarian, and Venetian armed forces, gaining experience with the techniques and discipline of traditional armies. In the end, this experience proved extremely useful in the struggle against Ottoman authority.[44]

Of course, what truly determined the success of the Greek and Serb insurrections was not the fighting ability of the rebels but the military and diplomatic policies of the Great Powers. In the case of the Serbs, the Great Powers had remained indifferent. The Greeks, however, were more fortunate. The intervention of Russia, France, and Britain extricated the Greek insurgents from a dangerous military predicament and prevented the Ottomans from completely crushing the incipient revolutionary movement.[45]

The Ottoman campaign against the Greek insurgents in southern and central Greece, the main theater of operations, was focused on reinforcing the dozen or so garrisons still held by forces loyal to the sultan and then fanning out to destroy pockets of resistance in the countryside. Conversely, the objective of the Greek rebels was to block the northern advance of the Ottomans, reduce the Ottoman-held fortresses, and capture the main towns in the Peloponnese. The Ottomans were constrained by geography. Only two passages were wide enough to allow large armies access through the mountains: Thermopylae in the east and the gates of Makrinos in the west. The weak Ottoman navy precluded the possibility of bringing reinforcements by sea to relieve the garrisons, and this forced the Ottomans to advance from north to south until they reached the Gulf of Corinth. At this point, the eastern and western flanks had to fight their way across the defiles of the isthmus of Corinth, which linked mainland Greece with the Peloponnese in the south. Tactically, this meant that the Ottoman armies had to proceed across broken coastal plains and at the same time maintain control over each gorge and mountain pass that lay behind them.

For two years, they attempted in vain to break through to the Peloponnese while fending off the constant harassment of the Greek irregulars. Finally, the sultan had little choice but to seek help from Muhammed Ali Pasha of Egypt. The Egyptian Ottoman viceroy, much like his namesake in the Balkans, had his own ambitious program, however, and Mahmut had to offer him the Peloponnese and Crete in exchange for his military support. By 1824, Ali's son, Ibrahim Pasha, was ready to move on southern Greece, and soon the Greek rebels were squandering all their military gains in fighting each other.

The conflict between the rebels exposed the regionalism that characterized nineteenth-century Greece. The *klepht* chiefs of the south became locked in a deadly struggle for control of the provisional government with the *klepht* leaders in the west and the Greek seamen and merchants of the islands. Ironically, the rebels were prepared for anything but success. Their early victories against the Ottomans raised the question of who would lead and who would follow. Unfortunately, the Phanariots, who had had the means to provide the political and intellectual leadership of the nascent Greek state, were either dead or scattered, and those who remained lacked the power base needed to influence events. The revolution, consequently, was marred by regional myopia, while most generals and political leaders fought only to secure the primacy of their respective regions.

The first phase of the Greek War of Liberation particularly highlighted the military limitations of the rebel forces. Inarguably, the *klephts* and the *armatoles* excelled in guerrilla warfare. When fighting in mountainous terrain and on ground of their own choosing, the irregulars performed with distinction and audacity. Indeed, the Greeks were able to win some of their greatest victories of the war by fighting in such conditions. For example, at the Battle of Dervenaki (August 6–8, 1822), Greek forces under the command of Theodore Kolokotronis were able to defeat the army of Mahmut Dramali Pasha. The Greek forces employed hit-and-run tactics against the Ottoman columns, at times surprising them and using the terrain to their advantage, bottlenecking and outflanking them until the Turkish regulars were beaten.[46]

Victories such as that of Ioannis Makriyannis at the Battle of Lerna (July 25, 1825), where a handful of Greek fighters in a well-fortified position were able to defy Ibrahim Pasha's European-trained Egyptian regulars, provided further proof of the effectiveness of irregular tactics in defensive warfare.[47] Unfortunately, the irregulars were no match for the same opponents on an open field, as had been demonstrated by the first encounter between Ibrahim's soldiers and the Greeks on April 19, 1825.[48] At that battle, the concentration of firepower from the well-disciplined Egyptians quickly scattered the Greek irregulars, and not without considerable casualties.

The irregulars' political reliability and devotion to the Greek cause were also uncertain. Throughout the war, some chiefs routinely abandoned the Greek cause when its fortunes were at a low ebb, only to side with the rebels once again when their odds seemed to improve. The chiefs, however, were probably not deliberately engaging in treason. Most likely, they perceived their repeated changes of allegiance as an extension of the customs and values of the old *armatolismos* system — a system that permitted frequent and relatively easy movement between spheres of legality and illegality. But in the context of the Greek liberation struggle, such actions were potentially disastrous, and the Western-educated leaders of the independence movement regarded behavior of this kind as contemptible and disgraceful.[49]

Another problem was the inability of the Greek leaders to effectively control the activities of the irregulars. In practice, the *armatoles* were loyal and obedient only to their own leaders, while the chieftains were answerable to no one but themselves.[50] These traditional relationships reinforced decentralizing tendencies and local autonomy, which impeded the establishment of a modern, centralized nation-state as envisioned by many of the Western-influenced Greeks. These fractious irregular bands, it soon became clear, had to be replaced with a military force that owed its allegiance exclusively to the state; indeed, this was to be the first step on the road to the eradication of local elites whose continued existence was incompatible with the dynamic of nineteenth-century nation-building.[51]

Between 1821 and 1825, this tension between these centralizing and decentralizing tendencies impeded the struggle for independence and nationhood. To be sure, the *klepht* and *armatole* bands eliminated the Ottoman presence in the Peloponnese, while the ships of the islanders kept the sultan's navy at bay. But very quickly, the bandit leaders, satisfied with their initial gains, reverted to their old habits and established individual fiefdoms, essentially assuming the role of the recently expelled Ottoman overlords. And unfortunately, the cause of independence fell by the wayside at precisely the moment when Ibrahim Pasha arrived in the Peloponnese with a fleet and a Western-trained army.

However, just as the Ottomans were poised to reclaim their lost territories, the Great Powers, led by Britain, stepped in. Britain's interest in Greece was to some extent sentimental, the result of the influence of Lord Byron and the philhellenes. But it was also practical. Greek ships had, during the course of the insurrection, established and maintained naval control over large sectors of the Aegean Sea, and more important, had become a threat to European maritime interests in the eastern Mediterranean. George Canning, Britain's foreign secretary, was not only cognizant of British interests in the Mediterranean, but also sympathetic to the Greek cause. On Canning's recommendation, the British government, in 1823, recognized the Greeks and the Ottomans as co-belligerents. This raised the Greeks above the status of insurgents, at least at sea, and gave the British security over their shipping. (Once the Greeks began to be treated as serious combatants, their attacks on neutral ships were considered piracy.)

In July 1827, Canning signed Britain, France, and Russia on to the Treaty of London, which proposed an armistice, mediation, and the creation of an autonomous Greek principality under the sultan's suzerainty. Additional secret clauses stated that if the sultan refused to accept these terms, the three European powers would enforce the blockade against the Ottoman fleet and establish commercial relations with Greece. Furthermore, it stipulated that the three powers would "jointly exert all their efforts to accomplish the object of such a compromise, without, however, taking any part in the hostilities between the two contending parties."[52] The Greeks quickly accepted, but the sultan refused.

The treaty was a masterpiece of ambiguity and the crowning touch of George Canning's diplomatic career. In only a few brilliant moves, he used the Greek revolution to dismantle the concert of Europe (as constructed by Count Metternich at the Congress of Vienna after the Napoleonic Wars) and reassemble it under British leadership. By the middle of September 1827, the combined fleets of Britain, France, and Russia had been deployed in southwestern Greece to enforce the armistice, and their commanders were instructed to "observe extreme care to prevent the measures which you shall adopt against the Ottoman marine from degenerating into hostilities . . . [and] not to make use of that force unless the Turks persist in forcing the passages which they [the admirals] had intercepted."[53] Never before had commanders in the field, except perhaps those under UN jurisdiction in the modern age, received such equivocal orders couched in such equally vague diplomatic language. The politicians simply transferred their responsibility to the three admirals, leaving them to accept either glory or blame — or both.

On October 20, 1827, after some confused negotiations with Ibrahim Pasha, the combined allied naval forces destroyed the Ottoman fleet at Navarino harbor. This military action made Greek independence a certainty, and three years later Greece emerged as a sovereign state, though with some limitations. Britain, France, and Russia carved out the boundaries, which included the Peloponnese, southern Roumeli, and a handful of islands close to the mainland. In the process, however, the protecting powers afflicted the nascent state with chronic irredentism. The Greeks, almost from the inception of their new country, endeavored to fight on until they had secured a rational frontier in the Balkans and the Aegean Sea.

The modern Greek state emerged not as the result of an organic process facilitated by domestic forces with support from the European powers; instead, it was a state created by Britain, France, and Russia to address their respective geopolitical concerns. For example, Czar Nicholas went to war not to support the Greeks, but because he objected to "the Turks' conduct to Russia." The French, for their part, went along out of pragmatism and to avoid leaving the settlement entirely to the British. And the Austrians supported the sultan and consequently were excluded from the final treaty, thus losing their chance to be one of the protecting powers. After Canning's death in August 1827, British policy toward Greek independence wavered, but the Duke of Wellington, Canning's successor, reluctantly went along in order to counter possible Russian designs in the Near East and particularly in India. The duke consoled himself by reflecting that "the Greek affair . . . has never cost us a shilling, and never shall."[54]

—◦◦◦—

For the next century, Greek society was pulled in many different directions. On one side was the regionalism of the *armatolismos* tradition and the Byzantine absolutism of the Orthodox clergy, and on the other was Western-oriented liberalism, as represented by the merchants, seafarers, and European-trained professionals. The principles of classical Greek antiquity and the intellectual constraints of Byzantium drove the cultural ideology of Greece in the modern era, and eventually, both traditions contributed to a cultural schizophrenia that manifested itself throughout the course of the nineteenth and twentieth centuries. The Greeks were the first subject peoples to sever ties with the Ottoman Empire, but within a few decades, they were followed by the other Balkan nations whose political boundaries were reflections of the European balance of power. For most citizens, however, the Balkan states were perceived as flawed and incomplete as long as their frontiers remained incongruent with local history and geography. The revolutions did not seem to have run their course, and thus they were unable to resolve the internal and external tensions inherent in countries that emerge out of upheaval. And with these states constantly in flux, the bandit leaders and warlords were only too happy to fill the vacuum. During the course of the nineteenth and twentieth centuries, the main challenge for the leaders of the Balkan states was to contain, and eventually control, the power of the regional warlords.

In Greece, the initial attempt to undermine the influence of the chieftains was led by Ioannis Capodistrias. Capodistrias had served as one of the czar's foreign ministers, was a conservative, and had abstained from the conspiracies that plagued many Greek political leaders. For these reasons, the various factions invited him to assume the position of president. His unique background as a Russian minister who had maintained his independence from the Russian court made him acceptable to the British and the French.

Capodistrias was sufficiently astute to realize that a wholesale dismissal of the irregular contingents and the establishment of a standing conscript army in their stead could create a wide range of social and political problems. Disbanding the irregulars without compensation would have exacerbated the problem of banditry by unleashing thousands of unemployed veterans on the countryside. Capodistrias knew that only proper remuneration, preferably in the form of land grants, could transform the former *klephts* and *armatoles* into obedient and responsible citizens by endowing them with a sense of respect for private property and authority.[55] At the time, however, the government lacked the resources to implement such a program. And Capodistrias was hesitant to reorganize the Greek armed forces along conventional lines for another reason: he feared that a conscript army — officered and trained by Western, primarily French, military personnel — could lose its autonomy or become a tool of his numerous political rivals.[56]

In the end, the strategy adopted by Capodistrias aimed to gradually integrate the irregular bands into a semi-regular military force organized according to the provisions of an 1829 law.[57] In practical terms, his policy was based on detaching the irregulars from their chieftains by making the former dependent on the government for pay and sustenance.[58] To undermine the warlords' authority even further, Capodistrias decided that positions of command in the new "army" would be entrusted to chieftains who were less prominent and influential, and thus less of a threat to the government.[59] The more powerful chieftains were either pensioned off or given commissions, which were commensurate with their rank but otherwise meaningless. Another way of undermining their authority was to place them in charge of small units in their respective districts.[60]

Capodistrias' military policy was only partially successful, however; implementation was hampered by a lack of funds, and recruits who joined the new units were frequently disappointed in their expectations of generous and timely pay.[61] In addition, the small size of the force created by Capodistrias — only fourteen battalions, with a total strength of no more than 5,000 of all ranks — meant that a significant number of the irregulars, perhaps as many as 4,000, were left unemployed. These men, most of whom were natives of Ottoman-controlled territories and thus unable to return home, simply reverted to brigandage, aggravating a social problem Capodistrias had wanted to curtail.[62] In the end, the military reorganization had the effect of antagonizing the irregulars and guaranteeing their permanent hostility to the state.[63] Predictably, their discontent boiled over into open revolt, with anti-government uprisings breaking out in May 1831 and July 1832.[64]

Whatever the deficiencies of Capodistrias' scheme, it was still far superior to the measures implemented by his successors after the president's assassination in September 1831. The assassins, predictably, were related to one of the regional warlords, and they killed Capodistrias because he had the leading members of the Mavromichali clan arrested. A year later, a government decree ordered the dismissal from service of all individuals who were not veterans of the War of Liberation. In November 1832, the decree was reinforced by another ruling, which called for the wholesale dismissal of all irregulars.[65] But the irregulars ignored these orders and remained in their encampments in the anticipation that King Otto, whose arrival in Greece was imminent, would reward them for their services.[66]

Otto was the price the Greeks had to pay for independence. The Great Powers would not accept a republic, and there was no Greek royalty to place on the throne. Otto was the second son of King Ludwig of Bavaria, and the protecting powers assumed that a young prince from a minor European monarchy would not give the donor state an undue advantage in Southeastern Europe. In March 1833, the new king was only seventeen, and a regency of Bavarian officials was established to rule in his name. The regents quickly issued a decree stipulating the dismissal of all irregulars who had enlisted after December 1, 1831 — in other words, those who were not veterans of the independence struggle.[67] From that point on, the Greek army was to be made up of the 3,500 Bavarian soldiers who had accompanied Otto to Greece.[68]

The 1833 decree was significant for two reasons. First, by leaving thousands of irregulars with no viable alternative employment except brigandage, it created a problem that was to plague Greece for most of the nineteenth century.[69] Second, it gave rise to feelings of animosity toward the Bavarians, whom the Greeks perceived "more as an occupying force than as part of the Greek army."[70] The hostility toward the Bavarians, and toward the concept of a regular army, intensified when the regency employed its regulars to suppress a peaceful demonstration of unemployed irregulars who had marched to Nauplion, the first capital of modern Greece, to demand bread.[71] Indeed, a negative attitude toward the regular military establishment continued to linger in Greece even after the departure of the Bavarians. For Greeks living in rural districts, the regular army was a severe economic burden. In the 1830s, peasants were required by law to provide food and shelter for troops scouring the countryside in an attempt to crush brigand uprisings.[72] In such circumstances, the majority of Greeks would hardly favor an even larger conventional army.

For years after the dismissal of the irregulars, the Greek government struggled with the problem of finding a lasting solution to brigandage. Soon the leaders of the new state resorted to enlisting the outlaws in the service of irredentism and the fulfillment of the territorial objectives of the so-called Great Idea. There were numerous advantages to using irregular bands for this purpose. First, the regular Greek army was itself inadequate for the task. Its small size restricted it to the role of a domestic security force; the protection of Greece's borders and sovereignty remained the official responsibility of the protecting powers.[73] Second, the protecting powers, whose desire to maintain the status quo was incompatible with Greek irredentist aspirations, were against using the regular army for irredentist purposes. This had the effect of making the use of irregulars to achieve those ends all the more attractive to the Greeks.[74] The upkeep of irregulars was actually more costly for the Greek state than the maintenance of regulars, but some individuals claimed that the expense was still preferable to raising more regular troops because it would help to avert the economic disruption that would undoubtedly occur with the conscription of productive peasants.[75]

For much of the nineteenth century, Greek military doctrine reflected the emphasis on irregular warfare as a vehicle of irredentism. Greece's political and military leaders believed that Hellenic unification could be attained only by means of peasant uprisings fomented in the Greek-speaking provinces of the Ottoman Empire by bands of irregulars who infiltrated from Greece.[76] In a curious reversal of standard military conventions, the regular army was to act merely as an auxiliary to the guerrilla forces operating in Ottoman-held territory. Its assistance was to be sought by the irregulars only as a last resort.[77] The tendency to marginalize the regular military establishment resulted in the progressive downsizing of the Greek army between 1835 and 1862.[78]

This policy provided the model for Greek operations in the irredentist upheavals of 1840, 1866–68, and 1877–78. The strategy adopted by irredentist organizations in all three instances had three stages. First, armed bands, many of them made up of refugees from unredeemed territories and led by local notables, attempted to seize towns near the border. Once the bands were in control of these localities, provisional governments were set up and declared their desire for union with Greece. The Greek regular army was to be partially mobilized to provide moral support, but the insurgents expected little else.[79]

Irredentist and revolutionary circles in other Balkan countries shared the Greek belief in the efficacy of what might be called the strategy of imported revolution. Gregori Rakovski, the nineteenth-century Bulgarian nationalist leader, was convinced that Bulgarian independence could be attained by the infiltration of armed bands, whose goal would be to provide the stimulus and leadership for a mass uprising.[80] Serbian nationalists advocated identical methods to fulfill their own irredentist aspirations.[81]

As appealing as such schemes appeared in theory, however, the complications of executing them demonstrated the misguidance of relying on irregular forces to execute irredentist policies. Time after time, the strategy of imported revolution failed to live up to the expectations of its advocates. In addition, the activities of the regular bands proved difficult to coordinate and control once these units had entered Ottoman territory.[82] With no clearly defined objectives or logistical system, the bands simply wandered aimlessly around the countryside, pillaging and robbing at will.[83] In some cases, as in 1854 and 1866–68 (the Cretan Uprising), many of the would-be liberators were actually criminals who had been released from Greek prisons and rehabilitated as freedom fighters, and thus such behavior was not altogether unexpected.[84] Clearly, however, imported revolution was not a substitute for an efficient regular army.

The creation of such a force was a difficult undertaking for all Balkan states, especially given the strong influence of the tradition of irregular warfare and brigandage. The romantic image of the *klephts, armatoles,* and *hayduks* powerfully held sway over Greek and Serb societies. The darker side of the bandits was easily forgotten, and contemporary writers routinely penned rhapsodies and panegyrics devoted to the mountain warrior. And when it came to military efficiency, the notions of independent action, personal initiative, manliness, courage, and contempt for authority clashed with the concepts of strict discipline and unquestionable obedience, principles that have formed the basis of all modern armies since the eighteenth century.

Ultimately, such strict military standards had to be applied to the Balkan peasants, who inevitably provided the bulk of the manpower for the new armies. Nevertheless, it remained a difficult task to accomplish. Potential recruits were deterred from enlisting by the prospect of having to submit to a Western-style military discipline whose precepts stood in direct opposition to the Balkan tradition of individualism and independence.

The irregulars were another pool of potential recruits, but they were equally reluctant to accept the military, since it ran counter to their conception of the warrior. Irregulars entering Capodistrias' semi-professional army, for example, were required to swear an oath of loyalty whose terms conflicted sharply with the ideas of personal independence that the *klephts* and the *armatoles* so dearly cherished. The oath forced the soldiers to obey commands, refrain from theft and murder, submit to limitations of movement between military camps, and refrain from intimidating civilians.[85] But obeying such regulations nullified all the advantages of being a mountain warrior.

Flagrant disregard of military discipline was also evident in Serbia. The peasant soldiers of the national militia were notorious for their inability to accept basic army regulations. Russian and Prussian observers who visited Serbia in 1863 and 1866, respectively, reported that obedience to commands was far from an established standard among the Serbs.[86] Officers were frequently compelled to resort to corporal punishment to accomplish their orders.[87] Common soldiers regarded typical training activities such as drill and target practice as a phenomenal waste of time that kept them away from the cultivation of their fields.[88]

The soldiers' reluctance to abide by the rules of military discipline was in large measure responsible for Serbia's disastrous showing in the ill-conceived war against the Ottoman Empire in 1876. Conventionally accepted tactics proved next to impossible to implement because of the soldiers' aversion to frontal attacks against enemy positions, reluctance to fight from static field fortifications, and preference for guerrilla-style ambushes.[89] Unauthorized retreats, false alarms, self-inflicted wounds, and desertions by individuals and even entire units were common occurrences. Serbian troops were particularly susceptible to outbreaks of panic, and even such trivial events as the sound of Ottoman artillery or the soldiers' inability to clear stoppages from their rifles were capable of producing mass hysteria.[90] Camp discipline was dismal, and soldiers could not be prevented from bringing their relatives and household chattel along on the campaign. The presence of so many non-combatants and so much impedimenta only compounded the panic that ensued when Serb forces were thrown on the defensive and had to retreat.[91]

As deeply entrenched in the Greek and Serbian national consciousness as the legacy of the Balkan mountain warrior was, it was not strong enough to resist the calls for military reform that began to be heard in both countries in the second half of the nineteenth century. Repeated military setbacks undermined the confidence that the leaders professed to have in the military effectiveness of irregular forces. By the end of the century, both countries had abandoned their policies of relying on irregular military organizations and gradually proceeded to establish regular armies that proved their worth in the Balkan wars of 1912–13. Nevertheless, the irregulars were not dispensed with entirely. Indeed, irregular warfare experienced a revival during the many-sided struggle for Macedonia at the turn of the century. In this contest, guerrilla-type warfare proved to be as important as it had been during the Greek and Serbian liberation struggles at the beginning of the nineteenth century.

———

What was to become known as the Macedonian Struggle or the Macedonian Question was rooted in the diplomatic arrangements that collectively settled the Great Eastern Crisis of 1876–78. Macedonia was not only the primary target of Greek, Serbian, and Bulgarian expansionism, but also a source of considerable consternation for the Great Powers. Then the Treaties of Berlin and Constantinople, which were concluded in 1878 and 1881, respectively, dramatically altered the geopolitical situation in the Balkans. The redistribution of Ottoman territory left Greece and Serbia in possession of areas that bordered the three Ottoman provinces that made up Macedonia. For the next four decades, Greek and Serb irredentists focused considerable energy on attempts to acquire the region for their respective states. This potentially explosive situation was compounded by the creation of an autonomous Bulgaria. When the Great Powers decided to revise the Treaty of San Stefano and exclude Macedonia from the new state, Bulgarian nationalist and irredentist circles in Sofia became determined to overturn the provisions and fulfill their dream of a Greater Bulgaria. It was not long before Bulgaria's aggressive designs on Macedonia came into conflict with Greek and Serbian aspirations in the same region, thus laying the foundations for a protracted and violent conflict.[92]

The first phase of the struggle, from the late 1870s to the mid-1890s, was relatively mild, compared to what would follow. Since Macedonia's population was largely defined by religious affiliation, rather than ethnicity, the three states interested in the region initially focused their attention on winning the "hearts and minds" of the locals through a vigorous nationalist propaganda campaign. By 1895, hundreds of Greek, Serbian, and Bulgarian schools, funded by irredentist associations such as the Bulgarian National Committee, the Greek Association of Hellenistic Letters, and the Serbian Society of Saint Sava, had been set up in Macedonia. These schools aggressively competed with one another in an effort to convert their pupils to the national causes of one of the three countries.[93] Considerable amounts of propaganda also emanated from the consulates that the three governments had established in Macedonia's major cities in the 1880s.[94]

The Macedonian Struggle was transformed in 1893, however, when a group of young intellectuals established the Internal Macedonian Revolutionary Organization (IMRO) in Thessaloniki. The organization's leaders rejected the Greek, Serb, and Bulgarian irredentist claims, and countered them with a vision of an autonomous Macedonia within the Ottoman Empire.[95] The IMRO then dedicated itself to creating conditions that would compel the Ottoman government to enact the provisions of article 23 of the Treaty of Berlin, which obliged the Porte to implement a series of internal administrative and electoral reforms, as well as a degree of self-government, in its European provinces.

Violence and terrorism were central to the IMRO's ideology. The leaders of the movement were convinced that the Ottoman government would implement article 23 only if pressured to do so by the Great Powers. In order to attract the attention of the Europeans and convince them to intervene with the Sublime Porte, the IMRO decided to unleash a campaign of revolutionary terror that would combine urban terrorist activity with a peasant-based uprising in the countryside. This strategy, the leaders of the IMRO believed, would reduce Macedonia to a state of utter political, economic, and social chaos, rendering the region unsafe for foreign investment and provoking Ottoman reprisals against the local population. They hoped that these developments would in turn thrust Macedonia to the forefront of the international agenda and force the Ottomans to grant the region the autonomy demanded by the revolutionaries.[96]

The IMRO leaders entrusted the organization's revolutionary program to its paramilitary wing, which was composed of armed units known as *chetas*. The tactics and ethos of these groups reflected the enduring Balkan tradition of guerrilla warfare. Each *cheta* unit ranged from fifteen to fifty men, known as *chetniks, komitas,* or *komitadjis* (men of the committee).[97] They were commanded by a *voivoda,* to whom they owed absolute obedience. Normally, the *voivodas* were veteran brigands or teachers who provided the IMRO with its intellectual leadership.[98] The organization also established a number of schools to train potential *voivodas.* The first of these was organized by Georgi Ivanov, a former sergeant major in the Bulgarian army and a veteran of the Serbo-Bulgarian War of 1885.[99] Under the name Marko Lerinski, Ivanov acquired a reputation for professionalism and effective leadership. In 1900 or 1901, he organized a model *cheta* that provided leadership training for promising *chetniks* and served as an example for other IMRO training schools.[100]

The *chetas* conformed strictly to the tactics and standards of irregular warfare. Their most important asset was mobility; in order to elude the authorities, each unit had to remain on the move.[101] They normally traveled at night and hid during the day. Typically, the *cheta* band was led by a scout, who was followed by the *voivoda* and then the main body of the band. Another scout guarded the rear of the column. The *chetniks* themselves marched in single file, separated by no less than four paces. They carried their rifles in their hands, rather than slung over the shoulder. Absolute silence was observed — even coughing was suppressed. Every hour or two the band rested, but the *chetniks* were not allowed to bunch together. Modern-day armies still use similar procedures to govern the conduct of infantry patrols and reconnaissance units.

According to regulations written around 1898 by Gotse Delchev, the IMRO's inspector of the *chetas*, the primary duties of the bands were to recruit new members and disseminate propaganda.[102] However, the *chetas* were also responsible for a variety of other tasks, including training peasants and demolishing bridges, roads, and telegraph lines. In addition, the *chetas* acted as terror squads, assassinating Ottoman officials and traitors, and kidnapping foreigners for ransoms that could be used by the IMRO to purchase weapons.

The *chetas* fought against Ottoman security forces, as well as bands sent into Macedonia by Serb and Greek irredentist societies.[103] They also had to contend with the delicate problem of other *chetas* operating on behalf of the Bulgarian Supreme Committee — an organization that was established in 1894 by Macedonian expatriates living in Sofia and that was dedicated to the goal of incorporating Macedonia into Bulgaria. Relations between the IMRO and the Supremists fluctuated between co-operation and outright hostility. Ultimately, they added yet another layer of complexity to the Macedonian problem.[104]

By 1903, the Supremists were able to convince the reluctant IMRO leaders to launch the long-awaited rebellion.[105] The Illinden Uprising began in August of the same year, and the Ottoman government quickly deployed 175,000 soldiers in an effort to crush it.[106] The insurgency exposed the limits of the military effectiveness of the *chetas*. As long as the bands restricted their activities to cutting communications, fighting small-scale engagements against isolated Ottoman units, and burning Muslim settlements and massacring their populations, they were able to survive to fight another day. However, as soon as they challenged the Ottoman forces in conventional combat, as was the case at Krushevo in August 1903, defeat was the inevitable result.[107]

By late October 1903, the uprising had been brutally suppressed by the Ottoman security forces, and the IMRO had lost much of its strength.[108] But the revolt did at least attract the Great Powers to the issue of Macedonia. Consequently, the Ottoman government was forced to agree to the implementation of reforms specified in the Muerzsteg Agreement, which was concluded between Austria-Hungary and Russia on September 30, 1903. Among other things, the reforms called for the reorganization of the Ottoman gendarmerie under the guidance of foreign military and police personnel.[109]

Unfortunately, this provision for what was essentially the first "peacekeeping" operation in history did not substantially contribute to stability and order in Macedonia. On the contrary, the weakening of the IMRO escalated the guerrilla war being waged in the region among the contending countries. Beginning in early 1904, Greek, Serb, Bulgarian, and even Romanian bands poured into Macedonia to take advantage of the IMRO's decline. By 1907, as many as 110 Bulgarian, 80 Greek, 30 Serbian, and 8 Romanian bands were operating in the region, fighting each other and the Ottomans in an effort to uphold their claims to the area.[110]

In the end, the Macedonian Question found resolution only in the course of the two Balkan wars of 1912 and 1913. In these conflicts, irregular contingents played only a limited role. Bulgarian and Macedonian irregulars, for example, were employed for intelligence-gathering activities and to harass the Ottoman armies' lines of communication. They were organized into twelve battalions of approximately 14,700 men.[111] During the First World War, the stalemate that characterized the Balkan front for most of the conflict precluded the use of irregular forces by either side. The only exception was a small contingent of Albanians used by the Allies for a brief period in the autumn of 1917. This unit operated with moderate success in the area around Lake Ohrid,[112] but it had ceased to exist by the middle of 1918.[113]

Although irregular warfare did not have a significant impact on the course of the Great War in the Balkans, it occupied a central place in the Second World War. The tactics, ethos, and even the physical appearance of members of the resistance movements that sprang up in Greece and Yugoslavia attested to the endurance of this Balkan military tradition. Today, the appeal of that tradition appears to be as strong as ever. Indeed, given events in the region in the 1990s, the allure of the brigand is unlikely to diminish. On the contrary, it will probably gain in strength, reinforced by the legends and myths that Balkan nationalists are probably already creating. The *klephts* and the *hayduks* of another era were reinvented as the paramilitaries of the former Yugoslavia, a sign that not all of the Balkan states have yet completed the cycle of revolution.

6

INTRACTABLE BOUNDARIES:
BALKAN BATTLEFIELDS

<del>~~⟋⟍⟋~~</del>

*The Balkans are not worth the bones
of a single Pomeranian grenadier.*

— OTTO VON BISMARCK

The Balkan states were formed
through compromises among the European powers, with little regard
for the actual or perceived national boundaries of these new countries. During the course of the nineteenth century, the Great Powers
followed a diplomatic minuet that first ignored each Balkan uprising,
then attempted to enforce a settlement between the sultan and the
rebels, and finally struck a deal that led to the creation of a new trun-
cated state.

The Balkan conundrum, as understood in the late nineteenth
century, was intertwined with the demise of the Ottoman Empire.
The fate of the "sick man" of Europe, as the Great Powers described
the Ottoman regime, was something the Europeans preferred not to
deal with. And this made the persistent independence demands of
the Balkan communities unwelcome and a nuisance. Only when the
situation brought Europe itself to the brink of war would the powers
reluctantly intervene, severing another chunk of Ottoman territory

while taking care not to further destabilize the empire. Accordingly, the newly created Balkan states were constituted in such a way as not to threaten the delicate balance of power in the Near East.

The Congress of Berlin in 1878 underscored this policy, and also exposed the triumphs and limitations of European diplomacy. Metternich's concert of Europe had disintegrated during the Crimean War and had been replaced by a patchwork of shifting alliances. Indeed, for the European powers, nationalism became a force that could be harnessed to serve the interests of the state. By the 1870s, not even the absolute czars of Russia could afford to ignore popular sentiment. During the final thirty years of the nineteenth century, each of the Great Powers would manipulate public opinion on occasion, evidence that government had become increasingly susceptible to popular sensitivities with respect to foreign policy. Nowhere was this more obvious — and potentially more dangerous — for the Europeans than in the Near East.

The ultimate goal of British policy on the Ottoman Empire in the nineteenth century was to prevent the Russians from controlling the Straits. In the post–Crimean War period, following the destruction of the Russian fleet, British interests were focused on the Suez Canal. With its construction in 1869, the canal turned the Mediterranean into a staging area for the protection of British assets in Asia. Containment of Russia, as essential as it was in Southeastern Europe, was critical in Central Asia, where the Great Game was waged with deadly earnestness.

The French, after their defeat in the Franco-Prussian War, were more consumed with reacquiring status and preparing for a future Franco-German conflict than they were with the Near East. Austria-Hungary, meanwhile, resisted any change that threatened to ignite nationalist feelings among its multicultural subjects, many of whom were linked by religious or ethnic ties to the sultan's subjects in Southeastern Europe. It therefore counted on the Ottomans to keep these Balkan ethnic groups under control, and to forestall the nightmare of new ethnic states on its eastern frontier. The Russians, for their part, were still recovering from the Crimean War and desperately needed to end their isolation from the Great Powers. In practical terms, this meant ignoring the Balkan Slavs and Christians, and securing the alliance of one or more of the Great Powers.

Effectively, the Balkan communities under Ottoman rule received support for their struggles for emancipation only when it was in the strategic interests of the Europeans, which invariably it was. The Greek War of Liberation, for example, was a near-death experience for the Ottoman Empire. But in the end, the Great Powers decided to limit the size of the new Greek state so that it could not pose a serious threat to the sultan's European domains. By compromising on the frontiers of the Greek state, they were able to suspend the Eastern Question for a generation. They could not put the genie back in the bottle, however. The Greek experience served as an example to the other Balkan peoples, and after 1870 new waves of national determination created more Balkan countries.

These new states were generally not viable economically or sociologically, and as soon as circumstances permitted, each one generated a shopping list of irredentist claims against both its neighbors and the Ottomans. The Romanians desired Transylvania; the Serbs wanted Kosovo, Bosnia-Herzegovina, Slovenia, and Croatia; the Greeks dreamed of securing Constantinople, Asia Minor, the Aegean Islands, Crete, and Macedonia; and the Bulgarians envisioned an outlet to the Aegean through the acquisition of Macedonia. In reality, the shopping list was a wish list that held few prospects of fulfillment unless a contender could secure an alliance with one or more of the Great Powers. The only asset each of the Balkan states could offer to potential allies was strategic location, however, and even this did not become essential to the Europeans until the end of the nineteenth century. Bulgaria was a case in point.

Bulgaria's proximity to Constantinople and the Straits is as much of a concern to Russia today as it was in the nineteenth century. But remarkably, Russia did not express an active diplomatic interest in Bulgaria until very late in that century. Between the last decade of the eighteenth century and the Great Eastern Crisis of the 1870s, the Danubian principalities, Serbia, and Greece were the focus of Russian diplomatic efforts in Southeastern Europe. Later, Britain and France overshadowed Russia's influence in Greece and Serbia, and the Russians replaced their policy of pan-Orthodoxy with one of pan-Slavism.

Bulgarian national consciousness was slow to develop, especially in comparison with Serbian, Greek, and Romanian nationalism. This might have been because Bulgaria was the Balkan province closest to the Ottoman imperial capital, and thus was easily susceptible to the administrative and political centralization that the Sublime Porte implemented after the first wave of nationalist uprisings in Serbia and Greece.[1] At the same time, Greek control over Bulgaria's ecclesiastical hierarchy and its cultural, educational, and economic institutions hindered the emergence of an indigenous intellectual and political elite with ties to the West.[2]

Russian foreign policy also inadvertently delayed the emergence of a Bulgarian liberation movement. Despite the numerous wars it had waged against the Porte in the second half of the nineteenth century, Russia attempted to maintain good relations with the Ottoman Empire, as well as with Britain and Austria-Hungary. Unfortunately, the Russians had suffered a serious military defeat in the Crimean War, and that defeat had left them diplomatically isolated. Russian policy in the aftermath of the conflict, therefore, was to overcome that isolation. But the price of a Europe-first policy was little or no support for Balkan independence struggles.[3] In fact, after Russia's defeat in the Crimean War, the new foreign minister, Alexander Mikhailovich Gorchakov, adopted the notion of retrenchment as the cornerstone of his policy. This was a sign that he recognized the need to relinquish, at least temporarily, an aggressive foreign policy and redirect Russia's resources and energies toward domestic reforms.[4] One and a half centuries later, the Russians faced the same dilemma in the Balkans, and once again they placed their interests in Southeastern Europe on hold while they attempted to deal with economic and political chaos at home.

In the post–Crimean War period, the idea of pan-Slavism began to take root among Russian intellectuals, politicians, and diplomats. In Bulgaria, Russian consular officials serving in the Balkans (regardless of official policy) fraternized with the small groups of revolutionaries and openly sympathized with them over the failed uprisings in Nis (1841) and Vidin (1850).[5] For the next two decades, however, official Russian policy toward Bulgaria was to discourage any drive for independence. During the 1860s and 1870s, the Russian government went so far as to pressure Romanian authorities not to harbor Bulgarian revolutionary *chetas* that were using their territory as a base from which to mount raids across the Danube and incite insurrection in Bulgaria.[6] Russia continued to follow this policy as late as the Bulgarian rebellion of 1876.

This Russian reluctance to actively support Bulgarian nationalism was reinforced by the fact that most Bulgarian revolutionary cadres in the mid-1800s were led by members of the "young" (or radical) faction. Some of these leaders, such as Khristo Botev and Stephen Stambulov, advocated leftist and nihilist ideas that they had acquired as students in Russia.[7] This hardly endeared the Bulgarian nationalists to the czar and his ministers, and undoubtedly contributed to the lukewarm policies of the Russian government toward the revolutionary movement in its early stages. Ultimately, the Russian government was not willing to support any Balkan liberation movement that it could not control.[8]

All this changed with the Great Eastern Crisis, which confounded European relations for the rest of the century and prepared the ground for the tragedies that have dogged the region, with brief respites, ever since. The Great Eastern Crisis took place because Ottoman decay was irreversible, especially after the empire had become hostage to European financial houses. The empire's voodoo economics did not follow any acceptable standard, and eventually became the cancer that ate away at the Ottoman system. In less than two decades, the Sublime Porte was so hopelessly indebted to French, British, and Austrian financial institutions that it was forced to declare de facto bankruptcy in 1875.[9] Between 1853 and 1875, the Ottoman Empire borrowed close to 200 million pounds, a debt that by 1875 required 43.9 percent of the empire's revenues to service.[10] All of these loans were squandered, and new loans were acquired to pay the interest on the debt. But these funds were also poorly managed, leaving the "sick man" of Europe on the brink of financial suicide.

These disastrous fiscal policies left the provincial subjects of the sultan at the mercy of tax collectors who resorted to extreme measures, such as seizing produce in the place of currency, whenever they were unable to settle up with the overburdened farmers. These high-handed policies, combined with crop failures, resulted in famine in the cities and towns, which further contributed to the erosion of the sultan's rule. Ironically, this was also a period of attempts at reform and modernization, a period that was supposed to establish equality between the Muslims and Christians of the empire, and through this define a secularized Ottoman identity to counter the threat of nationalism. But these efforts caused only greater disruption in the provinces. Few Muslim communities were willing to relinquish their superior status in the empire, and the provincial Ottoman elites resented any attempts to diminish their political prerogatives. The results were catastrophic. The Muslims in Herzegovina and Bosnia resisted these changes, and the Porte was forced to employ troops to overcome opposition. Ottoman control over these provinces weakened considerably, while the provinces themselves were left devastated by the fighting. At the same time, the economic collapse of the empire forced the sultan to increase taxes, which caused more misery in the provinces and spread the contagion of rebellion among the peasants.

After a decade of widespread unrest and intermittent fighting, the Christian peasants in Herzegovina rebelled in 1875, followed shortly by the peasants in Bosnia. This set in motion the first act of the Great Eastern Crisis. None of the European powers was inclined to intervene, and all preferred to maintain the status quo in the Balkans. Unfortunately for them, the rebellions in Bosnia-Herzegovina were followed by uprisings in Bulgaria, Serbia, and Montenegro. "Once the Slavs were astir," wrote A. J. P. Taylor in *The Struggle for Mastery in Europe*, "the Russian Government dared not let them fail; Austria-Hungary dared not let them succeed."[11]

France, as the primary lender, had a vested interest in preserving the Ottoman Empire, and both it and Britain got involved in the Balkan crisis to protect their interests in the Near East. The Italians also joined; they were willing to fight any battle and support any cause so long as Italy could be treated as a Great Power. The primary catalyst for the intervention of the Great Powers was the massacre of Bulgarians by Ottoman irregular troops, who spent more time slaughtering innocent civilians than actually fighting the revolutionaries. Although the Bulgarian uprising was crushed in a month, stories of mass killings and torture found their way into countless newspaper descriptions of the rebellion. Such brutal treatment was not exclusive to the Ottomans, of course; the Bulgarian revolutionaries also contributed to the atrocities, albeit on a smaller scale. The European press, however, focused only on the activities of the Turks, which had considerable impact on public opinion and ultimately could not be ignored by the European governments. In effect, the atrocities committed by the Turkish irregulars in Bulgaria, not for the last time, internationalized the crisis and created the conditions for intervention.

Russian diplomatic officials posted in both the Balkans and the Ottoman Empire exploited this barbarism by reporting, in considerable detail, the Ottoman massacres in Bulgaria. Yet the Russian government attempted to cling to the status quo — even after the diplomats pleaded that the killings were not legitimate reprisals against rebels, but crimes inflicted on innocent Bulgarians who had not participated in the uprising. Both Naidin Gerov, the Bulgarian-born Russian vice-consul in Plodiv, and Nicholas Pavlovich Ignatiev, the Russian ambassador in Constantinople, stated in their reports that the events in Bulgaria did not represent an organized revolution. Instead, the two diplomats claimed that the unrest had been incited by the Ottomans as an excuse to consolidate their control over the province.[12] This only caused further outrage and indignation among Russia's pan-Slavic circles, and contributed to the Russian government's decision to declare war on the Ottoman Empire in April 1877.

Fundamentally, Russia's reluctance to support the Bulgarians was rooted in its determination to maintain European alliances. This was compounded by the fact that Southeastern Europe was the weak link in the *Dreikaiserbund* (the Three Emperors' League), a tenuous diplomatic understanding among the rulers of imperial Germany, Austria-Hungary, and Russia between 1872 and 1873.[13] The Russian foreign ministry feared that the Three Emperors' League could collapse over misunderstandings about the Balkans between Russia and the Dual Monarchy (Austria-Hungary), leaving Russia in isolation.[14] That is why Gorchakov, the foreign minister, and his Austro-Hungarian counterpart, Julius Andrássy, attempted to persuade the sultan to implement reforms that would negate foreign intervention.[15]

The Ottoman promises, however, amounted to nothing, and the unrest in the empire's European provinces escalated. By spring 1876, 25,000 men from Serbia and Montenegro were waging a guerrilla war with 30,000 Ottoman troops against a backdrop of atrocities and counter-atrocities on both sides. Each bloody report of the fighting alerted the Russian public to the plight of the Slavs in the Balkans, and the influential pan-Slavic movement agitated for Russian intervention. Czar Alexander could not continue to ignore the situation in the Balkans. At the same time, the Russians could not organize a European coalition against the Ottomans, which left them with only one option: a new arrangement that offered Balkan spoils to Austria-Hungary.[16]

The Reichstadt Agreement, concluded between Russia and the Dual Monarchy in July 1876, had effectively committed Russia to coordinating its Balkan policy with that of its *Dreikaiserbund* partner. The treaty stipulated that in case of an Ottoman defeat in the Balkans, Russia could recover part of Bessarabia and Austria-Hungary could annex some or all of Bosnia. It further stipulated that if Serbia and Montenegro were defeated by the Ottomans, Southeastern Europe was to return to the status quo ante. If the Serbs proved victorious, however, then Russia and Austria-Hungary reserved the right to jointly sanction any territorial changes in the region.[17] Only if the Ottoman Empire collapsed entirely would the Russians consider the establishment of an autonomous Bulgaria. And even in that eventuality, Gorchakov and Andrássy agreed that the new entity would not constitute a large Slavic state in the Balkans. To maintain the balance of power, and imperial solidarity, Bulgaria's territorial boundaries would have to be limited, and would exclude Rumelia or any of the other areas that Bulgarian nationalists had claimed as part of their historical birthright.[18]

Unfortunately, this imperial camaraderie was not to last forever. Russia's restrained attitude toward Bulgaria had changed significantly by the time the Great Powers organized the Constantinople Conference of Ambassadors in December 1876. This conference was meant to diffuse tensions in the Balkans following the defeat of Serbia and Montenegro by the Ottomans. Ignatiev, the Russian delegate, demanded the creation of a greater Bulgaria, including Dobruja, Rumelia, most of Macedonia, and the districts around Nis and Kastoria. In addition, he suggested that a Russian army occupy Bulgaria until an administrative infrastructure was set up in the new state.[19] Lord Salisbury, the head of the British delegation, was willing to support Ignatiev if he agreed to seek modest changes. So Ignatiev proposed dividing Bulgaria into an eastern and a western half, with a

total area less than that of the greater Bulgaria he originally suggested. Furthermore, neither of the two regions was to have an outlet
to the Aegean.[20] The Ottomans, however, assumed that they could
count on British support, and rejected the sweeping reforms proposed by the Great Powers in Constantinople.

In the end, Russia's new Bulgaria policy emerged as one element
in a much greater diplomatic tour de force. While the Constantinople
Conference was still in session, the Russians concluded the Budapest
Convention with Austria-Hungary. The Budapest Convention was
designed to secure Austro-Hungarian consent to Russia's military
intervention against the Ottoman Empire. The terms of the convention stipulated that the Dual Monarchy would maintain benevolent
neutrality in case of a Russo-Ottoman war, and in return the Austrians
could occupy Bosnia-Herzegovina at a time of their own choosing.
Significantly, the convention made no mention of the fate of the
Bulgarian lands, aside from a provision that stated that no large Slav
state was to be established in the Balkans after a Russian victory.[21] The
convention's ambiguity toward Bulgaria and Bosnia-Herzegovina was
the price Russia had to pay to avoid resuscitating the anti-Russian coalition of the Crimean War. In fact, the Budapest and Constantinople
conventions irrevocably dissolved the Crimean coalition. The atrocities committed by the Ottomans made it impossible for the British to
aid them; the French were still weak after their defeat by Prussia; and
the new German Empire had little interest in the Balkans.[22]

Consequently, the outbreak of the Russo-Ottoman War in April
1877 paved the way for Russian intervention in Bulgaria and the
Balkans. In the initial stages of the conflict, Gorchakov displayed
every intention of conforming to the agreements between Russia and
the other Great Powers interested in the Balkans, especially Austria-
Hungary. He feared that a long war to secure more territory for a new
Bulgarian state was dangerous because it increased the potential for
foreign intervention and domestic revolutionary unrest in Russia.[23]

These relatively limited objectives were modified as the war
dragged on into the summer of 1877, however. Pressure from pan-
Slavic lobby groups, combined with the military's domination of
Russia's foreign policy, war aims, and peace terms, resulted in a
demand for the establishment of a greater Bulgaria. (This, in fact,
became the principal condition of Russia's postwar settlement with

the Ottoman Empire at San Stefano in March 1878.[24] The new Bulgarian state would consist of the territories that corresponded roughly with those first proposed by Ignatiev at the Constantinople Conference. In addition, Russian government officials were to assist in the organization of the new country's administration, and the Russian army was to continue to occupy Bulgaria for a period of two years.[25])

As the Russo-Ottoman War went on, the czar's armies had some success, and by June it appeared that the Russians would conquer all of the Ottoman territories in Europe. Then the course of events dramatically shifted. The Ottoman fortress of Plevna blocked the Russian drive to the south and prevented the capture of Constantinople. According to Taylor, "Most battles confirm the way that things are going already; Plevna is one of the few engagements which changed the course of history."[26] The Russians finally took the fortress in December, but by then the European powers had been able to check the Russian momentum, and eventually they were able to force an armistice. It is unlikely that the Ottoman Empire would have survived in Europe or Asia Minor had the Russians crowned their victory with the conquest of Constantinople. Still, the victory did give them a predominant position in Bulgaria and a strong foothold in the Balkans. Even the continued existence of the Ottoman Empire, at least for a short time, was at the mercy of Russian foreign policy.

Although the Ottomans grudgingly signed the San Stefano agreement, it caused a formidable backlash in Europe and a diplomatic crisis. The new territorial order in the Balkans was particularly troubling for Austria-Hungary because it contravened earlier Russo-Austrian agreements stipulating that no large Slav state was to be created in the Balkans.[27] Britain, for its part, feared that Bulgaria would be little more than a Russian pawn in the region, and that it would give the Russians access to the Mediterranean and control of Southeastern Europe.[28] Opposition was equally strong from the other Balkan states. By insisting on the creation of a greater Bulgaria, Russia had effectively alienated Greece and Serbia. The Greeks resented the incorporation into Bulgaria of territories that were historically theirs.[29] The Serbs, for their part, were just as disappointed with Russia's decision to give Bulgaria areas conquered by Serbian troops during that country's second war with the Ottoman Empire in 1877–78.[30]

But Russia's hegemony in the Balkans was shortly diminished by the Congress of Berlin, which averted a European war by altering the provisions of the Treaty of San Stefano. The congress itself was mainly ceremonial, since most of the agreements finalized in Berlin had been worked out between the Great Powers in advance. Yet representatives from the existing Balkan states, as well as from states in the process of being created, scurried to Berlin in hopes of gaining additional territory. The meetings, however, turned out to be little more than an opportunity to grandstand and humiliate the smaller states. The Serbs' request to present their demands was rejected; they were permitted to submit only a written document, which the delegates were free to ignore. The Albanians failed to make any impression at all, while the Greeks, who were admitted to the congress, literally put some of the delegates to sleep. According to Count Corti, one of the Italian delegates, even Salisbury, Beaconsfield, and Waddington, Greece's principal supporters, "slept the sleep of the just."[31] Although one of the objectives was to maintain the Ottoman Empire, the Great Powers did grant official recognition to Serbia, Montenegro, and Romania. This, however, did not prevent them from awarding Bessarabia, which was part of Romania, to Russia.

Bulgaria was divided into three sections — the area north of the Balkan range but including Sofia was to be an autonomous Bulgarian principality, the province of Eastern Rumelia was to remain under Ottoman suzerainty, and Macedonia was to be returned to the Ottoman Empire.[32] In other words, the Bulgarians got half of the territory they claimed. The Treaty of Berlin allowed Russia to maintain its influence in Bulgaria, but that was feeble compensation for the loss of Serbian, Greek, and Romanian sympathy, and a return to isolation.[33]

Even Russia's influence in Bulgaria quickly eroded. Friction with its Balkan protégé began to arise after Alexander of Battenberg was selected to be Bulgaria's ruler. Alexander, who had served with the Russian army against the Ottomans in the war of 1877–78, held the Russians in low esteem because of their inefficient conduct during that war.[34] The feeling was mutual. The Russians resented Alexander and his Bulgarian allies because the young ruler stubbornly placed Bulgaria's interests ahead of Russia's. In 1885, Alexander further exasperated the Russians by unilaterally reuniting Eastern Rumelia with Bulgaria, thus cheating Czar Alexander III of the same prize. To make matters worse, the Great Powers confirmed the new territorial arrangement. In a reversal of roles, the Russians appealed to the international community to enforce the Berlin treaty for the sake of the Ottoman Empire. Although Germany and Austria-Hungary, Russia's *Dreikaiserbund* partners, backed Russia's position, the British endorsed the unification.[35] In fact, the British now believed that a large Bulgaria, made possible through the union of Bulgaria and Rumelia under Alexander of Battenberg, was the way to go. They were convinced that a greater Bulgaria with an anti-Russian prince on the throne would be an effective barrier against future Russian designs on Constantinople and the Straits.[36] The Russians were stymied, and the Great Powers accepted the new union. Their rationale seemed to be that because it was not a Russian initiative, it therefore was in keeping with the aims of the Berlin set-tlement (that is, maintaining the status quo in the Near East). Clearly, change was acceptable as long as the Ottoman Empire sur-vived and Russian ambitions were checked.

This state of affairs might have suited the Europeans, but for the Balkans the Congress of Berlin was a harbinger of future conflict. The agreements made before and during the final settlement in the German capital reconfigured the Balkans in such a way as to guar-antee both another war in the region and friction between the Great Powers. Bosnia and Herzegovina were handed over to Austria-Hungary as part of Britain's maneuverings to keep the Russians away from the Straits and Constantinople.[37] The British had secured the agreement of the Germans and the Austro-Hungarians for a larger Bulgaria, and in exchange they supported the Austrian claim to Bosnia. At the same time, the British took over Cyprus from the Ottomans, thus planting the seeds for future Greco-Turkish conflicts in the Aegean. They justified their occupation of the island by arguing it was part of their "onerous obligation of a defensive alliance with Turkey."[38] With one stroke of a pen, the Great Powers in Berlin inad-vertently guaranteed that Southeastern Europe would repeat the Great Eastern Crisis in almost every subsequent generation.

—⚬⚬⚬—

In essence, the Berlin settlement addressed the security concerns of Western Europe and (indirectly) Central Asia; the interests of the

Balkan states, if considered at all, were secondary. The Great Powers shuffled land and peoples in the region with little regard for the consequences. In Bismarck's words, "The borders of Montenegro and Serbia, and places of which no one ever heard before,"[39] were not relevant. The overlapping and contradictory national territories of the emerging Balkan states were not a consideration. Remarkably, the disposition of Macedonia, perhaps the one issue that more than any other doomed the region to a future of conflict, was not even taken up seriously at the Congress of Berlin. The Great Powers were satisfied to return Macedonia to the Ottoman Empire and then forget about it. Yet Macedonia was a microcosm of the Balkans, a mosaic of Muslim, Greek, Bulgarian, Serb, Albanian, Vlach, Jewish, and Gypsy communities. And it sat at the crossroads of east and west, north and south. Thessaloniki was not only the largest city in the Ottoman province, but also the largest port in Southeastern Europe. In all, Macedonia was a strategic hub crucial to Greece, Bulgaria, Serbia, and the Ottoman Empire. Indeed, most of the Balkan states wanted to acquire this territory at almost at any cost. For the Europeans, meanwhile, Macedonia in the late nineteenth and early twentieth centuries was part of the overall Ottoman problem, a potential flashpoint for Bulgarian, Albanian, Greek, or Turkish aggression.

Indeed, even before the ink was dry on the Berlin treaty, the competition for territory dominated the interstate relations of the Balkan nations. The Albanians were the first to react to the changes. Abandoned by the Ottomans and ignored by the Congress of Berlin, the Albanians opted to defend those of their lands awarded to Montenegro by the Great Powers. From 1878 until 1881, the Albanians fought against a coalition of Montenegrin, Serb, and Ottoman forces. The Ottomans, pressured by the Great Powers to enforce the Berlin agreement, took no pleasure in killing their former subjects. Indeed in July, the Austro-Hungarians had to deploy more than a quarter of a million troops to occupy the former Ottoman province. Sarajevo exploded in violence as the Muslims tried to deny the city to the Dual Monarchy. In some parts of Bosnia, meanwhile, the Muslim resisters were joined by Serbs who opposed the Austro-Hungarian occupation. Fighting continued until October 1878, when the Austrians managed to subdue the rebels.

But resistance to foreign rule had not been quashed in either Bosnia or Albania. Instead, the struggle for independence transformed itself, alternating between guerrilla war in the mountains and sabotage and subversion in the cities. These tactics of terror achieved their fullest expression in Macedonia, which over the next thirty years was to be the target of political intrigues directed from the various Balkan capitals. The shift from conventional battles to irregular warfare, and thus the absence of large military establishments, also offered the Balkan states an opportunity to pursue their irredentist policies.

In the autumn of 1885, Serbia invaded Bulgaria, ostensibly because the Serbs had not been compensated for Eastern Rumelia. The two underlying objectives of the war, however, were to give Serbia an advantageous position from which to claim Macedonia, and to prevent Bulgaria from incorporating the former Ottoman province itself. In less than one week, the Serbian army was defeated and fell back across the Bulgarian frontier. Serbia was saved only by the intervention of Austria-Hungary, which threatened war unless the Bulgarian forces withdrew from Serbian territory. With this first round of the competition for territorial space going to Bulgaria, the Serbs switched tactics and began sending guerrilla bands into Macedonia.

In the aftermath of the Congress of Berlin, Russia, deprived of a firm foothold in Southeastern Europe, had temporarily shifted the focus of its foreign policy toward Central Asia and the Far East.[40] But the Russians avoided total isolation in Europe by joining the reconstituted Three Emperors' League in 1881. In May 1897, under the terms of the Goluchowski-Murayev Agreement, Russia and Austria-Hungary agreed to maintain the status quo in the Balkans, and to co-operate in preventing any other power from acquiring territory in the region.

With the Russian-Austrian rivalry in the Balkans temporarily suspended, the rulers of the Dual Monarchy could focus on solving their domestic problems, while Russia was free to pursue its goals in the Far East.[41] Both powers demonstrated their desire to avoid complications in the Balkans by dealing with the Macedonian Question through the Muerzsteg Agreement, which aimed to reduce ethnic tensions in Macedonia through gradual Ottoman reforms.[42] This agreement was evidence that the Russian government was still reluctant to support revolutionary upheavals in the region, or to become involved in another Balkan crisis that it could not control.

The turn of the century also witnessed a revival of friendly relations between Bulgaria and Russia. Bulgaria's new ruler, Ferdinand of Coburg, who had replaced Alexander of Battenberg in 1887, was able to normalize the relationship with Russia by 1896, when official diplomatic ties between the two countries were re-established. The unfortunate Alexander had been kidnapped by Bulgarian officers loyal to Russia in 1886, and after his release he was ordered by the czar to abdicate. By 1902, Russia and Bulgaria had concluded a secret military alliance designed to counteract a similar Austro-Romanian agreement. But a degree of suspicion persisted between Russia and Bulgaria, and it was clear to the Bulgarians that the Russians could not be counted on to support their ambitions in Macedonia. Russia's unwillingness to spark an international crisis in the Balkans meant that Bulgarian designs in the region would be unable to advance substantially.[43]

Russia's position in Southeastern Europe improved even more in the first years of the twentieth century with the establishment of closer economic and military ties between Serbia and Bulgaria. The 1903 coup that overthrew Alexander Obrenovic and brought Peter Karadjordjevic to the throne meant that a monarch who was unacceptable to Austria-Hungary ruled Serbia. Consequently, the Serbs gravitated even more toward Bulgaria. Between April 1904 and June 1905, the two Balkan states signed a series of political, military, and economic treaties, including an agreement that called for the establishment of a customs union by 1917. Many contemporary observers interpreted this agreement as the first step toward the founding of a South Slav state that would serve as a barrier to Austro-Hungarian expansion in Southeastern Europe.[44]

The rapprochement between Serbia and Bulgaria provided a firm base for Russian intrigues, especially those after the Bosnian Crisis of 1908–1909. The Russians were also in favor of a league of Balkan states whose goal would be to block Austro-Hungarian ambitions in the region. After 1909, and Austria-Hungary's decision to annex Bosnia-Herzegovina, the 1897 agreement that committed Russia and the Dual Monarchy to maintaining the status quo in Southeastern Europe had become a dead letter. Sergei Sazonov, who had been Russian foreign minister since October 1910, instructed Nicholas Hartwig and Anatol Nekliudov, the Russian ministers in Belgrade and Sofia, respectively, to encourage the governments of the two Balkan states to establish firmer diplomatic ties.[45] This was a difficult proposition, however, since Serbia and Bulgaria held divergent views on the future of Macedonia. The Serbs favored partitioning the territory among the Balkan states, but the Bulgarians advocated granting Macedonia autonomy as a prelude to annexation by Bulgaria. Earlier attempts at a closer Serbo-Bulgarian alliance had foundered on this same issue.[46]

What encouraged the Bulgarians to compromise on the matter this time was their unwillingness to accept a proposal to include the Ottoman Empire in a new Balkan alliance under the aegis of Russia. A Russian-Ottoman agreement would invariably have deprived Bulgaria of the opportunity to carry out an active and aggressive policy in Macedonia.[47] They agreed to the partitioning of Macedonia after they had convinced themselves that they could quickly defeat the Ottomans and occupy the entire region, thus precluding any need to divide the spoils with Serbia. When the Italians successfully attacked Ottoman Libya in September 1911, the Bulgarians took it as a sign of the imminent collapse of the empire, and cleared the way for a Balkan alliance.[48] On March 13, 1912, Serbia and Bulgaria concluded a secret treaty. Both countries agreed to the division of Macedonia into three zones: a Bulgarian zone, a Serbian zone, and a contested zone (whose ownership was to be mediated by the Russian czar).[49] In May, Bulgaria concluded a treaty of alliance with Greece. (The Greeks had initially refused to acknowledge an autonomous Macedonia, but the pace of events forced them to acquiesce — at least temporarily.[50]) Montenegro also signed treaties with Bulgaria and Serbia, completing the organization of the Balkan League.[51]

However, this new Balkan alliance did not resemble the arrangement envisioned by Russia. Far from constituting a barrier to Austria-Hungary, the Balkan League was a military and diplomatic coalition directed against the Ottoman Empire. By September 1912, the Russian government, still not wishing to see the Balkans explode into another international crisis, resorted to co-operating with Austria-Hungary in an effort to prevent the Balkan allies from going to war against the Ottomans. In a joint statement issued by Russia and the Dual Monarchy on behalf of the other powers of Europe, the Balkan states were warned that any change to territorial arrangements in Southeastern Europe would not be tolerated. At the same time, to mitigate this warning, Russia and Austria-Hungary promised to continue to exert pressure on the Porte to implement reforms in Macedonia.[52] This meant nothing to the Balkan allies, however, who cared little about Ottoman reforms and were more interested in annexing Macedonia.

Time was running out for the Ottoman possessions in the Balkans. The Italians had expanded their war against the Porte in the Aegean and the Straits, and there was a clear possibility that the Great Powers would recognize the autonomy of the remaining four Ottoman administrative districts in Albania. In early October 1912, Montenegro invoked a long-standing border dispute with the Ottomans and declared war. Serbia, Bulgaria, and Greece soon joined in, on the grounds that the Porte had failed to implement reforms in Macedonia as stipulated by the Congress of Berlin in 1878.

————⟞∕∅∕∅⟝————

The principal military operations of the First Balkan War took place in two theaters: Thrace (in the east) and Macedonia (in the west). In both regions, the Allies outnumbered the Ottoman forces. In Thrace, approximately 115,000 Ottoman troops faced an army of 200,000 Bulgarians (later substantially reinforced). The situation in Macedonia was similar. In this theater of operations, 175,000 Ottomans confronted 273,000 troops of the Balkan League.[53] But the Ottoman situation was by no means as hopeless as it appeared. In both regions, they enjoyed a number of advantages that resourceful commanders could have used to compensate for the numerical weakness of the forces at their disposal. In Macedonia, for example, the units assembled by the Porte occupied the central position, and the region's transportation network provided good interior lines of communication. The rail lines from Thessaloniki to Monastir and along the Axios-Vardar valley, as well as the military road connecting Monastir, Prilep, Veles, and Stip, offered the possibility of rapid concentration of forces along any one of the theater's fronts. Yet ultimately, none of these advantages was put to use in such a way to compensate for the structural weaknesses of the Ottoman military establishment.

Measured in terms of the amount of human and material resources committed by the belligerents, as well as the intensity of the fighting, the field campaign waged by the Ottoman and Bulgarian armies in Thrace was the most important of the First Balkan War. The Bulgarian general staff had given priority to the advance on Thrace, and planned to destroy the Ottoman field army, if nothing else. (Even the reduction of the fortress of Adrianople was relegated to a subsidiary role.[54]) To this end, the Bulgarians deployed three field armies in the broad triangle formed by the Marica and Tundja rivers. The Bulgarian high command ordered the Bulgarian Second Army westward along the Marica to surround and contain Adrianople. The Bulgarian Third Army was to advance southward along the Tundja toward Kirk Kilissa, with the objective of severing the Ottoman lines of communication with Constantinople. At the same time, the Bulgarian First Army was given the task of providing a link between the Second and Third armies by advancing into the region between Adrianople and Kirk Kilissa.[55] Other Bulgarian units — including the Seventh Rila Infantry Division, the Second Thracian Infantry Division, and the Macedonian-Thracian Volunteer Corps — were to operate in the Rhodope Mountains and western Thrace, and maintain contact with the Serbian forces in Macedonia.[56] Opposing the Bulgarians was Abdullah Pasha's Ottoman Eastern Army, with its four Nizam (regular) corps (First, Second, Third, and Fourth) and six Redif (reserve) corps (Fifteenth, Sixteenth, Seventeenth, Eighteenth, Twenty-third, and Twenty-fourth). These took up positions along the Adrianople–Kirk Kilissa line.[57]

Units of the three Bulgarian armies crossed the border into Thrace on the morning of October 18, 1912. The Bulgarian Second Army successfully encircled Adrianople, bottling up an Ottoman force of 45,000 men. The advance of the First and Third armies progressed rapidly despite Ottoman opposition,[58] and by October 24, the Bulgarians had taken possession of Kirk Kilissa, the region's second most important fortress. Although the Ottoman Eastern Army had been badly savaged, the Bulgarians did not attempt to pursue it. Instead, they paused their advance at Kirk Kilissa to rest and reorganize their forces.[59] The Ottoman forces took advantage of this unexpected respite and retreated to the southeast, taking up defensive positions behind the Karagatch River along a twenty-five-mile (40 km) front stretching from Lule Burgas in the south to Bunahisar in the north.[60]

On October 28, the Bulgarian armies resumed their advance.

When they encountered Ottoman forces along the Karagatch River, the Bulgarians launched a series of attacks against their position, thus initiating the largest engagement of the First Balkan War: the Battle of Lule Burgas. For four days, the Bulgarian high command attempted to outflank the Ottoman left wing and force them to withdraw to the northeast, where they would be trapped against the Istranja Balkan Mountains.[61] But the Bulgarian advance stalled, and the Ottomans stubbornly resisted until October 31. On that day, Abdullah Pasha, the commander of the Eastern Army, ordered a retreat to the Chatalja lines, the outer defenses of Constantinople, thus giving the Bulgarians possession of the battlefield. Still, the Battle of Lule Burgas was hardly a Bulgarian victory. They had lost more than 18,000 men, and were too exhausted to launch an immediate pursuit.[62] Heavy rains caused further delays.[63]

Again, the Ottoman Eastern Army was able to retreat in good order. When they reached the Chatalja lines in early November, the Ottomans immediately began the task of improving and strengthening their defenses, which had fallen into disrepair before the war.[64] On November 17, the Bulgarians resumed the offensive by launching a series of assaults against the Chatalja lines, though these proved more than sufficient at repelling the attacks. The combination of the exhaustion of their troops and the superiority of the Ottoman artillery meant the Bulgarians made little progress.[65] To make matters worse, they were waging a battle at the end of a tenuous and dangerously overextended line of communication. The resulting decline in the quality and quantity of logistical support took its toll on the morale of the troops.[66] As if that wasn't enough, a cholera epidemic broke out and claimed the lives of 1,600 Bulgarian soldiers. This was in addition to the nearly 16,000 casualties they had incurred during the fruitless three-day attack against the Chatalja lines.[67]

While the exhausted Bulgarian First and Third armies were resting in front of Chatalja, an armistice was concluded between the Ottoman Empire and the Balkan League (excluding Greece) on December 4, 1912. The agreement soon broke down, however, and hostilities resumed on February 3, 1913. But instead of renewing their offensive against Chatalja, the Bulgarians focused their energies on the reduction of Adrianople, which had been contained by the Bulgarian Second Army from the beginning of the war.[68] Before all the Bulgarian forces could be concentrated against that fortress, however, the high command redirected several units to neutralize the threat of an Ottoman counteroffensive. The Ottomans had intended to strike at the rear of the Bulgarian First and Third armies, thereby lifting the siege of Adrianople and reversing the strategic situation in Thrace.[69] To do this, they planned to launch coordinated offensives against two points in the Thracian theater. The Chatalja Army (as the Eastern Army was now being called) was to stage a series of diversionary attacks against the Bulgarian First and Third armies. At the same time, the newly organized Gallipoli Army was to advance to the north from Bulair, at the neck of the Gallipoli peninsula.[70]

To deal with the threat at Gallipoli, the Bulgarians created a new army, the Bulgarian Fourth Army, from units that had just arrived by sea from Macedonia, where the fighting had already ended. This formation was then ordered to advance from Demotika to Bulair, where it succeeded in halting the advance of the Gallipoli Army in a battle that lasted from February 4 to 9.[71] On February 8, the Ottomans landed their Tenth Corps at Rodosto, in an attempt to strike at the rear of the Bulgarian Fourth Army. However, Bulgarian counterattacks compelled the landing force to retreat.[72] Ottoman attempts to break through on the Chatalja front were equally unsuccessful, and the Ottoman counteroffensive as a whole petered out.[73]

Once the Bulgarians had dealt with the Ottoman counteroffensive, they concentrated their forces on Adrianople. The Ottomans were holding the fortress with one regular and three reserve divisions, ten field artillery regiments, and two heavy artillery regiments — in all, 40,000 men.[74] Although the Bulgarian Second Army had been surrounding the city since October, active operations did not begin until the failure of the armistice in February. By then, two Serb divisions had reinforced the Bulgarian Second Army; this brought the total number of allied forces to more than 100,000 men.[75] The main assault was launched on the evening of March 24, after a preparatory artillery bombardment that lasted for nearly eight hours. After two days of heavy fighting, the commander of the fortress surrendered.[76] The capture of Adrianople concluded the Thracian campaign of the First Balkan War.

In the Macedonian theater, meanwhile, the Ottomans faced an onslaught of the combined Serbian, Greek, and Montenegrin armies.

But the Serbian offensive launched south of Nish had the greatest impact on the course of the campaign in the west. The Serb high command decided to crush the Ottoman forces in the Skopje-Stip-Veles triangle with a classic double envelopment. To do this, they deployed three field armies along their frontier with Ottoman Macedonia. Crown Prince Alexander's Serb First Army was assembled in the upper Morava valley, around Vranje.[77] This unit was to advance along the valley and, after crossing the frontier, engage the Ottoman forces in the Ovce Polje region.[78] At the same time, Gen. Bozidar Jankovic's Third Army would march toward Pristina and then follow the line of the Mitrovica-Skopje railroad to envelop the Ottoman left flank.[79] The weakest of the Serb formations, the Second Army, was to direct its one Serb division and one Bulgarian division west from their original position at Kustendil, engaging the Ottoman right flank.[80] All three formations were to unite at Ovce Polje and defeat the Ottoman Western Army once and for all.[81] In addition, subsidiary operations in the district of Novi Bazar were undertaken by Gen. Mihail Zivkovic's small Army of the Ibar and the Javor Brigade, whose total strength amounted to 37,000 men and forty-four guns.[82]

But the Serb plan unraveled almost from the beginning. Zekki Pasha, the commander of the Ottoman Army of the Vardar, did not simply wait for the Serb offensive. Instead, he maneuvered his forces north from Ovce Polje and took up defensive positions near Kumanovo.[83] His intention was to defeat the Serb First Army before it could join up with the Second and Third armies, and then to destroy the weaker formations in turn. After clearing Macedonia of Serbian troops, Zekki planned to march on Sofia and divert the Bulgarians from their offensive in Thrace.[84]

Zekki's tactics unexpectedly complicated the original Serb plan. The Serb First Army clashed with his forces on October 23, in the two-day Battle of Kumanovo. The fighting on the first day was quite intense, since the Serbs were not able to commit all their forces. Once all the Serb units joined the engagement, however, the First Army was able to deal with the Army of the Vardar, even without reinforcements from the Second and Third armies. In the afternoon of October 24, the Ottoman left wing disintegrated, and the Ottoman center was exposed to newly arrived Serb units. The battle quickly degenerated into a rout, and the Ottoman forces withdrew rapidly toward Skopje.

Only the Ottoman right wing, composed of Djavid Pasha's army corps, retained its cohesion and fell back to Stip in an orderly manner.[85] But the Serb army once again failed to pursue the defeated Ottomans, preferring instead to occupy the fortifications abandoned by the enemy and regroup before any further advance.[86] Their failure to exploit their victory enabled the Ottomans to withdraw into southern Macedonia, consolidate their forces around Monastir, and fight another battle.

After resuming their advance, the Serbs took Skopje on October 27 and the high command decided to drastically reorganize his forces. The Serb Second Army was ordered to proceed to Thrace and assist in the siege of Adrianople.[87] The Third Army was given the task of pacifying the newly conquered countryside and dealing with the remnants of the Albanian irregular contingents.[88] The First Army, meanwhile, was divided into three groups and directed to Monastir to engage the Ottoman forces concentrated around the city. The eastern and western columns advanced through Stip and Kavadar, Tetovo and Kercevo, respectively, encountering little opposition. The central detachment, however, ran headlong into determined resistance south of Prilep, and managed to drive the Ottomans back only after suffering 3,000 casualties.[89]

The Ottoman resistance near Prilep did not seriously delay the Serb advance, but it did give Djavid Pasha the time to rush south from Monastir with a part of his force and defeat, at the Battle of Banica, the Greek column advancing toward Florina. Djavid, however, had neither the resources nor the official backing to exploit his victory. As a result, the future of the Ottomans in Macedonia depended on the outcome of a battle to be fought near Monastir.[90]

Although the Ottomans defended Monastir with determination and skill, the superiority of Serb artillery once again proved decisive.[91] In the course of a two-day engagement (November 16–18), the Army of the Vardar, or what was left of it, disintegrated and the remnants fled to Albania. Some Ottoman troops, including 15,000 soldiers under Zekki Pasha, were able to join the garrison of Ioannina, and thus contributed to the defense of that fortress against the Greeks. Another detachment, 16,000 men under Djavid Pasha, escaped into the Berat region of Albania. Their presence there prevented the Great Powers from intervening militarily in the region.[92]

—◦◊◦—

In addition to the main campaign in central Macedonia, the Serbs also undertook a series of subsidiary operations west of the Morava-Vardar corridor. On October 22, the Serb Army of the Ibar invaded the district of Novi Bazar. After sweeping aside some ineffectual Ottoman resistance, the Serbs joined up with Montenegrin forces at Plevje on October 24; at the same time, the Ottoman forces in the area crossed the border into Bosnia and were disarmed and interned by Habsburg authorities.[93] The Serb Third Army was then able to clear Kosovo of Ottoman forces and Albanian irregular detachments. By October 31, the Montenegrins had occupied Pec, the Army of the Ibar had taken Djakovo, and the Third Army had captured Prizren.[94]

The Serbs spent the next ten days reorganizing their forces and preparing to advance to the west to secure an outlet to the Adriatic. General Zivkovic's forces were left behind to pacify Novi Bazar, disarm the local Albanian population, and raise new regiments from among the local Serbs. The Third Army was broken up into two columns and proceeded through northern Albania under Jankovic's command. The larger detachment, made up of 8,700 soldiers of the Second Drina Division and supported by ten mountain artillery pieces and ten machine guns, advanced from Djakovo to Alessio, capturing that town on November 19. The other column, with its 7,000 soldiers from the First Sumadija Division, four mountain guns, and ten machine guns, departed Prizren on November 9 and reached Durazzo two weeks later. Both Serb columns marched under extremely difficult conditions. Their progress was hampered by frequent breakdowns in logistical support, inclement weather, rough terrain, inaccurate maps, and attacks by Albanian guerrillas. The attempt to secure access to the sea cost the Serbs 3,500 men, a sacrifice that was totally unnecessary, since the Great Powers had already decided to create an autonomous Albanian state.[95]

The Greeks contributed two field armies to the Balkan League's war effort. These were deployed on the frontier with the Ottoman Empire. Gen. Constantine Sapountzakis's Army of Epirus, though it amounted to little more than a division, was charged with the primary task of guarding the Epirote frontier. Later, this mission was modified, and Sapountzakis received substantial reinforcements that allowed him to take on offensive operations.[96] The Greek ground forces, meanwhile, were concentrated at Larissa, in central Greece, and included seven infantry divisions, one cavalry brigade, and four *evzone* (highlander) battalions. They were organized as the Army of Thessaly and placed under the command of Crown Prince Constantine.[97] The primary mission of the ground forces was the capture of Thessaloniki. Constantine's army was to deliver its main thrust north into the valley of the Aliakhmon, then follow that river to the northeast in the direction of the Kampania Plain and the Axios River. Light, fast-moving columns were posted on both wings of the Army of Epirus to protect its flanks. The Greek Seventh Division, operating on the army's extreme right, advanced along the coast of the Thermaic Gulf in an attempt to secure the bridges over the Axios and sever the Ottomans' route of retreat to the east.

The main obstacle to Constantine's advance was the Ottoman Eighth Redif (Reserve) Corps, with its three infantry divisions, one independent infantry brigade, and one cavalry regiment.[98] The Ottomans did not attempt to contest the Greek offensive right at the border, and instead allowed the Greeks to occupy Elasson on October 6.[99] The Ottoman commander intended to fight on ground of his own choosing, and thus he concentrated his men at Saranda-poron, approximately ten miles (16 km) south of the Aliakhmon and at the entrance to the Porta Petra Gorge, a naturally strong defensive position.

Leading elements of Constantine's forces encountered the Ottomans on the morning of October 22. The Eighth Redif Corps was deployed across the Elasson-Kosanie road, between the villages of Viglia and Glycovo.[100] To dislodge the Ottomans from their positions, Constantine ordered his First, Second, and Third divisions to launch a series of diversionary frontal attacks against the main line of the enemy's defenses. At the same time, the Greek Fourth Division was to execute a wide turn around the Ottoman right, through Metaxa, in an effort to seize the road junction at Kaldades and block the retreat of the Eighth Corps. To the left of the Third Division, Major-General Alexandros Soutsos's cavalry brigade (with the Fifth Division in support) had to carry out an even wider flanking movement to capture the Aliakhmon Bridge between Kosanie and Servia, thus trapping the Ottoman forces.[101]

The Greeks first attacked the Glycovo-Viglia position in the pouring rain at 7:00 a.m.[102] By nightfall, the Ottomans still had not been dislodged. However, by daybreak on October 23, it seemed that the Ottomans had retreated, and the Greek forces charged with turning the Ottoman right were now menacing the rear of the Eighth Corps.[103] In reality, the Ottomans probably exaggerated the threat posed to them by the Greek flanking force, since the grand envelopment envisioned by Constantine was only partially successful. The Fourth Division was able to occupy a commanding position near the Porta Petra Gorge, intercepting some of the retreating Ottoman troops. But the efforts to completely block the Ottoman retreat were unsuccessful. The Ottoman Eighth Corps abandoned twenty-two artillery pieces and all the wheeled transport, but most of this unit escaped to the northwest and lived to fight another day.[104] The Greeks also failed to capture the Aliakhmon Bridge after the Fifth Division encountered stiff resistance from a small Ottoman force at Lazaredes. The delay on the advance of Greek forces was just long enough to allow the majority of Ottoman troops to escape across the river. Thus the Greeks were unable to win a decisive victory.[105]

Following the clash at Sarandaporon, Constantine's army indulged in the customary period of rest and reorganization. On October 26, the advance resumed and the main body of the army followed the Aliakhmon to the northwest. The Fifth Division, however, was ordered north to block any Ottoman attempts to sever the vulnerable Greek lines of communication. The Greek supply line stretched back to Larissa, and became increasingly assailable with each advance the Army of Epirus made into Macedonia.[106] The Ottomans, for their part, did not seriously contest the Greek progress along the Aliakhmon. Only a few minor engagements were fought, and the Greeks easily swept aside whatever resistance the Ottomans were able to offer.[107] On October 29, the Third Division occupied Veria, thus severing the rail link between Thessaloniki and Monastir.[108] Two days later, however, the Greeks ran into determined Ottoman resistance. After emerging from the Aliakhmon valley into the Kampania Plain, the Army of Epirus encountered the Ottoman Eighth Corps drawn up for battle northwest of the town of Yannitsa.

The decision made by Hassan Taxim Pasha, the commander of the Eighth Corps, to challenge the Greeks at Yannitsa gave

Constantine another opportunity for the decisive victory that had eluded him at Sarandaporon. Accordingly, he ordered his First, Second, and Third divisions to advance directly on Yannitsa through the villages of Burgas, Drisari Vlach, and Krousari, respectively. The Fourth and Sixth divisions were to advance along the Vodena-Yannitsa road and attack the Ottoman right wing. The *coup de grâce* was to be delivered by the Seventh Division. Once this division approached Yannitsa, it was directed to interpose itself between the Eighth Corps and the Axios River, then seize the bridges and cut off the Ottoman route to Thessaloniki.[109] Hostilities commenced around noon on November 1. When the Second Division attempted to cross the Moglenica River, however, it suddenly came under long-range fire from Ottoman artillery batteries on the hills north of the town. The Greek advance was halted to allow the Army of Epirus to bring its own artillery forward. For the remainder of the day, both sides engaged in a protracted artillery duel, with the Greeks eventually proving more successful. By evening, the Second and Third divisions had crossed the Moglenica and closed to within two or three miles (3 to 5 km) of the Ottomans' main line of defense.[110]

The exchange of artillery fire was renewed at 6:00 a.m. Three hours later, the Greeks launched a general attack, which compelled the Ottomans to evacuate their positions and retreat to the east.[111] Yet again, as was the case at Sarandaporon, Constantine failed to achieve a decisive victory, and the Seventh Division did not capture the Axios bridges to cut off the Ottoman retreat. Although a company of the *evzone* battalion did manage to approach the bridges, it had to withdraw when the remainder of the division failed to come up in support.[112] The division's commander later claimed that he could not capture the bridges because a mist had covered the area, making it dangerous to attack over unfamiliar terrain.[113] Ultimately, the Seventh Division advanced only as far as the village of Plati, more than five miles (8 km) from the banks of the river. The only positive outcome for the Greeks was the Ottomans' failure to blow up the railroad bridge at Kavakli (although they did destroy the road bridge at Mentetsli, a few miles upstream).[114]

On November 6, the Greeks crossed the Axios after the railroad bridge had been modified to accommodate the passage of the army.[115] One day later, at the urging of the consuls of the Great

Powers, Hassan Taxim Pasha and Constantine began negotiating the surrender of Thessaloniki and the Ottoman garrison.[116] The talks dragged on for nearly a day and a half, until a protocol of surrender was concluded on November 8. The following day, the Seventh Division marched into the city to begin the process of disarming the Ottoman garrison; in the process, the Greeks took 1,000 Ottoman officers and 26,000 soldiers prisoner.[117]

The capture of Thessaloniki fulfilled part of the Greek government's political agenda, but the military operations were by no means over. On November 14, Constantine led four divisions out of the city and advanced into western Macedonia. He wanted to redress the dangerous state of affairs created in that region by the defeat of the Greek Fifth Division at Banica on November 2. After the Battle of Sarandaporon, the Fifth Division was made responsible for the Greek army's left flank, and the 11,000 men of that unit advanced boldly toward Florina.[118] But the commander of the division, to secure his own supplies and pacify the areas he passed through, was compelled to assign an increasing number of troops to protect the division's lines of communication. In the process, he reduced the combat power of his forces. By the beginning of November, only 7,000 men remained at the point of the advance.[119]

The depletion of the fighting strength of the Fifth Division provided the Ottoman commanders in the region with an invaluable opportunity. In an impressive display of strategic initiative, Djavid Pasha used the northwestern section of the Monastir-Thessaloniki railroad to bring together 11,000 to 12,000 troops at Banica.[120] Having assembled this superior force at a critical point in the theater of operations, Djavid attacked and defeated the Fifth Division on the night of November 2, capturing twelve artillery pieces that were later used by the Ottomans to defend Monastir from the Serbs.[121] Yet Djavid could not fully exploit his success. The Ottoman commander soon had to turn his attention to the threat posed to Monastir by the advance of the Serb forces. On November 19, the first units of the Army of Thessaly were already gathering in the region, and within a week, Ottoman military resistance in western Macedonia had collapsed. Florina, Kastoria, and Koritsa were captured by the Greeks between November 20 and December 20,[122] and the focus of the Greek war effort shifted to Epirus.

Initially, the Greek high command intended to limit military action on the Epirote front to defensive operations. In fact, the forces placed at the disposal of General Sapountzakis were negligible, and thus precluded any possibility of a Greek offensive. The grandly named Army of Epirus was, in fact, little more than a division-sized force, consisting of one regular infantry regiment, three *evzone* battalions, and one reserve infantry regiment. General Sapountzakis could also count on the services of 3,000 Cretan and Epirote irregulars, and a contingent of foreign volunteers led by a descendant of Giuseppe Garibaldi.[123] This meager force stood against 15,000 Ottomans under Essad Pasha.[124]

The Greek commanders routinely interpreted their orders in whatever manner suited the occasion, and General Sapountzakis was no exception. He could not accept the passive role he had been allocated and, disregarding the numerical inferiority of his forces, ordered his small "army" to invade Epirus on October 19. Initially, the Greek operations were directed against the port of Preveza, on the Ambrasian Gulf. Sapountzakis was determined to seize the town, thereby securing a logistical base for an attack against the Ottoman fortress at Ioannina.[125] After brushing aside the Ottoman detachments blocking his way at Gribovo, Sapountzakis took Preveza in less than two weeks (on November 3).[126] Then he turned north and occupied the Pente Pigadia position on November 10. At Pesta, five miles (8 km) to the north, Sapountzakis decided to wait for reinforcements. By the middle of November, 4,000 men of the Second Division, supported by twelve guns, marched across the passes of the Pindus range to join Sapountzakis and his men, and a month later (on December 12), the combined force reached Ioannina.[127]

Ioannina was one of the two greatest Ottoman fortresses in the western Balkans (Monastir was the other). Ioannina is located at the center of a plain surrounding a lake. It is shielded in the east, south, and southwest by a semi-circular range of hills, which dominate the major approaches to the town. Prior to the Balkan wars, the Ottomans augmented Ioannina's natural defenses by building a number of forts on the summits of the principal hills in a horseshoe-shaped barrier. A number of entrenched batteries were also constructed, to fill the gaps between the permanent forts.[128] When Sapountzakis approached, the garrison, having received reinforcements from the

Ottoman forces that had managed to escape from the Serbs at Monastir in the middle of November, held approximately 25,000 men and 100 artillery pieces.[129] Although outnumbered and outgunned, the Greeks launched a series of assaults against the fortress throughout December. Unable to make any headway, however, General Sapountzakis suspended the attacks around December 25 and decided to wait for reinforcements.[130]

In January 1913, Sapountzakis's force was strengthened by the arrival of the Fourth, Fifth, and Sixth divisions from Macedonia. In the second half of January, the Greek commander decided to make another attempt against the fortress. From January 20–23, the Greeks launched a major assault, supported by an intensive artillery bombardment, against Bezanie, the strongest of the forts surrounding Ioannina and the key to the entire defensive position. But the attack failed.[131] Two days later, Constantine arrived at Ioannina to assume direction of the siege. He immediately suspended all attacks and devoted the next month to preparing his army for a decisive, all-out assault.[132] On March 4, twenty-three Greek battalions, in three assault columns, were concealed in positions opposite the western and southwestern sectors of Ioannina's defenses. After an intense artillery bombardment, the three columns seized the Tsouca, Saba, and St. Nicholas redoubts, breaking the Ottoman line of defense and directly threatening the town of Ioannina itself.[133] The Ottoman commander, Essad Pasha, had little choice and capitulated on the night of March 5. Altogether, 1,000 Ottoman officers and 32,000 soldiers marched into captivity. But Essad Pasha himself was able to slip away to Albania.[134] Nevertheless, the Greeks had achieved most of their primary goals. With the capture of Ioannina and Thessaloniki, Greece was at last reunited with Epirus (in what was then Ottoman Albania) and a good chunk of Macedonia.

—⟨∾⟩—

The military operations of the Montenegrin army during the war, meanwhile, were focused on the town of Scutari, in northern Albania. For decades, the town had been at the heart of Montenegro's territorial aspirations. Scutari dominated the fertile coastal plains around the lake of the same name, and its capture would significantly enhance the economy of Montenegro, the smallest and poorest of the Balkan allies. In addition, Scutari would have given Montenegro a convenient outlet to the Adriatic around the mouth of the Bojana River.[135] The town was defended by Hassan Riza Pasha's Scutari Corps, which included 13,600 soldiers, 96 artillery, a reinforced regular infantry regiment of 3,750, and contingents of 2,000 Albanian irregulars. The Ottoman commander did not intend to assume offensive operations against the Montenegrins, but he was determined to defend and hold the town.[136]

Montenegro had declared war against the Ottoman Empire on October 8, 1912, and the following day its army crossed the border into enemy territory. After a number of preliminary engagements, the Montenegrins reached the fortress on October 25. For the next four days, the besiegers attempted to take the town by storm, but vigorous Ottoman counterattacks drove them from most of the positions they had initially captured.[137] The ineffectiveness of the siege was compounded by the failure to surround Scutari from all sides, which enabled the garrison to receive supplies and reinforcements from Albania.[138] Finally, in late November, after the Serb advance through northern Albania had taken Alessio and Medua, the Ottomans' lifeline was severed.[139] Ironically, this would ultimately protract the siege. Although he was cut off from all communication with Constantinople, Hassan Riza Pasha refused to recognize the armistice of December 4 and declined to surrender the fortress for more than a month.[140]

Frustrated in their efforts to capture the town, the Montenegrins requested support from the Serbs.[141] The plea for help was underscored by a sense of urgency generated by a conference in London. By late December, the representatives of the Great Powers had decided to create an independent Albanian state. Although King Nicholas of Montenegro was confident that Scutari would be awarded to his state "with one stroke of the pen," it was not an absolute guarantee. The Montenegrins felt they had to capture the town.[142] In response to their request for assistance, the Serb high command ordered three divisions to Scutari. Thus reinforced, the besiegers launched yet another major assault on February 7, 1913. The attack lasted for three days, and the Serbs and Montenegrins suffered 4,000 casualties. But the Ottomans still held the town.[143]

The next major attack was launched on March 31, but it also collapsed against the Ottoman fortifications.[144] This failure was indicative of the declining fortunes of the Montenegrins. Even before the latest attack, the Great Powers had decided to award Scutari to Albania. Moreover, Essad Pasha, who had succeeded Hassan Riza after an Albanian murdered him in late March, rejected all appeals to surrender and continued to resist.[145] The prospects of capturing the town diminished even further when the government of Serbia bowed to Austro-Hungarian pressure and ordered the withdrawal of all Serb units from Scutari.[146] Essad Pasha ultimately surrendered of his own volition on April 23, 1913, marching his troops out of the fortress with the honors of war and carrying off most of the supplies.[147] The Montenegrins had finally secured their prize, but it did not really matter — the Great Powers still awarded Scutari to Albania. Disgruntled, the Montenegrin army evacuated the town on May 4.[148]

On April 16, the Ottoman Empire and Bulgaria again concluded an armistice, shortly after the other belligerents had terminated their own military operations. International attention now shifted from the battlefields of Southeastern Europe to the conference rooms of London. Soon, the representatives of the combatants and the Great Powers became locked in a fierce diplomatic struggle over the distribution of the territorial spoils of war. The military successes of the Balkan allies meant that the Great Powers had to accept some revisions to the territorial order established by the Congress of Berlin. The Europeans, however, were looking beyond the Balkan horizon at the great rivalry between the Triple Entente (Great Britain, France, and Russia) and the Triple Alliance (Germany, Austria-Hungary, and Italy), and these considerations underscored the negotiations. In the end, the London settlement, finalized in May 1913, sparked only recriminations among the Balkan allies, thus making a lasting settlement unlikely.

Serbia refused to withdraw its troops from the parts of Macedonia allotted to Bulgaria. The Serbs wanted compensation for having been deprived of northern Albania and access to the Adriatic. Indeed, Nikola Pasic, the prime minister of Serbia, had insisted on a redefinition of the original zones of partition in Macedonia as early as February 1913,[149] and by April, Pasic had made his demands public. But the Bulgarians would not agree.[150] The Serbs countered this intransigence by concluding a secret military alliance with Greece in

May.[151] The resulting treaty provided for a common Greco-Serbian border east of the Vardar, and a partition of Macedonia west of the Vardar based on "effective occupation." In April, the Bulgarian government had asked the Russian czar to arbitrate the division of the Macedonian spoils. The Serbs, however, had raised the stakes and declined mediation; they would agree only to an arbitration of all of the partitioned zones of Macedonia.[152] Soon, the cries for a military solution to the dispute escalated, especially among the Macedonian refugees living in Bulgaria. These exiles made blood-curdling threats to assassinate any public figure who dared to oppose military action.[153] The Bulgarian army's high command, meanwhile, intoxicated by the victories against the Turks, also favored war. Gen. Mikhail Savov, the chief of the Bulgarian general staff, argued that the army must either fight or demobilize; discontent was brewing among the ranks, and he warned there would soon be lapses of discipline.[154]

The Russians, for their part, wanted to forestall the disintegration of the Balkan League and diffuse tensions between Bulgaria and its erstwhile allies. On May 8, Nicholas II made a personal appeal to Peter of Serbia and Ferdinand of Bulgaria to find a peaceful solution to their problems. Both rulers issued favorable replies, which prompted Sergei Sazonov, the Russian foreign minister, to invite the two prime ministers, Nikola Pasic and Stoyan Danev, to St. Petersburg to submit their territorial claims for Russian arbitration. At the same time, the Russian minister urged all the Balkan states to demobilize their armies.[155]

The Bulgarian Cabinet discussed the Russian proposal on June 22. General Savov made it clear that the Bulgarian army could not remain in a state of readiness for much longer; it was therefore imperative that the Macedonian issue be resolved quickly. The Cabinet, consequently, decided to accept the Russian offer of arbitration, on the condition that the Russian government reach a final decision within eight days.[156]

The Cabinet's decision was diplomatically fatal. Effectively, it soured Russian-Bulgarian relations and terminated the Balkan alliance. The tone of the Bulgarian note infuriated Sazonov, who interpreted the insistence on an eight-day time limit as an ultimatum. The Russian government assumed, wrongly, that the Bulgarians would not have worded their message in so haughty a manner without secret support from another Great Power, most likely Austria-Hungary.[157] To make matters even worse, Sazonov happened to be suffering from kidney troubles, and this condition did little to improve his mood.[158] On June 24, Sazonov met with Stefan Bobchev, the Bulgarian ambassador to Russia, and berated the hapless envoy over the imprudent note:

> Your announcement does not surprise me. I have been aware of the actions of your government for several days. You are acting on the advice of Austria. You are free. Thus the Serbs with their folly and you with your incorrect attitude have rejected Russia and Slavdom. The Russian emperor did not expect an ultimatum with a time limit in which to declare his decisions concerning the Serbian-Bulgarian difference. However, he would have fulfilled his difficult mission with expedition. Now, after your declaration, allow me to communicate ours to you! Do not expect anything from us, and forget the existence of any of our engagements from 1902 until today![159]

Sazonov's outburst shattered whatever impartiality Russia had enjoyed in the eyes of the Bulgarians. They became convinced that Russia was favoring Serbia in the dispute, a conviction that caused them to break with their traditional Great Power "liberator" and patron.[160] Bulgarian popular opinion was soon calling for war. On the night of June 29, the army attacked Serbian outposts near the Bregalnitsa River, initiating the short Second Balkan War and Bulgaria's final military and diplomatic defeat. Remarkably, Prime Minister Danev and King Ferdinand were aware of the attack, but the Bulgarian Cabinet found out only after the commencement of hostilities.[161]

The Bulgarian high command had single-handedly taken the decision to settle the territorial dispute by force. The principal goal was to occupy the disputed territory without a declaration of war.[162] The Bulgarians, consequently, deployed the majority of their troops along their borders with Serbia and Greece. The initial plan was to crush the Serbian forces in Macedonia by means of a double envelopment. The plan called for an advance by the First and Third armies into the Morava valley, followed by a sweep to the south-west. At the same time, the Fourth and Fifth armies were to push the

Serbs westward from the Bregalnitsa River, thus completing the encirclement.[163]

Not for the first time, political considerations intervened, and instead of a full-scale attack by all of its forces, the Bulgarian high command had to limit the assault to the Second and Fourth armies. The Bulgarian government wanted to give the impression that the conflict was only a limited spat between Balkan allies. For that reason, military operations were confined to Macedonia, since that disposition of the region was still in question.[164]

The Serbs and Greeks also deployed most of their armies in the disputed region. Radomir Putnik, the commander-in-chief of the Serbian army, sent 70 percent of his forces to Macedonia, leaving only light detachments to protect Serbia's frontier with Bulgaria and Albania.[165] Most of the striking power of the Serbian forces was distributed between Crown Prince Alexander's First Army, deployed southwest of Kriva Palanka, and General Jankovic's Third Army, which occupied positions from Krivolak (on the Vardar) to Zletovo. The Second Army stood guard over the old Serbo-Bulgarian frontier.[166] The Greek army,[167] meanwhile, commanded by Constantine, who was now king, was deployed around Thessaloniki.[168]

The Bulgarian attack against the Serbs came at midnight on June 29, 1913, without a formal declaration of war.[169] To achieve tactical surprise, they did not preface the assault with the usual artillery barrage.[170] The Bulgarians were able to cross the Zletovska River and make minimal gains along the entire length of the Fourth Army's sixty-eight-mile (110 km) front, particularly on the right wing, where the Macedonian Adrianople Division captured the fortified position of Redki-Buki.[171] The Serbian line held, but General Jankovic, commander of the Third Army, was alarmed and requested authorization to withdraw.[172]

Faced with Jankovic's request, Putnik had two possible courses of action. The first, Jankovic's, required withdrawal of the Third Army behind the St. Nikola River and the abandonment of most of Macedonia east of the St. Nikola–Svecin line. But Zivojin Misic, Putnik's deputy, argued in favor of making a stand on the original front line along the Kriva Lakavitsa, Bregalnitsa, and Zletovska rivers.[173] In the end, Putnik rejected Jankovic's proposal; he believed any retreat would affect the morale of the soldiers and discourage potential allies from intervening against Bulgaria. Instead, he opted to follow a variation of Misic's plan. Putnik ordered the Third Army to hold its ground against the Bulgarian advance and eventually go on the offensive. The First and Second divisions were to check a possible Bulgarian advance from Kustendil, thus allowing the rest of the First Army, as well as the First Morava, Second Sumadija, and Cavalry divisions, to launch a counterattack on Kocane.[174]

The Serbian counteroffensive began on July 1, 1913, and within a day the Serb First Army had driven the right wing of the Bulgarian Fourth Army across the Zletovska.[175] Two days later, the Serbs had captured Rajcanski Rid and were poised to sever the only avenue of retreat for the Bulgarians.[176] Unfortunately for the Serbs, the offensive began to lose momentum. The Bulgarian high command decided to shift the offensive against the southern end of the Serbian front line. The new plan called for a drive into the rear areas of the Serbian position, much of which was held by the Second Timok Division. Although the division fought against Bulgarian forces for nearly five days, it was forced to retreat across the Bregalnitsa on July 4.[177]

Fortunately, the successful counterattack of the Serb First Army, as well as the Greek army's victories against the Bulgarians near Dojran and Lahana, limited the damage caused by the withdrawal of the Second Timok. Yet the tone of Jankovic's report to Putnik created the impression that the Third Army was on the verge of disaster.[178] Putnik decided to transfer the First Sumadija Division from the Serbian left to reinforce Jankovic. This act diminished the offensive momentum of the First Army, however, and enabled the northern wing of the Bulgarian Fourth Army to withdraw intact through Kocane, escaping what might otherwise have been a decisive defeat.[179]

Nevertheless, the Bulgarian campaign was quickly unraveling. The high command now authorized its First and Third armies to invade Serbia. But it was too little, too late. Although the two formations crossed the Serbo-Bulgarian border on July 5, they were both forced to withdraw by July 17. The token forces left by Putnik to defend the area cautiously followed the Bulgarians, but no further major engagements took place.[180] Meanwhile, the Serb First Army resumed its pursuit of the retreating Bulgarians. Kocane was occupied on July 6, and by July 9 Stip and Radoviste were also in the hands of the Serbs.[181] The Serbian advance continued until July 14, when Kriva

Palanka was captured. The Bulgarians, meanwhile, took up defensive positions around Pehcevo.[182] Soon the Serbo-Bulgarian front was stabilized, since the mountainous terrain prevented either army from making significant gains. From July 21–27, the Bulgarians launched a series of counterattacks against the Serbs near Kriva Palanka and in the region west of Kocane, but they had little success.[183]

In late July, Bulgaria's strategic situation changed dramatically. Romania had mobilized its army on July 5, and the country declared war against Bulgaria five days later.[184] On July 15, the Ottoman army marched into Bulgarian Thrace, taking possession of Lule Burgas and occupying Adrianople on July 23. On the same day, the Romanian Fifth Army occupied southern Dobruja, while the main Romanian forces were closing in on Sofia.[185] With the majority of its units deployed against Serbia and Greece, the Bulgarian army found it impossible to offer any effective resistance to the Romanian and Ottoman invasions. Although the Bulgarian Second Army was more than holding its own against the Greeks in the valley of the Strymon, the future was bleak.

Bulgarian operations against Greek forces in southern Macedonia happened concurrently with the Fourth Army's attack on the Serbs at Bregalnitsa. On June 29, the Bulgarian Second Army drove the Greeks out of their forward positions at Gevgeli, between Lake Tahinos and the Gulf of Orfano.[186] A few days later, the Greek offensive began. The principal thrust was delivered in the west, where the Second, Third, Fourth, and Fifth divisions advanced toward Gevgeli, attacking the Bulgarian positions at Kilkis. In the east, the First and Sixth divisions moved toward Lahana, while the Seventh Division was directed against Nigrita.[187] The following day, the Bulgarians abandoned Kilkis. Greek forces then occupied Lahana and Nigrita, while the Tenth Division took possession of Gevgeli.[188]

After the success at Kilkis, the left wing of the Greek army continued to press north, driving the Bulgarians out of Dojran, their principal supply facility in the area.[189] Shortly thereafter, the Bulgarians abandoned Seres, which the Greeks occupied on July 11.[190] Next, the Greek army advanced toward the Thessaloniki-Adrianople railroad, which threatened to cut off the Bulgarian lines of supply and communication. Suddenly, the Bulgarians were confronted with a critical situation, and Gen. Nikola Ivanov was forced to order a general retreat. One part of the Bulgarian Fourth Army fell back across the Belasica River, to the valley of the Stumica, and another part withdrew north, through the Rupel Pass.[191] And the Bulgarians did not stop there. After reaching the Stumica valley, they turned to the east and continued their retreat toward Petric in an effort to rejoin the rest of the Fourth Army as it moved north along the Strymon. The Greeks followed closely, but they could not trap the Bulgarians. Detachments of *evzones* were sent to cut them off, but without artillery support, these lightly armed Greek troops could only watch helplessly from the crests of the Belasica as the Bulgarians made a clean getaway.[192]

The Bulgarian retreat continued until July 11, when Ivanov attempted to consolidate a defensive position at the Kresna Pass and link up with the Fourth Army on the upper Bregalnitsa.[193] The Bulgarians were lucky. The rugged nature of the terrain and the lack of good roads made it difficult for the Greeks to pursue them. The two armies came into contact again on July 21, when Constantine launched an assault against the Kresna positions. The king's goal was to outflank the Bulgarians from the east and force them to retreat within their old boundaries.[194] After three days of fighting, the Greek center drove through Kresna, pushing the Bulgarians north until they again managed to consolidate their positions near the town of Djumaia. At the same time, the Greek left took Pehcevo and the right occupied Mehomija.[195]

The rapid advance of the Greek army now placed its central divisions in a dangerous position. The Greek flanks lagged far behind the center, and the Second, Fourth, and Fifth divisions were dangerously exposed to a Bulgarian attack. The Bulgarian high command seized this opportunity and began to prepare for a counterstroke against the Greeks. On July 28, reinforced with 20,000 troops, the Second Army advanced. The Bulgarian plan was ambitious. Essentially, troops were to advance against both flanks of the Greek forces and envelop the bulk of Constantine's army in the valley of the Strymon. The Bulgarian Third Balkan Division, supported by the Dram and Ser bridges, was to hold the Greek center. At the same time, the Second Thracian and Sixth Bdin infantry divisions and the First Brigade of the Tenth Combined Division were to strike southeast, along the Breganitsa, toward Pehcevo and the Strymon valley.

In the east, the Samokov and West Rhodope detachments were given the task of advancing southwest, from Belica toward the Strymon, thus closing the ring around the Greeks.[196] Mehomija and Pehcevo had fallen to the Bulgarians by July 30, in spite of Greek counterattacks on the previous day. But before the Bulgarian offensive could make its full impact, a cease-fire was concluded at Bucharest and all military operations ended.

In true Balkan tradition, the suddenness of the cease-fire gave rise to considerable controversy over the probable outcome of the Greco-Bulgarian battle. The Bulgarians claimed that their offensive was on the verge of success, while the Greeks argued that the Bulgarian attack would have had a negligible effect.[197]

EPILOGUE:

A WEDDING IN SARAJEVO, 1992

———

Do you intend, he asked, to make
Yugoslavia your home after the war?
No sir, I replied. Neither do I, he said.
And that being so, the less you and I worry about
the form of government they set up the better.

— WINSTON CHURCHILL TO FITZROY MACLEAN, WHO LED THE
BRITISH MILITARY MISSION TO TITO'S PARTISANS IN 1943

Any attempt to reconstruct the past is invariably skewed by one's contemporary perspective. In the Balkans, the spectator's angle of vision is often determined by events that bring into focus elements of history previously overlooked. In the early nineteenth century, Greece attracted the interests of the Great Powers, while in the first years of the twentieth century, Macedonia figured prominently as a zone of insecurity. Between 1912 and 1913, the Balkan wars surprised and confounded Western policy-makers, and reconfigured the political geography of Southeastern Europe. But that conflict was not ultimately decisive. Bulgaria remained hostile, and Albania was created mainly to satisfy Austro-Hungarian paranoia over Serbia's domination of the Adriatic.

And it didn't end there. The First World War devastated Serbia, set the path toward the establishment of modern Turkey, and terminated Greek ambitions to resurrect a new Byzantine Empire. In the Second World War, Bulgaria attempted to redress the territorial failures she'd suffered in 1913 (though any gains were rolled back in 1945). The subsequent Greek Civil War (1946–49) ushered in the Cold War and gave Tito an opportunity to distance himself from Stalin. Indeed, the very creation of Yugoslavia in 1929 had started the clock ticking for the Balkan crises of the 1990s, and Tito's system only put tensions on ice until the Soviet Union began to unravel in 1989.

Soon the idea of Yugoslavian identity, like the concept of Yugoslavia itself, was consigned to the dustbin of history. In 1991 the world discovered Croatia, and in 1992 the words "Bosnia" and "ethnic cleansing" became part of diplomatic discourse. At the same time, Serbs learned that there are limits to self-determination. The Western allies were prepared to accept the independence of the former Yugoslav republics, but they could not concede equal treatment for Serb areas in Croatia and Bosnia. The result was war.

Yugoslavia failed as a federal experiment, but its death throes justified NATO's existence. Any doubts Slobodan Milosevic or anybody else had had about the American "new world order" were placed to rest with the bombings of Kosovo and Serbia. This was cold comfort for Yugoslavs, of course, who overnight became another disenfranchised Balkan ethnic group. Yet glimmers of peaceful co-existence occasionally emerged above the violence and ugly rhetoric. One time that glimmer came from a simple wedding in Sarajevo.

Weddings stir up anxiety even under the best of circumstances.[1] The bride and groom and their families fuss over the minutest details, from flowers to food to seating arrangements. Of course, getting married while your country is under siege poses an entirely different set of problems. But in August 1992, a wedding in Sarajevo captured for a fleeting moment the flicker of hope that sustains the human spirit under adversity. The couple in question typified that Balkan paradox: Muslims and Christians, one people, to paraphrase George Bernard Shaw, divided by religion and a common language.

When this couple decided to marry, the violence in Sarajevo had been going on for more than four months. Every major political meeting was accompanied by firefights in the streets of the Bosnian capital. Various parts of the city fell into and out of the control of either Muslim or Serb forces. In the middle of this deadly madness, the inhabitants of Sarajevo struggled to survive against the chaos of a divided and besieged city.

Emma, a Muslim, and Nicholi, a Serb, lived in downtown Sarajevo, which meant they were surrounded by forces hostile to one or the other of them. Daily life was dictated by patterns of frequently changing sniper zones and the diminishing prospect of securing food and water. Parts of the city had been reduced to rubble, while other sections were hardly touched by the routine shelling and gunfire. The people of Sarajevo had few hopes, but one was that their own neighborhood would somehow be spared. Emma and Nicholi were no exception.

At the beginning of the war, the shelling had usually started in the late afternoon. People had come to rely on the relative punctuality of the gunners, and could even plan activities accordingly. But within a few weeks, the artillery in the mountains had adopted a random schedule. Shells rained down everywhere and at any time — in the middle of the city, in the marketplace, or on houses and apartment buildings. Each day, the body count of civilians grew.

As the fighting intensified, a new kind of darkness descended over the city. The streetlights ceased to function, and the limited electricity supply forced everyone to conserve their indoor lighting. Telephone lines were cut and power outages became common. The quality of life deteriorated rapidly, and a survivalist mindset emerged. Most people were trapped in the dying city; only a lucky few could escape. Food reserves dropped to critical levels, and any food that could not be consumed immediately became spoiled. The black market thrived, and the price of most items was astronomical. Savings accounts were frozen and salaries were at best irregular. People survived by whatever gave them a cash income. Many believed — or had convinced themselves — that the fighting would end any day. No one dared to imagine that the war would continue for much longer.

To make matters worse, the machinery of opportunism and propaganda emerged. Gangsters reinvented themselves as freedom fighters, and began claiming they were defending the city; they were instantly popular among the locals, who wrote songs about them and celebrated them as heroes. Meanwhile, ordinary people continued to suffer. The weaker ones broke down, wandering through the city day and night despite the shelling or sniper fire. But most just pretended they were living normal lives, ignoring the dangers and the deprivations. Consistent behavior, even living in denial, was the way for them to maintain their sanity.

—⚬⚬⚬—

August 19, 1992, was a sunny day. To safeguard their friends and families, Nicholi and Emma had organized their wedding with the meticulousness of a military operation. The ceremony was to take place at Sarajevo's city hall. The event was restricted to a handful of people, and they had to be prepared to face bullets, mortars, and shelling. Nicholi could not tell his own father, Dragan, of his plans because the old man lived in an apartment in the middle of one of the city's war zones and he would have wanted the wedding to be held there.

Yet sorting out the guest list and deciding on the venue was only the beginning. There were still many more logistical problems to be solved. On the day of the wedding, for example, Nicholi and Emma decided to dress up. But how could they prepare their good clothes, which had to be pressed for the occasion? Electrical rationing meant they could not just plug in the iron and press a shirt or a dress. If they heated their electric steam iron over the gas cooktop, that meant no warm food for a couple of days. In the end, Emma's mother, Milicia, who lived in a relatively safe part of the city, assumed responsibility for preparing the wedding meal and the reception. This was not a simple task in a city where food was in such short supply, but she managed to get the job done.

The ceremony was to take place at around noon. Nicholi went to city hall by himself. Naturally, the bride and her three closest friends were late. Under normal conditions, they would have walked, but in 1992 it was too risky to be out on the city streets. Public transportation was unreliable but safer. On that particular day, the bus route had been changed, and when they finally got off, they were about one thousand feet (300 meters) past city hall. To get to where they wanted to be, they had to cross an intersection that was exposed to sniper fire. Emma feared for her life, and worried about her future husband. As the bridal party crept across the intersection, they could hear hand grenades exploding and the occasional bullet whizzing by. Meanwhile, Nicholi and his best man, Misha, stood nervously waiting inside. When the bride and the rest of her party finally arrived, the ceremony was quickly carried out. Signatures on the wedding certificate made it official.

Afterward, they all went to Dragan's apartment. Misha arrived first and broke the news. Initially, Nicholi's father was shocked, but he quickly accepted the situation and joined in the celebration. The meal consisted of broth with some noodles, a pilaf, a tomato-and-onion salad, and a well-traveled chicken that Dragan had been hiding away for a special occasion. After the tasty meal, traditional toasts were made, and young and old remembered the good old days. Sadly, the guests had to leave before dark so as not to be caught by the curfew.

—⁓—

The story of Nicholi and Emma — like the stories of so many other innocent victims of the Balkan *tableau grotesque* — was set in motion a century earlier. Indeed, there is a golden thread of historical memories and terror linking the experiences of Nicholi and Emma to the Balkan wars of 1912–13. Histories of that conflict, and that includes the account in the previous chapter, are too often clinical studies of strategy, tactics, battles, and sieges, and too rarely chronicle the human cost and collective scars left by war.

The Balkan wars lasted less than one year, but during that short span of time, the seeds of revenge were sowed. The 1914 report of the Carnegie International Commission on the Balkan Wars documents cruelties that were echoed only too clearly in the atrocities of the 1990s. On the Thracian front, for example, retreating Ottoman troops exacted a terrible revenge for their defeat in the First Balkan War. In village after village, Turkish soldiers, irregulars, and even ordinary Muslims exacted their pound of flesh. In the village of Haskovo, 450 of 700 male Bulgarians were led into a gorge and executed. In the same village, according to the Carnegie report:

> A woman . . . described how her little child was thrown up into the air by a Turkish soldier who caught it on the point of his bayonet.

Other women told how three young girls threw themselves into a well after their fiancés were shot. . . . About twenty women . . . confirmed this story, and added that the Turkish soldiers went down into the well and dragged the girls out. Two of them were dead; the third had a broken leg; despite her agony she was outraged by the Turks. Other women . . . saw the soldier who had transfixed the baby on his bayonet carrying it in triumph across the village.[2]

In other situations, the Muslims themselves fell victim to capricious barbarism. When the Bulgarians finally captured Adrianople, for instance, officers and enlisted men attacked civilians as well as the Ottoman garrison. According to a *Daily Telegraph* account given by a Russian officer:

> What the women of Adrianople had to endure is beyond imagination. Outrages were committed against Greek, Jewish, and even Armenian women, despite the Armenians' devotion to the Bulgarian cause. Naturally the worst violence was directed against the Turkish women. . . . Among the women violated there were as many girls of tender years as aged women. Many of these girls are now actually with child. And those who could do so have gone away to hide their shame in remote regions. Many have lost their reason. Most keep silent about their misfortune, for reasons easy to understand.[3]

Early forms of propaganda exacerbated ethnic hatred. Two popular posters displayed prominently in Athens and Thessaloniki were representative of the appeal to baser instincts. One poster showed a Greek *evzone* holding a Bulgarian soldier with both hands while he gnawed at his face; the other depicted a Greek soldier gouging out the eyes of a Bulgarian.[4] The attempts to dehumanize the enemy easily kept pace with the shift of alliances.

And those alliances were constantly shifting. In the Second Balkan War, for example, the Bulgarians massacred and terrorized their former allies. Remarkably, in many cases the culprits were ordinary civilians who indulged themselves by butchering their neighbors, for either revenge or profit. In the village of Doxato, the Bulgarians, before they withdrew, armed the local Muslims, with lethal results for the Greek inhabitants. Of 2,700 Greeks, 600 men, women, and children were exterminated, and the "slaughter was carried out with every conceivable circumstances of barbarity."[5] A British naval officer serving with the Greek armed forces reached the village after the massacre and provided a firsthand account to the Carnegie commission:

> In some of the gardens and courtyards we saw children's graves each with a few wildflowers on them, but they do not appear to have buried any except the children. Poor souls! After the horror of it all, one wonders how they buried anyone. . . . I saw rooms where the floors were soaked with blood, and rugs, mats and cushions were covered with blood and human remains. The very stones in the courtyards of these houses were stained with blood; it is said that most of those who were killed in these yards were stoned to death.[6]

The primary objective for both sides in the conflict was to eliminate potential hostile populations. The instruments of persuasion were village burnings, torture, fear, and conversions. The Carnegie report documents the scorching of thousands of buildings, noting that "the burning of villages and the exodus of the defeated population is a normal and traditional incident of all Balkan wars and insurrections."[7]

Sadly, the Carnegie report seems to have been completely accurate on this point. During the 1990s, burnt-out houses and scorched villages could be seen throughout Croatia and Bosnia. An example cited by the 1994 "United Nations Balkan War Crimes Report" indicates how little ethnic warfare has changed. "On 9 September 1993 Croat forces attacked the Medak Pocket, a collection of small rural villages and hamlets forming a finger of Serb-controlled land in Sector South [in Bosnia] jutting into Croat territory," the report reads. "The Croats quickly killed or routed the Serb defenders and overran the area. . . . The withdrawal was completed by 17 September. As UN forces entered the pocket, they found every building burning or demolished."[8] The rest of the description could just as easily have come from the eighty-year-old Carnegie report. "Houses and whole villages are reduced to ashes," the account continues, "unarmed and innocent populations massacred en masse, incredible acts of violence, pillage and brutality of every kind — such were the means which were employed by the Serbo-Montenegrin soldiery, with a view to the entire transformation of the ethnic character of regions inhabited exclusively by Albanians."[9]

In 1912 and 1913, too, the burnings and pillages were the least of the brutalities conquered communities had to endure. The usual pattern was for a single detachment of one army or another to approach a village — more often than not, there was no resistance — and set in motion the grim process of depopulating the place. In most cases, regular troops were accompanied by various paramilitary forces, and these assumed responsibility for the pending massacre. Males between the ages of fourteen and sixty, if they were lucky, were executed. Women and young girls, regardless of age or physical circumstances, were raped repeatedly. Dozens of reports filed by British and Russian consuls in the Balkans include references to the pitiless treatment of pregnant women and girls under the age of fourteen. No measure was considered too demeaning. Captain Boyle, the British naval attaché in Athens, commented in his dispatch that in the Turkish village of Emalu, the Bulgarian occupiers had forced "the women of the village . . . [to parade] naked in the street. I was at first inclined to think that this meant with uncovered faces, but my interpreter insisted that it meant in the nude."[10] According to another report, this one from H. E. W. Young, the British vice-consul at Philoppoli, in Macedonia, the Bulgarian army was met by emissaries as it approached the towns of Serres, Cavalla, and Xanthi. These emissaries were to

> formally surrender to him [the Bulgarian general] long before the troops (regular or irregular) reached these towns. Yet at Serres 400 persons were massacred; at Cavalla 200 were methodically tortured to death on successive days; and at Xanthi there were numerous murders and "disappearances," and innumerable isolated acts of violence. At Dedeagatch some 300 persons were massacred, and the Muslim quarter looted. Women were stripped and their ornaments torn from them. Everywhere one hears of outrages on women and children.[11]

In 1994, the "United Nations Balkan War Crimes Report," in an eerie echo, stated: "The pattern of rape involved individuals or groups

committing sexual assaults against women for the purposes of terror-
izing and humiliating them, often as part of the policy of 'ethnic
cleansing.'"[12] In practice, this meant public rapes. The same report
describes one witness who "saw an elderly woman and others raped in
front of a group of 100 detained villagers. The witness was herself
threatened with rape and she saw a number of men from the group
having their throats cut."[13]

During the Balkan wars in 1912–13, crusading priests followed on
the heels of the army units and paramilitaries and "persuaded" the
survivors, usually old men and women, to convert. The British consul
writes that the Bulgarians surrounded the "the village of Yasouren . . .
by a cordon while priests and *komitajis*, with threats and blows,
endeavored to force the people to renounce their religion." When
the British diplomat complained to the Bulgarian authorities, he was
told "that these fanatical Moslems had signed petitions of their own
free will begging the Government to send priests to baptise them,
and after the ceremony they had danced."[14]

The Serbs in Macedonia, meanwhile, persuaded Bulgarians to see
the light, and to accept religious and national transformation.
Everyone — from schoolteachers and municipal authorities to ordinary villagers — was encouraged to sign the following declaration:

> Five and a half centuries ago our forefathers were Serbs. They were
> conquered by the Turks. Whilst under Turkish rule they were
> forced by propaganda and terrorism to become Bulgars. We have
> now been given freedom by our kinsmen and have again become
> Serbs. The Bulgars did not make us free, but marched into Thrace
> and fought for non-Slavonic races there. And now they are waging
> war against Servia. Of our free will we accept the protection of
> King Peter and of his son, the heir to the Servian throne.[15]

Ironically, after less than thirty years and one world war had
passed, the Serbs themselves faced the dilemma of conversion or
death. After the German occupation of Yugoslavia in 1941, the Nazis,
in co-operation with Croatian Fascists, established an independent
state of Croatia. But large pockets of Eastern Orthodox Serbs posed a
problem for the Catholic-centric state. The solution was either extermination or conversion, and in many cases both. In July 1941,

members of the Ustashe (an extremist Croatian nationalist organization) descended on the town of Glina, in southern Croatia. Peasants
who had fled to hide in the woods were lured back with an offer of
amnesty if they accepted Roman Catholicism. Some 250 Serbs agreed
and assembled inside the local Orthodox Church. According to an
eyewitness account, after their conversion, they were locked in the
church and attacked. Many were killed with wooden hammers, others
were stabbed, and some were set alight with candles and slowly
burned. One poor man had his throat slit and was forced to sing, all
while the blood spurted from his body onto the remaining victims.[16]

For the rest of the war, the Ustashe turned Croatia into a slaugh-
terhouse, complete with death camps and other mechanisms of mass
killing. Their Nazi patrons were more interested in erasing the
Yugoslav Jews, however, and less concerned with the Serbs. In fact,
the local Nazi overlords eventually grew impatient with the excesses
against the Serbs, since such excesses drove many to join the armed
resistance and diverted resources from the extermination of the Jews.
But the members of the Ustashe were not alone in settling old scores
and adopting a program of depopulation. Some Bosnian Muslims
and ethnic Albanians also welcomed the German occupation, and
added religious homogeneity to the Nazi goal of ethnic purity. Many
Albanians in Kosovo joined the Scanderberg Waffen SS division,
while some Bosnian Muslims accepted work in the death camps. And
all sides used or forced Gypsies to do their dirty work.

The methods of execution were ghastly and macabre, and the
inmates of the camps faced a grisly and unimaginable end.
Hammers, hoes, iron bars, knives, axes, hatchets, explosives, and
guns of various types were all employed, depending on the victims
or the circumstances.[17] Mass rape was again used to humiliate and
torment. In the Loborgrad camp, 1,500 Jewish women and girls were
subjected to repeated rapes by the commandant and his guards.[18] At
least 60,000 Jews, 26,000 Gypsies, and 750,000 Serbs were killed in
Yugoslavia between 1941 and 1944.[19]

The Greeks fared little better. The Nazis awarded Macedonia and
Thrace to their Bulgarian allies in 1941, and 100,000 Greeks were
expelled and more than 30,000 killed in a mini genocide. The
Bulgarian government, determined to homogenize the region and
remove any vestiges of Hellenism, confiscated land and turned it over

to Bulgarian colonists. All evidence of Greek culture was systematically destroyed. Thousands sought refuge in Thessaloniki, but more went to Athens, where they fell victim to a familiar but faceless killer — famine. After the Axis occupation of Greece in 1941, the Germans confiscated all foodstuffs and livestock. Some Greek peasants saw an excellent opportunity to eliminate their debts by charging exorbitant prices for their produce, but in the process of satiating their avarice they contributed to the starvation of their countrymen.

The Bulgarians exacerbated the food crisis by seizing the wheat fields of Macedonia and Thrace, and the British compounded the problem with a blockade. More than 100,000 died of starvation and disease in Athens alone, and countless more perished in other cities and towns. Athens was transformed into a city of long lines of emaciated men, women, and children waiting for thin soup delivered once a day by the Greek Red Cross. The streets, meanwhile, were littered with decaying corpses, for the authorities did not have enough wagons and volunteers to carry the dead to mass graves outside the city.

After liberation, amazingly, the situation for Greece deteriorated. A destructive civil war between Greek Communists and government forces ravaged what was left of the infrastructure of the country. Entire villages in northern Greece were forcibly abandoned in a government scheme to deprive the Communist insurgents of their supplies.[20] Even today, Greece is recovering from the aftershocks of this social upheaval, which flooded the cities and towns with peasants. The urban sprawl that defines modern Athens and characterizes the Greek state is the culmination of that upheaval. The Greek countryside is now managed by land owners with farm workers who come mostly from Albania.

The trauma of occupation and civil war quickly resurfaced during the Yugoslav crisis, when the Greeks were suddenly confronted with the Macedonia issue. Few would have believed that in its bid for independence, this small former Yugoslav republic could have generated such hysteria. But Macedonia for the Greeks conjures up memories of starvation, forced conversions, executions, and mass killings, memories that dramatically re-emerged during Yugoslavia's death throes. After all, Macedonia had been devastated by an ugly guerrilla war before 1912–13, and during the occupation it was the scene of reprisals and executions whose ferocity was upstaged only by the massacres of the Greek Civil War. Today, the issue of Macedonia still threatens to ignite the Balkan powder keg.

In many ways, this small Yugoslav republic, which achieved independence in 1991 without the force of arms, has emerged as a microcosm of the Balkans. Although the Albanian minority is quickly reaching parity with the Slav majority, this is not the miracle of inclusion it would at first seem to be. Indeed, the government in Skopje is practicing the policies of exclusion, with probable lethal consequences for the future. A Macedonian republic implies a society of Macedonians alone, with no room for Albanians. With nowhere else to turn, the Albanian minority will doubtless press for the creation of a greater Albania to ensure their physical and cultural security.

Indeed, since the Serbian debacle in Kosovo in 1999, the call for a greater Albania has seduced Albanians throughout the former Yugoslav republics. NATO intervention in Kosovo has led Albanian nationalists to misunderstand Western policy toward the former Yugoslavia as a license to experiment with Balkan frontiers. It is an old game played with human currency, the only capital readily available in the Balkans. The results, however, are the same: war, death, destruction, atrocities, and thousands of refugees. Why does this pattern of conflict continue to haunt the Balkan peninsula?

One explanation is that in the twenty-first century, the only thing that has altered in the "great game" for control of Central Asia through Southeastern Europe is the players. The United States has replaced Britain as Russia's primary competitor in Asia, and this may explain why America is interested in the Balkans for more than just humanitarian reasons. U.S. policy in the region is guided by the same strategic considerations that once shaped Britain's approach toward Southeastern Europe and the Ottoman Empire. In fact, the Americans have gone one step further: the NATO protectorates of Bosnia and Kosovo are de facto satellites of the United States, and thus a potential base of operations from which to secure the northern approaches to Southeastern Europe and cast a long shadow across to Central Asia. Because of this geopolitical reality, the former Yugoslav republics continue to remain on the periphery of the "great game." They will be left on their own, even to drown in a sea of their own blood, only until their destabilization undermines the interests of the United States, Europe, and Russia.

—⟨∿∿⟩—

The Americans went to war against Serbia on March 24, 1999, because it became clear to Washington that the crisis in Kosovo could ignite a wider Balkan conflict and unravel the security of Southeastern Europe. President Clinton articulated this policy on the day the NATO bombing commenced by stating: "We act to prevent a wider war, to defuse a powder keg at the heart of Europe that has exploded twice before in this century with catastrophic results."[21] To some degree, the Balkans have not been able to shed the war fatigue of the past. After all, the Balkan battlefield has been consuming lives for more than a millennium, and certainly the past 600 years have offered only brief respites from conflict. The war in Kosovo was the most recent crisis — but almost certainly not the last.

Prior to the NATO intervention in Kosovo, 500,000 Albanians had fled from the terror of Slobodan Milosevic's security forces and the firefights between the Serb army and the Kosovo Liberation Army (KLA). Another 900,000 escaped to avoid the bombings.[22] From 1990 to 1999, the Serb security forces brutalized, executed, pillaged, and terrorized the Albanians with impunity. But when the Serbs surrendered to NATO in March 1999, the pendulum swung in favor of the Albanians, and the KLA became the new lords of Kosovo. It was now the Serbs' turn to suffer. The Serbian population of Kosovo has dropped from 200,000 before the war to less than 25 percent of that number today. Pristina, the capital, has only one thousand Serb residents left of its original 40,000.[23]

The grim cycle will undoubtedly resume, with the Serbs once again exacting vengeance. Victory or defeat in one war only prepares the ground for a renewed struggle in the future. But the antidote to war is security and material wealth. Although the Balkan map cannot be changed, it can be made less fractured through economic progress. Ultimately, the answer is not NATO occupation but economic peacekeeping,[24] the integration of the region into the European Union. The blurring of frontiers will provide the political, economic, and social security needed for distinct and ancient communities to adjust their cultural, religious, and linguistic boundaries without fear of retaliation. Only then will national chauvinism and insecurity die a quiet death.

NOTES

⟨✦⟩

Introduction: Memory of Terror

1 Roksanda Petrovic presently is living with her children and grandchildren in Vancouver. She generously and patiently provided the author with an account of her experience of the first night of the NATO bombing of Belgrade. Her family managed to bring her safely to Vancouver, but she plans to return to Belgrade in spring 2001.

Chapter 1: Assassination, Martyrdom, and Betrayal

1 A policeman almost intercepted Princip and could have prevented the assassination, but he was kicked in the knee by one of the other conspirators. This allowed Princip enough time to carry out his mission. Vladimir Dedijer, *The Road to Sarajevo* (New York: Simon & Schuster, 1966), 321.

2 According to R. W. Seton-Watson, the visit on the anniversary of the Battle of Kosovo was resented by the vast majority of Serbs in both Bosnia-Herzegovina and Serbia, and was seen as a provocation and a challenge. A. J. P. Taylor argues that Ferdinand's visit to Sarajevo was meant to provoke nationalist feeling, or rather to challenge it. He maintains that the visit deliberately coincided with Serbia's national day. R. W. Seton-Watson, *Sarajevo: A Study in the Origins of the Great War* (London: The Camelot Press, 1925); A. J. P. Taylor, *The Struggle for Mastery in Europe, 1848–1918* (Oxford: Oxford University Press, 1971), 520, n. 2.

3 Bosnia and Herzegovina were formally annexed by the Austro-Hungarians in 1908.

4 "The Archduke's Consort," *The Times*, June 29, 1914. The official list of recognized higher nobility was again revised and published in 1825. It included fourteen "princely houses" located within the empire and six old families headed by counts who were included because of special historical or genealogical factors. Once this list had been established, the door to the inner circle of

the Habsburg nobility was closed forever. Gordon Brook-Shepherd, *Victims at Sarajevo: The Romance and Tragedy of Franz Ferdinand and Sophie* (London: Harvill Press, 1984), 44.

5 Count Ottokar Czernin, *In the World War* (London: Cassell, 1919), 39.

6 Luigi Albertini, *The Origins of the War of 1914*, vol. 2, trans. and ed. Isabella M. Massey (London: Oxford University Press, 1952), 3.

7 Dedijer, *Road to Sarajevo*, 93.

8 "The Archduke's Consort."

9 Dedijer, *Road to Sarajevo*, 99.

10 Ibid.

11 Ibid., 102.

12 The morganatic marriage originated during the Roman Empire and defined the legal relationship between a free and a non-free person. The word "morganatic" stems from the German *morgen* (meaning "morning"), and referred to "the morning gift" a husband would bestow on a wife as a reward for the previous evening's physical relations. Over time, this particular type of marriage was used to accommodate the union of individuals of higher and lower status. Under its terms, the archduke had to assure the emperor that Sophie would never present herself at court or in high noble circles, and that she would claim no official role for herself or her future offspring. In effect, Sophie had agreed to remain invisible and simply serve as little more than a concubine (Brook-Shepherd, *Victims at Sarajevo*, 75).

13 Albertini, *War of 1914*, vol. 2, 2.

14 The only exception was Ferdinand's stepmother, Archduchess Maria Theresa.

15 Brook-Shepherd, *Victims at Sarajevo*, 55.

16 Ibid., 108.

17 Ibid.

18 Ibid., 221–22, 235.

19 Albertini, *War of 1914*, vol. 2, 18–19.

20 Ibid. Albertini cites a number of individuals close to the archduke whose accounts underline his uneasiness over the trip to Bosnia.

21 Alan Palmer, *Twilight of the Habsburgs: The Life and Times of Emperor Francis Joseph* (London: Grove/Atlantic, 1997), 319.

22 Brook-Shepherd, *Victims at Sarajevo*, 221; Albert von Margutti, *The Emperor Francis Joseph* (London: Hutchinson, 1921), 126–27; Count Carlo Collas, "Auf den Bosnischen Wegspuren der Kriegsschuldfrag," *Kriegsschuldfrag* (Jan. 1927): 11–27; A. J. P. Taylor, *The Observer*, Nov. 16, 1958.

23 A. Morsey, "Konopischt und Sarajevo," *Berliner Monatshefte* (June 1934): 64; Brook-Shepherd, *Victims at Sarajevo*, 240.

24 For a detailed description of the actual events surrounding the assassination, see Brook-Shepherd, *Victims at Sarajevo*, chapter 12, and Dedijer, *Road to Sarajevo*, chapter 14.

25 "Servian Condemnation," *The Times*, July 1, 1914.

26 In English, this translates to "the Field of Blackbirds."

27 However, by the fourteenth century, only candidates from the Eastern Orthodox

Church would be able to acquire legitimacy under all the various circumstances affecting succession to the throne.

28 W. Ensslin, "The Government and Administration of the Byzantine Empire," in H. M. Gwatkin and J. P. Whitney, eds., *The Byzantine Empire, Part II: Government, Church and Civilization*, vol. 4 of *The Cambridge Medieval History* (Cambridge: Cambridge University Press, 1967), 6.

29 M. Dinic, "The Balkans, 1018–1499," in ed. J. M. Hussey, *The Byzantine Empire, Part I*, vol. 4 of *The Cambridge Medieval History* (Cambridge: Cambridge University Press, 1966), 538–39.

30 Ibid., 539–40.

31 Ibid.

32 These dates are approximate.

33 John V. Fine, Jr., *The Late Medieval Balkans: A Critical Survey from the Late Twelfth Century to the Ottoman Conquest* (Ann Arbor, Mich.: University of Michigan Press, 1987), 409.

34 Ibid.

35 There is not a single primary source that reliably describes the events surrounding the Battle of Kosovo, and therefore each reconstruction is subjective. A combination of primary texts, commentaries, and authoritative secondary sources provides a reasonable account of the events before and after battle.

36 There is considerable literature on all the versions of the Battle of Kosovo, along with folktales and myths that have evolved over the centuries. Most can be consulted in an exhaustive study by Thomas A. Emmert, *Serbian Golgotha: Kosovo, 1389* (New York: Columbia University Press, 1990), passim.

37 Fine, *Late Medieval Balkans*, 409–10. Although ascribing the idea of betrayal to literary requirement, Fine does not entirely dismiss the notion that there may have been actual treachery.

38 Laonicas Chalcocondylas, "De Rebus Turcicis," in ed. Emmanuel Bekker, *Corpus Scriptorum Historiae Byzantinae* (Bonn: E. Weberi, 1843), 54. Chalcocondylas's account provides both the Turkish and Greek versions. According to the former, Murad was killed pursuing the Serbs; latter sources state that the sultan was assassinated before the battle. Ducas (3.1) suggests that the assassination took place during the course of the battle, and that the Ottoman officials kept the death secret. In *Byzantium, Europe, and the Early Ottoman Sultans, 1373–1513: An Anonymous Greek Chronicle of the Seventeenth Century*, trans. Mario Philippides (New York: Aristide D. Caratzas, 1990), the Turkish sources state that Murad led the charge against the Serbian forces and was killed by an arrow fired by a Serbian foot soldier. The anonymous writer also repeats the story of an assassin who approached Murad and stabbed him with a dagger. According to Philippides, the editor of the codex, it is quite evident, because of the references to Turkish and Roman sources, that the anonymous author based his account on that of Chalcocondylas (p. 125, n. 16).

39 Ducas (22.11) asserts that it was common practice to keep secret the death of a sultan until the new one assumed the title. This helped avoid turmoil and even rebellion among the Ottomans.

40 Ducas, 3.3.

41 Herbert Adams Gibbons, *The Foundation of the Ottoman Empire*, (London: Cass, 1968), 177–78.

42 It was customary for the Ottomans to place Christian units on the right wing and Turkish forces on the left when fighting in Europe and reverse the order for battles in Asia. Lord Kinross, *The Ottoman Centuries: The Rise and Fall of the Turkish Empire* (New York: William Morrow, 1977), 58.

43 The Battle of Nicopolis is one such example. Charles Oman, *A History of the Art of War in the Middle Ages, 1278–1485*, vol. 2 (New York: B. Franklin, 1924), 349.

44 Nicholas C. J. Pappas and Lee Brigance Pappas, "The Ottoman View of the Battle of Kosovo," in ed. Wayne S. Vucinich and Thomas A. Emmert, *Kosovo: Legacy of Medieval Battle* (Minnesota: University of Minnesota, 1991), 46.

45 H. A. Gibbons, *The Foundation of the Ottoman Empire*, 176, and Kinross (*Ottoman Centuries*, 58) also suggest that Vuk's withdrawal was either treason or desertion.

46 H. A. Gibbons, 182.

47 Fine, *Late Medieval Balkans*, 412.

48 Ibid., 411–12.

49 Ducas (15.2), in particular, laments the sacrifice of young girls and boys. It seems the sultan's tastes transcended gender boundaries, and included "lascivious sexual acts, indulging in licentious behavior with boys and girls."

50 H. A. Gibbons, 183.

51 Fine, *Late Medieval Balkans*, 425–26.

52 Warren Treadgold writes that Manuel, the Byzantine emperor, attempted to negotiate with the Venetians and Genoese, but his efforts did not yield any agreement. Instead, Byzantium, Venice, and Genoa concluded a treaty with Sulayman, one of the brothers who had taken control of the Ottoman European possessions. This treaty returned some territories to the Byzantines and granted favorable concessions and privileges to the Venetians and Genoese. Warren Treadgold, *A History of the Byzantine State and Society* (Stanford, Calif.: Stanford University Press, 1997), 789. Edward Gibbon, *The Decline and Fall of the Roman Empire*, vol. 6 (New York: Random House, 1994), 177–78, argues that the Byzantines, Venetians, and Genoese, instead of denying passage to the Ottomans trapped on the Asian side of the Dardanelles, competed with each other over who would offer the most help to the Turks.

53 H. A. Gibbons, 255, n. 1, and 256. Gibbons refers to Bayazid's wife as Despina. *An Anonymous Greek Chronicle*, 2. 34, relates that Timur's method of humiliating Bayazid was to have Olivera's dresses cut from the knee to the thigh. According to Gibbon (256, n. 1), exposure of women was a common symbol of conquest among the Mongols.

54 It is unclear whether Bayazid died of apoplexy or killed himself by smashing his head against the bars of his cell or cage (H. A. Gibbons, 256, n. 2).

55 Ibid., 261–62.

56 Halil Inalcik, *The Ottoman Empire: The Classical Age 1300–1600* (New York: Praeger, 1973), 17–18. Fine (*Late Medieval Balkans*, 503) argues that despite the civil war, neither the Serbians nor the Byzantines were in any position to rise up against the Ottomans. The only possibility was a coalition of all the Balkan Christians, but that did not happen. It is not known whether such a possibility was even considered.

57 Fine, *Late Medieval Balkans*, 426.

58 Ibid., 554–55.

59 Ibid., 409–10. Fine suggests that the Kosovo epic poems paralleled the New Testament, and thus the Christ-like Lazar required a Judas. H. A. Gibbons (*The Foundation of the Ottoman Empire*, 174–75) considers Lazar a minor Serbian chieftain with little authority. He further claims that Lazar began his rule by submitting cravenly to Murad, and that he survived the Battle of Kosovo only to be executed, bringing to an end an unspectacular career. Gibbons also notes, with some disgust, that Lazar gets far more candles at his shrine than the Lazar of Bethany.

60 Fine, *Late Medieval Balkans*, 413.

61 Ibid., 414.

62 Ibid., 576.

63 Emmert (*Serbian Golgotha*, 83) writes that by the end of the fifteenth century, the records of some observers had made the assassination of Murad a central theme.

64 Ibid., 105.

65 Ibid., 111.

66 Dedijer, *Road to Sarajevo*, 253.

67 Ibid., 255–57.

68 Ibid., 120.

69 "The Servian Tragedy," *The Times*, June 15, 1903.

70 "Murder of the King and Queen of Servia," *The Times*, June 12, 1903.

71 David MacKenzie, *The "Black Hand" on Trial: Salonika, 1917* (Boulder: Eastern European Monographs, 1995), 11–12; "The Servian Tragedy."

72 MacKenzie, *"Black Hand" on Trial*, 18.

73 "The Servian Tragedy."

74 "Murder of the King and Queen of Servia."

75 "The Servian Tragedy."

76 Ibid.; Rebecca West, *Black Lamb and Grey Falcon: A Journey through Yugoslavia* (London: Penguin, 1994), 11.

77 "The Servian Tragedy."

78 Ibid.

79 Ibid.

80 "Murder of the King and Queen of Servia."

81 Ibid.; MacKenzie, *"Black Hand" on Trial*, 11–12.

82 Dedijer, *Road to Sarajevo*, 440–51.

83 Albertini, *War of 1914*, vol. 2, 20; W. A. Dolph Owings, *The Sarajevo Trial*, trans. W. A. Dolph Owings, Elizabeth Pribic, and Nikola Pribic, 2 vols. (North Carolina: Documentary Publications, 1984), vol. 1, 68.

84 Dolph Owings, *The Sarajevo Trial*, vol. 1, 68.

85 Dedijer, *Road to Sarajevo*, 187–90.

86 Ibid., 192–93.

87 Ibid., 196–97.

88 Ibid., 197.

89 Albertini, *War of 1914*, vol. 2, 47, n. 2.

90 Dedijer, *Road to Sarajevo*, 319–20.

91 Dolph Owings, *Sarajevo Trial*, vol. 1, 56.

92 Ibid., xiii, 84–85.

93 Ibid., 68; Albertini, *War of 1914*, vol. 2, 86–87.

94 Dolph Owings, *Sarajevo Trial*, vol. 1, 28–29.

95 By accommodating the South Slavs, the Austrians not only would have balanced the Hungarian influence, but also would have countered the movement toward a Yugoslav state, eventually absorbing Serbia, voluntarily, into a Greater Austria. The South Slavs' desire for unification could have been achieved within the framework of the empire. Albertini, *War of 1914*, vol. 2, 13–15.

96 Dedijer, *Road to Sarajevo*; Seton-Watson, *Sarajevo*. Albertini (*War of 1914*, vol. 2, 86–88) had the opportunity to interview some of the participants or their relatives, and he maintains that the archduke's Slavophile attitude represented a major threat to the Serb nationalists.

97 Dolph Owings, *Sarajevo Trial*, vol. 2, 324.

98 Albertini, *War of 1914*, vol. 2, 36.

99 Dolph Owings, *Sarajevo Trial*, vol. 1, ii, and vol. 2, 324.

100 Albertini, *War of 1914*, vol. 2, 36.

101 Ibid., 36–37.

102 Brook-Shepherd, *Victims at Sarajevo*, 251; Albertini, *War of 1914*, vol. 2, 37.

103 Dolph Owings, *Sarajevo Trial*, vol. 1, 67.

104 Ibid., vol. 2, 325.

105 Ibid.

106 Brook-Shepherd, *Victims at Sarajevo*, 271–72. A black tablet was erected on the spot where Princip stood when he assassinated Archduke Ferdinand. The inscription read: "Here, in this historical place, Gavrilo Princip was the initiator of liberty, on that day of St. Vitus, the 28th of June, 1914." In 1996, the new Bosnian government removed the monument.

107 Dolph Owings, *Sarajevo Trial*, vol. 2, 527.

108 The two coffins were placed side by side on a dais draped with a golden cloth and surrounded by nearly one hundred long candles. On top of the archduke's coffin lay his prince's crown, archduke's hat, general's helmet and sword, and a velvet cushion pinned with his orders and medals. The top of Sophie's casket carried only a cushion with one decoration, the Order of the Star cross, and the black fan and white gloves that symbolized both a noblewoman and a lady-in-waiting. Brook-Shepherd (*Victims at Sarajevo*, 264) writes that the fan and the white gloves were not necessary, and that this was "an offensive token of Sophie's station."

109 Brook-Shepherd, *Victims at Sarajevo*, 266–67.

110 According to Dedijer (*Road to Sarajevo*, 19), more than three thousand books and pamphlets about the controversy have been published since 1939.

Chapter 2: The Ottoman Era: The Birth of Balkan Mythology

1 Cristobulus, "De Rebus Gestis Mechemetis," in ed. C. Muller, *Fragmenta historicorum graecorum*, vol. 5 (Paris: Ambrosio Firmin Didot, 1848–1885), 66–67. Also

see the English translation by C. T. Riggs, *History of Mehmet the Conqueror by Kritovoulos* (Princeton, N.J.: Princeton University Press, 1954).

2 According to the Koran, a city that did not surrender would be subjected to three days of pillaging.

3 Cristobulus, "De Rebus Gestis Mechemetis," 60–61; Makarios Melissenos, "The Chronicle of the Siege of Constantinople, April 2–May 19, 1453," in trans. Marios Philippides, *The Fall of the Byzantine Empire: A Chronicle by George Sphrantzes, 1401–1477* (Amherst, Mass.: University of Massachusetts Press, 1980), 119.

4 Nicolo Barbaro, *Diary of the Siege of Constantinople 1453*, trans. J. R. Jones (New York: Exposition Press, 1969), 61.

5 In 1439, at the Council of Florence, the two churches that had been divided by the Great Schism of 1054 were once again united. The union, however, was an act of desperation by the Byzantine and the Orthodox delegates. At the council, they were willing to accept almost any formula in order to secure military help from the West. The Orthodox patriarch, Joseph, agreed that the Latin formula of "the Holy Ghost proceeding *from* the Son" was the same as the Greek formula of "the Holy Ghost proceeding *through* the son" (emphasis mine). Unfortunately, he died shortly thereafter, and thus could not exert any influence over the anti-unionists in Constantinople. Steven Runciman cites a particularly unkind scholar, who remarked that after Joseph muddled his prepositions, what else could he do? On the general unwillingness of the Byzantines to fight, see Leonard of Chios, *The Siege of Constantinople 1453: Seven Contemporary Accounts*, trans. J. R. Melville Jones (Amsterdam: Hakkert, 1972), 28–29. See also Steven Runciman, *The Fall of Constantinople 1453* (Cambridge: Cambridge University Press, 1965), 17–180.

6 Steven Runciman argues that the Orthodox already living under Ottoman rule represented a flaw in the plan for the union of the two churches. In effect, union meant that these Eastern Christians would be excluded from the jurisdiction of the Orthodox Church. Runciman, *Fall of Constantinople*, 20–22.

7 Barbaro, *Diary of the Siege*, 77–78; Leonard of Chios, *Siege of Constantinople*, 26, 30. According to Chalcocondylas, Mehmet was motivated by lust ("De Rebus Turcicis," 54). The daughter of a Greek renegade in the Ottoman camp had a passionate affair with the sultan. Chalcocondylas, perhaps to underline Mehmet's depravity, states that the killings were conducted at the urging of the Greek woman's father, whose motives remain a mystery.

8 Runciman writes that although the Byzantines paid the price demanded for Western aid, in the end they were cheated. Runciman, *Fall of Constantinople*, 72.

9 Ducas, *Decline and Fall of Byzantium to the Ottoman Turk* (Detroit: Wayne State University Press, 1975), 148.

10 Ibid., 40-41; Leonard of Chios, *Siege of Constantinople*, 39–40.

11 Ducas, *Decline and Fall of Byzantium*, 36–37.

12 Ibid., 36.

13 Cristobulus, "De Rebus Gestis Mechemetis," 58–59.

14 Ducas, *Decline and Fall of Byzantium*, 39–40.

15 G. Ostrogorsky, "The Palaeologi," in *Cambridge Medieval History*, vol. 4, 386.

16 Edward S. Creasy, *History of the Ottoman Turks: From the Beginning of Their Empire to the Present Time* (Beirut: Khayats, 1961), 79, n. 1.

17 Steven Runciman, *The Kingdom of Acre and the Later Crusades*, vol. 3 of *A History of the Crusades* (Cambridge: Cambridge University Press, 1951), 131.

18 A typical casualty of the frequent dynastic quarrels that plagued Byzantium was Emperor Isaac. Isaac was deposed by his brother, Alexius. In keeping with tradition, Alexius had Isaac blinded and then thrown in prison with his son. Blinding was common practice, since those maimed would be permanently disbarred from the throne. In 1201, Isaac's son, also named Alexius, managed to escape from prison and seek refuge at his sister's court in Germany. With the help of Philip of Swabia, his brother-in-law, Alexius reached an understanding with the leaders of the Fourth Crusade and the pope. If he agreed to financial concessions and the unification of the churches, Alexius would receive their support for his claim to the Byzantine throne. Runciman, *History of the Crusades*, vol. 3, 111–13.

19 Ibid., 123.

20 A great deal of the violence inflicted on the inhabitants was random and the result of poorly disciplined troops. The leader of the crusade, Boniface, the marquis of Montferrant and the count of Flanders, had forbidden, on pain of death, the rape of married women, virgins, and nuns. His restrictions, however, were not met with respect to plunder. Most of the public and private wealth of the Greeks, whether in coins, works of art, icons, or ancient Greek and Roman antiquities, became the prize of the knights and their soldiers. The only condition was that all the booty collected by individuals had to be deposited in a common pool in one of three designated churches. (Any violation of this order was punishable by death, and early in the course of the pillage, one of the knights was made an example and hanged with his shield and coat of arms around his neck.) The amassed wealth was then divided between the French and the Venetians. The latter first deducted 50,000 marks to cover the debts owed them by the crusaders. Even so, the French portion of the pillage alone was worth 400,000 marks of silver (about seven times the annual revenue of England in Gibbon's time). A great deal of gold and priceless artifacts were also lost or wasted by the soldiers. Gibbon, *Decline and Fall*, vol. 6, 193–95.

21 Peter F. Sugar, *Southeastern Europe under Ottoman Rule, 1354–1804*, vol. 5 (Seattle: University of Washington Press, 1977), 9.

22 Fernand Braudel, *The Mediterranean and the Mediterranean World in the Age of Philip II*, vol. 2, trans. Sian Reynolds (Los Angeles: University of California Press, 1973), 661.

23 Sugar, *Southeastern Europe*, 11.

24 Michael VII Palaeologos expelled the Latins from Constantinople and reestablished the city as the capital of the empire.

25 Speros Vryonis, *The Decline of Medieval Hellenism in Asia Minor and the Process of Islamization from the Eleventh through the Fifteenth Century* (Berkeley: University of California Press, 1977), 136.

26 The period between 1261 and 1310 witnessed the establishment of the Ghazi principalities of Mentese, Aydin, Saruhan, Karesi, and Osmanli.

27 Sugar, *Southeastern Europe*, 12.

28 For most of the fourteenth century, the Byzantine Empire was the battleground for civil and dynastic wars aggravated by religious quarrels. In 1347, the bubonic plague hit the empire, killing close to one-third of the population. According to Runciman, the Ottomans took advantage of these upheavals and

penetrated farther into the Balkans. By the end of the century, they had reached the Danube. Runciman, *Fall of Constantinople*, 4.

29 Charles Oman, *A History of the Art of War in the Middle Ages, 1278–1485*, vol. 2, (New York: 1924), 340.

30 Sugar, *Southeastern Europe*, 187.

31 Ibid. The last third of the sixteenth century is considered, by most historians, to be the beginning of the Ottoman decline. Sugar, *Southeastern Europe*, 187.

32 It should be noted that Halil was also both Theodora's son and the grandson of a Byzantine emperor.

33 Ducas, *Decline and Fall of Byzantium*, 8.3.

34 Custom and tradition dictated humane treatment between Christian soldiers. After a battle was over, the victors could not execute their prisoners or mistreat them (other than to deprive them of their clothing). These rules, however, did not apply to non-Christian captives, who were usually put to death. Ibid., 8.4, 9.1.

35 Ibid.

36 Ibid.

37 Herbert Adams Gibbons, *The Foundation of the Ottoman Empire: A History of the Osmanlis up to the Death of Bayazid I, 1300–1403* (London: Cass, 1968), 108.

38 The Golden Horn is a curved inlet of the Bosporus; it forms the harbor of Constantinople.

39 Mehmet brought to the siege thirteen large and fifty-six smaller cannons. L. S. Stavrianos, *The Balkans since 1453* (New York: New York University Press, 1958), 55.

40 Cristobulus, "De Rebus Gestis Mechemetis," 60–65; Georgius Phrantzes, "Chronicon," in ed. E. Bekker, *Corpus Scriptorum Historiae Byzantinae* (Bonn, 1828–1897), 269–70.

41 The defenders could patch most of the damage to the walls because the Ottoman cannons could fire only at intervals and the large cannon constructed specially for the siege was good for only seven rounds. The Byzantines also used cannons, but they were slower and had less impact, and their recoil further undermined the structural integrity of the fortifications. Treadgold, *Byzantine State and Society*, 799.

42 Halil Inalcik, *The Ottoman Empire: The Classical Age 1300–1600*, trans. Norman Itzkowitz and Colin Imber (New York: Weidenfeld and Nicholson, 1972), 26.

43 This practice was essentially, although not exclusively, confined to rural communities. Muslim children were excluded, as were Romanians, since they were vassals, not subjects, of the sultan. The same held true for Jews, Gypsies, Wallachians, Moldavians, and Armenians (though these last were eventually included). Exceptions were also made for Muslims from Bosnia and Herzegovina, although they were included in the child levy by a firman in 1564. The majority of the Janissaries came from Greek and Slav villages; some were the children of slaves captured by Tartars in Russia and corsairs in the Mediterranean. Godfrey Goodwin, *The Jannissaries* (London: Saqi Books, 1997), 21–33.

44 Byzantine nobles such as Murat Pasha (originally a Palaeologos), Iskenderoglu (Alexander), and Mikhaloglu (Michael) changed sides and converted to Islam in order to protect their estates and even expand their wealth. Ibid., 33.

45 Another seven were in the despotate of Morea. Runciman, *Fall of Constantinople*, 20.

46 The nature and extent of the wound is disputed by contemporary accounts. Phrantzes writes that Giustiniani was hit in the foot ("Chronicon," 8–9), while Chalcocondylas states that he was wounded in the arm by a shot from a cannon ("De Rebus Turcicis," 201–14). Ducas's version is close to that of Chalcocondylas and attributes the wound to a shot that hit the arm above the elbow (*Decline and Fall of Byzantium*, 39.10). Leonard of Chios claims that it was an injury to the armpit that incapacitated Giustiniani (*Siege of Constantinople*, 36). According to the account of Cristobulus, Giustiniani was injured after a ball pierced his breastplate. Barbaro, on the other hand, mentions only that the Genoese deserted (*Diary of the Siege*, 65). Runciman, however, is convinced that there was a good probability that Giustiniani received a serious wound somewhere on his body (*Fall of Constantinople*, 224, n. 1).

47 Giustiniani managed to escape from Constantinople to the island of Chios, where he died a short time later. Leonard of Chios, *Siege of Constantinople*, 24–25.

48 Ibid., 39. According to the vivid description of Leonard of Chios, "women were raped, virgins deflowered and young men forced to take part in shameful obscenities. Later they were carried off as captives, whereas the nuns were left behind after the soldiers . . . disgraced [them] with foul debaucheries."

49 Ducas, *Decline and Fall of Byzantium*, 39.20.

50 Runciman, *Fall of Constantinople*, 147.

51 The description of the last day of the siege and sack of Constantinople is based on the following sources: Phrantzes, "Chronicon," 280–87; Barbaro, *Diary of the Siege*, 51–57; Leonard of Chios, *Siege of Constantinople*, 15–41; Cristobulus, "De Rebus Gestis Mechemetis," 67–71; Ducas, *Decline and Fall of Byzantium*, 39.351–61; Chalcocondylas, "De Rebus Turcicis," 354–56; Sa'ad ed-Din, *The Capture of Constantinople from the Taj ut-Tavarikh*, trans. E. J. Gibb (Glasgow, 1879), 21–28. The most exhaustive secondary source is still Runciman's *Fall of Constantinople*, which includes citations to additional primary accounts and histories.

52 Cristobulus claims that 4,000 were killed and 50,000 taken prisoner, including about 400 soldiers ("De Rebus Turcicis," 76, n. 255); Leonard of Chios suggests 60,000 captives (*Siege of Constantinople*, 39); Barbaro also mentions 60,000 captives (*Diary of the Siege*, 57); Ducas put the figure at 2,000 soldiers killed (*Decline and Fall of Byzantium*, 39.14).

53 Mehmet took as his booty allotment all the members of the great Byzantine families who had survived the massacre. He freed most of the females and gave them money to purchase the freedom of some of their relatives. The senior noblemen he had killed, and he kept particularly attractive young women and men for his seraglio. Runciman, *Fall of Constantinople*, 149.

54 Gibbon, *Decline and Fall*, vol. 6, 517.

55 Steven Runciman, *Byzantine Civilization* (New York: Longmans, Green & Co., 1956), 240

56 Paul Fregosi, *Jihad in the West: Muslim Conquests from the 7th to the 21st Centuries* (New York: Prometheus Books, 1998), 248. It is quite evident that Fregosi was moved by the plight of Yugoslavia; his book is dedicated to "a Serbian Christian and a Bosnian Muslim" who were both felled by an unknown sniper in Sarajevo on May 20, 1993.

57 *Ta Byzantina Chronia: Istoria E' Taxis* (The Byzantine years: grade five history) (Athens: Ministry of National Education and Religion, 1987), 201.

58 Ibid.

59 The destruction of the island of Chios by Kara Ali (April 6–7, 1822) and the fate of its inhabitants inspired not only Greek accounts of Turkish barbarism, but also a great number of newspaper articles, paintings, and drawings of the massacre by European writers and artists. Other stories intertwine images of brutality with the struggle against the Ottomans, including the capture of Athanasios Diakos by Pasha Omar Vryonis (April 23, 1821). Because Diakos had displayed considerable bravery, the pasha offered to free him if he would convert to Islam. Diakos turned the offer down and, in the process, made insulting comments about the Islamic faith. In response, Pasha Vryonis had Diakos trussed up and roasted over a spit. After independence, a statue of Diakos was placed in the center of the city of Lamia in honor of his bravery and self-sacrifice.

60 Sugar comments that the Ottoman social structure was basically the "skillful blending of traditional Muslim sociopolitical traditions with Turkish and Byzantine elements." The term "professional Ottomans" was coined by modern-day scholars. Sugar, *Southeastern Europe*, 31–33.

61 According to Alexis Alexandris, the jurisdiction of the Greek patriarch of Constantinople over the Bulgarians and all Orthodox subjects of the Ottoman Empire derived from the millet system and remained in force from 1454 to 1923. Alexis Alexandris, *The Greek Orthodox Minority of Istanbul and Greek–Turkish Relations, 1918–1974* (Athens: Center for Asia Minor Studies, 1983), 21–23.

62 Ibid., 22.

63 According to Inalcik, Mehmet considered himself the inheritor of the Byzantine throne and adopted the principle of executing any Greek of royal blood with a potential claim (*Ottoman Empire*, 26). However, Pius II refused to recognize the sultan's legitimacy unless Mehmet converted to Christianity. Franz Babinger, *Mehmed der Eroberer und seine Zeit* (Munich: F. Bruckmann, 1953), 212–13.

64 The status of the Orthodox Church in the Ottoman Empire was regulated by a *beret* (ordinance) that guaranteed that the patriarch was "untaxable and irremovable." The patriarch and the synod had the authority to settle all matters of doctrine, to control and discipline all members of the Church, to manage all Church property, and to levy dues on laity and clergy. In addition, Mehmet's ordinance granted full freedom of conscience. The followers of the Orthodox Church were free to keep sacred books and icons in their homes, and to attend church services unmolested. Finally, the *beret* invested the patriarch with considerable civil authority, making him head of not only the Orthodox Church, but also the Orthodox community. Ecclesiastical courts had the power to regulate and pronounce judgments on matters of marriage, divorce, and inheritance, and in a few years, the jurisdiction of the Church was extended to all civil cases. Stavrianos, *Balkans since 1453*, 103; Runciman, *The Great Church in Captivity: A Study of the Patriarchate of Constantinople from the Eve of the Turkish Conquest to the War of Independence* (Cambridge: Cambridge University Press, 1968), 181.

65 Operating under the jurisdiction of the Church, the courts employed Byzantine canon law and Byzantine civil and customary law. In civil cases, the judgment was in the form of arbitration and could be challenged in Turkish courts.

However, any case could be brought to a Turkish court in the first place at the request of either party. Runciman, *Great Church*, 172.

66 A royal minister and a member of the imperial council.

67 At least thirty-six churches were handed back by the Orthodox Church.

68 The Bulgarian patriarchate was eliminated in 1393 and the Serbian in 1459. Stavrianos, *Balkans since 1453*, 104.

69 In 1557, Grand Vizier Mohamed Sokolli, who was of Serbian origin, helped to establish the Serbian patriarchate of Pec in Kosovo.

70 A major exception, of course, was Russia.

71 Jason Goodwin, *Lords of the Horizon: A History of the Ottoman Empire* (New York: Henry Holt, 1998), 46.

72 The only exception was the patriarch.

73 Runciman, *Great Church*, 179.

74 This argument is especially endorsed by Stavrianos, *Balkans since 1453*, 105, and ibid., 180–81.

75 Various circumstances and conditions motivated conversion to Islam. For more details, see Stavrianos, *Balkans since 1453*, 105–7.

76 Ibid., 111.

77 A study by Achilleas A. Mandrikas, *Krypho Scholeio: Mythos E Pragmatikotita* (Secret school: myth or reality) (Athens: Ekdosis Kalentis, 1992), offers convincing evidence repudiating the myth of the secret schools, as well as an excellent bibliography of works that support this argument. The textbooks issued by the Greek ministry of education and religion include references to the secret schools in the elementary grades, but at the high-school level, the history texts drop all mention of these schools and refer instead to the establishment of the patriarchal academic institutions by the Orthodox Church. See N. Diamandopoulou and A. Kypriazopoulou, *Elliniki Istoria ton Neoteron Chronon* (Greek history of the modern years) (Athens: Organismos Ekdoseon Didaktikon Biblion, n.d.), 27–29, and Vassilis Vl. Sfyroera, *Istoria Neoteri kai Synchrony* (History: modern and current) (Athens: Organismos Ekdoseon Didaktikon Biblion, 1991), 116–17.

78 Stavrianos has considered in great depth the sociological, economic, and political factors of the Ottoman educational policies in the Balkans. He contends (and the historical record endorses his conclusions) that the Balkan peoples were "living in a static and self-contained Orthodox theocracy, [and thus] they remained oblivious to the new learning, the scientific advances, and the burgeoning of the arts that were transforming and reviving the Western World." Stavrianos, *Balkans since 1453*, 111–12.

79 Ibid., 114.

80 The description of events surrounding Euphrosyne and the other Greek women of Ioannina is based on the accounts of George Finlay, *History of the Greek Revolution, and of the Reign of King Otho*, vol. 1 (London: Zeno, 1971; originally published in 1877), 60–63, and William M. Leake, *Travels in Northern Greece*, vol. 1 (Amsterdam: Hakkert, 1967; originally published in 1835), 401–4.

81 Leake records that Euphrosyne was the niece of the bishop of Greneva (*Travels in Northern Greece*, vol. 1, 403).

82 J. C. Hobhouse, *A Journey through Albania* (New York: Arno Press, 1971), 111.

83 Finlay states that the Muslim tradition called for women to be drowned at night, with the body placed in a sack. Leake suggests that drowning was an ancient Greek custom. To this end, he cites the examples of Periander, the king of Corinth, and Cleomenes, the tyrant of Methymna, both of whom had ordered "women of irregular conduct to be sewn up in sacks and thrown into the sea." Finlay, *History of the Greek Revolution*, vol. 1, 62; Leake, *Travels in Northern Greece*, vol. 1, 404, n. 1.

84 According to Leake, the account of the husband's reprehensible behavior came from the wife's family. The husband, Kyr N. G. of Kalarytes, denied having any foreknowledge of Ali Pasha's plan to drown the women. Ibid., 402.

85 Leake adds that in addition to Euphrosyne, the inhabitants of Ioannina boasted of a bookstore and two colleges as proof of their superior civilization. Ibid., 403.

86 Barbara Jelavich, *History of the Balkans: Eighteenth and Nineteenth Centuries*, vol. 1 (Cambridge: Cambridge University Press, 1983), 52.

87 Ibid., 52.

88 Finlay, *History of the Greek Revolution*, vol. 1, 10.

89 Leake, *Travels in Northern Greece*, vol. 4, 281.

90 Finlay, *History of the Greek Revolution*, vol. 1, 64.

91 This group of privileged Orthodox Christians, most of whom were Greek (though some families were Hellenized Italians, Romanians, and Albanians), took their name from the Phanar, or lighthouse, district of Constantinople, where they maintained their homes. By the middle of the seventeenth century, they had developed great fortunes through their association with the Ottoman government, and thus they exercised considerable influence. Jelavich, *History of the Balkans*, vol. 1, 54.

92 This phrase is referred to in *The Decline of the American Empire*, a film by Denys Arcand, 1986.

Chapter 3: Bandits with Attitude

1 Complete details of the episode are found in Romilly Jenkins, *The Dilessi Murders: Greek Brigands and English Hostages* (London: Prion, 1998). The actual events of April 11, 1870, are described on pp. 77–82.

2 "Captured and Murdered by Brigands," *The Times*, Apr. 26, 1870.

3 Ibid.

4 A series of agreements, starting with the Treaty of London in 1827, led to the establishment of a sovereign Greek state in 1830, and assigned Great Britain, France, and Russia the status of protecting powers. The three Great Powers were responsible for maintaining the constitutional integrity of the country.

5 Domna Dontas, *Greece and the Great Powers, 1863–1875* (Thessaloniki: Institute for Balkan Studies, 1966), 168.

6 Simon Winchester, *The Fractured Zone: A Return to the Balkans* (New York: HarperCollins, 1999), 19–20.

7 C. M. Woodhouse, *The Philhellenes* (London: Doric Publications, 1969), offers a well-researched account of the nineteenth-century philhellene. Woodhouse himself can qualify as a philhellene of the nineteenth-century variety, partly because of his postings in Greece during the Second World War and partly because of his numerous publications on Greek history.

8 F. S. N. Douglas, *An Essay on Certain Points of Resemblance between the Ancient and Modern Greeks* (London: J. Murray, 1813), 165, see note.

9 Leake, *Travels in Northern Greece*, vol. 1, 149.

10 Edward Dodwell, *A Classical and Topographical Tour through Greece* (London: Rodwell and Martin, 1819), 59, 74.

11 Quoted in Woodhouse, *Philhellenes*, 46.

12 Jenkins, *Dilessi Murders*, 109.

13 Quoted in John L. Comstock, *History of the Greek Revolution: Compiled from Official Documents of the Greek Government* (New York: W. W. Reed and Co., 1828), 97.

14 Mao Tse-tung, "Problems of War and Strategy," in *Selected Works*, vol. 2 (London: Lawrence and Wishart, 1954), 224.

15 Dontas, *Greece and the Great Powers*, 165–67.

16 S. G. W. Benjamin, *The Turk and Greek; or Creeds, Races, Society, and Scenery in Turkey, Greece and the Islands of Greece* (New York: Hurd and Houghton, 1867), 223.

17 John S. Koliopoulos, *Brigands with a Cause: Brigandage and Irredentism in Modern Greece 1821–1912* (Oxford: Oxford University Press, 1987), 189.

18 Thanos Veremis, *The Military in Greek Politics: From Independence to Democracy* (London: Hurst and Company, 1997), 40.

19 Jenkins, *Dilessi Murders*, 115–16.

20 Tzvetan Todorov, *The Morals of History*, trans. Alyson Waters (Minneapolis, Minn.: University of Minnesota Press, 1995), 90.

21 Julie A. Mertus, *Kosovo: How Myths and Truths Started a War* (Berkeley, Calif.: University of California Press, 1999), 2.

22 William Mure, *Journal of a Tour in Greece and the Ionian Islands*, vol. 2 (London: W. Blackwood and Sons, 1842), 294–95.

23 Elgin was made ambassador to Constantinople in 1799. In 1801, the sultan rewarded Elgin for the British victory over Napoleon in Egypt with a firman that allowed the young diplomat to make copies of the sculptures on the Acropolis. Elgin naturally took the sultan's permission to the next level and simply had the sculptures removed. Unfortunately, the actual firman has not survived and there is no extant copy of the document, thus rendering irresolvable the debate over how Elgin acquired the Marbles.

24 Concise surveys of the historical geography of the Balkans may be found in John V. Fine, *The Early Medieval Balkans: A Critical Survey from the Sixth to the Late Twelfth Century* (Ann Arbor, Mich.: University of Michigan Press, 1983), 1–4; Stavrianos, *Balkans since 1453* (New York: New York University Press, 2000), 2–8.

25 Fine, *Early Medieval Balkans*, 2.

26 Koliopoulos, *Brigands with a Cause*, 21–24; Irwin T. Sanders, "Balkan Rural Societies and War," in eds. Bela K. Kiraly and Gunther E. Rothenberg, *Special Topics and Generalizations on the Eighteenth and Nineteenth Centuries*, vol. 1 of *War and Society in East Central Europe* (New York: Social Science Monographs, 1979), 151–52.

27 Koliopoulos, *Brigands with a Cause*, 24, 26.

28 Ibid., 25; Sanders, "Balkan Rural Societies," 152.

29 Koliopoulos, *Brigands with a Cause*, p. 25; Sanders, "Balkan Rural Societies," 153.

30 Koliopoulos, *Brigands with a Cause*, 25–26.

31 John V. Fine Jr., *The Late Medieval Balkans: A Critical Survey from the Late Twelfth Century to the Ottoman Conquest* (Ann Arbor, Mich.: 1987), 416.

32 Koliopoulos, *Brigands with a Cause*, 31; also see Barbara Jelavich, *History of the Balkans: Eighteenth and Nineteenth Centuries*, vol. 1 (Cambridge: Cambridge University Press, 1983), 61.

33 Jelavich, *History of the Balkans*, vol. 1, 61.

34 Wayne S. Vucinich, "Serbian Military Tradition," in Kiraly and Rothenberg, *War and Society*, vol. 1, 287.

35 Koliopoulos, *Brigands with a Cause*, 260.

36 Vucinich, "Serbian Military Tradition," 287.

37 Koliopoulos, *Brigands with a Cause*, 260–61; Mure, *Journal of a Tour*, vol. 2, 149.

38 According to the description offered by William Mure, the fire was built on top of green wood, and thus the ground was not stained (ibid., 150).

39 Vucinich, "Serbian Military Tradition," 292; Sanders, "Balkan Rural Societies," 153–54.

40 Dimitrije Djordjevic and Stephan Fischer-Galati, *The Balkan Revolutionary Tradition* (New York: Columbia University Press, 1981), 42.

41 Koliopoulos, *Brigands with a Cause*, 32–33.

42 David Urquhart, *Spirit of the East*, vol. 2 (London: H. Colburn, 1839), 145.

43 Koliopoulos, *Brigands with a Cause*, 33.

44 Henry M. Baird, *Modern Greece: A Narrative of a Residence and Travels in That Country; with Observations on Its Antiquities, Literature, Language, Politics, and Religion* (New York: Harper and Brothers, 1856), 346.

45 Ibid., 346.

46 Koliopoulos, *Brigands with a Cause*, 282.

47 Stavrianos, *Balkans since 1453*, 144.

48 Koliopoulos, *Brigands with a Cause*, passim.

49 Ibid., 282.

50 Ibid., 285–86.

51 Ibid., 26.

52 Dennis S. Skiotis, "Mountain Warriors and the Greek Revolution," in eds. V. J. Parry and M. E. Yapp, *War, Technology and Society in the Middle East* (London: Oxford University Press, 1975), 310.

53 Ibid., 310–11; Koliopoulos, *Brigands with a Cause*, 27.

54 Skiotis, "Mountain Warriors," 311; Koliopoulos, *Brigands with a Cause*, 27.

55 Skiotis, "Mountain Warriors," 311.

56 Ibid., 312.

57 Koliopoulos, *Brigands with a Cause*, 27.

58 Ibid., 27–28.

59 Sanders, "Balkan Rural Societies," 153.

60 Skiotis, "Mountain Warriors," 313–14; George A. Kourvetaris, "Greek Armed

Forces and Society in the Nineteenth Century, with Special Emphasis on the Greek Revolution of 1821," in ed. Bela K. Kiraly, *East Central European Society and War in the Era of Revolutions, 1775–1856*, vol. 4 of *War and Society in East Central Europe* (New York: Social Science Monographs, 1984), 284.

61 In the fifth century B.C., Xerxes, the king of Persia, employed the same tactic to protect the exposed frontier of the empire on the steppe. Chinese rulers also hired tribes to defend their borders against similar tribes of raiders. In both cases, the system broke down when boundary guards joined the marauders, either because they were not paid or because they hoped for greater remuneration in the form of plunder. William H. McNeill, *The Pursuit of Power: Technology, Armed Forces, and Society since A.D. 1000* (Chicago: University of Chicago Press, 1982), 16.

62 Koliopoulos, *Brigands with a Cause*, 32–34.

63 Thucydides, *The Peloponnesian War*, trans. Steven Lattimore (Indianapolis, Ind.: Hackett, 1998), vol. 1, 5.6.

64 Fine, *Early Medieval Balkans*, 12.

65 Ibid., 12–13.

66 Ibid., 13–14, 21.

67 Ibid., 23.

68 Nicholas Cheetham, *Medieval Greece* (New Haven, Conn.: Yale University Press, 1981), 19.

69 Ibid., 65.

70 Fine, *Late Medieval Balkans*, 19.

71 Ibid., 23–24.

72 Ibid., 316.

73 Ibid., 317.

74 Ibid., 337.

75 Ibid., 408; M. C. Bartusius, "Brigandage in the Late Byzantine Empire," *Byzantion* 51 (1981): 403.

76 Fine, *Late Medieval Balkans*, 370–71, 460–61.

77 Ibid., 408.

78 Ibid.

79 Bartusius, "Brigandage in the Late Byzantine Empire," 389.

80 Ibid., 390.

81 See, for example, Bistra Cvetkova, "The Bulgarian Haiduk Movement in the 15th to 18th Centuries," in eds. Gunther E. Rothenberg, Bela K. Kiraly, and Peter F. Sugar, *East Central European Society in the Pre-Revolutionary Eighteenth Century*, vol. 2 of *War and Society in East Central Europe* (Boulder, Colo.: Social Science Monographs, 1982), 301–38.

82 Stephen Fischer-Galati, "Military Factors in the Balkan Revolutions," in Kiraly and Rothenberg, *War and Society*, vol. 1, 184.

83 Djordjevic and Fischer-Galati, *Balkan Revolutionary Tradition*, 14–15.

84 Ibid., 12.

85 Vladimir Corovic, *Istorija Srba* (History of Serbia) (Beograd: Beograd izdavacko-graficki zavod, 1995), 522–23.

86 Ibid., 31.

87 Ibid., 32.

88 *Timars* were temporary land grants awarded by the sultan to the Ottoman cavalrymen. For the most part, the *timar* holders were absentee landlords who left the local peasants alone as long as they fulfilled their obligations to pay taxes and provide labor. Eventually, as central authority declined, the *timar* holders were able to establish a hereditary right over their lands, which were then called *chifliks*, and as a result, they came to play a greater role on these estates, while demanding higher taxes and imposing harsher encumbrances on the peasants.

89 For the process of Ottoman decline in the Balkan context, see Stavrianos, *Balkans since 1453*, 117–53.

90 Skiotis, "Mountain Warriors," 315.

91 George Finlay, *A History of Greece*, vol. 6 (New York: AMS Press, 1970), 85.

92 Douglas Dakin, *The Greek Struggle for Independence, 1821–1833* (London: Ernest Benn Limited, 1973), 72.

93 Ibid.; Finlay, *History of Greece*, vol. 6, 85.

94 Dakin, *Greek Struggle for Independence*, 73.

95 William St. Clair, *That Greece Might Still Be Free: The Philhellenes in the War of Independence* (London: Oxford University Press, 1972), 37; Finlay, *History of Greece*, vol. 6, 85.

96 St. Clair, *That Greece Might Still Be Free*, 39.

97 Ibid., 38.

98 Ibid., 39.

99 Baird, *Modern Greece*, 347.

100 George Waddington, *A Visit to Greece in 1823 and 1824* (London: J. Murray, 1825), 149.

101 Koliopoulos, *Brigands with a Cause*, 282; Dakin, *Greek Struggle for Independence*, 73.

102 St. Clair, *That Greece Might Still Be Free*, 37.

103 Dakin, *Greek Struggle for Independence*, 73.

104 Edward Blaqueiere, *Letters from Greece: With Remarks on the Treaty of Intervention* (London: J. Ilbery, 1828), 108–9.

105 Koliopoulos, *Brigands with a Cause*, 282.

106 Ibid., 283–84.

107 On the few examples of *klephts* having affairs or maintaining families, see ibid., 282–84.

108 Ibid., 72.

109 For the Souliots, see Finlay, *History of Greece*, vol. 6, 42–51.

110 Ibid., 40.

111 Ibid., 41.

112 St. Clair, *That Greece Might Still Be Free*, 232.

113 Stavrianos, *Balkans since 1453*, 496; Jelavich, *History of the Balkans*, vol. 1, 80.

114 Stavrianos, *Balkans since 1453*, 497.

115 Stevan K. Pavlowitch, *A History of the Balkans, 1804–1945* (New York: Longman, 1999), 10.

116 J. C. Hobhouse was impressed by the Albanian consciousness of Muslims, Orthodox Christians, and Catholics in the region (*Journey through Albania*, 131). Pavlowitch estimates that by the eighteenth century, about two-thirds of Albanians had converted to Islam (*History of the Balkans*, 10).

117 Pavlowitch, *History of the Balkans*, 10.

118 Miranda Vickers, *Between Serb and Albanian: A History of Kosovo* (New York: Columbia University Press, 1996), 17–18.

119 Stavrianos, *Balkans since 1453*, 497.

120 Pavlowitch, *History of the Balkans*, 12.

121 Comstock, *History of the Greek Revolution*, 86–87.

122 Pavlowitch, *History of the Balkans*, 13.

123 Stavrianos, *Balkans since 1453*, 497.

124 Misha Glenny, *The Balkans: Nationalism, War, and the Great Powers, 1804–1999* (New York: Viking, 2000), 23.

125 These were the equivalent of prime ministers in the Ottoman administration.

126 Stavrianos, *Balkans since 1453*, 501.

127 Hobhouse, *Journey through Albania*, 133.

128 Ibid., 132–33.

129 Mure, *Journal of a Tour*, vol. 2, 291–92.

130 Hobhouse, *Journey through Albania*, 134.

Chapter 4: Ethnicity versus the Nation-State

1 Leake writes that Lake Ioannina was often beset by furious thunderstorms and occasional frosts (*Travels in Northern Greece*, vol. 1, 403–4).

2 Unfortunately, little is known about the role of women during this period. Ali's favorite wife, Vasiliki, was the love of his life, and was very much respected by Greeks and Albanians alike.

3 Douglas Dakin, *The Unification of Greece, 1770–1923* (New York: St. Martin's Press, 1972), 24.

4 Comstock, *History of the Greek Revolution*, 140n.

5 Fortunately, the bodyguard either failed in his attempt or could not carry out the order, and Vasiliki was not killed. Finlay, *History of the Greek Revolution*, vol. 1, 94, n. 1.

6 There are several stories about Ali's death. The one cited is based on the account of François Pouqueville, *Histoire de la régénération de la Grèce* (History of the regeneration of Greece), 4 vols. (Paris: Didot père et fils, 1824), 374–76. According to Finlay (ibid.), Kurshid Pasha had arranged a meeting between Ali and Mohamed Pasha, Kurshid's successor as governor of the Peloponnese. When the discussion was over, the two pashas rose and bowed. At that moment, Mohamed pulled out his dagger and plunged it into Ali's chest. However, Finlay also relates that he visited the site of the monastery, and according to local tradition, Ali and his men fought it out with Kurshid's soldiers and Ali was mortally wounded in the melee. In this version, Ali's men, who were stationed on the cliff above the monastery and thus covered the courtyard, did not fire on the Ottoman troops because one of their comrades was standing too close to the gate. Kurshid's men were then able to gain access to the building and, by firing through the wooden floors, finally killed Ali. All accounts agree

that Ali's head was cut off and sent to the sultan, where it was displayed outside the palace.

7 Pavlowitch, *History of the Balkans*, 23.

8 Stavrianos, *Balkans since 1453*, 217.

9 They were known as *kodjabashi* in Greece, *chorbaji* in Bulgaria, and *knezes* to the Serbs.

10 Stavrianos, *Balkans since 1453*, 224.

11 Ivo Banac, *The National Question in Yugoslavia: Origins, History, Politics* (London: Cornell University Press, 1984), 35–37; John R. Lampe, *Yugoslavia as History* (Cambridge: Cambridge University Press, 1996), 28–29.

12 The influence of the Ottomans also drove Romania closer culturally and spiritually to Constantinople. Keith Hitchins, *Rumania 1866–1947* (Oxford: Oxford University Press, 1994), 3.

13 R. W. Seton-Watson, *A History of the Roumanians* (Cambridge: Cambridge University Press, 1934), 127.

14 For some interesting commentary on the attitude of the Phanariots toward the French Revolution, see Cyril Mango, "The Phanariots and the Byzantine Tradition," in ed. Richard Clogg, *The Struggle for Greek Independence: Essays to Mark the 150th Anniversary of the Greek War of Independence* (London: Macmillan, 1973), 56.

15 Athanasios Ypsilantis, *Ta Meta tin Alosin* (The events after the conquest) (Constantinople, 1870), 263.

16 Pavlowitch, *History of the Balkans*, 24.

17 Mango, "Phanariots and the Byzantine Tradition," 56–57.

18 Ibid., 58–59.

19 Finlay, *History of the Greek Revolution*, vol. 1, 98.

20 Ibid.; Dakin, *Unification of Greece*, 29–33.

21 Finlay, *History of the Greek Revolution*, vol. 1, 99.

22 Tasos Vournas, *Istoria tis Neoteris Elladas, Apo tin Epanastasi tou 1821 os to kinima tou Goudi* (The history of modern Greece, from the revolution of 1821 to the coup of Goudi) (Athens, n.d.), 64.

23 Pavlowitch, *History of the Balkans*, 33.

24 Dakin, *Unification of Greece*, 257.

25 Pavlowitch, *History of the Balkans*, 26; Benedict Anderson, *Imagined Communities: Reflections on the Origins and Spread of Nationalism* (London: Verso, 1983), offers an interesting insight into the use of history as a mechanism for the creation of national identity.

26 Recreating the Byzantine Empire was an ongoing proposition for the Phanariots.

27 Mango, "Phanariots and the Byzantine Tradition," 48.

28 Cited in Comstock, *History of the Greek Revolution*, 139–40.

29 Finlay, *History of the Greek Revolution*, vol. 1, 42.

30 Ibid., 59.

31 Ibid., 59.

32 Ibid., 45–46. According to Miranda Vickers, the population of Suli was 12,000.

Taking into account the extended families that were common among Albanians at this time, it is not improbable that 450 families would represent such a number. Miranda Vickers, *The Albanian: A Modern History* (New York: I. B. Tauris Publishers, 1999), 20.

33 Finlay, *History of the Greek Revolution*, vol. 1, 42.

34 Leake, *Travels in Northern Greece*, vol. 1, 502.

35 Finlay, *History of the Greek Revolution*, vol. 1, 45.

36 Leake writes that the incident between Ali and the Tzevellas family was witnessed by the Greek interpreter of the French consulate at Thessaloniki (*Travels in Northern Greece*, vol. 1, 507, n. 1).

37 Ibid., 506.

38 Ibid., 513.

39 Finlay, *History of the Greek Revolution*, vol. 1, 51. Leake gives neither the exact number of Suliots at Zalongo nor the number of women who jumped off the cliff. He does write that twenty men were killed and 150 (or three-fourths) managed to escape (*Travels in Northern Greece*, vol. 1, 519–20).

40 Ibid. Leake also provides part of Ali's biography, and he bases his description of the destruction of the Suliots on the manuscript of an untitled poem by a Muslim Albanian (ibid., 463ff.). According to Leake, the author was conversant with the colloquial Greek of Albania but not educated in Greek, and the language of the poem represents the vulgar dialect of the region. He includes another account of the Suliots and their war with Ali Pasha, this one based on a summary of a published work (*A Brief History of Suli and Parga*), which was written by a native of Parga who became a major in one of the regiments stationed in the Ionian Islands (ibid., 501ff.).

41 N. Diamandopopou and A. Kyriazopoulou, *Elliniki Istoria ton Neoteron Chronon* (Modern Greek history) (Athens, n.d.), 51.

42 Finlay, *History of the Greek Revolution*, vol. 1, 74; Comstock, *History of the Greek Revolution*, 130.

43 Finlay, *History of the Greek Revolution*, vol. 1, 75.

44 Ibid., 74–77.

45 Sir Hamilton Gibb and H. Bowen, *Islamic Society and the West*, vol. 1 (London: Oxford University Press, 1950), 101–92.

46 Richard Clogg, "Aspects of the Movement for Greek Independence," in Clogg, *Struggle for Greek Independence*, 6. See also note 20 for additional sources of the incident.

47 Glenny, *The Balkans*, 5.

48 Alan Palmer, *The Decline of the Ottoman Empire* (New York: J. Murray, 1992), 70–71.

49 Vladimir Dedijer et al., *History of Yugoslavia*, trans. Korddija Kveder (New York: McGraw-Hill, 1975), 263, suggest a population of around 368,000.

50 According to Glenny, of the 12,000 people listed in the Janissary rolls of Constantinople in 1790, only 2,000 actually provided military service (*The Balkans*, 4). By 1809, there were more than 110,000 registered Janissaries in the empire.

51 Ibid., 2; Michael Boro Petrovich, *A History of Modern Serbia, 1904–1918*, vol. 1, (New York: Harcourt Brace Jovanovich, 1976), 28; Lovet F. Edwards, ed., *The*

Memoirs of Prota Matija Nenadovic (Oxford: Oxford University Press, 1969), 50–51.

52 Petrovich, *History of Modern Serbia*, vol. 1, 28; Edwards, *Memoirs of Prota Matija Nenadovic*, 51.

53 Edwards, *Memoirs of Prota Matija Nenadovic*, 53.

54 Ibid., 51; Glenny, *The Balkans*, 2.

55 Glenny, *The Balkans*, 2; Petrovich, *History of Modern Serbia*, vol. 1, 28.

56 Petrovich, *History of Modern Serbia*, vol. 1, 28–29.

57 Barbara Jelavich, *The Ottoman Empire, the Great Powers, and the Straits* (Bloomington, Ind.: Indiana University Press, 1973), 16–17.

58 Clogg, "Aspects of the Movement for Greek Independence," 7–8.

59 The Russians acquired several strategic enclaves on the north shore of the Black Sea. In the east, they gained the port of Azov, part of the province of Kuban, and the Kerch peninsula between the Azov and Black seas. In the west, the Russians kept the estuary formed by Dnieper and Bug rivers. The Ottomans also gave up the Crimean peninsula, which according to the treaty was to become an independent state, though the Russians quickly took over. For the complete text of the treaty, see J. C. Hurewitz, *Diplomacy in the Near East*, vol. 1 (Princeton, N.J.: Princeton University Press, 1956), 54–61.

60 The treaty is named after an obscure Bulgarian village south of the Danubian town of Silistria. Today it is called Kainardzhi.

61 James Stotwell and Francis Deak, *Turkey at the Straits: A Short History* (New York: Books for Libraries Press, 1940), 22.

62 Palmer, *Decline of the Ottoman Empire*, 46–47, suggests that article 7 obliged the sultan to protect all Christians, regardless of denomination, and did not give the Russians any right to intervene on behalf of the Orthodox Church or its followers.

63 Cited in Roderic H. Davison, *Essays in Ottoman and Turkish History* (Austin, Tex.: University of Texas Press, 1990), 32; Stavrianos, *Balkans since 1453*, 192.

64 Stavrianos, *Balkans since 1453*, 246.

65 Glenny, *The Balkans*, 13–14.

66 Technically, the holy war was declared by the mufti of Constantinople, who issued a *fetva* proclaiming the Serbs enemies of all Muslims.

67 Stavrianos, *Balkans since 1453*, 247.

68 Glenny, *The Balkans*, 14–16; Pavlowitch, *History of the Balkans*, 29; Jelavich, *History of the Balkans*, 200–202; Stavrianos, *Balkans since 1453*, 247.

69 Lawrence P. Meriage, *Russia and the First Serbian Insurrection, 1804–1812* (New York and London: Garland Publishing, 1987).

70 Glenny argues that Karageorge's choice was not unreasonable, but he adds that the decision to fight linked the success of the uprising to the presence of Russian troops in the Balkans (*The Balkans*, 15–16).

71 Jelavich, *History of the Balkans, Eighteenth and Nineteenth Centuries*, 199.

72 Ibid., 199.

73 Karageorge concluded the alliance with the czar on June 10, 1807.

74 The Treaty of Bucharest was signed on May 28, 1812. Article 8 of the treaty

dealt specifically with Serbia. The salient points were that the Ottomans would occupy all of Serbia, re-establishing Ottoman garrisons and offering an amnesty to Serbs. For the details, see Edward Hertslet, *The Map of Europe by Treaty*, vol. 3 (London, 1875–91), 2030–32.

75 A. Boppe, *Documents inédits sur les relations de la résurrection de la Serbie, 1804–1834* [The unedited documents of Serbian insurrection] (Belgrade, 1888), 6.

76 Petrovich, *History of Modern Serbia*, 67.

77 One Ottoman brigade, commanded by Ahmed Pasha, invaded Serbia from Vidin; another, commanded by Karsli Ali Pasha, invaded from Nis; and a third, commanded by Ali Pasha, invaded from Bosnia.

78 Petrovich, *History of Modern Serbia*, 81.

79 Ibid., 81.

80 Ibid., 82.

81 Ibid., 84.

82 Ibid., 28–29.

83 Ibid., 79.

84 Glenny, *The Balkans*, 16.

85 Ibid., 17. Petrovich defines these as monarchic centralism, oligarchic regionalism, and constitutional centralism (*History of Modern Serbia*, 45).

86 Glenny, *The Balkans*, 18.

87 Pavlowitch, *History of the Balkans*, 29.

88 In the end, the Ottoman reprisals against the Serbs served only to instigate another uprising. In April 1814, the Serbs again went to war, but this time their objectives were considerably more limited. Their leader, Milos Obrevonic, was content to alter the substance, if not the form, of Ottoman rule in Serbia. He was now willing to accept the sultan's authority, but only if the Sublime Porte would recognize a Serbian political hierarchy under his leadership. The sultan, faced with the prospect of another prolonged rebellion, agreed to the terms, and Serbia at last emerged as a semi-autonomous province.

Chapter 5: Fire, Sword, and Blood: The Birth of the Balkan State

1 Robert Walsh, *A Residence at Constantinople*, vol. 1 (London: F. Westley and A. H. Davis, 1836), 315.

2 Finlay, *History of the Greek Revolution*, vol. 1, 186.

3 The execution of the patriarch and subsequent actions against the Greek Orthodox in Constantinople are elaborately described by Robert Walsh (*Residence at Constantinople*). Walsh was present at the hanging of Gregorius, and he also witnessed the persecution and brutal treatment of the Greek Orthodox by the mobs and by official Ottoman representatives. He went to great lengths to verify accounts of atrocities, and is quite scrupulous in separating fact from fiction. Despite the danger, he traveled throughout the city to ascertain the veracity of various accounts of brutality.

4 Walsh, *Residence at Constantinople*, vol. 1, 315.

5 Finlay, *History of the Greek Revolution*, vol. 1, 187.

6 Ibid., 186; Walsh, *Residence at Constantinople*, vol. I, 314–17.

7 Ibid., 184.

8 A. Otetéa, "L'Hétairie d'il y a cent cinquante ans" (The Hetaira of 150 years ago), *Balkan Studies* 6, no. 2 (1965): 261.

9 Walsh, *Residence at Constantinople*, vol. 1, p. 329.

10 Ibid., 316–17; Palmer, *Decline of the Ottoman Empire*, 87.

11 Walsh, *Residence at Constantinople*, 307.

12 Ibid., 337.

13 Ibid., 337.

14 Palmer, *Decline of the Ottoman Empire*, 87.

15 William L. Cleveland, *A History of the Modern Middle East* (Boulder, Colo.: Westview Press, 1994), 76.

16 Runciman, *Great Church*, 406.

17 Ibid., 406.

18 Stavrianos, *Balkans since 1453*, 280.

19 Ibid.

20 According to the 1991 census, the Muslims were at 43.7 percent, the Croats 17.3 percent, the Serbs 31.4 percent, and others 5.5 percent. Lenard Cohen, *Broken Bonds: Disintegration of Yugoslavia* (Boulder, Colo.: Westview Press, 1993), 236.

21 Yugoslav Telegraph Service, July 11, 1993.

22 Harry J. Psomiades, *The Eastern Question: The Last Phase* (Thessaloniki: Institute for Balkan Studies, 1968), 63–64.

23 According to Michael L. Smith, Nureddin called to the crowd that "Chrysostomos was theirs to judge and deal with." Michael L. Smith, *Ionian Vision: Greece in Asia Minor 1919–1922* (New York: St. Martin's Press, 1973), 308.

24 Jean de Murat, *The Great Extirpation of Hellenism* (Florida: A. Triantafillis), 137–38; Marjorie Housapian Dobkin, *Smyrna 1922: Destruction of a City* (New York: Newmark Press, 1998), 133–34.

25 William Shawcross, *Deliver Us from Evil: Peacekeepers, Warlords and a World of Endless Conflict* (New York: Simon and Schuster, 2000), 168.

26 Dakin, *Unification of Greece*, 236.

27 Dobkin, *Smyrna 1922*, 150.

28 Ward Price, cited in Smith, *Ionian Vision*, 310.

29 Mark O. Prentiss, "Eyewitness Story of Smyrna's Horror; 200,000 Victims of Turks and Flames; Kemal Demands Greeks Quit Thrace," *New York Times*, Sept. 18, 1922.

30 Michael Smith, *Ionian Vision*, 309–10.

31 Dakin, *Unification of Greece*, 256; Smith, *Ionian Vision*, 310.

32 Prentiss, "Eyewitness Story of Smyrna's Horror."

33 Philip Mansel, *Constantinople: City of the World's Desire, 1453–1924* (New York: St. Martin's Press, 1995), 407.

34 Psomiades, *Eastern Question*, 60.

35 Finlay, *History of the Greek Revolution*, vol. 1, 218–19 and n. 3.

36 Strangford to Castlereagh, July 23, 1821. Cited in Palmer, *Decline of the Ottoman*

Empire, 86.

37 The trade in provisions was terminated by Kyriakuli Mavromichalis, one of the senior Greek commanders. Finlay, *History of the Greek Revolution*, vol. 1, 216.

38 Ibid., 217–18.

39 John R. Elting, *Swords around a Throne: Napoleon's Grande Armée* (New York: Free Press, 1988), 371.

40 Stavrianos, *Balkans since 1453*, 213. The regiment's most famous member was Theodore Kolokotronis, whose experiences as a British soldier can be found in his *Memoirs from the Greek War of Independence, 1821–1833* (Chicago: Argonaut Publishers, 1969), 118–28.

41 Skiotis, "Mountain Warriors," 319.

42 Djordjevic and Fischer-Galati, *Balkan Revolutionary Tradition*, 69.

43 See Gavro Skrivanic, "The Armed Forces in Karadjordje's Serbia," in ed. Wayne S. Vucinich, *The First Serbian Uprising, 1804–1814* (New York: Columbia University Press, 1982), 303–39.

44 See Vucinich, "Serbian Military Tradition."

45 Fischer-Galati, "Military Factors in the Balkan Revolutions," 185–87.

46 See Kolokotronis, *Memoirs*, 180–89; Dakin, *Greek Struggle for Independence*, 96–99.

47 Ioannis Makriyannis, *The Memoirs of General Makriyannis, 1797–1864* (London: Oxford University Press, 1966), 83–92.

48 Dakin, *Greek Struggle for Independence*, 133; St. Clair, *That Greece Might Still Be Free*, 235–36.

49 Koliopoulos, *Brigands with a Cause*, 49.

50 Veremis, *Military in Greek Politics*, 20.

51 Ibid., 2.

52 Cited in C. M. Woodhouse, *The Greek War of Independence* (New York: Russell and Russell, 1975), 122.

53 Ibid., 123.

54 Ibid., 127.

55 Koliopoulos, *Brigands with a Cause*, 73.

56 Veremis, *Military in Greek Politics*, 13.

57 Koliopoulos, *Brigands with a Cause*, 67.

58 Ibid., 67.

59 Ibid., 70.

60 Ibid., 69–70.

61 Ibid., 69.

62 Veremis, *Military in Greek Politics*, 21.

63 Ibid., 21.

64 Koliopoulos, *Brigands with a Cause*, 74–75.

65 Ibid., 75.

66 Ibid., 76.

67 Ibid.; Veremis, *Military in Greek Politics*, 26; Dimitris Michalopoulos, "The

Evolution of the Greek Army (1828–1812)," in Kiraly, *East Central European Society*, 320.

68 For the organization of the Greek army in the 1830s, see ibid., 321.

69 Koliopoulos, *Brigands with a Cause*, passim.

70 Michalopoulos, "Evolution of the Greek Army," 321.

71 Kourvetaris, "Greek Armed Forces and Society," 294.

72 Michalopoulos, "Evolution of the Greek Army," 324.

73 Koliopoulos, *Brigands with a Cause*, 156.

74 Evangelos Kofos, "War and Insurrection as Means to Greek Unification in the Mid-Nineteenth Century," in Kiraly, *The Crucial Decade: East Central European Society and National Defense, 1859–1870*, vol. 14 of *War and Society in East Central Europe* (New York: Social Science Monographs, 1984), 345–46.

75 Koliopoulos, *Brigands with a Cause*, 124.

76 See Michalopoulos, "Evolution of the Greek Army."

77 Evangelos Kofos, "Greek Insurrectionary Preparations, 1876–1878," in eds. Bela Kiraly and Gale Stokes, *Insurrections, Wars and the Eastern Crisis in the 1870s*, vol. 17 of *War and Society in East Central Europe* (New York: Social Science Monographs, 1985), 182.

78 See Michalopoulos, "Evolution of the Greek Army," 321–23.

79 Kofos, "War and Insurrection," 347.

80 Simeon Damianov, "The Bulgarian National Liberation Movement and the Wars in Europe in the Fifties and Sixties of the Nineteenth Century," in Kiraly, *The Crucial Decade*, 288.

81 Dimitrije Djordjevic, "Balkan Revolutionary Organizations in the 1860s and the Peasantry," in Kiraly, *The Crucial Decade*, 273–74.

82 Koliopoulos, *Brigands with a Cause*, 146.

83 Ibid., 147.

84 Ibid., 145, 177.

85 Michalopoulos, "Evolution of the Greek Army," 317–18.

86 Milorad Ekmecic, "The Serbian National Army in the Wars of 1876–1878: National Liability or National Asset?" in Kiraly and Stokes, *Insurrections, Wars and the Eastern Crisis*, 281.

87 Ibid., 284.

88 Ibid., 297.

89 Dimitrije Djordjevic, "The Serbian Peasant in the 1876 War," in Kiraly and Stokes, *Insurrections, Wars and the Eastern Crisis*, 309.

90 Ekmecic, "Serbian National Army," 283, 289, 294–95.

91 Djordjevic, "Serbian Peasant," 312.

92 For the origins of the Macedonian struggle, see Stavrianos, *Balkans since 1453*, 513–17; Nadine Lange-Akhund, *The Macedonian Question, 1893–1908* (New York: Columbia University Press, 1998), 19–25; Douglas Dakin, *The Greek Struggle in Macedonia, 1897–1913* (Thessaloniki: Institute for Balkan Studies, 1993), 26–34; and Duncan M. Perry, *The Politics of Terror: The Macedonian Liberation Movements, 1893–1903* (Durham, N.C.: Duke University Press, 1988), 2–8.

93 Stavrianos, *Balkans since 1453*, 518–21; Lange-Akhund, *Macedonian Question*, 26–33; Dakin, *Greek Struggle in Macedonia*, 16–23; Perry, *Politics of Terror*, 27–30; and Djordjevic and Fischer-Galati, *Balkan Revolutionary Tradition*, 177.

94 Djordjevic and Fischer-Galati, *Balkan Revolutionary Tradition*, 177–78.

95 Perry, *Politics of Terror*, 38; Stavrianos, *Balkans since 1453*, 519–20; Dakin, *Greek Struggle in Macedonia*, 46–48; and Lange-Akhund, *Macedonian Question*, 36–37.

96 For examinations of the IMRO's ideology, see Perry, *Politics of Terror*, passim; and Lange-Akhund, *Macedonian Question*, 93–94.

97 Perry, *Politics of Terror*, 157.

98 Ibid.

99 Mercia MacDermott, *Freedom or Death: The Life of Gotse Delchev* (London: Journeyman Press, 1978), 201.

100 Ibid.; Perry, *Politics of Terror*, 158.

101 Perry, *Politics of Terror*, 159.

102 Ibid., 157; MacDermott, *Freedom or Death*, 200.

103 See Koliopoulos, *Brigands with a Cause*, 215–36; Lange-Akhund, *Macedonian Question*, 54–61.

104 An analysis of the Supreme Committee and its early relations with the IMRO may be found in Perry, *Politics of Terror*, 42–48, 51–57, 62–68, 72–106, and passim.

105 Djordjevic and Fischer-Galati, *Balkan Revolutionary Tradition*, 190.

106 Lange-Akhund, *Macedonian Question*, 124.

107 For the Illinden Uprising, see Perry, *Politics of Terror*, 133–40; Lange-Akhund, *Macedonian Question*, 118–30; and Dakin, *Greek Struggle in Macedonia*, 92–106.

108 The effects of the Illinden Uprising on the IMRO are examined in Perry, *Politics of Terror*, 141–42; and Lange-Akhund, *Macedonian Question*, 201–7.

109 For the Muerzsteg Agreement and the subsequent reforms, see Lange-Akhund, *Macedonian Question*, 141–200; and Dakin, *Greek Struggle in Macedonia*, 112–16.

110 Djordjevic and Fischer-Galati, *Balkan Revolutionary Tradition*, 194.

111 Ernst Helmreich, *The Diplomacy of the Balkan Wars, 1912–1913* (Cambridge: Cambridge University Press, 1938), 40.

112 Alan Palmer, *The Gardeners of Salonika* (New York: Simon and Schuster, 1965), 159–60.

113 Ibid., 195.

Chapter 6: Intractable Boundaries: Balkan Battlefields

1 Barbara Jelavich, *Russia's Balkan Entanglements, 1806–1914* (Cambridge: Cambridge University Press, 1991), 159.

2 Stavrianos, *Balkans since 1453*, 366–67; Richard J. Crampton, *Bulgaria, 1878–1918: A History* (Boulder, Colo.: East European Monographs, 1983), 4–7.

3 Jelavich, *Balkan Entanglements*, 159–60.

4 Ibid., 145–46.

5 Ibid., 160–61; Mark Pinson, "Ottoman Bulgaria in the First Tanzimat Period: The Revolts of Nish (1841) and Vidin (1850)," *Middle Eastern Studies* 11, no. 2

(May 1975): 103–46.

6   Jelavich, *Balkan Entanglements*, 163.

7   Stavrianos, *Balkans since 1453*, 375–78; Crampton, *Bulgaria, 1878–1918*, 10.

8   Jelavich, *Balkan Entanglements*, 163.

9   Bernard Lewis, *The Emergence of Modern Turkey* (London: Oxford University Press, 1968), 159.

10 Ibid., 446–47.

11 Taylor, *Struggle for Mastery*, 229.

12 Ibid., 168–69.

13 Ibid., 219–20.

14 Stavrianos, *Balkans since 1453*, 394.

15 Ibid., 400; Taylor, *Struggle for Mastery*, 234; M. S. Anderson, *The Eastern Question, 1774–1923* (London: Macmillan, 1966), 182.

16 Taylor, *Struggle for Mastery*, 241.

17 The Serbo-Ottoman war ended on February 17, 1877. The reorganized and better-trained Ottoman forces routed the Serb armies very quickly. A complete collapse was averted when the Russian government warned the Porte that unless the Ottomans agreed to an armistice, Russia would intervene on behalf of the Serbs.

18 Anderson, *Eastern Question*, 185–86; Jelavich, *Balkan Entanglements*, 171; Stavrianos, *Balkans since 1453*, 404–406; Taylor, *Struggle for Mastery*, 237–38.

19 Jelavich, *Balkan Entanglements*, 171; Anderson, *Eastern Question*, 191.

20 Anderson, *Eastern Question*, 191; Stavrianos, *Balkans since 1453*, 405.

21 Taylor, *Struggle for Mastery*, 242–44; Stavrianos, *Balkans since 1453*, 406; Anderson, *Eastern Question*, 193.

22 Taylor, *Struggle for Mastery*, 239–41.

23 Ibid., 195.

24 Ibid., 195–96, 199.

25 Jelavich, *Balkan Entanglements*, 175.

26 Taylor, *Struggle for Mastery*, 245.

27 Ibid., 176.

28 Stavrianos, *Balkans since 1453*, 409.

29 Charles Jelavich, *Tsarist Russia and Balkan Nationalism: Russian Influence and the Internal Affairs of Bulgaria and Serbia, 1879–1880* (Berkeley, Calif.: University of California Press, 1962), 11.

30 Ibid., 12–13.

31 W. N. Medlicott, *The Congress of Berlin and After: A Diplomatic History of the Near Eastern Settlement, 1878–1880* (Hamden, Conn.: Archon Books, 1963), 89.

32 Anderson, *Eastern Question*, 211.

33 Jelavich, *Tsarist Russia*, 13.

34 Anderson, *Eastern Question*, 228. The prince was not alone in his dislike of Bulgaria's liberators. Indeed, the Bulgarians themselves were resentful of Russia's tendency to meddle in their domestic politics. They were especially indignant about the predominance of Russians in the officer corps of the

Bulgarian army. All ranks above captain were held by Russians. See also Jelavich, *Balkan Entanglements*, 182–83.

35 Jelavich, *Balkan Entanglements*, 187.

36 Stavrianos, *Balkans since 1453*, 432; Anderson, *Eastern Question*, 320–31.

37 Taylor, *Struggle for Mastery*, 250.

38 The Greeks accepted the transfer of Cyprus to Britain in the mistaken belief that eventually it would make it easier for them to acquire the island themselves. Medlicott, *Congress of Berlin*, 112–14.

39 Ibid., 38.

40 Jelavich, *Tsarist Russia*, 195.

41 Stavrianos, *Balkans since 1453*, 522.

42 Ibid., 523.

43 Ibid., 440.

44 Ibid., 523–24.

45 Jelavich, *Balkan Entanglements*, 228–29; Edward C. Thaden, *Russia and the Balkan Alliance of 1912* (University Park, Penn.: Pennsylvania State University, 1965), 65–81.

46 Crampton, *Bulgaria, 1878–1918*, 406.

47 Ibid., 407.

48 Pavlowitch, *History of the Balkans*, 196.

49 Andrew Rossos, *Russia and the Balkans: Inter-Balkan Rivalry and Russian Foreign Policy, 1908–1914* (Toronto: University of Toronto Press, 1981), 45–46; Helmreich, *Diplomacy of the Balkan Wars*, 53–57.

50 Pavlowitch, *History of the Balkans*, 197.

51 Stavrianos, *Balkans since 1453*, 533.

52 Jelavich, *Balkan Entanglements*, 231–32.

53 Kemal Soyupak and Huseyin Kabasakal, "The Turkish Army in the First Balkan War," in eds. Bela K. Kiraly and Dimitrjie Djordjevic, *East Central Europe and the Balkan Wars* (Boulder, Colo.: Social Science Monographs, 1987), 159.

54 R. W. Seton-Watson, *The Rise of Nationality in the Balkans* (New York: H. Fertig, 1966), 176.

55 Momchil Yonov, "Bulgarian Military Operations in the Balkan Wars," in Kiraly and Djordjevic, *East Central Europe*, 64.

56 Ibid., 65.

57 Soyupak and Kabasakal, "The Turkish Army," 158, 160.

58 For a summary of operations in the early stages of the Thracian campaign, see ibid., 66–69.

59 Seton-Watson, *Nationality in the Balkans*, 179; Yonov, "Bulgarian Military Operations," 70.

60 Seton-Watson, *Nationality in the Balkans*, 179.

61 Ibid., 180; Yonov, "Bulgarian Military Operations," 72.

62 Yonov, "Bulgarian Military Operations," 72.

63 Seton-Watson, *Nationality in the Balkans*, 181.

64 Ibid., 182–83.

65 Ibid., 184.

66 Yonov, "Bulgarian Military Operations," 74.

67 Ibid., 75.

68 Seton-Watson, *Nationality in the Balkans*, 207.

69 Yonov, "Bulgarian Military Operations," 75–76.

70 Ibid., 76.

71 Ibid.; Seton-Watson, *Nationality in the Balkans*, 208.

72 Yonov, "Bulgarian Military Operations," 77; Seton-Watson, *Nationality in the Balkans*, 208.

73 Yonov, "Bulgarian Military Operations," 76.

74 Ronald Tarnstrom, *Balkan Battles* (Lindsborg, Kans.: Trogan Books, 1998), 58.

75 Seton-Watson, *Nationality in the Balkans*, 209.

76 For the siege of Adrianople, see ibid., 209–10; and Yonov, "Bulgarian Military Operations," 78–80.

77 The First Army included five infantry divisions, one cavalry division, and 154 pieces of artillery guns. Borislav Ratkovic, "Mobilization of the Serbian Army for the First Balkan War, October 1912," in Kiraly and Djordjevic, *East Central Europe*.

78 Ibid.

79 This army comprised the First Sumadija, Second Drina, and First and Second Morava divisions, and ninety-six field artillery (ibid.). See also Petar Opacic, "Political Ramifications of Serbo-Bulgarian Military Co-operation in the First Balkan War," in Kiraly and Djordjevic, *East Central Europe*, 90.

80 Ratkovic, "Mobilization of the Serbian Army," 155.

81 Opacic, "Political Ramifications," 90.

82 Ratkovic, "Mobilization of the Serbian Army," 155.

83 Opacic, "Political Ramifications," 90.

84 Seton-Watson, *Nationality in the Balkans*, 173.

85 For the Battle of Kumanovo, see ibid., 188.

86 Savo Skoko, "An Analysis of the Strategy of Vojvoda Putnik during the Balkan Wars," in Kiraly and Djordjevic, *East Central Europe*, 20.

87 Ibid., 22.

88 Seton-Watson, *Nationality in the Balkans*, 190–91.

89 Ibid., 191–92.

90 Ibid., 192–93.

91 Ibid., 193–94.

92 Ibid., 195.

93 Ibid., 195.

94 Ibid., 196.

95 Ibid.; Skoko, "Strategy of Vojvoda Putnik," 24.

96 Hellenic Army History Directorate, Army General Headquarters, "Hellenic Army Operations during the Balkan Wars," in Kiraly and Djordjevic, *East*

Central Europe, 100; D. J. Casavetti, *Hellas and the Balkan Wars* (London: T. F. Unwin, 1914), 76.

97 Casavetti, *Hellas and the Balkan Wars*, 76.

98 Hellenic Army, "Hellenic Army Operations," 100.

99 Ibid., 101; Casavetti, *Hellas and the Balkan Wars*, 78.

100 Ibid., 80.

101 Ibid., 80.

102 Hellenic Army, "Hellenic Army Operations," 101.

103 Casavetti, *Hellas and the Balkan Wars*, 81.

104 Ibid.

105 Ibid., 82.

106 Ibid., 95–96.

107 See ibid., 88–89.

108 Hellenic Army, "Hellenic Army Operations," 101.

109 Casavetti, *Hellas and the Balkan Wars*, 90.

110 Ibid., 90–91.

111 Ibid., 91.

112 Ibid., 91.

113 Ibid., 91–92.

114 Ibid., 92.

115 Ibid., 101.

116 Seton-Watson, *Nationality in the Balkans*, 198.

117 Casavetti, *Hellas and the Balkan Wars*, 104: The Greeks also seized 70 artillery pieces, 30 machine guns, 70,000 rifles, and 1,200 horses (Hellenic Army, "Hellenic Army Operations," 102).

118 Seton-Watson, *Nationality in the Balkans*, 200.

119 Casavetti, *Hellas and the Balkan Wars*, 116.

120 Ibid., 117.

121 Seton-Watson, *Nationality in the Balkans*, 200.

122 Hellenic Army, "Hellenic Army Operations," 103; Casavetti, *Hellas and the Balkan Wars*, 119–24.

123 Casavetti, *Hellas and the Balkan Wars*, 134–35.

124 Ibid., 138.

125 Ibid., 139.

126 Seton-Watson, *Nationality in the Balkans*, 201–2; Hellenic Army, "Hellenic Army Operations," 104.

127 Seton-Watson, *Nationality in the Balkans*, 202; Casavetti, *Hellas and the Balkan Wars*, 140; Hellenic Army, "Hellenic Army Operations," 104.

128 For a description of Ioannina's defenses, see Casavetti, *Hellas and the Balkan Wars*, 141–42.

129 Ibid., 141; Hellenic Army, "Hellenic Army Operations," 104.

130 Casavetti, *Hellas and the Balkan Wars*, 143.

131 Ibid., 144–46.

132 Hellenic Army, "Hellenic Army Operations," 104.

133 Casavetti, *Hellas and the Balkan Wars*, 148–52.

134 Hellenic Army, "Hellenic Army Operations," 104; Seton-Watson, *Nationality in the Balkans*, 213.

135 Mitar Durisic, "Operations of the Montenegrin Army during the First Balkan War," in Kiraly and Djordjevic, *East Central Europe*, 126.

136 Ibid., 127.

137 Ibid., 129–30; Seton-Watson, *Nationality in the Balkans*, 175.

138 Durisic, "Operations of the Montenegrin Army," 130.

139 Seton-Watson, *Nationality in the Balkans*, 175.

140 Ibid., 175–76.

141 Ibid., 214.

142 Durisic, "Operations of the Montenegrin Army," 135.

143 Ibid., 136–37.

144 Ibid., 138.

145 Seton-Watson, *Nationality in the Balkans*, 215.

146 Ibid., 216.

147 Ibid., 217.

148 Durisic, "Operations of the Montenegrin Army," 139.

149 Crampton, *Bulgaria, 1878–1918*, 417.

150 Ibid., 417.

151 Rossos, *Russia and the Balkans*, 177–79.

152 Crampton, *Bulgaria, 1878–1918*, 419.

153 Stavrianos, *Balkans since 1453*, 439.

154 Crampton, *Bulgaria, 1878–1918*, 420.

155 Ibid., 420.

156 Rossos, *Russia and the Balkans*, 186.

157 Ibid., 187.

158 Stavrianos, *Balkans since 1453*, 539.

159 Stephen Constant, *Foxy Ferdinand, Tsar of Bulgaria* (New York: Franklin Watts, 1980), 277.

160 Ibid., 278.

161 Crampton, *Bulgaria, 1878–1918*, 422.

162 Seton-Watson, *Nationality in the Balkans*, 258.

163 Skoko, "Strategy of Vojvoda Putnik," 26.

164 Ibid., 26.

165 Ibid., 27.

166 Ibid., 28.

167 The Greek army included 147,000 men and 230 guns.

168 George I, Constantine's father, was assassinated by a deranged man in

Thessaloniki in 1913.

169 Seton-Watson, *Nationality in the Balkans*, 262; Skoko, "Strategy of Vojvoda Putnik," 27.

170 Lord Courtney, ed., *Nationalism and War in the Near East* (New York: Arno Press, 1971), 268.

171 Seton-Watson, *Nationality in the Balkans*, 262.

172 Skoko, "Strategy of Vojvoda Putnik," 27.

173 Ibid., 28.

174 Ibid.; Seton-Watson, *Nationality in the Balkans*, 264.

175 Skoko, "Strategy of Vojvoda Putnik," 31; Seton-Watson, *Nationality in the Balkans*, 266.

176 Seton-Watson, *Nationality in the Balkans*, 266.

177 Skoko, "Strategy of Vojvoda Putnik," 30.

178 Ibid., 30–31.

179 Ibid., 31; Seton-Watson, *Nationality in the Balkans*, 267.

180 Skoko, "Strategy of Vojvoda Putnik," 31; Seton-Watson, *Nationality in the Balkans*, 280.

181 Skoko, "Strategy of Vojvoda Putnik," 31.

182 Seton-Watson, *Nationality in the Balkans*, 272.

183 Ibid., 281.

184 Ibid., 271.

185 Ibid., 280.

186 Ibid., 274; Hellenic Army, "Hellenic Army Operations," 106.

187 Hellenic Army, "Hellenic Army Operations," 107; Seton-Watson, *Nationality in the Balkans*, 275; Casavetti, *Hellas and the Balkan Wars*, 326.

188 Casavetti, *Hellas and the Balkan Wars*, 326; Hellenic Army, "Hellenic Army Operations," 109.

189 Casavetti, *Hellas and the Balkan Wars*, 327.

190 Seton-Watson, *Nationality in the Balkans*, 276.

191 Ibid., 275.

192 Casavetti, *Hellas and the Balkan Wars*, 328.

193 Seton-Watson, *Nationality in the Balkans*, 276.

194 Ibid., 281.

195 Hellenic Army, "Hellenic Army Operations," 108.

196 Momchil Yonov, "Bulgarian Military Operations," 80–81; Seton-Watson, *Nationality in the Balkans*, 282.

197 Yonov, "Bulgarian Military Operations," 81; Seton-Watson, *Nationality in the Balkans*, 283; Casavetti, *Hellas and the Balkan Wars*, 333.

Epilogue: A Wedding in Sarajevo, 1992

1 This account is based on the experiences of a young couple from Sarajevo who kindly provided the author with the story of their wedding. The names have been changed to protect the identity of the couple. After the wedding, Emma and Nicholi survived two more years of war. Every day, they recollect, was more

difficult then the previous one, more dangerous, with more fear. They took the first chance they had to get out of the besieged city, leaving on March 14, 1994.

2 Carnegie Endowment for International Peace, Division of Intercourse and Education, "Report of the International Commission to Inquire into the Causes and Conduct of the Balkan Wars" (Washington: Carnegie Endowment for International Peace, 1914), 131.

3 Ibid., 327.

4 Ibid., 97.

5 Ibid., 79.

6 Ibid., 286.

7 Ibid., 73.

8 Paul Lewis, "The Balkan War Crimes Report: If There Ever Were a Nuremberg for the Former Yugoslavia," *New York Times*, June 12, 1994.

9 Carnegie Endowment, "Report of the International Commission," 51.

10 Captain Boyle to Sir F. Elliot, Public Records Office (PRO), Great Britain, Unpublished Documents, Foreign Office (FO) 371/1830, 173.

11 Vice-Consul Young to Sir H. Bax-Ironside, PRO, FO 371/1782, 410. Young's report, which was forwarded to Edward Grey, the foreign minister, cites numerous examples of atrocities committed in Macedonia.

12 Lewis, "Balkan War Crimes Report."

13 Ibid.

14 Young to Bax-Ironside, PRO, FO 371/1782, 410.

15 The declaration was summarized by the British vice-consul, C. A. Greig, in Monastir (PRO, FO 371/1830).

16 Vladimir Dedijer, *The Yugoslav Auschwitz and the Vatican* (New York: Prometheus Books, 1988), 166–69.

17 Wooden hammers were used to keep mass killings as quiet as possible. A carpenter's hatchet was the instrument of choice for mass killings of women and children, although bombs were also used against children. Iron bars and knives were applied to women and children in equal measure. Machine guns were reserved for special occasions, with the victim shot in the legs, then the stomach, and finally through the breast. Revolvers and rifles were used only for public executions of selected individuals, professionals, and political opponents. Death came quickly, except when the executioner decided to "torment the criminal a bit." In those instances, the victim was shot at an angle so he would take hours to die. For a more detailed account of the choices of weaponry, see ibid., passim.

18 Glenny, *The Balkans*, 501.

19 *Encyclopedia Judaica*, vol. 16 (New York: Macmillan, 1971–72), 867–85; Martin Gilbert, *The Atlas of the Holocaust* (London: Michael Joseph, 1982), 170–77. After the war, Marshal Tito claimed the total was closer to 1.7 million dead, but even before the break-up of Yugoslavia, a fierce debate had been waged over that figure.

20 American military advisers conceived this plan and later tried the same experiment in Vietnam.

21 Francis X. Clines, "NATO Opens Broad Barrage against Serbs As Clinton Denounces Yugoslav President," *New York Times*, Mar. 25, 1999.

22 John Kifner and Ian Fisher, "Crisis in the Balkans: The Sickening Scenes of Atrocities," *New York Times*, June 16, 1999.

23 Peter Finn, "NATO Losing the Battle for Kosovo Minds," *Manchester Guardian Weekly*, Aug. 12–18, 1999.

24 A colleague, James Dean, professor of economics at Simon Fraser University, first coined the term "economic peacekeeping."

BIBLIOGRAPHY

—⟨∞⟩—

Books

Albertini, Luigi. *The Origins of the War of 1914*. 3 vols. Translated and edited by Isabella M. Massey. London: Oxford University Press, 1952.

Alexandris, Alexis. *The Greek Orthodox Minority of Istanbul and Greek–Turkish Relations, 1918–1974*. Athens: Center for Asia Minor Studies, 1983.

Anderson, Benedict. *Imagined Communities: Reflections of the Origins and Spread of Nationalism*. London: Verso, 1983.

Anderson, M. S. *The Eastern Question, 1774–1923*. London: Macmillan, 1966.

Anonymous. *Byzantium, Europe, and the Early Ottoman Sultans, 1373–1513: An Anonymous Greek Chronicle of the Seventeenth Century*. Translated and annotated by Marios Philippides. New York: Aristide D. Caratzas, 1990.

Babinger, Franz. *Mehmed der Eroberer und seine Zeit* (Mehmed the conqueror and his time). Translated by Ralph Manheim. Princeton, N.J.: Princeton University Press, 1978.

Baird, Henry M. *Modern Greece: A Narrative of a Residence and Travels in That Country; with Observations on Its Antiquities, Literature, Language, Politics, and Religion*. New York: Harper and Brothers, 1856.

Banac, Ivo. *The National Question in Yugoslavia: Origins, History, Politics*. London: Cornell University Press, 1984.

Barbaro, Nicolo. *Diary of the Siege of Constantinople 1453*. Translated by J. R. Jones. New York: Exposition Press, 1969.

Bekker, Emmanuel, ed. *Corpus Scriptorum Historiae Byzantinae*. Bonn: E. Weberi, 1843.

Benjamin, S.G.W. *The Turk and Greek; or Creeds, Races, Society, and Scenery in Turkey, Greece and the Islands of Greece*. New York: Hurd and Houghton, 1867.

Blaquiere, Edward. *Letters from Greece: With Remarks on the Treaty of Intervention*. London: J. Ilbery, 1828.

Boppe, Auguste. *Documents inédits sur les relations de la résurrection de la Serbie,*

1804–1834 (The unedited documents of Serbian insurrection). Belgrade: State Printer, 1888.

Bourke, Joanna. *An Intimate History of Killing: Face-to-Face Killing in Twentieth-Century Warfare.* London: Granta Books, 1999.

Braudel, Fernand. *The Mediterranean and the Mediterranean World in the Age of Philip II.* 2 vols. Translated by Sian Reynolds. Los Angeles: University of California Press, 1973.

Brook-Shepherd, Gordon. *Victims at Sarajevo: The Romance and Tragedy of Franz Ferdinand and Sophie.* London: Harvill Press, 1984.

Casavetti, D. J. *Hellas and the Balkan Wars.* London: T. F. Unwin, 1914.

Cheetham, Nicholas. *Medieval Greece.* New Haven, Conn.: Yale University Press, 1981.

Cleveland, William L. *A History of the Modern Middle East.* Boulder, Colo.: Westview Press, 1994.

Clogg, Richard, ed. *The Struggle for Greek Independence: Essays to Mark the 150th Anniversary of the Greek War of Independence.* London: Macmillan, 1973.

Cohen, Lenard. *Broken Bonds: Disintegration of Yugoslavia.* Boulder, Colo.: Westview Press, 1993.

Comstock, John L. *History of the Greek Revolution: Compiled from Official Documents of the Greek Government.* New York: W. W. Reed and Co., 1828.

Constant, Stephen. *Foxy Ferdinand, Tsar of Bulgaria.* New York: Franklin Watts, 1980.

Corovic, Vladimir. *Istorija Srba* (History of Serbia). Beograd: Beograd izdavacko-graficki zavod, 1995.

Courtney, Lord, ed. *Nationalism and War in the Near East.* New York: Arno Press, 1971.

Crampton, Richard J. *Bulgaria, 1878–1918: A History.* Boulder, Colo.: East European Monographs, 1983.

Creasy, Edward S. *History of the Ottoman Turks: From the Beginning of Their Empire to the Present Time.* Beirut: Khayats, 1961.

Czernin, Count Ottokar. *In the World War.* London: Cassell, 1919.

Dakin, Douglas. *The Greek Struggle for Independence, 1821–1833.* London: Ernest Benn Limited, 1973.

———. *The Greek Struggle in Macedonia, 1897–1913.* Thessaloniki: Institute for Balkan Studies, 1993.

———. *The Unification of Greece, 1770–1923.* New York: St. Martin's Press, 1972.

Davison, Roderic H. *Essays in Ottoman and Turkish History, 1774–1923: The Impact of the West.* Austin: University of Texas Press, 1990.

Dedijer, Vladimir. *The Road to Sarajevo.* New York: Simon and Schuster, 1966.

———. *The Yugoslav Auschwitz and the Vatican.* New York: Prometheus Books, 1988.

Dedijer, Vladimir, et al. *History of Yugoslavia.* Translated by Korddija Kveder. New York: McGraw-Hill, 1975.

Diamandopopou, N., and A. Kyriazopoulou. *Elliniki Istoria ton Neoteron Chronon* (Modern Greek history). Athens: Organismos Ekdoseos Didaktikon Vivlion, n.d.

Djordjevic, Dimitrije, and Stephan Fischer-Galati. *The Balkan Revolutionary Tradition.* New York: Columbia University Press, 1981.

Dobkin, Marjorie Housapian. *Smyrna 1922: Destruction of a City.* New York: Newmark Press, 1998.

Dodwell, Edward. *A Classical and Topographical Tour through Greece.* London: Rodwell and Martin, 1819.

Dontas, Domna. *Greece and the Great Powers, 1863–1875.* Thessaloniki: Institute for Balkan Studies, 1966.

Douglas, F.S.N. *An Essay on Certain Points of Resemblance between the Ancient and Modern Greeks.* London: J. Murray, 1813.

Ducas. *Decline and Fall of Byzantium to the Ottoman Turks.* Translated by H. Magoulias. Detroit: Wayne State University Press, 1975.

Edwards, Lovet F. *The Memoirs of Prota Matija Nenadovic.* Oxford: Oxford University Press, 1969.

Elting, John R. *Swords around a Throne: Napoleon's Grande Armée.* New York: Free Press, 1988.

Emmert, Thomas A. *Serbian Golgotha: Kosovo, 1389.* New York: Columbia University Press, 1990.

Fine, John V. *The Early Medieval Balkans: A Critical Survey from the Sixth to the Late Twelfth Century.* Ann Arbor, Mich.: University of Michigan Press, 1983.

———. *The Late Medieval Balkans: A Critical Survey from the Late Twelfth Century to the Ottoman Conquest.* Ann Arbor, Mich.: University of Michigan Press, 1987.

Finlay, George. *A History of Greece.* 7 vols. New York: AMS Press, 1970.

———. *History of the Greek Revolution, and of the Reign of King Otho.* 2 vols. London: Zeno, 1971.

Fregosi, Paul. *Jihad in the West: Muslim Conquests from the 7th to the 21st Centuries.* New York: Prometheus Books, 1998.

Gibb, Hamilton, and H. Bowen. *Islamic Society and the West.* London: Oxford University Press, 1950.

Gibbon, Edward. *The Decline and Fall of the Roman Empire.* 6 vols. New York: Penguin Press, 1994.

Gibbons, Herbert Adams. *The Foundation of the Ottoman Empire: A History of the Osmanlis Up to the Death of Bayazid I, 1300–1403.* London: Cass, 1968.

Gilbert, Martin. *The Atlas of the Holocaust.* London: Michael Joseph, 1982.

Glenny, Misha. *The Balkans: Nationalism, War, and the Great Powers, 1804–1999.* New York: Viking, 2000.

Goodwin, Godfrey. *The Janissaries.* London: Saqi Books, 1997.

Goodwin, Jason. *Lords of the Horizon: A History of the Ottoman Empire.* New York: H. Holt, 1999.

Helmreich, Ernst C. *The Diplomacy of the Balkan Wars, 1912–1913.* Cambridge: Harvard University Press, 1938.

Hertslet, Edward. *The Map of Europe by Treaty.* 4 vols. London: Butterworths, 1875–91.

Hitchins, Keith. *Rumania, 1866–1947.* Oxford: Oxford University Press, 1994.

Hobhouse, J. C. *A Journey through Albania.* New York: Arno Press, 1971.

Hussey, J. M., ed. *The Cambridge Medieval History.* 8 vols. Cambridge: Cambridge University Press, 1964–67.

Inalcik, Halil. *The Ottoman Empire: The Classical Age, 1300–1600.* New York: Praeger Publishers, 1973.

Jelavich, Barbara. *History of the Balkans: Eighteenth and Nineteenth Centuries.* Cambridge: Cambridge University Press, 1983.

———. *The Ottoman Empire, the Great Powers, and the Straits.* Bloomington: Indiana University Press, 1973.

———. *Russia's Balkan Entanglements, 1806–1914.* Cambridge: Cambridge University Press, 1991.

Jelavich, Charles. *Tsarist Russia and Balkan Nationalism: Russian Influence and the Internal Affairs of Bulgaria and Serbia, 1879–1880.* Berkeley: University of California Press, 1962.

Jenkins, Romilly. *The Dilessi Murders: Greek Brigands and English Hostages.* London: Prion, 1998.

Kinross, Lord. *The Ottoman Centuries: The Rise and Fall of the Turkish Empire.* New York: William Morrow, 1977.

Kiraly, Bela K., and Dimitrjie Djordjevic, eds. *East Central Europe and the Balkan Wars.* New York: Social Science Monographs, 1987.

Kiraly, Bela K., et al., eds. *War and Society in East Central Europe.* 17 vols. New York: Social Science Monographs, 1979–85.

Koliopoulos, John S. *Brigands with a Cause: Brigandage and Irredentism in Modern Greece, 1821–1912.* Oxford: Oxford University Press, 1987.

Kolokotronis, Theodore. *Memoirs from the Greek War of Independence, 1821–1833.* Chicago: Argonaut Publishers, 1969.

Lampe, John R. *Yugoslavia as History.* Cambridge: Cambridge University Press, 1996.

Lange-Akhund, Nadine. *The Macedonian Question, 1893–1908.* New York: Columbia University Press, 1998.

Leake, William M. *Travels in the Morea.* 3 vols. Amsterdam: Hakkert, 1968.

———. *Travels in Northern Greece.* 4 vols. Amsterdam: Hakkert, 1967.

Leonard of Chios. *The Siege of Constantinople 1453: Seven Contemporary Accounts.* Translated by J. R. Melville Jones. Amsterdam: Hakkert, 1972.

Lewis, Bernard. *The Emergence of Modern Turkey.* London: Oxford University Press, 1968.

Lewis, Geoffrey L. *Modern Turkey.* New York: Praeger, 1974.

Margutti, Albert von. *The Emperor Francis Joseph.* London: Hutchinson, 1921.

MacArthur, John R. *Second Front: Censorship and Propaganda in the Gulf War.* New York: Hill and Wang, 1992.

MacDermott, Mercia. *Freedom or Death: The Life of Gotse Delchev.* London: Journeyman Press, 1978.

MacKenzie, David. *The Black Hand on Trial: Salonica, 1917.* Boulder, Colo.: East European Monographs, 1995.

Maclean, Fitzroy. *Eastern Approaches.* London: Jonathan Cape, 1949.

Makriyannis Ioannis. *The Memoirs of General Makriyannis, 1797–1864.* London: Oxford University Press, 1966.

Malcolm, Noel. *Bosnia: A Short History.* London: Papermac, 1996.

Mandrikas, Achilleas A. *Krypho Scholeio: Mythos E Pragmatikotita* (Secret school: myth or reality). Athens: Ekdosis Kalentis, 1992.

Mansel, Philip. *Constantinople: City of the World's Desire, 1453–1924.* New York: St. Martin's, 1995.

McNeill, William H. *The Pursuit of Power: Technology, Armed Forces, and Society since A.D. 1000.* Chicago: University of Chicago Press, 1982.

Medlicott, W. N. *The Congress of Berlin and After: A Diplomatic History of the Near Eastern Settlement, 1878–1880.* Hamden, Conn.: Archon Books, 1963.

Meriage, Lawrence P. *Russia and the First Serbian Insurrection, 1804–1812.* New York and London: Garland Publishing, 1987.

Mertus, Julie A. *Kosovo: How Myths and Truths Started a War.* Berkeley: University of California Press, 1999.

Mojzes, Paul, ed. *Religion and War in Bosnia.* Atlanta, Ga.: Scholars Press, 1998.

Muller, C., ed. *Fragmenta historicorum graecorum,* 5 vols. Paris: Ambrosio Firmin Didot, 1848–1885. (Also see the English translation by Riggs, C. T. *History of Mehmet the Conqueror by Kritovoulos.* Princeton, N.J.: Princeton University Press, 1954.)

Murat, Jean de. *The Great Extirpation of Hellenism and Christianity in Asia Minor.* Florida: A. Triantafillis, 1999.

Mure, William. *Journal of a Tour in Greece and the Ionian Islands.* 2 vols. London: W.

Blackwood and Sons, 1842.

Nikolic-Ristanovic, Vesna, ed. *Women, Violence and War: Wartime Victimization of Refugees in the Balkans.* Budapest: Central European University Press, 2000.

Oman, Charles. *A History of the Art of War in the Middle Ages, 1278–1485.* New York: B. Franklin, 1924.

Owings, W. A. Dolph. *The Sarajevo Trial.* 2 vols. Translated by W. A. Dolph Owings, Elizabeth Pribic, and Nikola Pribic. Chapel Hill, N.C.: Documentary Publications, 1984.

Palmer, Alan. *The Decline of the Ottoman Empire.* New York: J. Murray, 1992.

——. *The Gardeners of Salonika.* New York: Simon and Schuster, 1965.

——. *Twilight of the Habsburgs: The Life and Times of Emperor Francis Joseph.* London: Grove/Atlantic, 1997.

Parry, V. J., and M. E. Yapp, eds. *War, Technology and Society in the Middle East.* London: Oxford University Press, 1975.

Pavlowitch, Steven K. *A History of the Balkans, 1804–1945.* New York: Longman, 1999.

Perry, Duncan M. *The Politics of Terror: The Macedonian Liberation Movement, 1893–1903.* Durham, N.C.: Duke University Press, 1988.

Petrovich, Michael Boro. *A History of Modern Serbia, 1904–1918.* 2 vols. New York: Harcourt Brace Jovanovich, 1976.

Philippides, Marios, trans. *The Fall of the Byzantine Empire: A Chronicle by George Sphrantzes, 1401–1477.* Amherst, Mass.: University of Massachusetts Press, 1980.

Psomiades, Harry J. *The Eastern Question: The Last Phase.* Thessaloniki: Institute for Balkan Studies, 1968.

Rossos, Andrew. *Russia and the Balkans: Inter-Balkan Rivalry and Russian Foreign Policy, 1908–1914.* Toronto: University of Toronto Press, 1981.

Runciman, Steven. *Byzantine Civilization.* New York: Longmans, Green and Co., 1956.

——. *The Fall of Constantinople 1453.* Cambridge: Cambridge University Press, 1965.

——. *The Great Church in Captivity: A Study of the Patriarchate of Constantinople from the Eve of the Turkish Conquest to the War of Independence.* Cambridge: Cambridge University Press, 1968.

——. *A History of the Crusades.* 3 vols. Cambridge: Cambridge University Press, 1951.

St. Clair, William. *That Greece Might Still Be Free: The Philhellenes in the War of Independence.* London: Oxford University Press, 1972.

Seton-Watson, R. W. *A History of the Roumanians.* Cambridge: Cambridge University Press, 1934.

——. *The Rise of Nationality in the Balkans.* New York: H. Fertig, 1966.

——. *Sarajevo: A Study in the Origins of the Great War.* London: Camelot Press, 1925.

Sfyroera, Vassilis. *Istoria Neoteri kai Synchrony* (History: modern and current). Athens: Organismos Ekdoseon Didaktikon Biblion, 1991.

Shawcross, William. *Deliver Us from Evil: Peacekeepers, Warlords and a World of Endless Conflict.* New York: Simon and Schuster, 2000.

Smith, Michael L. *Ioanian Vision: Greece in Asia Minor 1919–1922.* New York: St. Martin's Press, 1973.

Stavrianos, L. S. *The Balkans since 1453.* New York: New York University Press, 1958.

Stotwell, James, and Francis Deak. *Turkey at the Straits: A Short History.* New York: Books for Libraries Press, 1940.

Sugar, Peter F. *Southeastern Europe under Ottoman Rule, 1354–1804.* Seattle: University of Washington Press, 1977.

Tarnstrom, Ronald. *Balkan Battles.* Lindsborg, Kans.: Trogan Books, 1998.

Taylor, A.J.P. *The Struggle for Mastery in Europe, 1848–1918.* Oxford: Oxford

University Press, 1971.

Thaden, Edward C. *Russia and the Balkan Alliance of 1912*. University Park, Penn.: Pennsylvania State University Press, 1965.

Thucydides. *The Peloponnesian War*. Translated by Steven Lattimore. Indianapolis, Ind.: Hackett, 1998.

Todorov, Tzvetan. *The Morals of History*. Translated by Alyson Waters. Minneapolis, Minn.: University of Minnesota Press, 1995.

Treadgold, Warren. *A History of the Byzantine State and Society*. Stanford, Calif.: Stanford University Press, 1997.

Tse-tung, Mao. *Selected Works*. 2 vols. London: Lawrence and Wishart, 1954.

United States Holocaust Memorial Museum. *Historical Atlas of the Holocaust*. New York: Macmillan, 1996.

Urquhart, David. *Spirit of the East*. 2 vols. London: H. Colburn, 1839.

Veremis, Thanos. *The Military in Greek Politics: From Independence to Democracy*. London: Hurst and Company, 1997.

Vickers, Miranda. *The Albanian: A Modern History*. New York: I. B. Tauris Publishers, 1999.

———. *Between Serb and Albanian: A History of Kosovo*. New York: Columbia University Press, 1996.

Vournas, Tasos. *Istoria tis Neoteris Elladas, Apo tin Epanastasi tou 1821 os to kinima tou Goudi* (The history of modern Greece, from the revolution of 1821 to the coup of Goudi). Athens: Ekdosis Adelphon Tolidi, n.d.

Vryonis, Speros. *The Decline of Medieval Hellenism in Asia Minor and the Process of Islamization from the Eleventh through the Fifteenth Century*. Berkeley, Calif.: University of California Press, 1971.

Vucinich, Wayne S., ed. *The First Serbian Uprising, 1804–1814*. New York: Columbia University Press, 1982.

Vucinich, Wayne S., and Thomas A. Emmert, eds. *Kosovo: Legacy of Medieval Battle*. Minnesota: University of Minnesota Press, 1991.

Waddington, George. *A Visit to Greece in 1823 and 1824*. London: J. Murray, 1825.

Walsh, Robert. *A Residence at Constantinople*. 2 vols. London: F. Westley and A. H. Davis, 1836.

West, Rebecca. *Black Lamb and Grey Falcon: A Journey through Yugoslavia*. London: Penguin Books, 1994.

Winchester, Simon. *The Fractured Zone: A Return to the Balkans*. New York: HarperCollins, 1999.

Woodhouse, C. M. *The Greek War of Independence*. New York: Russell and Russell, 1975.

———. *The Philhellenes*. London: Doric Publications, 1969.

Ypsilantis, Athansios. *Ta Meta tin Alosin* (The events after the conquest). Constantinople: G. Aphthonidis, 1870.

Zurcher, Eric J. *Turkey: A Modern History*. London: British Academic Press, 1993.

Articles

"The Archduke's Consort." *London Times*, June 29, 1914.

Bartusius, M. C. "Brigandage in the Late Byzantine Empire." *Byzantion* 51 (1981).

"Captured and Murdered by Brigands." *London Times*, Apr. 26, 1870.

Clines, Francis X. "NATO Opens Broad Barrage against Serbs As Clinton Denounces Yugoslav President." *New York Times*, Mar. 25, 1999.

Collas, Count Carlo. "Auf den Bosnischen Wegspuren der Kriegsschuldfrag." *Kriegsschuldfrag* (Jan. 1927).

Finn, Peter. "NATO Losing the Battle for Kosovo Minds." *Manchester Guardian Weekly*, Aug. 12–18, 1999.

Hemingway, Ernest. "Waiting for an Orgy." *Toronto Star*, Oct. 19, 1922.

Kifner, John, and Ian Fisher. "Crisis in the Balkans: The Sickening Scenes of Atrocities." *New York Times*, June 16, 1999.

Lewis, Paul. "The Balkan War Crimes Report: If There Ever Were a Nuremberg for the Former Yugoslavia." *New York Times*, June 12, 1994.

Morsey, A. "Konopischt und Sarajevo." *Berliner Monatshefte* (June 1934).

"Murder of the King and Queen of Servia." *London Times*, June 12, 1903.

Otetéa, A. "L'Hétairie d'il y a cent cinquante ans" (The Hetairia of 150 years ago). *Balkan Studies* 6, no. 2 (1965).

Pinson, Mark. "Ottoman Bulgaria in the First Tanzimat Period: The Revolts of Nish (1841) and Vidin (1850)." *Middle Eastern Studies* 11, no. 2 (May 1975).

Prentiss, Mark O. "Eyewitness Story of Smyrna's Horror; 200,000 Victims of Turks and Flames; Kemal Demands Greeks Quit Thrace." *New York Times*, Sept. 18, 1922.

"Servian Condemnation." *London Times*, July 1, 1914.

"The Servian Tragedy." *London Times*, June 15, 1903.

Public Documents

Carnegie Endowment for International Peace, Division of Intercourse and Education. "Report of the International Commission: to Inquire into the Causes and Conduct of the Balkan Wars." Washington: The Endowment, 1914.

London. Public Record Office. Foreign Office (FO) 78/99/71. July 23, 1821, Strangford to Castlereagh.

———. FO 371/1782. Vice-Consul Young to Sir H. Bax-Ironside.

———. FO 371/1830. Captain Boyle to Sir F. Elliot.

———. FO 1830. British Vice-Consul C. A. Greig in Monastir.

INDEX

---〜〜〜---

Index

Index